P9-DTL-156

CONTENTS

ACKNOWLEDGMENTS

I've learned to be rather picky about whom I let help me with this sort of thing: better to drag a few unlucky souls through the muck of recipe testing and paper-crumpling edits than bother everybody I know. To those select few, then, who were kind or naïve enough to take part in this searing saga, I am truly indebted.

The recipe-testing bait was taken by a powerful triumvirate of culinarily talented friends and family. My brother Peter applied his meticulous approach to classical music to the testing of sauces. My cookbook author mother Julie Riven Jaye helped with marathon sessions in my tiny kitchen; carefully applied guilt trips might have got her there, but her energy, palate, and organization were instrumental. And the cheerful willingness of Andrew "Moneyman" Pease could always be counted on to inspire every step of this process.

Sharon Bowers, my agent, is responsible for nurturing this project from its inception. It is valuable, almost indispensable, to have someone like Sharon always at the ready with encouragement.

Susie Middleton, in addition to being a great friend, gave thoughtful counsel on many of the sauces in this book. And Giuliano Bugialli, for years a wonderful mentor, received Italian cooking questions with his trademark mix of wit and impatience. I'm also grateful to the many members of the *Fine Cooking* family who have continued to push me along through the years, including Rebecca Freedman, Jennifer Armentrout, Abby Dodge, Molly Stevens, Pam Anderson, and Sarah Jay. And thank you to the b.good team who allowed me the freedom to both write and cook.

The structure of this book was due in large part to its editor Geoff Stone, who helped mold the original concept into a sophisticated formula. Also from Running Press, Cisca Schreefel guided the manuscript through its many stages of editing, Martha Whitt helped tidy it up, and the publicity department led by Seta Zink got it out there.

And, finally, Marguerite played the role of on-call guidance counselor and resident dishwasher with love and without complaint. Thank you.

INTRODUCTION

It's best you sit down first. I don't take you for the fainting kind (introduction readers generally aren't), but this book contains potentially explosive elements that are intended to alter the very way you live. OK, fine . . . alter the way you cook, which, of course, could change the way you live . . . stay with me here.

No worries, I've no interest in your daily donut dalliances or late-afternoon chocolate dealings. It's dinner that I care about and dinner where I can help. I'm particularly focused on that brief, dangerous period when you get home each night, hungry and tired and uncertain of what to make or, more simply, what to eat. Studies show . . . ok, my studies show . . . that hungry, tired people tend to make bad food decisions. That is unless these same hungry, tired people are somehow presented with a better option, an easier way. This book is that better option and its ramifications are why you're now seated.

By the end of your journey through *Sear, Sauce, and Serve*, you will be able to feed yourself and your loved ones better and more quickly than ever before. And you'll do this through the help of a very basic formula, a simple two-step cooking process that pairs four high-heat cooking methods with a vast array of jazzy, but immensely easy sauces. Continue reading and you will learn how to make dinner in a setting that is far more real and pressure-packed than any *Iron Chef* Kitchen Stadium. It's called Monday night. And that secret ingredient? It may feel like just that . . . a @#$%!! secret. But you'll take a deep breath and channel this formula and soon enough you'll pick up all sorts of secret ingredients and little tricks to prepare them.

I don't know whether this book will help you sleep more soundly or influence others more profoundly, but it will help you cook better and, damn it, good-cooking, well-fed people do well in life.

Before I explain how this whole formula works and how it will change all things cooking for you, I might as well tell you how I came to it myself. The story begins back when I was a little guy. As most moms do, mine always insisted that I make my bed and fold my clothes before leaving the house. Unlike most kids, though, I took to the whole thing in a mildly OCD way. This neatness bug stuck with me, and by the time I was cooking in restaurant kitchens in my teens, I was mentally organizing and reorganizing every technique I came across. And this wasn't all bad; it helped me quickly discover that cooking well wasn't so much about memorizing recipes as it was about understanding, absorbing, and mastering the basics. "Build this foundation," I thought to myself (yes, like in one of those sitcom voice-overs when a character writes a letter), "and one day you'll be able to get all cool and creative."

Sopping Up Every Last Drop

Dan Freedberg's house was halfway between mine and my elementary school. So every morning my little brother and I would shoot down Nobscot Road, through the Connors' driveway, over a little fence, down Dan's backyard, up the back steps, and into the kitchen where we would ask Dan, breathlessly, if he wanted to join us on the walk to school.

The scene in the kitchen was almost always the same. Dan would have a plate of over-easy eggs before him and one of his parents would be nearby, part pleading, part imploring him to eat. Dan would usually eat some of the eggs, but he always left large swaths of the runny yolks behind.

Those abandoned egg yolks killed me. I loved eggs and I was always hungry and there sat those yolks, untouched and unready for the dishwasher. Cereals (and we're not talking sugar cereals either, but healthy O's and flakes) were the only things doing in my house for weekday breakfasts. Eggs were weekend food, special food. And not only did Dan get eggs every morning, but they were so plain to him that he left the best part behind. I eyed those yolks longingly, thinking if only they had been mine.

I'm not going to get all dramatic and claim that those untouched yolks were the genesis for my writing a book on sauces—some sort of emotional hole that needed to be filled through high-heat cooking. But I do believe that at a young age, we become the kind of people who either finish our plates (or are forced to do so) or not. And not only was I a finish-my-plate type, but even as a kid I was a sauce-picker-upper; the type to grab a hunk of bread and sop up whatever liquid (or yolk) remained. I think people who love to eat start that way and just keep on eating. The savory pull that draws us to sauces in the first place keeps us there 'til they're all gone.

I never went to cooking school so I had to build this foundation on my own. And because I'd somehow managed to work my way into Boston's fanciest kitchens by my early twenties, I had to teach myself quickly so I wouldn't be exposed by all the slick CIA (the Culinary Institute of America, not the agency) grads darting past me. So I began a manic game of catch-up, spending many late nights in my dingy bachelor's apartment turning vegetables or practicing hollandaise sauce or butchering skate wing: in essence, sorting out (and re-sorting) most everything there was to learn about cooking.

I wasn't dating much back then. To be honest, I wasn't dating at all. Worse, I always smelled like food, and not chocolate cake or blueberry pie, mind you, but onions and garlic and shallots (yeah, oh my). After a couple of years of this self-inflicted kitchen crash course, I finally caught up. And, along the way, I fine-tuned my slightly obsessive approach to cooking. I would take the core techniques and deconstruct them to their base parts ("The first step to sauté scallops is to pat them completely dry to avoid sticking and encourage caramelization. Next, heat up the pan until it's ripping hot . . . ") and then build them back up in my mind, kind of like those car enthusiasts who take apart an engine only to reassemble it. From this approach, I learned not only how to sauté scallops but also what this technique had in common with grilling shrimp or broiling chicken breasts. Clearly, I wasn't building a fuel cell or mapping DNA strains, but the experience was revelatory, and because I mostly taught myself I got good at teaching others.

The second piece to my sear-and-sauce story took place a handful of years later when I started cooking at home more regularly. I was still working in restaurants then, but I had a cushy gig where I could get home at a reasonable hour and sleep when the rest of the world sleeps, and do the happy things that most hardworking cooks can't like go to a movie or watch the sun set or make dinner for the family. And as I cooked more at home, a couple of things started to happen. First, I began to really understand home cooking. Don't get me wrong—it's not like restaurant kitchens are on Mars, but they're different. At home you have to be more gentle and thoughtful. You can't sling food around like it's an arena football game. There's no time for two-hour reductions, no need for architectural presentations, and no money for caviar. The nightly goal is more basic: get something good to the table and fast. For this reason, most restaurant- and chef-driven cookbooks (even those under the guise of "*Famous Chef X Cooks at Home*") are as useful for the home cook as an eighteen-wheeler's manual is for the owner of a compact car.

Also, after a year or two of home cooking, I noticed that all my meals tended to follow a simple pattern. They were quick and relatively simple, relied on high heat for intense browning, and called on big, complementary flavors to pull it all together. I would take some sort of meat or fish or vegetable, season it generously (often with just salt and pepper), give it a quick sear, and then finish it with a simple but jazzy sauce. And I would usually accompany the main-course sear with something starchy or green or both. And it worked, so much so that I started thinking that this method was something worth sharing, worth writing about.

Of course, I'm not going to pretend like I invented this sear and sauce method. It's been around for as long as there's been fire and salt. But I've organized it in a way that only a slightly neurotic cook could: taking the four essential high-heat techniques (broiling, grilling, sautéing, and stir-frying) and connecting them in such a way that after a couple of times grilling steaks or sautéing salmon, you will absorb what one technique shares with another and understand the basics of high-heat cooking. And it's this knowledge that will transform you from a recipe follower into a confident cook.

This is *Sear, Sauce, and Serve*'s real goal: to empower you to become a calm and thoroughly proficient cook, running the show in your kitchen on a Wednesday night, free to create whatever you're in the mood for and not dependent on cookbook recipes like some sort of tethered weeknight weakling. This method-centric tack intentionally veers far astray from traditional cookbooks' recipe-centric approach. Sure, other cookbooks may teach you good dishes, but you will always have to rush back to the book to make sure you're doing things "right." I'm more like that cookbook mom or dad who loves you, but wants you out of the house, out on your own, spreading your culinary wings. It's best for you, but it will also let me go to Boca and take a break.

So, what is a *Sear, Sauce, and Serve* recipe? Sure, you could broil a steak, slather it with ketchup, and call it "seared and sauced." Likewise, a filet mignon with truffle butter and a scoop of osetra caviar, by definition, would also fit the method's profile. This book celebrates dishes that happily fall somewhere in between: meals that are dressy enough to feel special, but quick enough to fit into the weeknight routine. Things like grilled pork tenderloin brushed with the Rosemary-Balsamic Glaze (page 88), sautéed chicken breasts (page 31) topped with the Jalapeño-Parmesan Cream (page 201), or Spicy Stir-Fried Sesame Beef (page 60). These dishes may sound good and slightly fancy, but they're within reach with twenty to thirty minutes of work. And because there are so many combinations in this book, you won't ever get bored. Even if you just want to sauté or grill chicken breasts from here on out, you'll have hundreds of sauce options to keep things fresh and lively.

Now that I've got you all pumped up to become a powerful home cook, it's time to stand up, light up that flame (or broiler), and start searing. Remember, you'll only need my help for a bit. Soon enough, this weeknight approach will be all your own. Think fondly of me then.

PREP AND COOK TIMES

Throughout this book, I list prep and cook times for each sause (when there's actually cooking involved) as a guide to help you choose what to make for dinner tonight (some nights, that 5-minute, no-cook dipping sauce is a lot more attractive than the 15-minute sauté sauce). Prep time is relatively subjective—everybody dices a tomato or minces garlic at a different speed. This book is built on a fast-lane approach to cooking, though, so my estimates lean toward the aggressive. They demand a reasonable but focused effort on your part—put down the Blackberry and mute Judge Judy.

WHAT IS A SEAR?

This isn't one of those metaphysical topics that you're supposed to ponder for days. It's a basic question with a two-part answer: what you can sear and how you can sear it. The ingredients can vary. Once upon a time, searing was the exclusive domain of meat—steaks, chops, and the like. However, dry, high-heat cooking can also be applied to fish, poultry, and vegetables, too. Searing generally involves something hot—a pan or skillet or grill grates—coming in direct contact with the ingredient. A bond is created between the heating element and the meat or vegetables that brands the latter with a browned crust that is as dramatic in its intensity of flavor as it in its accompanying sights, sounds, and smells. Consider the sizzle of a steak hitting the grill grates, the splash of chicken being dropped into a wok, or the aroma of onions browning in a pan. These dramatic sensory characteristics are not only what we think of when we think of cooking but also, like a high-heat Pavlovian bell, the things that make us hungry, that pull us to the dinner table or into that greasy burger joint or over to the neighbor's barbecue.

In this book, meat, poultry, fish, seafood, and vegetables are all subjects for searing. And the four high-heat techniques I classify as "searing"— grilling, broiling, sautéing, and stir-frying—consist of the sear and little more. They all start with a blast of high heat and then end shortly thereafter. Compare that to braises or stews that begin with a sear, but then follow with lengthy, slow cooking. Paring searing down to these four quick, high-heat methods not only creates a uniform formula for fast weeknight cooking but also highlights those universal rules that run throughout these techniques. And by learning to build on these high-heat culinary tenets, you'll become a damn good home cook.

dipped, dabbed, or dunked, all with the singular and noble goal of making each bite of what they accompany that much better.

So although some of the mixtures in this book might lack traditional sauce status, that's just the point. They're meant to be daring and different so that, yes, dinner can be a pork chop with that plain marinara sauce (page 135), or it can also be a spice-crusted steak with a Mango and Grilled Pepper Chutney (page 223). Options are good. Loosen up and prepare to think differently about sauces.

WHAT IS A SAUCE? (THE ONE-BITE PRINCIPLE)

There are two ways to define a sauce: the first is by its physical consititution or appearance—a liquid mixture that can be loose or thick or hot or cold but always . . . well, saucy. Like pornography, it's one of those things where you know it when you see it. The second is by what it does—acting as an integral supporting player in flavoring and adorning the metaphorical meat of a meal.

My definition of a sauce focuses more on the latter, on what a sauce does rather than how it looks. In this book, I include all kinds of things that don't have a traditional sauce appearance—like pestos, chutneys, or salsas—but certainly do what a sauce does. I admit, drawing that line where a sauce ends and something altogether different begins is tricky. That's why I propose a new definition for sauces: the **ONE-BITE PRINCIPLE.** To me a sauce is something meant to be eaten in the same bite with whatever it accompanies—in this book, it's seared food. Sauces are things that can be not only drizzled or spooned, but also spread, shmeared,

CHAPTER: 1

SEAR, SAUCE, SERVE, AND YOU

UNDERSTANDING THE METHOD AND WHAT YOU'LL NEED TO GET STARTED

I'M ONE OF THOSE YO-YOS WHO DOESN'T READ INSTRUCTIONS. IF I CAN'T FIGURE OUT HOW TO PUT TOGETHER A TOY OR A BOOKCASE BY JUST LOOKING AT IT, THE TASK IS PROBABLY TOO COMPLICATED FOR ME IN THE FIRST PLACE. THIS BOOK FOLLOWS THIS NO-INSTRUCTIONS-NECESSARY PRINCIPLE. IF YOU'VE READ THE TITLE OF THIS CHAPTER AND WANT TO BREEZE ON BY TO THE MEAT OF THE BOOK, YOU'LL BE JUST FINE. FOR TYPE-A'S WHO ARE STILL WITH ME (OR FOR THOSE OF YOU WHO'VE LIKED THE RECIPES ENOUGH TO GET THE BACKGROUND), **THIS CHAPTER WILL HELP YOU BETTER UNDERSTAND THE BASIC FORMULA.**

I. THE METHOD

As you've probably already figured out, there are three basic steps to our high-heat formula—sear, sauce, and serve. Follow all three and you'll produce a dressy main-course dish in thirty minutes or less; that is our basic objective.

How you follow these sear and sauce recipes is a little different than most, though. Unlike most cookbooks where recipes start and finish on one page, each recipe in *Sear, Sauce, and Serve* is broken up into two sections of the book—the searing techniques, which you will learn about in chapter 2, and the sauces, which you will select from chapters 3 and 4—so you can mix and match flavors as you wish. Think of it as the culinary version of those Choose-Your-Own-Adventure books, which were probably your thing if, like me, your parents refused to get you Nintendo.

This is how it works:

(1) SEAR: Start by choosing a meat, fish, or vegetable. Then decide on one of the four high-heat cooking techniques in chapter 2—broiling, grilling, sautéing, or stir-frying.

(2) SAUCE: Pick out one of over 225 sauces from chapters 3 or 4 to go with the sear. (There are also some rubs and marinades in chapter 2.)

(3) SERVE: Finally, pair the seared main course with a starchy side from chapter 5, some seared vegetables, a green salad, or whatever it is you like to eat with a main course.

So you may decide you want to make sautéed chicken breasts (page 31), with a Porcini and Pea Sauce (page 148), and serve with Buttered Egg Noodles with Chives (page 233). Or you may be in the mood for salmon on the grill (page 78) with a Spicy Hoisin Glaze (page 89), some grilled zucchini (page 80) and steamed jasmine rice.

This mix-and-match approach to recipes might be a little more cumbersome than your basic cookbook, but the goal is to give you options to make all sorts of different dishes and a basic structure on which to build a weeknight repertoire. Once you create your own favorites, they'll be locked into your memory, and you can graduate from this book to successful solo weeknight cooking.

"THERE ARE RULES HERE!"

Unlike Walter Sobchak in *The Big Lebowski*, I'm not a big rules guy, but I do adhere to a couple of basic ones in this book—like each sauce must have eight or fewer ingredients (not including salt, pepper, and a cooking oil) and the preparations (both searing and sauce) should take thirty minutes from start to finish. My hope is that working within these constraints will make your life easier without sacrificing any taste. I readily admit that some of the finest sauces around are intricate and involved, whether it's a thirty-ingredient Mexican mole or a painstakingly reduced French jus. But the prep times for these sauces are prohibitive and stocking all the ingredients for them is a chore, not what you're looking for on a busy weeknight.

Caveman and Carême, the Original Creators of Searing and Saucing

One can safely assume that as far back as cavemen, most weeknights (all right, every night that there was something to cook) included some form of searing: throw a stick with some meat over a fire and char until done. By Latin and Greek times, sauces had achieved prominence, too. These liquid accompaniments, literally "salted" concoctions (going back to the Latin root *salsus*), were meant to add both moisture and flavor to a dish. It would be almost another two thousand years before sauces would fully evolve into things which you and I would recognize. Part of the credit for the West's leap into modern sauce making goes to Antonin Carême, the early nineteenth-century French chef and one of the founders of haute cuisine. Not only was Carême instrumental in creating many of the rich, intense sauces central to classical French cuisine, but he also organized them into four basic categories, the mother sauces. And while Carême and the French were perfecting their version of searing and saucing, cultures around the globe were doing the same. In Mexico, the chile salsas and spiced purées of the Aztecs and Mayans were fusing with the rice-and-meat-based cuisine of the Spanish colonists. Sauces and high-heat cooking were flourishing both in the strong regional stir-fries of China as well as the sautés and grill-roasted fare of Italy. Thai cooks were merging the chiles of South America with their own native spices and seafood into intense curries and broths. Tomes have been written about how each of these cuisines evolved and fused and the role that sauces and high-heat cooking played in this evolution. The relevant point for us is simple, though: searing and saucing is universal, and its importance around the globe helps color this formula with a bright spectrum of flavors, textures, and spices.

STEP 1: SEAR

PREP TIME: less than 5 minutes

COOK TIME: Usually 5 to 10 minutes; no more than 20 minutes.

The first step in the method is the high-heat sear. The twenty-five techniques in chapter 2 help you choose what to sear—chicken, meat, fish, or vegetables—and how to sear them—sauté, stir-fry, broil, or grill. These high-heat techniques cover pretty much anything that can be cooked quickly. All of them are fast, weeknight-friendly, and full of information and tips so you'll be fine whether you decide to sear shrimp or summer squash.

Why sear? Or better said, what makes searing so special? Quite simply, high-heat cooking produces tasty food that both sounds good (think of the sizzle a steak makes on the grill) and looks good (envision that perfectly browned crust on grilled chicken or sautéed scallops) in a short amount of time. Grill marks connote flavor. Similarly, it's the crisp crust on sautéed, broiled, or stir-fried meats and vegetables that marks the flavorful effects of those high-heat techniques.

The process by which seared ingredients brown is explained by the Maillard reaction, an interaction between amino acids and sugars, often facilitated by heat. The French chemist Louis-Camille Maillard was the first to chronicle this process in the early twentieth century. But you don't need me to break down the intricacies of Maillard's work (nor could I) to understand that nicely browned food tastes good.

What searing does not do is "seal in the juices." This phrase has been used so often that it sounds right. But going back as far as the 1930s, and explained most concisely by Harold McGee in his food science masterpiece, *On Food and Cooking* (New York: Scribner, 2004), scientists have proven that high-heat cooking does nothing of the sort. Rather loss of moisture in meat is ultimately affected by the meat's temperature—the hotter it is, the more its protein strands contract, causing juices to be squeezed out (whether or not the meat has been properly browned). This is one reason why it's important to let meat rest (see Let Steaks and Chops Rest After Searing on page 70), and cool slightly after cooking and before slicing.

But even if meat or fish does lose some moisture during searing, it acquires a crisp crust, which, along with the increased flavor, makes searing a net positive no matter your culinary or scientific slant.

TIP: Simultaneously Sear and Sauce for Speediest Results

If you were to add up the maximum prep and cook times I've listed for some of the longer searing techniques and sauces, you could end up cooking for more than the promised half hour limit. The best way to avoid this is the mother of all weeknight techniques: multitasking. Make the sauce while you sear.

SEARING STEP 1A: SEASON

— ∙ — ∙ — ∙ — ∙ — ∙ — ∙ — ∙ — ∙ — ∙ —

INGREDIENTS: 6 or less for rubs and marinades (plus
salt and pepper)
PREP TIME: 5 minutes or less

Before you sear anything, you need to season it. You
can grill the most expensive beef tenderloin or
sauté up the most exotic of wild mushrooms, but if
the seasoning is off—too much or too little—the
dish will fall short. Salt is the primary seasoning,
but it can be complemented by spices and herbs.
Because the seared food in this book is paired with
a sauce, this seasoning step doesn't have to be complicated. In most cases, salt, pepper, and a little olive
oil will do the trick. Some techniques may be a little more involved, though. Stir-fried meat, chicken,
and seafood get a quick marinade of soy sauce,
cornstarch, and sherry. Cutlets are dusted with flour
before sautéing. And grilled and broiled foods have
optional rubs and marinades (see pages 14 to 19).

RUBS

— ∙ — ∙ — ∙ — ∙ — ∙ — ∙ — ∙ — ∙ — ∙ —

Pat (or rub) these mixtures onto meat, chicken, or
fish right before grilling or broiling (or up to 24
hours ahead for best results). The herb mixes also
go nicely with most vegetables, and in some cases
you can add the spice rubs to meat or chicken
before sautéing, though you'll want to make sure
to sear them gently so the spices don't scorch. If
you do feel so moved, do freshly grind whole
spices (like cumin or coriander or even black peppercorns) for these rubs. It's a tasty and not terribly
time-consuming step.

Sweet Southern Rub

Substitute one minced garlic clove for the garlic powder for a fresher, more intense flavor.

YIELD: 3 TABLESPOONS, ABOUT 4 SERVINGS

2 teaspoons kosher salt
2 teaspoons light brown sugar
2 teaspoons chile powder
2 teaspoons paprika
½ teaspoon freshly ground black pepper
½ teaspoon garlic powder
¼ teaspoon chipotle powder or pimentón de la Vera

Mix all the ingredients well in a small bowl (the
brown sugar may clump a bit) and sprinkle on just
before grilling or broiling or up to 24 hours ahead.

PAIRINGS: Add to chicken (mix with a little olive oil if
you're using boneless, skinless breasts to give them a
little moisture), pork chops or tenderloin, shrimp or
salmon. Finish these cuts with a glaze like the Chipotle
Honey Glaze (page 92) or serve with the Quick
Homemade BBQ Sauce (page 95).

Moroccan Spice Crust

YIELD: SCANT 3 TABLESPOONS, ABOUT 4 SERVINGS

2 teaspoons light brown sugar
2 teaspoons kosher salt
1 teaspoon chile powder
1 teaspoon ground cumin
1 teaspoon ground coriander
½ teaspoon freshly ground black pepper
¼ teaspoon ground cinnamon
¼ teaspoon espelette powder or ground cayenne

Mix all the ingredients well in a small bowl (the brown sugar may clump a bit) and sprinkle on just before grilling or broiling or up to 24 hours ahead.

PAIRINGS: Lamb chops and chicken are the most natural pairings for this fragrant rub, though you can add a light sprinkling to grilled vegetables like eggplant or zucchini. Pair with a complementary sauce from the region like Toasted Chermoula Sauce (page 215) or Lemony Tahini Sauce (page 174).

Tex-Mex Spice Rub

YIELD: SCANT 3 TABLESPOONS, ABOUT 4 SERVINGS

2 teaspoons kosher salt

2 teaspoons chile powder

1 teaspoon ancho chile powder (if unavailable, just use more chile powder)

1 teaspoon ground cumin

1 teaspoon granulated sugar

½ teaspoon freshly ground black pepper

½ teaspoon garlic powder

¼ teaspoon chipotle powder

Mix all the ingredients in a small bowl and sprinkle on just before grilling or broiling or up to 24 hours ahead.

PAIRINGS: Sprinkle on chicken (mix with a little olive oil if you're going to add to boneless, skinless breasts to give them a little moisture), pork chops, or flank steak. Pair with a mild salsa like the Tomatillo Salsa Verde (page 155) or Avocado and Corn Salsa (page 158).

Greek Garlic and Oregano Rub

YIELD: ¼ CUP, ABOUT 4 SERVINGS

2 tablespoons olive oil

2 tablespoons chopped fresh oregano or 1 teaspoon dried oregano

1 teaspoon chopped fresh thyme

1 large garlic clove, minced (about 1 teaspoon)

1½ teaspoons kosher salt

¾ teaspoon freshly ground black pepper

Mix all the ingredients in a small bowl and sprinkle on at least a half hour before grilling or broiling or up to 24 hours ahead.

PAIRINGS: This rub goes nicely with grilled chicken, lamb, or beef. Try to add it at least a couple of hours ahead of time so the garlic gently infuses its flavor. Pair with the Greek Dill-Cucumber Tzatziki (page 202) or the Greek Dressing (page 181).

Lemon-Herb Rub

Freshly grated lemon zest imparts a measured hit of citrus to this rub without affecting a seared ingredient's texture the way lemon juice would.

YIELD: SCANT ¼ CUP, ABOUT 4 SERVINGS

2 tablespoons olive oil

2 teaspoons chopped fresh thyme or rosemary

1½ teaspoons kosher salt

1 medium garlic clove, minced (about ¾ teaspoon)

Freshly grated zest of 1 lemon (about 1 teaspoon)

¾ teaspoon freshly ground black pepper

Mix all the ingredients in a small bowl and rub on at least a half hour before grilling or broiling or up to 24 hours ahead.

PAIRINGS: This rub goes nicely with grilled chicken, lamb, or beef. Then pair it with assertive Rosemary-Buffalo Sauce (page 166) or mild Chive and Black Truffle Butter (page 198) sauces alike.

MARINADES AND PASTES

This grouping of liquids and pastes are best added a couple of hours, if not a full day, ahead so their flavors can soak in. Pastes lie somewhere between marinades and rubs, blending spices and herbs with aromatics (garlic, shallots, and ginger) and some oil or yogurt. Marinades are mostly about flavoring; their ability to tenderize has been largely debunked. And then there are brines, straight liquid mixtures that infuse flavor like a marinade, but also add moisture.

TIP: About Salt and Pepper

I've included an approximate amount of how much salt and pepper I used when testing recipes in my own kitchen. You can use this as a guide or set aside the measuring spoons if you feel comfortable and sprinkle away. I call for kosher salt—it has a far cleaner flavor and easier texture for sprinkling than iodized table salt. If you're dead set on using table salt, use about one-third less than my suggested amounts.

Basic Brine

A brine is a mix of salt and water (and sometimes sugar) that adds moisture and flavor to lean cuts—like pork tenderloin, pork chops, or chicken breasts—so they don't dry out during cooking. Because the cuts in this book are on the small side, all it takes is one to two hours for a brine like this one to do its thing. Double this recipe if you're making something large like chicken parts or bone-in pork chops.

YIELD: 2¼ CUPS, ABOUT 4 SERVINGS

2 cups water

3 tablespoons kosher salt

2 tablespoons granulated sugar

1 garlic clove, minced

1 teaspoon chopped fresh herbs (like thyme)

Whisk the ingredients in a large bowl until thoroughly dissolved and then add steaks, chops, or chicken parts 1 to 2 hours before grilling or broiling.

PAIRINGS: Brine chicken breasts (or parts) or pork (chops or tenderloin) and then baste with a glaze on the grill or under the broiler to give the cuts a nice caramelized crust.

TIP: When you use this brine, make sure to omit the salt in the searing technique.

Soy Ginger Marinade

YIELD: ½ CUP, ABOUT 4 SERVINGS

2 tablespoons dry sherry

2 tablespoons canola oil

2 tablespoons soy sauce

1 tablespoon toasted sesame oil

1 tablespoon chopped fresh ginger

2 garlic cloves, chopped (about 2 teaspoons)

Mix all the ingredients in a small bowl. Marinate meat or chicken in a large baking dish or a zip-top bag at least 2 hours before grilling or broiling or up to 24 hours ahead.

PAIRINGS: This is the perfect marinade for any sort of Asian grilling or broiling. Try it with beef, chicken, pork, or even shrimp (for a short spell). Finish with the Spicy Hoisin Glaze (page 89) or serve with the Korean Steak Sauce (page 169) or Thai Peanut Dipping Sauce (page 167).

Red Wine and Rosemary Marinade

This is an old-school marinade, the kind of hearty mixture that goes well with a large cut of beef or lamb. It may not tenderize them, but it will give them a fine flavor profile.

YIELD: 1½ CUPS, ABOUT 4 SERVINGS

½ cup red wine

¼ cup olive oil

1 tablespoon kosher salt

1 tablespoon chopped fresh rosemary

1 large garlic clove, chopped (about 1 teaspoon)

1 teaspoon coarsely cracked black pepper

Mix all the ingredients in a small bowl. Marinate meat or chicken in a large baking dish or a zip-top bag at least 2 hours before grilling or broiling or up to 24 hours ahead.

PAIRINGS: This marinade is perfect for steaks, lamb, or even chicken parts. You can even marinate the steaks before sautéing—just make sure to pat them dry before cooking. After searing, top with a pat of Café de Paris Butter (page 200) or the Toasted Garlic Aioli (page 194).

Tandoori Yogurt Marinade

YIELD: ¼ CUP, ABOUT 4 SERVINGS

¾ cup plain yogurt

2 tablespoons minced ginger

1 garlic clove, minced (about 1 teaspoon)

2 teaspoons curry powder

2 teaspoons paprika

2 teaspoons kosher salt

1 teaspoon freshly ground black pepper

¼ teaspoon cayenne

Mix all the ingredients in a small bowl and marinate meat, chicken, or fish at least 1 hour before grilling or broiling or up to 24 hours ahead.

PAIRINGS: This tandoori-like paste is perfect for adding moisture to dry cuts like chicken or pork. After grilling or broiling, pair with the cooling Cucumber-Mint Raita (page 203) or punch it up with the Spicy Indian Tomato-Onion Chutney (page 223).

Jamaican Jerk Paste

I like to leave the jalapeño seeds in so they offer a little zing, though you can remove them if you like.

YIELD: ½ CUP, ABOUT 4 SERVINGS

2 tablespoons olive oil

1 large or two small shallots, diced (about ¼ cup)

1 jalapeño, stemmed and diced (about ¼ cup)

1 tablespoon chopped fresh ginger

2 teaspoons kosher salt

1 teaspoon freshly ground black pepper

½ teaspoon allspice

⅛ to ¼ teaspoon ground nutmeg

⅛ to ¼ teaspoon ground cloves

Add all the ingredients to a mini-chop or food processor and purée until finely chopped; you may need to scrape down the sides. Marinate meat or chicken in a large zip-top bag or a shallow baking dish at least 1 hour before grilling or broiling or up to 24 hours ahead.

PAIRINGS: Grilled chicken parts are the classic pairing for this jerk marinade, though I also like it with pork or even shrimp (the latter shouldn't sit in this paste for more than 1 hour). Finish with the Mango, Roasted Red Pepper, and Habanero Salsa (page 161).

SAUCES WHILE SEARING		
Sauce Type	**Description**	**Pair with . . .**
Glazes and BBQ Sauces	Thick, sweet mixtures armed with a healthy punch of acid and spice. Fresher and more sophisticated than anything you can find in a jar	Baste onto grilled or broiled steak or chops toward the end of cooking so these sugary mixtures don't burn.
Pan Sauces	These boozy concoctions are the rock stars of the book, dressy but quick. These creations range from sharp, acidic jus to rich, creamy reductions to light herb broths.	Meaty sautéed ingredients. Whisk booze, broth, or cream into the skillet after sautéing (and after removing the seared steak or chop) to pick up any caramelized crust left behind.
Sauté Sauces	Unlike pan sauces, these are prepared apart from the sear (either in another pan or in a bowl) and then added to the sautéed ingredients during the final stage of cooking.	Add to sautés of beef, chicken, seared shrimp, or hearty vegetables like cauliflower for dishes that are a cross between saucy sautés and quick braises.
Stir-Fry Sauces	These sauces traverse the flavor borders of South East Asia, ranging from light Chinese broths to heavier Thai curries.	Make these mixtures in a separate vessel from the stir-fry and then toss with seared meat or vegetables for the last minute or two of cooking.

SAUCES AFTER SEARING

Sauce Type	Description	Pair with . . .
Salsas	Yes, there's *salsa* salsa in here, but all sorts of other bright vegetable and fruit mixtures as well, some spicy and some not, many of them from Latin or South America.	Nap over seared steak or fish or set out for dipping at the table when the weather's warm and the garden is in bloom.
Vinaigrettes	Not just for salads, vinaigrettes perk up seared ingredients with their tangy balance of richness and acidity.	Drizzle over grilled or broiled chops or steaks. Or go the salad route: set seared ingredients on top of greens and drizzle with these vinaigrettes.
Dressings and Emulsions	Mayo serves as the base for the creamy dressings and flavored mayonnaises in this section. There's a master recipe for home-made mayonnaise or use the jarred stuff if you prefer.	Spread flavored mayos over a grilled burger or dollop on top of seared fish, steaks, or chicken. Partner dressings with asparagus, beans, or hardy salad greens.
Dipping Sauces	These sauces hit most every point on the globe—from a Thai peanut dipping sauce to an Indian raita—but all are meant to be either dipped or drizzled.	Use as finishing sauces for grilled or broiled meats and fish. Set into small bowls and let your guests dip away.
Infused Dairy and Oils	This group uses oil or dairy as the vehicle to carry intense flavors. Infused oils had their heyday in the 80s, but they're still a quick, flavorful accompaniment to all sorts of seared ingredients. Compound butters—herbs and aromatics folded into softened butter—are richer, if not more dressy.	Baste the oils on grilled or broiled steaks or drizzle on vegetables or fish fillets after broiling. Melt infused butter or cream onto everything from a vegetable sauté to grilled corn on the cob.
Relishes and Chutneys	These fruit and vegetable combinations tend to be more spiced, sweet, and sour than salsas.	Use these chunky, intensely flavored mixtures to punch up plain grilled or broiled meat, fish, or chicken.
Seared Vegetable Toppings	No, grilled balsamic onions or sautéed wild mushrooms are not saucy sauces, but they fit the One-Bite Principle (page 9), enhancing each bite of a seared ingredient.	Smother these flavor-soaked vegetables on seared chops or steaks.
Pestos, Pastes, and Purées	Pulse together in a blender or food processor and then spread or melt on seared ingredients like a colorful infused butter.	Spread, dip, or toss with lighter grilled or broiled vegetables, fish, or chicken.

STEP 2: SAUCE

INGREDIENTS: 8 or less (not including salt, pepper, and cooking oil)
PREP/COOK TIME: Usually about 10 minutes and no more than 15 minutes

The sauce should complement both the cooking technique (a stir-fry sauce goes with stir-fries, a glaze goes with broiled or grilled food, and so on) and the actual seared ingredient (a sweet, acidic pan sauce pairs well with sautéed pork chops, for instance). The types of sauces in this book may be familiar (like a pan sauce, gravy, or glaze) or exotic (like a relish, chutney, or flavored oil), but I've organized them into two categories based on when they're added: Sauces While Searing (SWS) in chapter 3 and Sauces After Searing (SAS) in chapter 4. All are quick and easy and packed with flavor to jazz up whatever you're searing (see preceeding chart for description).

This brings up one of the more important questions of this book: what constitutes a sauce? My list of 250 sauces intentionally stretches to include unconventional (non-liquid-based) mixtures, pushing the definition of a sauce from its standard liquid (or saucy) constitution to a broader complementary role in everything from purées and infused butters to quick pickles and seared vegetables (see the One-Bite Principle on page 9). And this isn't because I ran out of sauce ideas. Rather, I wanted there to be a wide range of options to make this sear-sauce-and-serve method full of all sorts of possibilities.

STEP 3: SERVE

This last step is part of your nightly culinary responsibility, so I offer options in chapter 5 for simple starchy sides with which to pair the main-course seared meat, fish, or vegetables. I also suggest how to put the whole meal together in both the final step of each high-heat searing technique as well as the pairings' section for the sauces. I won't tell you to go with the white tablecloth instead of the green, but I try to guide you toward the season and occasion for which each sear and sauce might go best.

II. THE EQUIPMENT

I'm a firm believer in working with what you've got. It's hard enough to find time to cook, but add to that the expense of outfitting a kitchen and most beginner cooks will likely stay just that. For this reason, I've tried to list the bare essentials for this book, about how much you should expect to pay, and their relative priority for your kitchen. You're better off working through this list one at a time, buying good pieces as you go (one good skillet is worth far more than two crappy pans).

BASTING BRUSH/SPATULA/WHISK: One of the few major innovations in kitchen equipment in the last ten years or so has been the appearance of silicone in the form of spatulas, basting brushes, and whisks. This material is generally heat-proof up to 500°F (no melting in the pan), easy to clean in the dishwasher (unlike old-fashioned pastry brushes), and won't scratch up nonstick cookware.

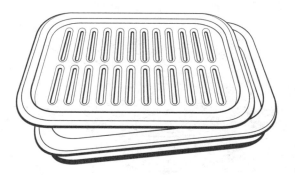

BROILER PAN: A broiler pan consists of a slotted tray set over a shallow baking pan. This two-pan configuration is designed to allow grease and juices to drain from whatever you're broiling so the food stays crisp, the cooking juices don't spatter all over the oven, and the kitchen stays relatively smoke-free.

TIP: The Importance of Being Sturdy

While it may be tempting to purchase a cheaper skillet, a pan's cost and its sturdiness are generally intertwined (unless it's a cast-iron pan, which is both heavy and cheap). Thickness and sturdiness are important because they help a pan retain its heat, which allows it to evenly cook whatever you're searing without fear of scorching or sticking.

Love the Broiler You're With

Chances are the broiler you're presently using is what you'll have for the foreseeable future. The cost of a new oven is substantial, so unless you've come into money (or a sweet wedding registry), you're best served learning to master what you have.

If you are looking for a new grill, there are whole books and stores devoted to the subject. So in this space, I'm not going to dare try to solve that riddle. Purists favor the flavor and intense heat of charcoal, and at about $75, a kettle grill is a good buy. Gas grills are far more quick and convenient, if not quite as hot. A decent gas grill will run somewhere between $150 to $500 and offer maximum efficiency for the techniques in this book.

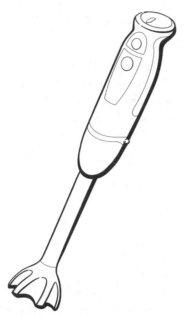

KNIVES: When you pick up a good, sharp knife after working with dull blades all your life, everything becomes so much easier. Big, sturdy chef's knives can cover most slicing tasks. A 10-inch blade runs about $100, which isn't much when you consider that it should last you a lifetime. A French or German chef's knife allows you to rock it back and forth on a cutting board; Japanese-style knives have flat blades that demand straight up-and-down slicing. For smaller tasks (like finely dicing a shallot), you can use a paring knife. I like the serrated Victorinox paring knives which are cheap (about $10) and sturdy. At some point, you can build up your knife drawer to include a boning and slicing knife for more advanced slicing techniques.

SAUCEPAN: The cooked sauces in this book mostly yield small amounts, meaning that a small saucepan (something with a handle that holds about 1½ quarts) will do the trick. Because the sauce preparations generally don't involve much more than browning onions or sweating garlic, there's no need to buy a particularly expensive saucepan (about $30 should do).

IMMERSION BLENDER: There's nothing wrong with your basic, old-fashioned blender, but I love the flexibility these handheld, sticklike blenders offer. You can purée a sauce right in the pan instead of having to do a back-and-forth transfer.

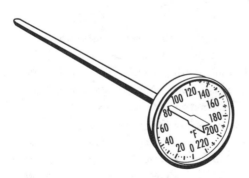

INSTANT-READ THERMOMETER: This is the best purchase you can make to ensure that your steaks or chicken are cooked just right. These pen-sized probes give you a quick and accurate reading of meat or poultry's internal temperature. One note: for thinner steaks and chops (of which there are many in this book), these probes won't give you a proper reading, so you're better off using touch and feel.

SAUTÉ PAN: These are like skillets only with straight, not sloping sides, and often come accompanied by a lid (whereas skillets are usually without). The straight edge limits the searing surface area, but does make it easier to contain brothy pan sauces. Most sauté pans are priced similar to skillets (up to $100 for a good 12-inch pan). If you have to choose between one or the other, go with a skillet for its enhanced searing capabilities.

SKILLET: The most versatile of all pans, a skillet's slopping sides create more surface area for searing and also offer clearance for flipping or moving seared ingredients around the pan. Surface area is important because it allows more space between each ingredient, which both encourages browning and prevents sticking. The pan's material is also significant. Cast iron is inexpensive (a good skillet is about $20) and offers the highest levels of performance, but it requires maintenance: properly heating it before cooking, washing it while hot, and avoiding soap and scouring. Nonstick pans are convenient, and perfect for delicate fish, but they don't brown foods well and need to be treated more gently. Finally, stainless steel holds up nicely to high heat, browns food beautifully, and is relatively easy to clean. It tends to be expensive, though (about $100 for a 12-inch skillet). If you only have a 10-inch pan, you might have to cook pork chops, chicken breasts, or steaks in batches—not ideal on a hurried weeknight.

TONGS: These can become an extension of a cook's fingers, the most versatile of tools for grabbing, flipping, twisting, or turning food in a pan, under the broiler, or on the grill. Locking tongs are convenient if you want to store them in a drawer or fit them neatly in the dishwasher. Make sure to use silicone-tipped tongs with a nonstick pan.

WOK: A wok's large surface area vibes with stir-frying's goal of quick, nonstick cooking. The vessel's rounded shape doesn't fit the contour of a flat stove top though (see illustration on page 59). Woks are traditionally set on a cylindrical stand so the heat can access most all of the pan. The flat burners on a home range mostly only heat a wok's relatively narrow bottom. For this reason, I generally go with skillets for stir-fries at home.

WHAT YOU CAN SEAR AND SAUCE

These charts cover all the different cuts and types of meat, fish, and vegetables that fit the time profile of our book. So while spareribs or brisket can most certainly be seared and sauced, they just can't be done within our time constraints.

CHARTS:
PAGES 24-27

	Ingredient	Saute (page)	Stir-Fry (page)	Grill (page)	Broil (page)	Information	Prep Notes	Preferred Doneness
CHICKEN — Boneless	Boneless breasts	31, 34, or 36		71	63	Easy and versatile; plain flavor fits just fine with our formula.	Butterfly or gently pound to speed up and even out cooking.	Cooked through, firm to the touch; 165°F.
Boneless	Boneless thighs	31, 34, or 36	56	71	63	More flavorful than breasts, but slower cooking.	Trim off fatty patches and pound for quick cooking.	Cooked through, firm to the touch; 165°F.
Bone-in	Split-breasts			73	63	Juicier than boneless, but thickness makes them hard to cook quickly.	Cut in half (widthwise) to cook quicker, more evenly.	
Bone-in	Bone-in thighs			73	63	Slow cooking; big flavor goes wonderfully with intense spiced sauces.	Trim excess skin, fatty patches. Cut in half through bone for quick cooking.	Cooked through, firm to the touch; 170°F.
Bone-in	Drumsticks			73	63	Cheap, easy to cook. Grill or broil and then toss with dipping sauce.	Cut off, discard chewy tendon near bottom of drumstick.	
Bone-in	Wings			73	63	Often more nosh than main course; perfect summer searing fare.	Cut off and discard wing tip, separate wing at the joint.	Cooked through; too small to temp.
BEEF — Chewy, Tasty	Flank Steak	34, 38	60	75	64	A bargain no more. Full flavored; tender (or less tough) when thinly sliced.	Very little fat to trim. A marinade-friendly cut.	Make a nick in the beef with a paring knife. Medium Rare = uniformly pink with a little red at center (130°F). Medium = light pink (135°F). Medium Well = touch of pink in center (150°F). Well = almost no pink (160°F).
Chewy, Tasty	Skirt Steak	34, 38	60	75	64	Similar to flank steak, but smaller, more gamey. Great for fajitas.	Relatively lean with little fat to trim.	
Chewy, Tasty	Flap Steak (Sirloin Tips)	34	60	75	64	Marbled, pleasantly chewy chunks. Best marinated and then grilled.	Trim any sheaths of fat. Cook whole or thinly slice and saute.	
Good value	Chuck-Eye Steak			75		One of the best beef bargains: full flavor makes up for tough texture.	Try to marinate if you have the time.	
Good value	Round Steak	38	60	75		Tender, but plain (occasionally with a livery flavor). Not my favorite.	Best thinly sliced and stir-fried.	
Good value	Top Sirloin			75	64	A great, affordable cut for a crowd. Tender and easy to grill.	Leave the fat lining the perimeter of this lean cut.	
Special Occasion	Rib Eye	38		75	64	Tender, great flavor/marbling. "Prime rib" in restaurants, from the rib roast.	Trim fatty patches, which are many.	
Special Occasion	Tenderloin	34, 38		75	64	Tender texture, plain flavor, big price.	Trim outside silverskin if you seek perfection.	
Special Occasion	Strip Steak	38		75	64	Big, beefy texture and flavor; too pricey for a stir-fry.	Trim off fat, if you like, for easy eating.	

Ingredient	Saute (page)	Stir-Fry (page)	Grill (page)	Broil (page)	Information	Prep Notes	Preferred Doneness
PORK							
Bone-In Chops	38		75	64	Look for center cut which, like a beef T-bone, has both loin and tenderloin meat.	For quick, even sauteing, buy ones about 1 inch thick.	Medium give when you press down on the center of a thicker chop; light pink in the center; 145°F.
Boneless Chops	38	60	75	64	Center-cut chops tend to be more tender.	A quick brine prevents this cut from drying out.	
Tenderloin	34	60	75	64	Like chicken breasts, convenient but plain. Pair with big flavors.	Grill or broil whole or sauté medallions.	
Country-Style Ribs			75		Inexpensive but fatty. Different muscles complicate even cooking (and doneness).	Trim off excess fat, which is considerable.	Well 150°F—(to cook off some of the fat).
Sausage	34		75	64	Perfectly good for searing and saucing.	Grill whole links or saute in pieces.	Cooked through with no traces of pink.
Ham Steak	38		75	64	Tasty and quick. Sear for just a couple of minutes on each side to brown.	NA. There's really no prep necessary.	Already cooked, so just heat through.
LAMB							
Shoulder Chops	38				Affordable but tough. Look for chops from near the rib area.	The wet heat of a quick saute/braise can tenderize this cut.	Tender and cooked through.
Rib Chops	38		75	64	Pricey chops from rack of lamb. Fattier, but more flavorful than loin chops.	Trim off excess fat.	Medium rare, uniformly pink, internal temperature of 130°F.
Loin Chops	38		75	64	Dressy and expensive T-bones. Lean and good eating.	Trim off excess fat.	
Sirloin Chops/Steak	38	60	75	64	The best buy of the group; nice balance of texture and flavor.	Trim off excess fat.	
OTHER							
Veal Cutlets	36				Now, with more veal humanely raised back on the tables this cut is an option for many cooks.	Buy pre-sliced cutlets for simplicity.	Just cooked through and firm to the touch.
Veal Chops	38		75		Thick bone-in veal chops are slow to cook, but are great seared and sauced.	Trim off excess fat.	Medium doneness, light pink—135°F.
Turkey Breasts	31		71		Not just holiday fare; convenient, flavorful alternative to chicken breasts.	Slice into cutlets and saute or butterfly and grill or broil.	Cooked through.—165°F.
Ground Meat	40		76		Grind yourself (page 41) or buy pre-ground; try fish like salmon or tuna, too.	Grind yourself: pulse in food processor or use a grinder.	Cooked through—165°F.

FISH/SEAFOOD

	Ingredient	Saute (page)	Stir-Fry (page)	Grill (page)	Broil (page)	Information	Prep Notes	Preferred Doneness
Non-Shell Shellfish	Shrimp	46	60	78	66	Farm-raised shrimp are affordable, easy, but can lack in flavor, texture.	Pre peeled, deveined save time. Rinse well and pat dry.	Just firm and cooked through.
	Scallops	46	60		66	Make sure to buy "dry" scallops. Sauteing and scallops are a perfect fit.	Remove the muscle, rinse well, and pat dry.	Slightly soft and pink in the center (medium).
	Calamari	46	60	78		The tenet (cook squid a little or a lot) is true; I lean towards the former here.	Slice bodies into rings (unless grilling); keep tentacles whole.	Just firm, opaque but still tender.
Shell Shellfish	Clams	48		78		Relatively easy and quick to cook. Pick out smaller varieties (like littlenecks).	Rinse or soak gritty clams in salt water with cornmeal.	Shells opened; discard unopened.
	Mussels	48				Affordable, quicker cooking than clams. Versatile with saute sauces.	Rinse and pull off stringy beards from sides of shells.	Shells opened; discard unopened.
Gamey, full-flavored and -textured fish	Salmon	42		78	66	Farm-raised is affordable, available year-round but, less flavorful than wild.	Leaving the skin on helps it hold together on the grill.	Medium, pink in the center.
	Tuna	42		78	66	Pair with intense Mediterranean or Asian sauces. Avoid frozen steaks.	Cut off dark (strong flavored) patches if you like.	Medium rare: uniformly pink in the center.
	Swordfish	42		78	66	Similar to tuna in steak-y texture. Pair with big Mediterranean flavors.	Cut off dark (strong flavored) patches if you like.	Medium well; just a little pink in the center.
Mild White Fish	Halibut	42		78	66	Great texture and mild flavor. Versatile with many sauces, techniques.	Steaks are easier to grill, filets easier sauté.	Medium well; a little glossy in the center.
	Cod (Haddock)	44			66	Very mild; gateway fish for the seafood-phobic. Adapts well to many flavors.	Rinse well; mild cod can be rather fishy if not.	Medium-well, just starting to flake.
	Sole	44			66	Delicate and dressy; thin, wide shape necessitates batch sauteing. Easy broiling.	Gently rinse and pat dry.	Just firm to the touch and cooked through.
	Tilapia	44			66	Fish for the future: cheap, sustainable, and tasty. Similar in shape to sole.	Gently rinse and pat dry.	Just firm to the touch and cooked through.
	Trout/Artic Char	44		78	66	Different colors, same species. Thin, but sturdy, especially on the stovetop.	Skin is mild and helps hold the filets together.	Medium well; a little pink in the center.

Ingredient	Saute/Stir-Fry (pg)	Grill (page)	Broil (page)	Information	Prep Notes	Preferred Doneness
Broccoli	50			Cheap, healthy, and tasty (no matter what the 1st President Bush might say).	Cut into 1½-inch florets; peel stalks and thinly slice.	Crisp tender, browned, and bright green.
Cauliflower	52			Slow sauté until a perfect wintry change of pace from gourds and squash.	Cut into 1-inch florets; thinly slice the core.	Browned and tender, but not mushy.
Green Beans (Wax Beans, Romano Beans)	50			Best when local in summer months, but, like broccoli, passable year-round.	Trim stems and sauté whole or in pieces.	Tender but still slightly toothy.
Asparagus	50	80	65	They wow when in season (spring) and in hemisphere (your own).	Snap off woody ends; grill/broil whole or cut in pieces.	Crisp tender, browned, and bright green.
Zucchini (Summer Squash)	50	80	65	Sweet flavor, soft texture intensify when browned over high-heat.	Buy smaller squash and cut off some of the seed core.	Tender but still slightly toothy
Eggplant	50	80	65	Sear well and pair with big flavors to highlight its meaty texture.	Slice 1/4 inch thick and salt ahead to pull out moisture.	Soft, completely cooked through.
Snap Peas (Snow Peas)	50			Either variety is fine raw; so sear quickly just to brown.	Trim snap peas and peel off the seams.	Browned but slightly crisp.
Corn	50	82		Be patient and buy corn that's local and in season so it's good and sweet.	Cut into kernels to saute or leave on husk for grilling.	Lightly browned and tender.
Spinach	53			Fresh bunches are more delicate, though cellophane bagged stuff is fine.	Slice off the stems from the bunch leaves or pick out thick stems from bagged spinach.	Wilted, but still a little toothy
Carrots	52			Slow sauteing both caramelizes and softens these root vegetables.	Peel and cut in julienne strips or 1/2-inch disks.	Lightly browned and tender.
Bell Peppers	50	80	65	Complementary in sauces, they can be the lead when grilled in large pieces.	Halve or quarter for grilling; cut in strips for stovetop.	Browned and just tender.
Onions	50	82		Central to many sauces in this book, though also fine vegetable sides.	Cut into disks for grilling or thinly slice for stovetop.	Browned and tender.
Bok Choy	53			Cross between spinach and cabbage; pair with high heat and Asian flavors.	Cut in 1-inch pieces, soak and spin dry.	Wilted, but still a little toothy.
Chinese Broccoli	50			Pleasantly bitter with an earthy edge. Not just for Asian stir-fries.	Leave greens whole; slice stems into 1/2-inch pieces.	Greens wilted, stems crisp-tender.
Swiss Chard, Kale, Collard Greens	53			Hardier greens need prolonged cooking. Pair with garlic and earthy flavors.	Use your thumb and index finger to stem (page 55).	Wilted, but still a little toothy.
Cabbage (Napa, Green, Red, Savoy...)	53			Cook quickly to brown lightly and then pair with sweet and sour sauces.	Cut in half, core, and then thinly slice.	Wilted, but still a little toothy.
Brussels Sprouts	52			Cook quickly with big flavors.	Halve or break into individual leaves.	Browned, wilted but a little toothy.

CHAPTER: 2

THE SEAR

FOUR COOKING MEDIUMS, TWENTY-FIVE HIGH-HEAT TECHNIQUES, AND ALL THE INFORMATION YOU'LL EVER NEED TO GET THEM JUST RIGHT

IN THIS CHAPTER, YOU'LL FIND OVERVIEWS OF ALL FOUR HIGH-HEAT METHODS AS WELL AS TWENTY-FIVE INDIVIDUAL SEARING TECHNIQUES. THE OVERVIEWS ARE LIKE SEARING *CLIFF'S NOTES*, A CONDENSED BLOCK OF CULINARY WISDOM THAT ANSWERS THE HOW'S AND WHY'S TO MY APPROACH TO HIGH-HEAT COOKING. THERE'S NOTHING OUT OF THE ORDINARY—NO NEED TO STAND ON YOUR HEAD OR CHEW GUM WHILE YOU GRILL—BUT I DO BREAK DOWN IN DETAIL SOME OF THE LITTLE TRICKS THAT YOU WOULD HAVE PICKED UP OVER TIME, BUT ARE BEST SERVED LEARNING UP FRONT.

THEN IT'S ON TO THE TWENTY-FIVE HIGH-HEAT TECHNIQUES, WHICH ARE YOUR BLUEPRINTS FOR SAUTÉING, STIR-FRYING, BROILING, OR GRILLING MOST ANYTHING, QUICKLY. THE TECHNIQUE INSTRUCTIONS ARE RELATIVELY GENERIC SO THAT WHETHER YOU'RE STIR-FRYING BROCCOLI OR SAUTÉING CLAMS, YOU CAN EASILY PLUG THE INGREDIENT INTO THE SEAR.

HOW THE HIGH-HEAT TECHNIQUES ARE ORGANIZED

In a perfect world, I'd include an individual high-heat technique for every ingredient that can be seared. However, since stir-frying pork is similar to stir-frying beef is similar to stir-frying shrimp, I've merged all of the similar-cooking ingredients into one technique to avoid redundancy, and to also allow you to see what searing one ingredient has in common with the next.

On this count, it's not a question of importance which ingredients are paired together. Rather, it's just what fits with what. The same goes for the high-heat techniques. There are ten sautéing methods in this book and only three broiling methods. This isn't because I think sautéing is more important. It's just that it's easier to fit a host of ingredients under the same broiling umbrella. Sautéing is a little more fickle, demanding more specific instruction based on what you're searing.

I. SAUTÉING

No doubt you've seen one of those Red Lobster commercials where a pan full of shrimp ride a wave of stove-top flames to a waiting dinner plate. (These ads run at every NFL timeout as a sort of Pavlovian seafood experiment.) The visual might not be enough to get you in the restaurant (I've never been), but it is instructive on the basics of sautéing: start with a sturdy pan and high heat (no worries, you don't need the dancing flames); add seafood, vegetables, or meat (or all of the above); sear and toss; and then finish with a splash of booze or a sauce.

That's the formula, but there are a couple of smaller but equally important steps. Like if you're cooking chicken or fish, it's a good idea to give them a rinse to wash off any funk from packaging. Then (1) **PAT EVERYTHING DRY** (even if it hasn't been rinsed). A wad of paper towels will do the trick and this drying step helps avoid sticking and ensures that the ingredients brown nicely (and browning = flavor).

....

TIP: Pat Ingredients Dry Before Searing

Any water clinging to the meat or vegetables creates steam and this vapor will upset the bond between what you're searing and the pan or grill.

Next, make sure to (2) **CUT ALL THE INGREDIENTS UNIFORMLY.** The idea is not to spend hours dicing fussy French food (though have at it if you like), but rather to cut uniform pieces so they all cook at the same rate. If you sloppily slice a chicken breast into uneven chunks, some pieces are either going to over- or undercook when you sear them. The idea is to be precise but not obsessive. Practice will help improve your knife skills. Until then, do your best to balance speed with precision.

Now it's on to the cooking. The pan you choose is important. (3) **USE A STURDY, HEAVY-BASED SKILLET.** You don't have to throw loads of money around to find one. I do the majority of my sautéing in a $20 cast-iron pan. But the vessel does need to be heavy enough to retain and evenly transfer high heat; see page 22 for a more thorough rundown of pan essentials.

Next up is a double step: (4) **GET THE PAN RIPPING HOT** and open up a window. If you're one of the lucky few to have a high-powered exhaust hood, forget the window. But if you're like me, you'll need to rely on kitchen windows to prevent the smoke alarm from sounding. Even in January, it's worth cracking open a window for the five minutes or so it takes to conduct the searing step—think of the momentary chill as the price for good food and a fresh-smelling abode.

Once you've got the ventilation going, you can heat up the pan. This is a Goldilocks-type task—not too hot, not too cold, but just right. Any culinary crazy can get a pan so hot the food recklessly scorches or lose his nerve and fail to get it hot enough to create a good sear. The real skill lies in guiding the heat of the pan somewhere in between. It needs to be hot enough that a droplet of water instantly evaporates upon hitting its surface, but not so hot that the droplet nervously skitters around the pan like a Mexican jumping bean hopped up on daytime cold medication. It takes about a minute or two on my electric stove top over medium-high heat to get to this instant-evaporation stage. Keep testing with a water droplet until you're there.

Now that the pan is hot, add a healthy splash of oil (I generally call for olive). It should almost immediately shimmer (but not smoke) and easily slide back and forth in the pan. At last, it's time to sauté. (5) **DON'T FUSS WITH THE FOOD** once it's in the pan. (This is also known as "playing it cool" in the sauté world.) When you're staring down a skillet full of sizzling food, the tendency is to make like a Benihana's grill chef and bang your spatula and tongs all over the place, messing with this and clattering at that. Resist this temptation. The bond between pan and sautéing food will only take if it's let be for at least one or two minutes. So, hold tight and ignore the itch to fiddle with the food until you can see it start to brown around the edges (and a corner easily releases when you gently lift it).

From this point, we can cruise past the flipping and cooking right to the sauté's endgame: pulling the meats or vegetables from the heat. A pilot once told me that landing is the hardest part of flying. Sautéing is kind of like that. You can buy the most wonderful piece of meat, prepare a beautiful red wine reduction to go with it, and if you lose your nerve or get distracted, that expensive cut can go to gray. No worries, I'm here to teach you how to (6) **POKE OR PARE** to see when sautéed fare is just done. For every recipe in this book, I take pains not just to give you an approximate cook time, but also what it should smell, feel, and look like when it's done. And when all else fails, there are always instant-read thermometers (the best $10 searing investment you'll ever make; see General Tools and Accessories on page 22) to tell you what's doing inside.

If you want to finish a sauté with a sauce, mix a pan sauce or sauté sauce with the browned crust left on the bottom of the pan from the sear. The French call this caramelized crust a "fond" and it's these browned bits that serve as the base for a good sauce. (7) **SCRAPE THE FOND** to incorporate it into the pan sauce. I'm not talking hair-raising, nails-on-chalkboard scraping. Just the opposite, a wooden spoon gently incorporates the fond, pulling it clean from the bottom of the pan.

Now that the sauté has safely landed, you can sauce it, arrange it on dinner plates, and serve with a crusty baguette or some sort of side. You've got a fine, even fancy, meal in a matter of minutes.

WHAT'S THE DIFFERENCE BETWEEN SAUTÉING AND STIR-FRYING?

There's no definitive food bible, but common sense and practice demonstrate the basic variables between these two methods. Both involve a combination of tossing and high heat. Stir-frying generally works with smaller pieces of meat or vegetables and involves constantly stirring the seared ingredients for a shorter cook time. Sautéing can be a little bulkier and not quite as fast. The ingredients can be either large or small (think a steak or thinly sliced beef) and are often left untouched in the pan for much of the cooking—almost like stove-top grilling—to encourage browning and avoid sticking.

In the restaurant setting, these two techniques will vary more, particularly in regard to the equipment. Restaurants have gas stove tops specifically designed for stir-frying. The burners look like the tail of a jet engine, which is far different than the standard Western range for sautéing.

Sautéed Chicken Breasts or Thighs
(Whole boneless breasts or thighs)

Sure there are all kinds of bland chicken preparations that fail to scream elegance or excitement (the TV-dinner industry has made a fortune on rubbery, pallid poultry). But add high heat and a dressy sauce (and, if you can swing it, good, local chicken) and you get a dish that's worthy of company, if not an "ahhh!" Though it's easy enough to sauté bone-in chicken (particularly if you finish cooking it in the oven), this technique calls for boneless for the sake of speed and convenience. If you are trying to impress someone, bone a split breast and leave the skin on (see How to Bone a Chicken Breast on page 32); or go a step further and stuff a chicken breast with a savory filling before searing it (see How to Stuff a Boneless Breast on page 33).

The Cut and the Prep

I like to gently pound boneless chicken breasts and thighs to about ½-inch thick before searing them. It gives them a uniform thickness so they cook more quickly and evenly. Use a meat mallet or even the side of a can.

Boneless chicken breasts: *Trimmed of excess fat and gently pounded*—about 4 medium.

Bone-in split chicken breasts: *Boned* (see How to Bone a Chicken Breast on page 32)—about 4 medium.

Boneless, skinless chicken thighs: *Trimmed of fatty patches and gently pounded to even out their thickness*; spread the thighs flat when sautéing so they cook quickly and evenly—about 6.

YIELD: 4 SERVINGS

PREP TIME: up to 5 minutes
COOK TIME: 4 to 10 minutes

1½ pounds boneless chicken breasts or thighs, cut as you like (see The Cut and the Prep)
About 1¼ teaspoons kosher salt
About ½ teaspoon freshly ground black pepper
1 tablespoon unsalted butter
1 tablespoon olive oil

1. SEAR: Season the chicken generously with salt and pepper. Set a large, sturdy skillet over medium-high heat for 1 minute, or until a droplet of water instantly evaporates once it hits the pan's surface. Heat the butter and oil until the butter melts and most of its foam cooks off, about 1 minute. Add the chicken, evenly spaced, and cook, without touching, until it browns around the sides, its opaque, cooked color stretches almost halfway up the sides, and it easily releases from the pan when you pick up an edge, about 2 minutes. Flip and cook the other side until browned and until the chicken is firm to the touch and just cooked through, 2 to 4 more minutes; check by slicing into a thicker piece—it should be opaque but juicy. Or check with an instant-read thermometer—it should register 165°F for breasts or 170°F for thighs.

2. SAUCE: Add an SWS sauté sauce (pages 132–150) and cook, tossing for 1 to 2 minutes, so the chicken soaks up its flavors and the liquid thickens. Or, transfer the cooked chicken to a plate, tent with foil, and make an SWS pan sauce (pages 97–114). After making the sauce, return the chicken to the pan to flip a couple of times to reheat through. Or, serve sautéed breast with a dipping sauce or drizzle with a vinaigrette (pages 175–185).

3. SERVE: Create a dressy meal by pairing whole breasts with a pan sauce like the Fresh Grape and Balsamic Pan Sauce (page 107) or the Orange and Caramelized Fennel Pan Sauce (page 105). Spoon the sauce over the chicken and serve with some sautéed greens (page 53) and something rich like the Herbed Goat Cheese Polenta (page 237) or Rosemary Roasted Fingerling Potatoes (page 235). Or make a quick braise with chicken thighs and the Cacciatore Sauce (page 136) or Spanish Stewed Chorizo and Garbanzos (page 139). Serve in shallow bowls with a crusty baguette and sautéed kale (page 53).

How to Bone a Chicken Breast (but Leave the Skin On)

A boneless, skin-on chicken breast combines the best of both worlds: convenience mixed with a touch of richness and flavor. Though you'd be hard-pressed to find boneless, skin-on breasts at the supermarket, it's easy enough to do at home. Pick up some bone-in split breasts and set them flat on a cutting board. Using a boning or paring knife, slice down just inside the breast bone (trace it with your fingers) until you get all way the way to the rib bones, then cut parallel to these bones so you can slice the breast meat (and the tenderloin) clean.

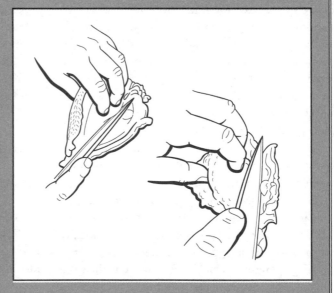

How to Stuff a Boneless Breast

Stuffing is a great way to jazz up a plain chicken breast. Use a chef's knife to slice into the fatter, outer edge, make a horizontal cut almost all the way through to the other side of the breast, and open it up like a book. Gently pound to even out the breast's thickness and then top the open breast with some combination of sautéed spinach, Parmigiano, sun-dried tomatoes, black olives, and prosciutto. Fold the halves back together, seal with toothpicks (two should do the job), and sauté. Because the stuffed chicken will take more time to cook, you may want to finish cooking it in a 425°F oven for about 5 minutes.

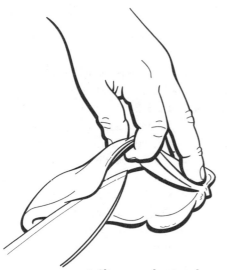

1. Slice a pocket into breast.

2. Pound to even out thickness.

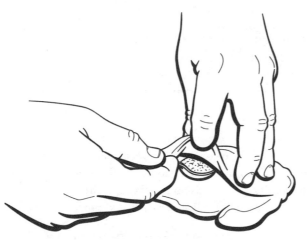

3. Spoon in stuffing.

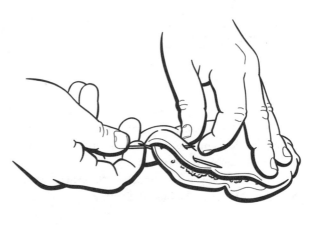

4. Seal with toothpicks.

Sautéed Strips or Chunks

(Chicken, Beef, Pork)

This technique is similar to stir-frying except you want to brown the meat by employing a hands-off approach at the start of cooking; avoid flipping (or even touching) the seared ingredients until they start browning at the edges, 1 to 2 minutes. Then toss with some sort of sauté sauce (or even a stir-fry sauce to mix mediums). You can dust the ingredients with flour before sautéing to offer a protective coating and help thicken any sauce you add to the pan.

YIELD: 4 SERVINGS

PREP TIME: up to 5 minutes
COOK TIME: 3 to 7 minutes

1¼ pounds boneless beef, pork, lamb, or chicken, cut as
    you like (see The Cut and the Prep)

About 1 teaspoon kosher salt

About ½ teaspoon freshly ground black pepper

1 tablespoon all-purpose flour (optional)

1 tablespoon unsalted butter

1 tablespoon olive oil

The Cut and the Prep

CHICKEN: I favor cutting thighs into smaller pieces so they cook through more quickly; this also makes it easier to sear off their fattiness.

Boneless, skinless breasts: *Trimmed of excess fat and cut into thin strips or uniform chunks (between 1 and 2 inches).*

Boneless, skinless thighs: *Trimmed of excess fat and cut into uniform chunks (between ¾ and 1½ inches).*

BEEF: It's unnecessary to use an expensive cut of beef for a sauté like this one, but if you're feeling flush, go crazy.

Tenderloin or strip steak: *Cut into uniform chunks (between 1 and 1½ inches).*

Flap meat, skirt, or flank steak: *Thinly sliced.*

PORK: Conventional pork loin or tenderloin is relatively affordable, but can be overly lean. Try to buy locally raised pork, which tends to have more fat and flavor. Cuts like country-style ribs, though generally boneless, have tough, fatty patches that are better gently braised.

Loin: *Trimmed of excess fat and cut into thin strips or uniform chunks (between 1 and 2 inches).*

Tenderloin: *Silverskin removed if you like and cut into thin strips or uniform chunks (between ¾ and 1½ inches).*

TIP: Less Meat = Even Cooking

Many of the broiling and grilling techniques in this book call for 1½ pounds of meat or chicken to serve 4 people (about 6 ounces per person) while the sauté and stir-fry recipes only call for 1¼ pounds. Part of the reason for the smaller portions on the stove top is that many sautés and stir-fries include vegetables in addition to the sauce. The other reason for this smaller portion is that it's all you can fit in a single layer in a 12-inch skillet (if you crowd in any more meat or fish, it will either stick or steam).

1. SEAR: Season the meat or chicken generously with salt and pepper and toss with the flour, if using. Set a large, sturdy skillet over medium-high heat for 1 minute, or until a droplet of water instantly evaporates once it hits the pan's surface. Heat the butter and oil until the butter melts and starts to foam, about 1 minute. Add the meat or chicken pieces in a single layer and cook, without touching for at least 1 minute, until the pieces brown around the edges, the raw coloring diminishes up the sides, and they easily release from the pan, about 2 minutes. Flip (if the pieces are large) or stir (if the pieces are smaller) and cook until they mostly lose their raw coloring on the outside, 1 to 2 minutes; remember, you don't want to cook them all the way through as they will finish cooking with the sauce in step 2.

2. SAUCE: Add an SWS stir-fry or sauté sauce (pages 115–150) and toss for 1 to 2 minutes so the meat or chicken just cooks through (slice open a bigger piece with a paring knife to check for doneness), the sauce heats through, and the flavors mix and meld.

3. SERVE: Depending on your mood and the season, this technique can produce a quick, wintry braise, a bright stir-fry, or a light spring sauté. Make a dressy pork sauté with the Sautéed Bacon and Browned Apples (page 143) and serve with Cheddar Cheese Grits (page 237). Or take beef in a springlike Italian direction with the Porcini and Pea Sauce (page 48) and serve over Creamy Saffron Risotto. Or turn chunks of chicken into a quick, but hearty braise with the New Mexican Green Chile Sauce (page 144) and a stack of warm tortillas.

TIP: Skip the Instant-Read Thermometer Here

Normally, I'm a big fan of instant-read thermometers (see General Tools and Accessories on page 22), but they're not much good for this technique. These strips or chunks are too small to get an accurate reading with the probe. So you'll have to use your senses—particularly, touch and sight—to let you know when the meat or chicken is properly cooked.

Sautéed Cutlets

(Chicken, Pork, Turkey, Veal)

This technique is the base for many old-school, Italian-American specialties: *piccata*, *saltimbocca*, and *marsala*, to name a few. The flour in this recipe serves a dual purpose: it gives the cutlets a protective coating so they stay moist and tender during cooking and it also helps make a rich base for a pan sauce (kind of like a lazy man's roux). Because these cutlets are thin and wide, you'll need to cook them in batches. They cook quickly, though, so this won't be much of a nuisance. I haven't included beef in this technique because its texture would become rubbery and the inside would gray. Shaved steak, the more common version of beef cutlets, would go best in the preceding technique (see page 34).

• •

The Cut and the Prep

Most supermarkets carry presliced cutlets though it's cheap and easy to cut your own (see How to Make Cutlets on page 37).

CHICKEN: Boneless, skinless breasts (about 3 medium), *trimmed of fat, cut into ¼-inch-thick pieces on the diagonal (6 to 8 pieces) and pounded to about ⅛-inch thick.*

PORK: Center-cut pork loin, *cut into medallions about ¼-inch thick (about 8) and pounded to ⅛ inch thick.*

TURKEY: Piece of boneless, skinless turkey breast, *cut into ¼-inch-thick pieces on the diagonal (6 to 8 pieces) and pounded to about ⅛ inch thick.*

VEAL: Because most supermarkets don't sell veal in portioned cuts, you might be best off buying 1¼ pounds of presliced cutlets.

YIELD: 4 SERVINGS

PREP TIME: up to 8 minutes (if you cut the cutlets yourself)
COOK TIME: 6 to 10 minutes

1¼ pounds pork, chicken, or veal cutlets, pounded to ¼-inch to ⅛-inch thickness
¾ teaspoon kosher salt
½ teaspoon freshly ground black pepper
½ cup all-purpose flour
2 tablespoons unsalted butter
1 tablespoon olive oil

1. SEAR: Season the cutlets generously with salt and pepper. Set the flour in a large shallow bowl (like a pie plate), dredge the cutlets, shaking off any excess flour, and transfer to a large plate.

Set a large, sturdy skillet over medium-high heat for 1 minute, or until a droplet of water instantly evaporates once it hits the pan's surface. Heat half of the butter and all of the oil until the butter melts completely and its foam subsides, about 1 minute. Add half of the cutlets and cook, without messing with them, until they just start to brown around the sides and easily release from the pan, 1 to 2 minutes. Flip and cook the other side until just firm to the touch (they should have just a little give when pressed) and cooked through (slice into one if you're unsure), about 1 minute. Transfer to a large plate and tent with foil. Melt the remaining butter, cook the remaining cutlets in the same manner, and transfer to the plate with the other cutlets.

2. SAUCE: Add an SWS pan or sauté sauce (pages 97–114) and cook, following its instructions (return the cutlets to the pan after cooking the pan sauce to flip a couple of times and pick up the flavors). Or, serve with an SAS (pages 152–231).

3. SERVE: This technique produces the kinds of dressy sautés you might order at your favorite Italian restaurant. Pair the Crisp Caper and Lemon Sauce (page 102) with most any cutlet for a jazzed-up take on your basic piccata; serve it with Spaghetti with Pecorino and Black Pepper (page 233). Try veal cutlets with the Morel and Chive Pan Sauce (page 110) or pork cutlets with the Fresh Grape and Balsamic Pan Sauce (page 107). Pair either with roasted potatoes and sautéed asparagus (page 50).

TIP: If you're going to add a sauté sauce, undercook chicken cutlets a bit—so they're still a little soft to the touch—as they will continue cooking with the sauce for another 1 to 2 minutes. Chicken thighs don't dry out quite as easily, so you can cook them all the way through before adding the sauce.

How to Make Cutlets

Though many butchers sell cutlets already prepared, you can cut them yourself quite easily and save a little bit of money while doing so. The trick is to slice boneless cuts into medallion-like pieces about 4-inches wide and ¼-inch thick (2 to 3 ounces). Then pound these pieces to a thickness of about ⅛ inch and 5 or 6 inches wide. With cylindrical cuts like pork loin or tenderloin, cutting the medallions is easy; just slice straight down. Try to slice flat cuts like chicken breasts or turkey breasts on the diagonal to get medallions. As long as you pound the pieces to a uniform thickness, they will cook evenly.

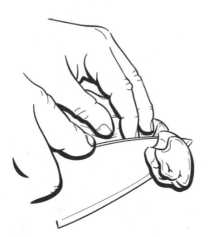

Sautéed Steaks and Chops

(Pork, Beef, Lamb, Veal)

Steakhouses are great, but needlessly expensive. You can go to a high-end butcher, pick up a fine cut, grab a nice bottle of wine, and use the savings toward flowers or chocolates or a college fund. And preparing that steak or chop like the pros is really quite easy: use high heat, season the meat well, don't fiddle with it much once it's in the pan, and you're there. Perhaps the hardest part is knowing when to pull the meat from the pan; look to the chart on page 24 for help with the doneness tests.

YIELD: 4 SERVINGS
PREP TIME: up to 2 minutes
COOK TIME: 4 to 8 minutes

1½ pounds boneless or 2½ pounds bone-in steaks or chops, cut as you like (see The Cut and the Prep)
About 1½ teaspoons kosher salt
About ¾ teaspoon freshly ground black pepper
1 teaspoon chopped fresh thyme or rosemary (optional)
2 tablespoons olive oil

PORK:

Boneless center-cut chops: Four 1-inch-thick chops will be about 1½ pounds. Leave the fat on the sides—it's easy enough to cut off at the dinner table and it adds moisture to lean, boneless pork during cooking.

Bone-in center-cut chops: Four 1-inch-thick chops will be about 2¼ pounds. Center-cut chops are the equivalent of a T-bone steak with pieces of both the loin and tenderloin.

Tenderloin: Trim the silverskin. You can sear the tenderloin whole or cut it into 1-inch steaks on the diagonal.

BEEF:

Tenderloin or rib eye: Trim these tender but pricey steaks of excess fat; try to buy steaks of similar thickness so they cook uniformly.

Flank or skirt: Trim off excess fat.

LAMB:

Rack of lamb: Best sear-roasted instead of simply seared.

Shoulder chops: More reasonably priced and just as flavorful.

1. SEAR: Season the meat generously with salt and pepper and the herbs, if using. Let sit at room temperature for 10 to 20 minutes while the grill heats.

Set a large, sturdy skillet over medium-high heat for 1 minute, or until a droplet of water instantly evaporates once it hits the pan's surface. Heat the oil until it's shimmering hot and easily glides from one side of the pan to the other, about 1 minute. Set the meat in the pan, evenly spaced (there should be at least ½ inch on each side if possible) and cook, without touching, until it browns around its edges and easily releases from the pan when you lift up a corner, 2 to 3 minutes. Reduce the heat to medium, flip, and cook the other side until browned, 2 to 4 minutes. Check for doneness: medium rare beef or lamb should be just slightly firm to the touch and a reddish pink when you make a nick into a thicker piece (130°F on an instant-read thermometer), while medium well pork should be medium-firm and just a little pink on the inside (about 145°F for medium well). Continue cooking and flipping until done to your liking.

2. SAUCE: Transfer the cooked meat to a plate, tent with foil, and make an SWS pan sauce (pages 197–114); you can either drizzle the pan sauce over the cooked meat or return the meat to the pan and flip a couple of times to reheat through. Or, serve with an SAS sauce (pages 152–231).

3. SERVE: Because doneness is so important with these large cuts, I generally don't use sauté sauces, which can complicate the timing of the cooking. A good sautéed steak, like a strip or even a chuck eye, goes perfectly with a boozy pan sauce like the Brandy and Dried Cherry Pan Sauce (page 101) or something rich like the White Truffle and Parmesan Cream (page 114). Serve with the Rosemary-Parmesan Mashed Yukon Potatoes (page 235) and some sautéed broccoli rabe (page 50). The Warm Mint Pan Sauce (page 109) will freshen up the gaminess of seared lamb chops, while the sweet fruitiness of the Apple Cider and Crisp Sage Pan Sauce (page 101) is just the sort of sweet and sour partner for pork chops; serve with Roasted Yukon Potato Wedges with Bacon and Thyme (page 236) and sautéed carrots (page 52).

TIP: Deglaze No Matter the Sauce

Even if you aren't making a pan sauce, you should use the flavorful caramelized crust left in the pan. Simply add ½ cup chicken broth, wine, or even water to the empty pan after sautéing, raise the heat to high, and cook, gently scraping the pan with a wooden spoon, until the liquid is reduced to just a couple of tablespoons and the caramelized crust has been incorporated into it. Drizzle onto the seared fare or whisk it right into the sauce if you prefer.

TIP: Pork Should Be Pink

In the 1950s when trichinosis was a scourge, undercooked pork was a danger and generations of Americans were taught to cook pork until well done. Two things have happened since then. New food safety standards have been applied to the pork industry and pork has been bred to be superbly lean (part of "The Other White Meat" campaign). Today not only is it unnecessary to cook pork until well done, but if you do, you'll get tremendously dry and flavorless meat. Instead, shoot for a medium-well doneness (around 145°F) so that the meat is still a little pink and moist.

TIP: Individual Doneness Tests

I've never been a big fan of corresponding meat doneness to how different parts of the hand feel when pressed; you spend more time trying to figure out your hand than you do the steak. And because each of these cuts has a unique shape and distinct texture (beef tenderloin is tender to start with while a flank steak, by nature, is firmer no matter its level of doneness), you're better off using an instant-read thermometer or making a little nick to check the level of pinkness. For more specific information on the doneness of each cut, check out the chart on page 24.

Sautéed Ground Meat

(Chicken, Beef, Lamb, Pork, Sausage, Turkey)

Anybody who grew up on Sloppy Joes or Ortega tacos (the ones with the spice packets and those ridiculously crunchy shells) knows that browning ground beef is pretty easy. It's up there with frying an egg or boiling spaghetti as something that everyone should be tested on before being let loose on the world. Despite its simplicity, there are so many great, even jazzy preparations you can make with this technique, so I've included it.

The Cut and the Prep

There really isn't much prep to this technique unless you choose to grind the meat yourself (see How to Grind Your Own on page 41).

Chicken: Breast meat grinds very lean and can have an overly soft texture. Thighs have more flavor and their fattiness offers a little more texture to the grind.
Beef: Ground chuck (from the shoulder of the animal) has the best balance of flavor and fat; ground round or sirloin (from the rear of the animal) tends to be leaner and not as tasty. Shoot for 85 percent lean, which has enough fat so it won't dry out.
Lamb: Generally, what you see is what you get for ground lamb at the butcher. Pick out some nicely marbled stew meat if you're going to grind it.
Pork: Try to buy ground pork from the butt (actually the shoulder of the animal), which tends to have some fattiness to it that holds up well.
Sausage: Buy bulk Italian sausage to avoid having to remove the meat from the casing. Cook it to the longer end of the range to melt off some of the fat.
Turkey: Most supermarkets carry decent ground turkey. If you want to grind your own, keep in mind that the thighs can have a slightly gamey flavor.

YIELD: 4 SERVINGS
PREP TIME: 2 minutes (up to 7 minutes if you grind your own)
COOK TIME: 4 to 8 minutes

1¼ to 1½ pounds ground meat
About 1 teaspoon kosher salt
About ½ teaspoon freshly ground black pepper
1 to 2 tablespoons olive oil (depending on the fattiness of the meat)

1. **SEAR:** Season the meat generously with salt and pepper. Set a large, sturdy skillet (I like to use my cast-iron pan) over medium-high heat for 1 minute. Heat the oil until it's shimmering hot, about 1 minute. Add the ground meat, spreading it in a thin layer, and cook, without touching it, until it starts to brown, 1 to 2 minutes. Using a wooden spoon or a heat-proof spatula, begin to chop at the meat to both flip it and break it up into small pieces. Continue cooking and breaking up until the meat completely loses all of its raw color, about 2 more minutes.

2. **SAUCE:** Add an SWS sauté or stir-fry sauce (pages 115–150), bring to a boil, and then simmer, stirring occasionally, so the meat completely cooks through and the flavors meld, 2 to 4 minutes.

3. **SERVE:** This technique produces a rather saucy dish (one easier to eat with a large spoon than a fork), so accompany it with something starchy like a warm tortilla, rice, or noodles. Pair sautéed ground pork with the Poblana Spiced Taco Sauce (page 146) and wrap in a corn tortilla with shredded green cabbage. Pair ground beef with Floating Rock's Chile-Basil Sauce (page 130) and serve with Cold Peanut Noodles with Mint and Thai Chiles (page 233). You could also make a fine meat sauce for pasta with any combination of ground beef, pork, sausage, or veal and the Quick Marinara (page 135) or Fresh Tomato and Fennel Sauce (page 133).

GROUND MEAT

Buying Ground Beef

These days, whenever there is a meat recall, the culprit is usually ground beef (as opposed to a steak or a whole cut). It's not that ground beef, in and of itself, is dangerous. Rather it's where and how the meat is ground. Unfortunately the large meat-processing plants in the Midwest still regularly incur bacterial contamination from dangerous strains like *E. coli*. The best solution to avoid this risk of food-borne illness is to either grind the beef yourself (see How to Grind Your Own) or buy it from a trusted, local source. Short of that, always cook pre-ground beef all the way through (past 160°F) to eliminate the risk of bacteria; this, of course, also applies to the burger technique on page 77.

Brown Early and Often

You need to chop and move ground meat around quite a bit during searing to cook it through evenly. This constant movement doesn't offer much opportunity for browning. To get some, spread the ground meat across the skillet in a single layer and let it ride untouched during the first minute or two of cooking so it starts to brown and color. After this, stir and chop up the meat with a wooden spoon or metal spatula until it cooks through. The browned flavor from this initial sear will give the dish a good flavor base.

How to Grind Your Own

After all the hamburger recalls over the years, it's tasty and perhaps safer to grind it yourself. Start by looking for full flavored steaks like chuck or even something exotic like brisket. Cut the meat into 1-inch pieces; don't worry about trimming off the fat or gristle as they'll be mixed into the grind. Freeze the meat for ten minutes; this will make it easier to pass through a grinder attachment on your stand mixer or to pulse in small batches in a food processor. The food processor won't grind meat quite as fine, but it is still perfect in burgers.

Sautéed Firm Fish Filets

(Halibut, Salmon, Swordfish, Tuna)

These firm-fleshed fish aren't all that hard to sear—they hold together nicely and flip relatively easily. This is a good thing because fresh tuna and swordfish can be rather pricey so you want to get your money's worth. Like a steak, doneness for fish is important (see Different Fish, Different Doneness on page 43). Most of these are best cooked to about medium. I suggest treating these fish as though they had been grilled or broiled. Their strong flavor and oily texture fish would overpower a pan sauce, leaving the whole thing tasting rather fishy. Instead, pair them after searing with a dipping sauce, vinaigrette, or even an infused butter. You can tuck them into a sauté sauce, though make sure to transfer the fish to the pan with the sauce instead of vice versa.

. . . .

The Fish and the Prep

Rinse and pat dry these filets very well.

. . . .

Salmon: I prefer to remove the skin before sautéing; if you do keep the skin on, start the sear skin side down.
Tuna: Slice off the darker patches (the fish's bloodlines) if you like; they can have a strong flavor.
Halibut: It's OK to use slightly thicker filets (up to 1½ inches).
Swordfish: Slice off the darker patches (the fish's bloodlines) if you like; they can have a strong flavor.

YIELD: 4 SERVINGS
PREP TIME: up to 2 minutes
COOK TIME: 5 to 10 minutes

1½ pounds firm-fleshed fish filets
About 1 teaspoon kosher salt
About ½ teaspoon freshly ground black pepper
1 teaspoon chopped fresh thyme or rosemary (optional)
2 tablespoons olive oil

1. SEAR: Season the fish generously with salt and pepper and herbs, if using. Turn on the oven fan and open up the kitchen windows. Set a large (preferably 12-inch), heavy-bottomed skillet over medium-high heat for 1 minute. Heat the oil until shimmering hot, about 1 minute. Add the fish, evenly spaced (about ½ inch on each side if possible), and cook, without touching, until it just starts to brown around the edges and easily releases from the pan (check by lifting up a corner with a spatula), 2 to 3 minutes. Flip, preferably with a fish spatula; use a pair of tongs to guide the fish onto the spatula if necessary. Cook the other side until the fish is just firm to the touch and reaches your desired level of pinkness when you slice into a thicker piece with a paring knife (see Different Fish, Different Doneness on page 43), 2 to 4 more minutes.

2. SAUCE: Transfer to a separate pan with an SWS sauté sauce (pages 132–150) and cook for a minute or two so the flavors mix and meld. Or, serve with an SAS sauce (pages 152–231).

3. SERVE: When you get a proper sear on these fish filets, the results are dressy. Go with that vibe. Spoon a dollop of flavored mayonnaise like the Black Pepper, 195) over sautéed salmon and serve with Roasted Rosemary Fingerling Potatoes (page 235) and sautéed spinach (page 53). Tuck sautéed tuna filets into a Mediterranean-inspired sauté sauce like the Venetian Agradolce Sauce with Raisins and Pine Nuts (page 142) and serve with Quinoa with Fennel and Feta (page 236) Or try simmering sautéed halibut in the Puttanesca Sauce (page 137) and serve over Garlicky Smashed Red Potatoes (page 235) with a side of sautéed green beans (page 150).

FISH

Choosing Fish

The fish in this technique are all popular and present tough decisions for the consumer, in part because of this popularity. Questions regarding the sustainability of farm-raised salmon or the mercury counts in large fish like tuna and swordfish are complex. Fortunately, there's a lot of great information around to assist with your decisions. The Natural Resources Defense Council provides a mercury counter on their Web site at www.nrdc.org or check out Montgomery Bay Aquarium's Seafood Watch guide at www.montereybayaquarium.org.

Different Fish, Different Doneness

There are some fish like swordfish or halibut that you want to cook nearly all the way through (about 140°F), or medium well, so they're mostly firm to the touch, but moist and just a little translucent in the center—use a paring knife to check. And then there are those fish whose flavor and texture are at their best when cooked to a medium or medium-rare doneness, like tuna or salmon (just think of the kinds of fish you might eat as sushi). These should be springy to the touch, almost uniformly pink in the center, and register about 130°F on an instant-read thermometer. As with a steak, though, how you cook fish is really up to you and how you like it.

Portion Fish After Searing

I suggest waiting to cut fish into portions until after searing it. Some filets aren't easy to portion evenly and in trying to do so, you can create uneven pieces (some thick, some thin) which won't cook uniformly. If you're uncertain, ask your fishmonger to cut the pieces to your liking or simply wait until after searing (when even cooking is no longer a concern).

Coat Tuna with a Flavor Crust

This is a neat trick to give tuna an extra hit of flavor and a dressy look. Rub thick steaks with a little oil, sprinkle some cracked black peppercorns or sesame seeds onto a large plate, and gently press down the filets so the pepper or seeds stick to them. You can use a nonstick pan to ensure you don't lose any of the crust, though it won't stick in a properly heated pan.

Open 'Em Up

This is perhaps the smelliest technique in the book. Seared fish is wonderful eating but its essence can linger long after the meal is done. Here's how to game plan it: Just before sautéing, open up a couple of windows (even if it's cold), close the bedroom door—you don't want that fish smell to get into your clothes!), and light a few scented candles. Five minutes after cooking, close the windows, but let the candles linger a bit. By the time you sit down to eat you'll be in a fresh-smelling abode.

Sautéed Delicate Fish

(Arctic Char, Cod, Haddock, Sole, Tilapia, Trout)

The fish in this grouping can vary quite a bit from one to the next—compare thick, flaky cod to light and delicate sole—but they all share an unfortunate tendency to break up when seared. This technique employs two basic steps to avoid this obstacle. A nonstick skillet goes a long way toward solving the problem. It won't give the fish the same browned crust as a stainless steel skillet, but it will ensure an easy flip. The other part of the solution is to focus on the flip itself (see Flipping Delicate Filets tip on right), so that all your hard work doesn't go for naught. Stay loose (deep, relaxed breaths) and flip easy.

> **TIP: Flipping Delicate Filets**
>
> Good fish spatulas make flipping delicate fish easier. A fish spatula is longer and thinner than most spatulas, allowing you to gently tuck it under the filet to flip it. Even better, a silicone fish spatula won't scratch your nonstick pan.

The Cut and the Prep

Rinse these fish and then pat dry them dry well with paper towels before sautéing.

Trout and Arctic char: I prefer to leave the skin on trout filets as it's mildly flavored and helps them hold together. Whole trout aren't hard to sauté, but they take extra time on the stove top and can be cumbersome to serve (unless you're in the mood to filet them tableside).

Cod and haddock: If you have a mix of thin and thick filets, fold over the thinner ones so they're the same thickness.

Sole: These filets are so thin that you won't be able to brown them much before they cook through.

Tilapia: This fish doesn't have the prestige of sole and isn't as familiar as cod, but it has stepped to the fore with its strong reputation for sustainability. It is a little thicker than sole, so it can get a nice browned crust.

YIELD: 4 SERVINGS

PREP TIME: up to 2 minutes
COOK TIME: 5 to 10 minutes

1¼ pounds fish filets
About 1 teaspoon kosher salt
About ½ teaspoon freshly ground black pepper
1 teaspoon chopped fresh herbs (like thyme or rosemary) (optional)
1½ tablespoons olive oil (1 more tablespoon if cooking in batches)

1. SEAR: Season the fish generously with salt and pepper and the herbs, if using. Heat the oil in a large, heavy-based nonstick skillet over medium-high heat until shimmering hot, about 1 minute. Add the fish, evenly spaced (about ½ inch on each side if possible—you may need to work in batches with sole or tilapia), and cook, without touching, until it just starts to brown or become opaque around the edges, 1 to 2 minutes. Flip, preferably using a fish spatula and a pair of tongs to guide the fish onto the spatula if necessary. Reduce the heat to medium and cook the other side until the fish is mostly firm to the touch and almost completely opaque when you slice into it (or pry open between cod flakes) with a paring knife, 2 to 4 more minutes (see Different Fish, Different Doneness on page 43).

2. SAUCE: Add an SWS sauté sauce (pages 132–150) and cook for 1 to 2 minutes, spooning the sauce over the filets, so they soak up its flavors and the liquid thickens. Or, transfer the cooked fish to a plate, tent with foil, and make an SWS pan sauce (pages 97–114; see Pan or Sauté Sauces for Mild Fish; drizzle the pan sauce over the cooked fish. Or, serve with an SAS sauce (pages 152–231).

3. SERVE: Most all of these fish are mild so you can go crazy with the pairings, pumping them up with assertive ingredients or letting them shine with more complementary flavors. Match Brown Butter and Rosemary Sauce (page 143) with sautéed sole and serve with Roasted Yukon Wedges with Bacon and Thyme (page 236). Take trout in a Spanish direction with a drizzle of the Salamanca Sherry-Thyme Vinaigrette (page 179) and serve with sautéed greens and a crusty baguette. I love making quick braises with cod using curries and Asian broths like the Fragrant Ginger and Lemongrass Coconut Broth (page 129) or a tomato-based sauce like the Fresh Tomato and Fennel Sauce (page 133). Serve either over steamed rice.

TIP: Pan or Sauté Sauces for Mild Fish

Unlike the sturdy but fishy fish in the technique (page 42), these delicate fish tend to be more mild, making them a go with pan sauces or sauté sauces. The only catch is that you have to treat them as gently during the saucing step as you do during the sear so they don't break up.

Sautéed Seafood

(Scallops, Shrimp)

The beauty of this technique is that it's exceedingly easy but can produce dishes that have a fancy, elegant feel. Shrimp and scallops are very different in shape and makeup. But the goal when cooking them is similar: give each a good sear to enhance its flavor and texture and then pair with bright sauces. The searing step is particularly important for scallops, whose flat sides acquire a beautiful crust when properly sautéed. The one big no-no for shrimp and scallops is overcooking: their tender texture quickly turns rubbery and tough.

The Seafood and the Prep

Rinse and then make sure to pat dry with paper towels very well before sautéing; this seafood won't brown properly if it's even just a little wet.

Scallops: *Muscles removed* (just grab them with your fingers and pull—these white tabs will come off like Velcro), *rinsed well, and patted dry.*

Shrimp: 21–26 count, *peeled, deveined, rinsed, and patted dry.*

YIELD: 4 SERVINGS
PREP TIME: up to 5 minutes
COOK TIME: 4 to 6 minutes

1¼ pounds shrimp or 1 pound scallops (see The Seafood and the Prep)
About ½ teaspoon kosher salt
About ½ teaspoon freshly ground black pepper
2 tablespoons olive oil

1. SEAR: Season the shrimp or scallops with salt and pepper; remember each tends to be naturally salty and are even more so if they've been treated (see Avoid STP on page 47). Set a large, heavy-based skillet (I like using my cast-iron pan to give the seafood a really good browned crust) over medium-high heat for 1 minute. Add the oil and heat until it's shimmering hot, about 1 minute. Add the seafood (if they're large try placing them one by one with tongs or your fingers so each has space to sear and brown properly) and then cook without touching until they brown around the edges and easily release from the pan when you lift up a corner, 2 to 3 minutes. Flip and cook until the scallops firm up slightly but are still a little translucent in the center when you slice open a thicker piece or the shrimp are firm to the touch and opaque if you slice into a thicker one, about 2 to 4 more minutes.

2. SAUCE: Add an SWS sauté sauce (pages 132–152) and toss for 1 to 2 minutes so the seafood soaks up its flavors. Or, transfer the cooked seafood to a plate, tent with foil, and make an SWS pan sauce (pages 97–114). After making the sauce, return the seafood to the pan to flip a couple of times to reheat. Or, serve with an SAS sauce (pages 152–231).

3. SERVE: Both scallops and shrimp go great with sauté or pan sauces. These sauces may wash off some of the browned crust you've worked so hard to create, but the melding of flavors makes up for it. Pair scallops with something bright like Orange and Caramelized Fennel Pan Sauce (page 105) or drizzle with a flavored emulsion like Sun-Dried Tomato and Lemon Beurre Blanc (page 205). Pair either with a bright grain salad like the Bulgur with Cherry Tomatoes, Mint, and Mozzarella (page 236). Turn sautéed shrimp into a *scampi* by tossing with the Garlicky White Wine and Butter Sauce (page 150) and serve over Orzo with Wild Mushrooms and Baby Spinach (page 233). Or make with a dressy Creamy Pea and Pancetta Sauce (page 149) and serve with Pesto Mashed Potatoes (page 235).

SHRIMP

Shrimp at the Market

There are quite a few choices when buying shrimp. Here is my take on the options.

FRESH OR FROZEN: Of course it's always better to buy fresh shrimp, but the majority of shrimp at the market has already been frozen. So if you can't find fresh-caught, domestic shrimp, it's actually better to do the defrosting yourself: buy a bag of instant quick frozen (IQF) shrimp and defrost them on the fly under cold, running water.

WILD OR FARM-RAISED: Only about 10 percent of the shrimp sold in the United States is wild caught. If you can find it, buy it. Its flavor and texture is superior to farm raised. From a sustainability standpoint, look for shrimp that has been farm raised in the United States or wild shrimp that has not been caught by trawling; ask your fishmonger for assistance.

PEELED AND DEVEINED: Call me crazy, but I actually like peeling and deveining shrimp. I consider it quiet time. But on a busy weeknight, it's perfectly fine to have the fishmonger do the work or buy a bag of already cleaned shrimp.

SIZE: Shrimp are sold by the count, which is the number of shrimp that make up a pound. Choosing which count to buy is a balancing act. The bigger they are the meatier their texture, but also the more expensive. I find 26-to-30-count to be the best buy, big enough to be good eating (and easy peeling), but not unreasonably priced.

TIP: Avoid STP

STP is a sodium solution that sounds well intentioned—it adds liquid to shellfish to avoid it from drying out—but is nothing of the sort. STP is bad for at least two reasons: (1) it adds water weight, which you end up paying for, and (2) it gives shellfish an unnatural, rubbery texture (think deli luncheon meat), which makes it harder to brown them (a thorn in the side of any good sear). By law, fishmongers must state whether shellfish are "dry" (without STP) or "wet" (with STP). Look for "dry."

Sautéed "Shell" Shellfish

(Clams, Mussels)

Technically this technique is not a sear. After all, how can you sear a hard, rounded shell? Rather, the method starts with an initial blast of heat to coax the shells partly open and then finishes with a secondary braise to gently finish cooking them. No matter what you call it, this technique is quick, super easy, and produces dressy results. The liquid you use for this secondary braise can be a sauté sauce, white wine, clam juice, or most anything that will combine with the shellfish's natural juices to create an intensely flavored broth.

The Seafood and the Prep

Clams: I prefer smaller varieties like Littlenecks or Manilla clams (generally the smaller they are the more tender). Rinse them well and soak if particularly gritty (see How to Clean Shellfish tip on page 49).

Mussels: *Beards removed* (see How to Clean Shellfish tip on page 49) and rinsed well.

YIELD: 4 SERVINGS

PREP TIME: up to 3 minutes
COOK TIME: 4 to 8 minutes

2 tablespoons olive oil

2 cloves garlic, smashed

2 pounds mussels or 2½ pounds clams (see How to Clean Shellfish tip on page 49)

Sauté sauce (pages 132–150) or ½ cup dry white wine, clam juice, or chicken broth

Kosher salt and freshly ground black pepper

1. SEAR: Heat the oil with the garlic in a large, heavy-based sauté pan or Dutch oven over medium-high heat until it sizzles steadily and becomes fragrant, about 1½ minutes. Add the seafood (scatter the shells around so they're in a single layer) and cook, shaking the pan and stirring occasionally with a wooden spoon, until some of the shells start to open, about 2 minutes for mussels or 3 minutes for clams.

2. SAUCE: Add an SWS sauté sauce (pages 132–150) or the white wine, clam juice, or chicken broth, cover, and cook, shaking the pan occasionally, until most all of the shells open up, 1 to 2 more minutes for the mussels or 2 to 4 minutes for the clams. At this point, you can cook the clams or mussels another minute or two to try to get any stragglers to open, though no longer than this as the tender texture of the remaining bivalves can start to toughen. Discard any unopened clams or mussels. They were mostly likely DOA and shouldn't be eaten. Season the broth with salt and pepper to taste (remember, the shellfish are salty to start with). Ladle into large shallow bowls with the broth.

3. SERVE: Steep the mussels in a Thai curry broth and serve with steamed jasmine rice or simmer with the Lemon Artichoke Sauce (page 142) and pair with french fries for a homemade twist on moules frites. Make a ciopino-like stew with both mussels and clams in a Fresh Tomato and Fennel Sauce (page 133) or pair clams with the Spanish Stewed Chorizo and Garbanzos (page 139); serve either with a baguette.

TIP: Choose a Pan with Straight Edges
This is one of the few high-heat methods in this chapter where I call for a wide cooking vessel with straight edges, like a sauté pan or a Dutch oven, as it will comfortably contain all the broth this technique produces.

How to Clean Shellfish

Clams can have quite a bit of grit, which can make eating them as much fun as a picnic sandwich that's been dropped at the beach. To clean the clams of this grit, wash them with a couple rinses of cold, running water. If they're still gritty, soak the clams in a large bowl of cold salt water (to replicate the brininess of the ocean) and ¼ cup cornmeal. The clams will open up their shells to feed on the cornmeal, which, in turn, will cause them to release some of the grit. For the mussels a rinse of water should be sufficient, although you may have to pinch off any "beards," or byssal threads, on the sides of their shells.

Sear-and-Steam Vegetables

(Sautéed/Stir-Fried Asparagus, Broccoli, Eggplant, Green Beans, Zucchini)

As a chef part of my day job involves tasting a lot of meat. I'm not complaining. But by the time dinner rolls around, often all I want are some seared vegetables. So many nights, this technique is what feeds me: I'll sear some vegetables, splash them with some sort of a stir-fry or sauté sauce, and accompany them with rice or noodles. The healthfulness of the meal is just a pleasant bonus.

As opposed to the meat or fish techniques where stir-fries and sautés are kept separate, this umbrella "sear-and-steam" is a hybrid of both methods with a dash of braising thrown in there. Start by searing the vegetables over high heat so they brown in places, then add a little chicken broth or water, cover, and cook for a minute or two until the vegetables are just crisp-tender. Toss with a sauce and you're there. I have listed some optional aromatics you can sear with the vegetables to boost their flavor. Pick what you like based on the sauce you make.

. . . .

The Vegetable and the Prep

You may want to sauté or stir-fry peppers or onions on their own, but they go great with any of the vegetables below. Thinly slice them, add them to the pan at the same time as the vegetables, and cook until crisp-tender; they should take about the same amount of time as the other vegetables.

. . . .

Asparagus: *Woody stems snapped off (peel the bottoms if they're thick) and cut on the diagonal into 1½-inch pieces.*

Broccoli: *Cut into 1½-inch florets, peel the stems (if any) and thinly slice.*

Chinese broccoli: *Soaked and spun dry, green leaves separated from the stems; slice the stems into ½-inch pieces and sear both leaves and stems together.*

Eggplant: I prefer Japanese or Thai eggplant here. They are smaller and tend to have a more delicate texture than the larger globe eggplants. *Thinly sliced on the diagonal.*

Green beans: *Stem ends trimmed.*

Snap peas or snow peas: *Ends trimmed and seams pulled off.*

Zucchini or summer squash: *Trimmed and cut into ¼-inch disks on the diagonal or into 2-inch rods.*

YIELD: 4 SERVINGS
PREP TIME: up to 5 minutes
COOK TIME: 4 to 8 minutes

2 tablespoons olive or canola oil

¾ to 1 pound vegetables, cut as you like (see The Vegetable and the Prep above)

2 garlic cloves, smashed, or 1 shallot, cut into thin disks, or one 1-inch knob ginger, peeled and thinly sliced (optional)

About ¾ teaspoon kosher salt

About ½ teaspoon freshly ground black pepper

¼ cup low-sodium chicken broth or water

1. **SEAR:** Set a large, heavy-based skillet (I like using my cast-iron pan, which really browns vegetables) over medium-high heat for 1 minute. Heat the oil until shimmering hot, about 1 minute. Add the vegetables and optional aromatics, sprinkle generously with salt and pepper, and cook, shaking the pan occasionally and tossing the vegetables with a wooden spoon, until they brown in places and soften slightly (also, green vegetables like asparagus or broccoli should brighten), 2 to 3 minutes. Add the chicken broth or water and partially cover. (Note: I like to leave the lid slightly askew so that some of this liquid reduces and so the vegetables don't full-on steam, which can sog them out.) Cook, shaking the pan occasionally, until the vegetables are just crisp-tender, 1 to 2 more minutes.

2. **SAUCE:** Add an SWS sauté sauce (pages 132–150) or stir-fry sauce (pages 115–131) and toss for 1 to 2 minutes, uncovered, so the vegetables soak up its flavors and the mixture heats through. Discard the optional aromatics if you like before serving (I leave them in).

3. **SERVE:** These vegetables go best with light sauté and stir-fry sauces (stay away from broths, which will water them down). I love matching green beans or broccoli with sweet and spicy mixtures like the Spicy Hunan Stir-Fry Sauce (page 119) or Oyster Stir-Fry Sauce (page 123). Make a meal out of either with Chinese Egg Noodles with Scallions and Shiitakes (page 233). Toss seared zucchini and summer squash with the Basil Pesto (page 210) or the Spicy Thai Peanut and Mint Sauce (page 124); pair either with angel hair pasta. Take eggplant in a Mediterranean direction with a drizzle of the Sun-Dried Tomato and Caper Vinaigrette (page 180) or pair Japanese eggplant with Floating Rock's Chile-Basil Sauce (page 130).

TIP: Adding Tofu

I haven't listed tofu as a searing ingredient. It's not that I don't like tofu (I do), but rather because it really doesn't need to be seared, more just heated through. Add it to this technique with the sauce and then cook it, stirring, for a minute or two until it heats through. I particularly recommend the prefried tofu available at Asian markets, which has a great texture and flavor.

TIP: Defining "Crisp-Tender"

I like sautéed or stir-fried vegetables to be crisp-tender, similar to the toothy *al dente* doneness that Italians look for in pasta. These vegetables should be firm and crunchy, but with a little give to the tooth. Slightly undercooking also ensures that green vegetables stay green and that all of their wonderful vitamins and minerals are left intact, too.

Slow-Sautéed Hearty Vegetables

(Brussels Sprouts, Carrots, Cauliflower, Parsnips)

This is my technique of choice once the leaves start turning and the light and lovely produce of summer segues into autumn's hardier harvest. Both the browning and the steaming stages here are similar to those for the quick-cooking vegetables on the preceding pages, only they're conducted over a lower flame and are more prolonged so the vegetables become tender without burning.

....

The Vegetable and the Prep

Brussels sprouts: *Halved, quartered, or broken up into leaves* (see How to Cut Brussels Sprouts tip on page 53 for how to prepare). These are part of the cabbage family so cook them quickly so they're a little toothy and maintain their mild flavors.

Carrots: *Peeled and cut in ¼-inch-thick slices or half-moons.*

Cauliflower: *Cut into 1 to 1½-inch florets*; the inner core can be thinly sliced and added to the sear along with the florets.

Parsnips: *Peeled and cut in ¼-inch-thick slices or half-moons.*

YIELD: 4 SERVINGS
PREP TIME: up to 6 minutes
COOK TIME: 7 to 10 minutes

2 tablespoons olive oil

1 to 1¼ pounds hearty vegetables

2 garlic cloves, smashed, or 1 shallot, cut into thin disks (optional)

1 teaspoon chopped fresh herbs (like thyme or rosemary) (optional)

About ¾ teaspoon kosher salt

About ½ teaspoon freshly ground black pepper

¼ cup low-sodium chicken broth or water

1. SEAR: Set a large, heavy-based skillet (I like using my cast-iron pan to give the vegetables a nice browned crust) over medium-high heat for 1 minute. Heat the oil until it's shimmering hot, about 1 minute. Add the vegetables, optional aromatics, and herbs, sprinkle generously with salt and pepper, lower the heat to medium, and cook, shaking the pan occasionally and tossing the vegetables with a wooden spoon, until they brown in places and start to soften slightly, 3 to 4 minutes. Pour in the chicken broth or water, cover with the lid partially ajar, and cook, shaking the pan occasionally, until the vegetables are tender but just a little toothy (you should be able to cut through them with the side of a fork), 2 to 4 more minutes. Add a splash more liquid if the pan is dry but the vegetables still aren't tender.

2. SAUCE: Add an SWS sauté sauce (pages 132–150) or stir-fry sauce (pages 115–131), raise the heat to high, and cook, scraping the bottom of the pan with a wooden spoon to incorporate any caramelized crust, until it reduces by about half, about 2 minutes.

3. SERVE: Most of these mild, earthy vegetables go well with bright, intense flavors like citrus, spice, and fresh herbs as well as something rich, be it a sprinkling of cheese or a pat of butter. Braise the cauliflower with the Indian Tikka Masala (page 127) or the Spicy Tomato Vodka Sauce (page 136); serve the former over Curried Basmati Rice with Currants and Almonds (page 234) or toss the latter with a sturdy pasta like penne or ziti. Pair the carrots with the Spiced Moroccan Olive and Orange Sauce (page 147) or Toasted Sesame-Ginger Stir-Fry Sauce (page 119) and serve with a steak. Brussels sprouts, a nice side for pork chops, go well with fruit and acid like the Sautéed Bacon and Browned Apples (page 143) or the Sun-Dried Tomato and Rosemary Butter (page 199).

TIP: Using Whole Aromatics

TIP: Using Whole Aromatics

You may notice that throughout this book I often stir-fry or sauté large pieces of aromatics—thinly sliced ginger, smashed garlic cloves, shallots wedges, smashed lemongrass, and even dried chiles—instead of chopping them up. Using large aromatics offers the best of both worlds. They infuse their flavor more delicately than chopped ingredients would. And they require less prep: just drop them in a skillet or wok and go.

TIP: Quick Cooking Keeps the Flavors Fresh

Cauliflower and Brussels sprouts are part of the brassica family (cabbage), a group of vegetables that can become rather smelly (or sulfurous, to be exact) when subjected to lengthy cook times. For this reason, I like to cook these vegetables quickly so they're a little toothy. Not only will their flavor be more subtle and sweet, but this texture allows them to hold up nicely to a brief braise with a sauté sauce.

TIP: How to Cut Brussels Sprouts

Part of the reason that Brussels sprouts have gotten such a bad rap is that they're not prepared properly. Cooking Brussels sprouts whole, a traditional approach, might make for easy prep, but it means that you have to sear them for a long spell, during which the outsides may turn to mush before the insides cook through. Worse, this long cook time can cause the sprouts to pick up an unpleasant, stinky flavor. Cutting the Brussels sprouts prior to cooking can solve this problem, shortening the cook time and offering more surface area to brown. Halve smaller ones or quarter large ones. Or core the Brussels sprouts and then break them into individual leaves and sauté them like a cabbage (see Sautéed Greens method on right).

Sautéed Greens

(Bok Choy, Cabbage, Kale, Spinach, Swiss Chard)

Of all the high-heat techniques in this book, this one is least likely to serve as dinner alone unless you're deep, deep, *deep* in diet mode or you pair these greens with a hearty sauté sauce—see the pairings below). Still the method is exceedingly simple and the resulting greens are a perfect side for most any meal.

This technique covers both quick-cooking greens like spinach as well as hardier leaves like beet greens, Swiss chard, and even cabbage. Start by gently sautéing garlic so it gets a light toasted flavor, but not so much that it becomes acrid. Then add the greens and sauté until they start to wilt and soften—at this point, delicate greens like spinach are basically done. The hardier greens need to be quickly braised: add a splash of chicken broth, cover the pan, and cook for a couple of minutes, flipping occasionally, until just tender.

NOTE: I've left a range for the garlic, based on your affinity for it. I stick to the lower end.

What and How to Prepare

All of these greens, with the exception of the cabbage, should be soaked and spun dry following The Trick for Washing Greens tip on page 55.

Bok choy: *Halve baby bok choy or cut large bok choy into 2-inch pieces, then soak and spin dry.*

Cabbage (Napa, Savoy, red, or green): *Tough outer leaves discarded, halved, cored, and sliced ¼ to ½-inch thick (the more delicate the cabbage, the larger you can leave the pieces).*

Collard greens: *Stemmed, cut into 2-inch pieces, washed and spun dry.*

Escarole: *Tough outer leaves discarded, cored, cut into 1½-inch pieces, washed and spun dry.*

Kale (Dinosaur kale is my favorite variety): *Stemmed and sliced into 1-inch pieces, washed and spun dry.*

Spinach: *Stemmed (at least, if the stems are large), washed, and spun dry.*

Swiss chard: *Stemmed and sliced into 1½-inch pieces, washed and spun dry.*

YIELD: 4 SIDE DISH SERVINGS
PREP TIME: up to 4 minutes
COOK TIME: 2 to 6 minutes

2 tablespoons olive oil
1 to 2 garlic cloves, minced (1 to 2 teaspoons)
1 pound greens, soaked, spun dry, and stemmed
   (if the stems are large)
About ¾ teaspoon kosher salt
¼ cup low-sodium chicken broth or water (optional)

TIP: Heat the Garlic with the Oil

Generally, I recommend heating a pan before adding the oil. But garlic can burn quickly so I like to heat it together with the oil (and the pan) so it gently infuses its flavor. By the time the oil is shimmering hot, the garlic will be steadily sizzling and just turning ever lightly brown at its edges, just the time to add the greens.

TIP: How to Sauté Greens in One Batch

If you've ever sautéed spinach, you know how deflating it can feel when that big handful of leaves cooks down to a meager clump. The trick to cooking a lot of spinach (or greens) at once is to sauté more than you can initially fit in the pan. To do this, add half of the greens (about ½ pound) to a large skillet (preferably 12 inches wide), and cook for 1 minute so the greens on the bottom start to wilt. Then, using tongs, flip the wilted greens over so they're on top of the raw ones. Then add the remaining greens (they should now all fit if you press them down) and cook, flipping and tossing, until the greens are just wilted. Remove the pan from the heat because the greens' heat will continue cooking them and you don't want to overcook them.

1. SEAR: Heat the oil and garlic in a large (preferably 12-inch wide) skillet over medium-high heat, stirring often, until the garlic sizzles steadily, becomes fragrant, and just starts to turn a light, light brown at the edges, about 1 minute. Add the greens (you may only be able to fit half at first until some of the greens wilt, see The Trick to Sautéing Greens in One Batch tip on left), sprinkle generously with salt, and cook, tossing and flipping over with tongs, until the greens start to wilt and soften, about 3 minutes. Go straight to the sauce stage with spinach or for hardier greens, add the chicken broth or water, cover with the lid partially ajar, and cook, stirring occasionally, until just tender (I like hardy greens like collard or kale to be a little toothy), 2 to 6 minutes.

2. SAUCE: Add an SWS sauce (pages 85–150) and cook, stirring, until it heats through and melds with the greens. Or, serve with an SAS sauce (pages 52–231).

3. SERVE: This is one technique which is fine to go without the sauce. Garlicky sautéed spinach or collard greens are plenty tasty on their own or simply garnished with any combination of the umami triumvirate of crisp bacon, shredded Parmigiano, or white truffle oil (just a drop or two). But you can pair these greens with any number of wonderful sauces, too. Drizzle sautéed spinach or escarole with the Lemon-Rosemary Oil (page 208) just before serving or make a quick creamed spinach by stirring in the Wild Mushroom and Herb Béchamel (page 206) and sprinkling with toasted panko bread crumbs. Or turn sautéed kale or collard greens into a stewy main course braise with Stewed Cannellini Beans with Rosemary and Crisp Bacon (page 141) or the Spanish Stewed Chorizo and Garbanzos (page 139); serve with a good sourdough loaf. Toss sautéed cabbage with Spicy Szechuan Chili and Black Bean Oil (page 209) and serve with Cold Peanut Noodles with Mint and Thai Chiles (page 233).

GREENS

TIP: The Trick to Washing Greens

I have strong opinions on washing greens and though these ideas may not be super exciting, they are important. Grit can ruin beautifully seared greens. Even if spinach's cellophane bag says it's been quintuple-washed or those collard greens look clean, they're worth washing again. Grit just isn't something to be taken lightly. To wash the greens, first soak them in cold water. I like doing this in the salad spinner itself so there's one less dish to wash. Pick up the inner basket (so that the remaining water and any grit are left behind), dump the water, and then spin dry.

TECHNIQUE: How to Stem Greens

The stems on heavy greens like Swiss chard or kale are so hardy that you're best off removing them and either discarding them or else thinly slicing them and cooking them separately. To stem greens, set the point where the stem meets the leaf between your thumb and index finger and squeeze those two fingers together (around the stem) while pushing up the stem. By doing this, you will scrape the green clean from the stem. It's rather easy and therapeutic after a long, stressful day.

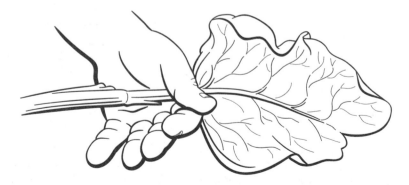

II. STIR-FRYING

If you're like me and grew up watching *Yan Can Cook* on PBS Saturday mornings, you already know the basics of stir-frying. If not, pay attention. Your first step is to **(1) SLICE AND DICE EVERYTHING UNIFORMLY**. Stir-frying's great reward, its remarkable quickness, comes with a price: you need to get everything organized prior to cooking. There are two reasons for this attention to detail. The first is that mismatched pieces (particularly meat or chicken) won't cook uniformly. The second is because the technique's quick cooking leaves little time for last-minute chopping. So think of stir-frying as an opportunity to get in touch with your obsessive side: cut everything just so and then arrange the prepared ingredients in small bowls near the stove top so you can grab them on the fly like a high-heat surgeon.

(2) **MARINATE (IF ONLY FOR A COUPLE OF MINUTES)**. This step is important as the short cook time for most stir-fries doesn't offer seared ingredients a chance to soak up much flavor. Tossing meats and seafood in a quick bath of soy sauce, sherry, and cornstarch gives the seared ingredients a coating that both starts to infuse flavor and also helps them hold up to the high heat.

Before you start cooking, you'll want to (3) **VENTILATE THE KITCHEN**. Just as with sautéing and broiling (and most all good cooking for that matter), stir-frying creates smoke, and so it's a good idea to crank up the fan (even if it only circulates air like my crappy microwave fan) and open the kitchen windows. (4) **HEAT UP A WOK OR SKILLET** (see information on page 59 to see why you might be better off with a skillet) with a neutral-flavored oil. The hot pan helps avoid sticking and also cooks the seared ingredients quickly. Though I love olive oil, I generally go with canola or peanut oil for stir-fries. Each has a high smoke point and mild flavor that won't compete with the other ingredients. Heat up the pan for a minute or

so, pour in the oil, and when it's shimmering hot (it should slide quickly from one side to the other if you tilt the pan), you're ready to start cooking.

(5) **KEEP THE SEARED INGREDIENTS MOVING** once they're in the pan. Unlike my sautéing or grilling advice where I stress leaving the seared ingredient alone for the first minute or two of cooking (so it browns nicely), stir-frying depends on constant movement to ensure even cooking during the technique's relatively short cook time (usually under 5 minutes). Use a long metal spoon or a wooden spatula to shift things back and forth in the pan. (6) **COOK UNTIL THE SEARED INGREDIENTS JUST LOSE THEIR RAW COLOR AND THEN SAUCE** (and add blanched vegetables). Because most stir-fry ingredients are on the smallish size, you want to avoid cooking them all the way through so they'll still be moist when you toss them with the sauce. The moment they lose their raw exterior (they should still be plenty soft to the touch—about medium done, if you will), it's time to add the sauce. Stir for 1 or 2 minutes with the sauce over high heat to bring the whole dish together.

Stir-Fried Chicken

(Boneless Strips, Large Chunks)

My first solo cooking expeditions involved stir-fried chicken when I was twelve years old and my mom was out of the house. Inspired by Martin Yan's culinary feats on PBS, I would grab a whole bird from the freezer, pull out every Asian condiment from the pantry, and proceed to saw through the frozen chicken like a lunatic with a bread knife. I'd cook the pieces in my mom's nonstick wok, and when the chicken was mostly cooked through and the kitchen was smoking, my younger brother and I would eat. The truth is that these stir-fries were actually pretty good—good enough that I would keep on stir-frying through my teenage years whenever my mom was gone for the day. I learned a lot about seasoning foods, making sauces, slicing frozen chicken (see Slicing Frozen

Chicken tip below), and how to clean up the kitchen so that my mom had only a vague sense of the madness that had taken place while she was gone.

The Cut and the Prep

I generally stay away from stir-frying chicken thighs because the quick cooking doesn't adequately render the thighs' fatty patches. If you do choose to go with chicken thighs, add another minute or two to the cook times.

Boneless skinless chicken breasts: *Trimmed of excess fat and thinly sliced, cut into strips or into ½-inch dice.*

Boneless, skinless chicken thighs: *Trimmed of excess fat and cut in uniform ½-inch pieces.*

YIELD: 4 SERVINGS

PREP TIME: up to 6 minutes

COOK TIME: 3 to 5 minutes

1¼ pounds boneless, skinless chicken breasts or thighs, cut as you like (see The Cut and the Prep)

2 teaspoons soy sauce

2 teaspoons dry sherry (or mirin if you have)

1 teaspoon cornstarch

½ teaspoon kosher salt

2 tablespoons canola oil

1. SEAR: Toss the chicken with the soy sauce, sherry, cornstarch, and salt. Set a large, heavy-based skillet or a wok over medium-high heat for 1 minute. Pour in the oil and heat until it's shimmering hot, about 1 minute. Add the chicken and cook, simultaneously shaking the pan and tossing the chicken with a wooden spoon, until it loses most but not all of its raw color on the outside (it should still be plenty soft to the touch and mostly pink if you slice into a piece with the side of a fork), about 2 to 3 minutes.

2. SAUCE: Add an SWS stir-fry sauce (pages 115–131) and toss for 1 to 2 minutes so the chicken just finishes cooking through (cut into a piece to check that it's completely opaque) and soaks up the sauce's flavors. Add a splash of water or chicken broth if the sauce starts to over thicken before the chicken cooks through.

3. SERVE: The chicken from this method goes well with most all of the stir-fry sauces (page 115–131) in this book. Toss thinly sliced stir-fried chicken breasts and blanched asparagus with the Spicy Black Bean Sauce (page 116) or the Thai Black Pepper Sauce (page 125) and serve with the Curried Rice Noodles (page 234 dice chicken thighs small and pair with the Kung Pao Sauce (page 120) and Thai Coconut Rice. This technique can also veer in a heavier braiselike direction with sauces like the Indian Tikka Masala (page 127 in some sautéed cauliflower if you like—or the Thai Red Curry (page 130).

TIP: Slicing Frozen Chicken

Raw chicken's soft, almost slimy texture can make it difficult to slice uniformly. If you have the time, you can make slicing chicken easier by freezing the chicken for 10 to 15 minutes before cutting. It will firm up and offer more of the resistance needed for getting a uniform cut.

TIP: Undercook the Chicken Before Adding the Sauce

Overcooked chicken is simply not very tasty in stir-fries. So make sure to lean toward the undercooked side of things when you add the sauce as the two will cook together for another minute or two. And if the sauce starts to thicken up too much before the chicken is done, just add 2 or 3 tablespoons of chicken broth or water to thin it out.

STIR-FRYING

Quick Marinades Before Stir-Frying

Whereas most of the techniques in this book rely simply on salt and pepper for the seasoning step prior to cooking, I toss meat, chicken, or shellfish with a mix of cornstarch, soy sauce, and sherry (or Shaoxing Chinese cooking wine) before stir-frying. Even if it's only for a couple of minutes, the mixture coats the seared ingredient (the cornstarch protects it the same way flour does a sautéed cutlet) and also begins the process of soaking in flavors.

Stir-Fries with Blanched Vegetables

Most stir-fries generally marry some sort of meat or fish with a vegetable. Though the techniques in this section focus on one or the other, it's not hard to stir-fry both meat and vegetables at the same time. Just add blanched vegetables to stir-fried meat or seafood at the same time as the sauce. To blanch vegetables, bring a generous amount of salted water (2 or 3 quarts) to a boil, drop in sliced vegetables, and cook for 30 seconds to 1 minute. Drain immediately under cold, running water and add to the stir-fried meat, chicken, or seafood during the saucing stage. Then just heat them up with the sauce, so they soak up the flavors and the whole dish comes together.

Beef and Broccoli

Seemingly for as long as there have been Chinese restaurants in the United States, there's been beef (or chicken) and broccoli. To recreate this restaurant classic, blanch the broccoli (see how to blanch vegetables above), and then add to the stir-fry at the same time as the sauce (try the Hoisin Stir-Fry Sauce (page 124) or the Spicy Hunan Stir-Fry Sauce (page 119) and toss for a minute or two to heat through and meld the flavors.

TIP: To Wok or Not?

A properly seasoned high-carbon steel wok is a thing of beauty: nonstick, quick to heat up and possessing a large, sloping surface that's great for quickly searing and stir-frying. The chief problem with woks is how their rounded shape fits a home stove top's flat surface. It only heats up the pan's narrow bottom and little of the sloping sides. You can purchase a metal ring for a gas stove top to replicate a traditional Chinese range, but the pan will still be further removed from the heat source than you'd like. The better solution is to simply stir-fry in a large skillet so the heat gets more evenly distributed.

Stir-Fried Meat or Seafood

(Beef, Lamb, Pork, Scallops, Shrimp, Squid)

It may seem strange that seafood is grouped together with meat in this technique, but all of these ingredients are alike in that they don't need to be cooked quite all the way through. Not only is this technique quick cooking, but, with the exception of the seafood, it can be affordable eating. No need to call on filet mignon or center-cut pork chops for the meat—their expense would be largely lost in the shuffle of high heat and big flavors. Instead go with full-flavored tough cuts (see Slicing Against the Grain on page 74), which maintain a pleasant chew when thinly sliced and seared.

The Cut and the Prep

I generally like to cut meat into thin slices or strips for stir-frying, as opposed to chunks—the quick high heat of a stir-fry overcooks the outside of large pieces before the inside has a chance to cook through.

Beef: Flank or skirt steak, *thinly sliced on the diagonal or butterflied and sliced into thin strips.*

Lamb: Boneless leg or shoulder steaks, *trimmed of fat and thinly sliced or cut into strips.*

Pork: Tenderloin or boneless pork chops, *trimmed of fat and cut into thin strips.*

Scallops: *Beards removed (just grab these white tabs with your fingers and pull—they'll come off like Velcro), rinsed well, and patted dry.*

Shrimp: 21–26 count, *peeled, deveined, rinsed, and patted dry.*

Squid: *Tentacles and bodies, rinsed well and patted dry, and bodies sliced into ¼-inch rings.*

TIP: Go Big with Lamb

Lamb's gaminess can overpower a stir-fry. If you do want to stir-fry lamb, the trick is to let spice and heat match its intensity. Try any of the stir-fry sauces with the word "spicy" in the title like the Spicy Black Bean Sauce (page 116) or the Spicy Hunan Stir-Fry Sauce (page 119).

INFORMATION: Squid Is Different

Well, not just how it cooks, but also what it is for many people. As much as squid has gained in popularity recently (further proving that if something's fried, folks will eat it), it still is not in the mainstream like shrimp or scallops. Call it calamari if it makes you less squeamish, but squid is wonderful eating and easy to cook. It does sear a little differently than shrimp and scallops, going better with more moderate heat—a real sharp sear can turn it tough.

YIELD: 4 SERVINGS
PREP TIME: up to 5 minutes
COOK TIME: 3 to 7 minutes

1¼ pound beef, pork or lamb or ¾ pound shrimp, scallops,
 or calamari cut as you like (see The Cut and the Prep)
2 teaspoons soy sauce
2 teaspoons dry sherry (or mirin if you have)
1 teaspoon cornstarch
½ teaspoon kosher salt
2 tablespoons canola oil

1. **SEAR:** Toss the meat with the soy sauce, sherry, cornstarch, and salt in a medium bowl. Set a large, heavy-based skillet or a wok over medium-high heat for 1 minute. Pour in the oil and heat until it's shimmering hot, about 1 minute. Add the meat or seafood (try to spread it in a single layer) and cook for 1 minute without touching. Start tossing the meat or seafood with a wooden spoon and gently shaking the pan until the meat or seafood mostly loses its raw color on the exterior and becomes slightly firm to the touch, about 2 to 3 minutes total.

2. **SAUCE:** Add an SWS sauce and toss for 1 to 2 minutes so the meat or seafood soaks up its flavors and just cooks through (check by slicing into a thicker piece—it's OK if it's still a little pink).

3. **SERVE:** Try pairing pork with something familiar like the Old-School Sweet and Sour Sauce (page 120) or different like the Vietnamese Caramel Sauce (page 126). Beef goes nicely with most any sauce, though I particularly like it with the Toasted Sesame-Ginger Stir-Fry Sauce (page 119); throw in some blanched green beans. Meanwhile, lamb demands big flavors (see page 50), like the Spicy Szechuan Garlic and Double Chile Sauce (page 117). Serve these stir-fries with the sorts of things you'd get at an Asian restaurant: steamed rice, udon noodles drizzled with a touch of sesame oil, or even something a little more exotic like the Orzo with Wild Mushrooms and Baby Spinach (page 223).

III. BROILING

For most folks, a broiler is like that fancy juicer you get for your wedding. A nice idea, but one that's soon forgotten (if not banished to the farthest reaches of the attic with the fondue pot and Pilates ball). But not for me. I'm a broiling booster, proselytizing on behalf of this underappreciated technique whenever possible. Of all the cooking methods (and not just the four in this book), broiling may offer the greatest balance of quickness (beautifully browned food in minutes) and simplicity (hands-free, indoor "grilling"—it is like an upside-down grill when you think about it). And broiling is fair game on most any night, unlike grilling, which marginalizes those folks in patio-less apartments or cold climes.

Admittedly, there's not much to broiling: stick food under fire, cook until browned but not burnt, and you're done. If anything, it's this browned/burnt equilibrium that proves most demanding. Like cooking a marshmallow over a campfire, broiled foods can go from lovely to charred in an instant. For this reason, your first task is to (1) **GET TO KNOW YOUR BROILER** and learn where to position your oven rack accordingly. More than most pieces of culinary equipment, broilers vary greatly from one oven to the next. Some electric broilers cycle on and off and work best when the oven door is open (so they don't cycle off). Some powerhouse gas broilers are so strong that food should be set ten inches away. No matter your oven, after a couple of broiling excursions, you should have a decent sense of its strength and how close to the element to set food.

As with roasting or baking, make sure to (2) **GIVE THE BROILER SOME TIME TO PRE-HEAT** (five minutes should do). Use this time to prepare a sauce.

Because a broiler is like an upside down grill, you need to (3) **GET A PAIR OF LONG TONGS AND A BROILER PAN** to work with its unique heat. The tongs help avoid singeing arm hairs while the broiler pan, a slotted pan set over a shallow tray (see page 21), allows the fat to drain down into the bottom pan instead of spattering all over the oven.

Once the food is in the oven, browning and bubbling away, listen to that little voice telling you, **"(4) STAY NEAR THE OVEN!"** Whereas my main sautéing advice revolves around acting cool and reserved, a little paranoia is fine for broiling because it so quickly takes food from golden brown to charred (like that campfire marshmallow). I generally keep the oven door open at an angle to watch the progress through the crack.

The doneness tests for broiled meats or vegetables aren't too demanding, because the cuts that I use for this method tend to be thin and quick cooking. So the basic rule is **(5) WHEN THE MEATS OR VEGETABLES ARE PROPERLY BROWNED, THEY'RE DONE.** Make a nick with a paring knife to make sure they're cooked to your liking, and then hit them with a glaze or some sort of salsa or dipping sauce.

For the most part you will **(6) BROIL FIRST AND THEN SAUCE LATER.** If you want to use a sugary glaze, broil the meat or vegetables until they're just done, then brush with some of the glaze and cook another minute or two until the glaze browns but doesn't burn.

TIP: A Few Broiling Tips

Grilling and broiling are both interactive processes. Though the heat of a broiler can be more predictable than a grill, broiling can be more complicated because it's harder to access whatever you're searing. Try rotating the pan a couple of times during broiling to ensure even cooking. When checking food for doneness, consider removing the pan from the oven and checking it on the top of the stove. This will eliminate singed arm hairs from leaning into the oven. And as always when broiling, stick close by to avoid charring.

TIP: Presalting Chicken

Chicken is one of those ingredients that greatly benefits from seasoning ahead. It doesn't even need to be as involved as a brine or marinade. In the morning before leaving for work, simply sprinkle generously with salt, pepper, and fresh herbs all over. If using skin-on parts, let them sit uncovered in the refrigerator so the skin starts to dry out a bit and turns crackly crisp in the oven.

Broiled Chicken

(Bone-in or Boneless Breasts, Thighs, Drumsticks)

This technique is my home-cooked wintry version of a tropical bar party; you know the ones where they truck in a boatload of sand and everyone rocks Hawaiian shirts. No, it doesn't make me forget that my grill is covered in snow or that my skin is pasty, but broiled chicken fills the kitchen with a little smoke and spice and that's good enough for me.

Broiling chicken does demand your undivided attention. The skin can go from crisp to burnt in a matter of moments, so stay close. Unlike grilling chicken where I use different techniques for boneless and bone-in parts, broiled chicken all fits under this one umbrella. The cook times will vary depending on the size of the pieces, but everything else in the technique will stay more or less the same.

The Cut and the Prep

Bone-in split breasts: *Cut in half widthwise* (you'll need to use a little force to cut through the breast bone).

Boneless, skinless breasts: *Gently pounded to even out thickness.*

Boneless, skinless thighs: *Trimmed of excess fat and gently pounded to even out thickness.*

Bone-in drumsticks: You can remove the piece of cartilage toward the bottom of the drumsticks if you like.

Bone-in thighs: *Trimmed of any excess skin as well as fatty patches.*

YIELD: 4 SERVINGS
PREP TIME: up to 2 minutes
COOK TIME: 5 to 12 minutes

1½ pounds boneless or 3 pounds bone-in chicken parts, cut as you like (see The Cut and the Prep on left)
About 1½ teaspoons kosher salt
About ¾ teaspoon freshly ground black pepper
1 teaspoon chopped fresh thyme or rosemary (optional)
1 tablespoon olive oil

1. **SEAR:** Season the chicken generously with salt, pepper, and herbs, if using (or coat the chicken with a couple of tablespoons of a spice rub, see pages 14–15), and rub with oil.

Heat the broiler to high and position an oven rack about 6 inches away from the heating element. Set the chicken on a broiler pan (or a rack set over a rimmed baking sheet) and cook until it starts to brown but doesn't burn, 3 to 5 minutes. Flip, rotate the pan (front to back), and cook until the other side is browned, about 3 more minutes. At this point, check breasts for doneness; they should be firm to the touch and cooked through (check by slicing into a thicker piece or check that the chicken registers 165°F on an instant-read thermometer). Or for chicken parts, rotate the broil pan again and continue cooking and flipping until properly cooked through—3 to 5 more minutes; slice into a thicker thigh to check that it's cooked through or it should register 170°F on an instant-read thermometer.

2. **SAUCE:** Brush with an SWS glaze (pages 86–94) or barbecue sauce (pages 94–96) and cook for another 1 to 2 minutes, basting a few times, until the sauce browns. Or, serve with an SAS sauce (pages 152–231).

3. **SERVE:** Go with the indoor grilling theme by basting chicken parts with something sassy like the Coffee BBQ Sauce (page 96) or the Scorched Habanero and Mango Glaze (page 87); accompany with some Dirty Rice (page 234) and sautéed collard greens (page 53). Or try tossing broiled chicken breasts with one of the SAS dipping sauces like the Rosemary-Buffalo Sauce (page 166) and sandwich with toasted ciabatta, crumbled blue cheese, and thinly shaved cucumber and carrot strips.

Broiled Steaks and Chops

(Beef, Lamb, Pork)

I'll be straight: a broiled steak doesn't match the flavor of a grilled or even a sautéed one because it's hard to get the same caramelization under a broiler that you can with those other heat sources. Broiling does have its advantages, though. For one, it's a year-round option. Also, when properly executed, broiling steaks and chops can be quite precise and effortless (for this reason, most steakhouses use this method, though with commercial broilers that are quite powerful). So once you are able to feel out the strength of your own broiler and get down the timing with a 1¼-inch steak (see The Cut and the Prep), you've got a quick entrance to fancy eating.

· ·

The Cut and the Prep

I find veal chops are too bulky for this technique. Like other thick steaks and chops, they can take a while to cook; the exterior of the meat can overcook and dry out long before the inside reaches the desired doneness. You're better off picking cuts about 1¼-inches thick, which are large enough to feel ample, but not so big that even cooking is an issue.

· ·

Beef: Flank or skirt steaks are great for broiling. They brown quickly and are easy to cook.

Pork: Bone-in chops hold up well to the dry heat. You can trim off some of the fat to avoid smoking or burning.

Lamb: Sirloin chops are my favorites for broiling. A rack from the loin is pricey and its layer of fat can make it susceptible to burning.

YIELD: 4 SERVINGS
PREP TIME: up to 2 minutes
COOK TIME: 5 to 10 minutes

1½ pounds boneless or 2½ pounds bone-in steaks or chops
About 1¼ teaspoons kosher salt
About ½ teaspoon freshly ground black pepper
1 teaspoon chopped fresh thyme or rosemary (optional)
1 to 2 tablespoons olive oil

1. SEAR: Heat the broiler to high and position an oven rack about 4 inches away from the heating element. Sprinkle the meat generously with salt and pepper and the herbs, if using, and then drizzle with oil. Note: let the steaks come to room temperature for 20 minutes while you conduct the rest of your dinner preparations; it will help them cook more quickly and evenly.

Set the steaks or chops on a broiling pan (or a rack set over a rimmed baking sheet). Cook until the meat starts to brown but doesn't burn, 3 to 5 minutes. Flip and cook the other sides until browned; beef or lamb should be slightly firm to the touch and solidly pink when you make a nick into a thicker piece (130°F for medium rare), while a pork chop should be medium-firm and just a little pink on the inside (about 145°F for medium well), 2 to 4 minutes.

2. SAUCE: Brush with an SWS sauce (pages 86–150) and cook, basting another 1 to 2 minutes, so the sauce browns. Or, serve with an SAS sauce (pages 152–231).

3. SERVE: Because this method is conducted indoors and is mostly hands-free, you can take on more involved sauces. Melt a couple of pats of Café de Paris Butter (page 200) over a broiled strip steak and serve with Traditional Rice Pilaf (page 234) and sautéed broccoli (page 50). Brush bone-in pork chops with the Spiced Fuji Apple Glaze (page 92) and accompany with sautéed Brussels sprouts (page 52) and Parmesan and Sun-Dried Tomato Polenta (page 237). Or drizzle broiled lamb chops with a Lemongrass-Chile Vinaigrette (page 184) and serve with broiled asparagus (page 65) and lightly dressed watercress.

TIP: Carryover Cooking

When you pull a steak out from under the broiler or off the grill, its residual heat keeps on cooking it five to ten degrees more depending on its thickness—the thicker the steak, the more it will continue to cook. To compensate for this carryover effect, the rule of thumb is to pull a steak off the heat just before the desired doneness. If you want a medium steak (140°F), take it out of the oven at medium rare (about 135°F) and for medium well pork pull it out at 145°F when the meat is still pink.

INFORMATION: Is Meat More Tender at the Bone?

In a word, no. But meat near the bone is generally less cooked than the rest of the steak or chop, which gives it the appearance of being more tender (if not more juicy). As Harold McGee explains in *On Food and Cooking*, though bones are better heat conductors than the actual meat, they have a hollow structure that inhibits the transfer of heat. This means that the bone slows down the cooking, and accordingly the doneness, of the meat around it. So if you don't mind your meat a little undercooked, gnawing on bones is good eating.

Broiled Vegetables

(Asparagus, Zucchini, Plum Tomatoes, Scallions)

Broiling is as easy and hands-free as vegetable cookery gets. Round vegetables like asparagus, cherry tomatoes, and scallions can be flipped by just giving the baking sheet* a good shake every couple of minutes. Unfortunately, slow-cooking or delicate vegetables like carrots, greens, and onions don't fit this technique's narrow profile. And you do need to stay near the oven while the vegetables broil to know when to flip or pull them. But considering the quick cook times (6 or 7 minutes) and prep work (a couple of minutes), you can't beat oven broiling.

*NOTE: Because these vegetables don't have any fat to spatter all over the oven, a baking sheet (and not a broiler pan) will do just fine; line it with some aluminum foil for easy cleanup.

What and How to Prepare

Asparagus: *Woody ends snapped off and peeled if very thick.*
Cherry/Grape Tomatoes: *Stemmed.*
Eggplant: *Trimmed and cut lengthwise into ¼-inch disks.*
Plum Tomatoes: *Cored and halved.*
Red Peppers: *Quartered and cored.*
Zucchini: *Trimmed and cut in ¼-inch slices.*

YIELD: 4 SERVINGS
PREP TIME: up to 4 minutes
COOK TIME: 4 to 8 minutes

1 to 1½ pounds vegetables or 1 pint cherry tomatoes (see What and How to Prepare)
1 to 2 tablespoons olive oil
About 1 teaspoon kosher salt
About ½ teaspoon freshly ground black pepper
1 teaspoon chopped fresh thyme or rosemary (optional)

1. **SEAR:** Heat the broiler to high and position an oven rack about 6 inches away from the heating element. Line a large, rimmed baking sheet with aluminum foil. Top with the vegetables, and toss with the olive oil and sprinkle generously with salt, pepper, and the herbs, if using.

Broil the vegetables until they start to brown, 2 to 3 minutes. Pull the oven rack out slightly so you can access the sheet pan (without singeing any arm hair) and flip the vegetables (or slide the vegetables back and forth), rotate the baking sheet front to back, and cook until the vegetables are uniformly browned and tender, 2 to 4 more minutes. If the vegetables still aren't tender, continue cooking, rotating the pan front to back and flipping the vegetables, until done to your liking.

2. **SAUCE:** Brush with an SWS glaze (pages 86–94) and cook, basting another 1 to 2 minutes, so it caramelizes on the vegetables' surface. Or, serve with an SAS sauce.

3. **SERVE:** Drizzle broiled tomatoes with an herb vinaigrette like the North End Rosemary Vinaigrette (page 176) or the Italian Garlic and Hot Chile Oil (page 206) and serve with broiled chicken breasts (page 63), lightly dressed baby arugula, and a baguette. Brush pieces of eggplant and zucchini with the Toasted Sesame Teriyaki Sauce (page 90), and set atop steamed rice with warm tofu and thinly sliced broiled scallion. Or make a warm composed salad with thick spears of broiled asparagus, broiled cherry tomatoes, Parmesan shavings, Boston lettuce, and the Lemon-Basil Vinaigrette (page 178).

TIP: Saucing Broiled Vegetables

The meaty textures and mild flavors of zucchini and eggplant allows you treat them as if they were meat: sprinkle them lightly with a spice rub before broiling or brush with a glaze while broiling so they become caramelized and sweet. You can even soak eggplant in the Soy Ginger Marinade (page 17) for 10 minutes or so before broiling—the vegetable's spongelike ability to soak up liquids actually serves it well in this case.

Broiled Fish/Seafood

(Cod, Halibut, Salmon, Scallops, Shrimp)

Somewhere in the mid-eighties, at least five years ahead of most Americans, my mom became obsessed with Omega 3 fatty acids and their potential health benefits. So we started eating a whole lot of fish in our house, enough that we actually started missing the plain roast chicken that we had vehemently protested in the preceding years. Most nights, Mom would broil the fish and then dress it with some sort of glaze or vinaigrette and the truth was that we learned to like it. And my mom was on to something—not just that fish was good for you, but that broiling is an efficient way to prepare it. It's basically just a slide in and out of the oven; these fish and seafood cook so quickly, you really don't need to flip them during cooking. Enjoy this convenience, get one side properly browned, and be on your way.

The Fish and the Prep

These cuts all tend to be delicate and quick cooking. I avoid broiling heavy fish steaks (like tuna or swordfish), because they need to be flipped and, even then, they don't brown as nicely in the oven as they would in a sauté pan or on the grill. *Rinse and pat dry each very well before cooking.*

Cod, haddock: 1-inch filets; fold thinner pieces over so they cook at the same rate as thicker pieces.

Halibut: 1-inch filets as thicker pieces.

Salmon: 1-inch steaks or filets.

Scallops: *Muscles removed* (just grab them with your fingers and pull—they'll come off like a white Velcro tab).

Shrimp: 21–26 count, *peeled and deveined.*

Sole, arctic char, tilapia: Let these filets rest on paper towels for a couple of minutes after rinsing; they're so thin that they will steam or stick if not completely dry.

YIELD: 4 SERVINGS

PREP TIME: up to 2 minutes

COOK TIME: 5 to 10 minutes

1½ pounds fish or 1¼ pounds shellfish (see The Fish and the Prep, page 66)

About 1 teaspoon kosher salt

About ½ teaspoon freshly ground black pepper

1 teaspoon chopped fresh thyme or rosemary (optional)

1 to 2 tablespoons olive oil

Oil cooking spray

1. SEAR: Heat the broiler to high and position an oven rack about 6 inches away from the heating element. Sprinkle the fish or seafood generously with salt, pepper, and the herbs, if using, and drizzle with the olive oil.

Coat a broil pan with the spray (be generous) and top with the fish (skin side down if it has skin). Broil until the fish or seafood starts to brown but doesn't burn, 2 to 4 minutes. Rotate the baking sheet front to back and cook until the fish is nicely browned and mostly firm to the touch and the interior hits the desired level of pinkness (check the chart on page 26 for specific doneness tests; check by slicing into a thicker piece with a paring knife), 2 to 5 more minutes.

2. SAUCE: Brush with an SWS glaze (pages 86–94) and cook, basting another 1 to 2 minutes, so the sauce browns. Or, serve with an SAS sauce (page 152–231).

3. SERVE: For an upscale (and healthy) take on fish and chips, sprinkle cod or sole with some Ritz cracker crumbs or herbed coarse bread crumbs (page 231), broil, and then pair with the French Cornichon and Tarragon Tartar Sauce (page 193) and the Roasted Rosemary Fingerling Potatoes (page 235). Brush broiled salmon with the Maple and Crushed Cumin Glaze (page 91) and serve with Couscous with Cinnamon and Oranges (page 237). Or make a warm salad with broiled scallops, broiled asparagus (page 65), baby romaine and the Sesame-Miso Dressing (page 182).

TIP: Rubs for Broiled Fish

You can use a spice rub for broiled fish the same way you do for grilled fare. Just sprinkle and broil. Top fresh sea scallops with Spanish paprika, fresh thyme, and a little olive oil or with a dusting of the Lemon-Herb Rub (page 15) and then sear until browned and tender. The Tex-Mex Spice Rub (page 15) was made for broiled shrimp. After broiling, drizzle with fresh lime juice, serve with Spanish Yellow Rice (page 234), and life is good.

IV. GRILLING

Though technically both gas and charcoal grills are part of the same happy family, they are very different. As an acknowledgment of these differences, I've included separate but simultaneous directions for both throughout the book. What's your fire? Most hard-core grillers swear by charcoal, and while I readily agree that nothing matches its flavor and intense heat, gas grills fit better with this book's streamlined approach. Light up the grill by just flipping a few knobs, go back into the kitchen to get your ingredients ready, and when you head back outside, the fire will magically be ready to go. If you don't mind the extra time charcoal demands, have at it. Or you can always have it both ways: add a little smoke to your gas grill by using a smoker pouch (see How to Add Smoke to a Gas Grill technique on page 70). There are a few basic steps to proper grilling.

1. **LIGHT THE FIRE** before you do anything else (see How to Build a Charcoal Fire technique on page 69). This book's quick prep can be completed well within the time it takes a gas grill to heat or a charcoal fire to catch. Generally, I call for a two-zone fire with medium-high and medium-low zones. Though most of the grilling in this book is conducted over the hot zone, the cooler zone offers both a safety spot in case anything starts to burn and also more gentle heat for finishing slower-cooking ingredients.

2. **CLEAN AND OIL THE GRILL GRATES.** These are small steps, but they make a world of difference to help prevent sticking and off flavors. Heat up the grill grates a bit and then scrape with a wire brush to loosen any debris from your last grilling excursion. Drizzle some oil on a wad of paper towel or an old dish towel and wipe over the grates to add another level of insurance against sticking.

3. **SET THE INGREDIENTS ON THE GRILL AND TAKE A DEEP BREATH**. Grilling, especially over charcoal, is an interactive process. Fire is unpredictable. But you do want to stay strong and try to avoid fiddling with the grilled ingredients so they can get good grill marks and not stick. If you're using a gas grill, keep the lid closed. This keeps in some of the heat, replicating the convection of an indoor oven so what a gas grill loses in surface heat, it gains in even, uniform cooking.

4. **FLIP AND THEN FLIP AGAIN IF NEEDED**. As with the sautéing, don't touch the meat or fish until it's browned and ready to flip. How to know when a steak or chop is browned if you can't see its underside? Grab one of its corners with tongs, gently lift it up a touch, and take a peek underneath to look for good grill marks and make sure it easily releases from the grates. If it sticks, let it ride for another minute or two, at which point it should easily release.

5. **IF YOU'RE BASTING, KEEP IT COOL**. Like toasting marshmallows, basting with a sweet glaze must tip-toe an ephemeral line between golden brown and completely charred. Sugar and fire can be a combustible pairing, so tread lightly. Brush the glaze on only once the grilled ingredient is more or less cooked and do so over a cooler zone. One to two minutes should be enough to brown the glaze, without it crossing over to the burnt side.

6. **GRILLED MEAT, ESPECIALLY LARGER STEAKS AND CHOPS, SHOULD REST** for a few minutes before slicing (see Let Steaks and Chops Rest After Searing tip on page 70). It can be a tough battle against temptation. Dinner is cooked and it's only natural to want to dig in. Resist this urge and instead wait for a couple of minutes. This step follows the same logic that your mother used when letting that Sunday roast or holiday turkey sit for a while before carving. The juices in meat need a chance to redistribute, something which will only happen if the meat can cool for a couple of minutes. If you slice the meat right away, all those juices will run out onto the cutting board.

TIP: Taking the Grill's Temperature

The accepted way to measure a fire's intensity is to set your hand about 6 inches above the grill and see how long you can hold it there—2 to 3 seconds is hot, 4 to 5 seconds medium, and so on. This practice has always seemed a little silly to me; testing one's pain threshold is a little subjective. Many grills, particularly gas grills, have thermometers on the outside, but these only tell you the grill's radiant temperature, not the temperature on the grates. I prefer a more accurate and less painful approach: surface thermometers. Rest them on the grill grates and they will quickly tell you when you hit that 400°F to 450°F window preferred for searing in this book.

TECHNIQUE: How to Build a Charcoal Fire

How much charcoal you use determines how hot the fire will be. I usually apply enough charcoal to fill a grill chimney. Once it's hot, I pour it into the grill to create a hot and a cool zone. To do this, spread two-thirds of the coals to one side of the grill (for the hot zone) and the remaining one-third to the other side for the cooler zone. You shouldn't need to add any more charcoal for the short grill times in this book.

TECHNIQUE: How to Add Smoke to a Gas Grill

Charcoal purists rightly argue that a gas grill can't truly replicate the flavor and intensity of a real, live fire. But there is one trick that can bridge the disparity between the two mediums: a smoker pouch. Wrap some soaked wood chips (I like mild apple or cherry wood) in aluminum foil. Make a couple of holes in the foil (so the smoke can escape) and set this hand-size packet under the grill grates and over one of the burners on the grill. Once the burners heat up, the smoke will start flowing. Then cook with the grill covered so whatever you're searing can pick up that smoky flavor in just a matter of minutes. Try smoking something as simple as chicken breasts and you'll see the difference.

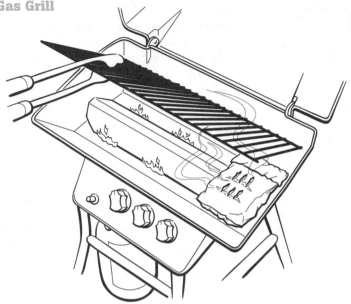

TIP: Let Steaks and Chops Rest After Searing

Whether you're broiling or grilling meat, it's best to let larger cuts rest for about 5 minutes after cooking and before slicing. As Harold McGee explains in *On Food and Cooking*, this cooling period gives meat a chance to firm up, which, in turn, allows its water capacity to increase. Stated simply, a couple of minutes of cooling allow the steaks to hold on to its juices. If you were to get antsy and slice the steak the moment it's off the grill, these juices would run out onto the cutting board instead of staying in the meat, the difference between a juicy and a not-so-juicy steak.

TIP: Forget About Hatch Marks

Somewhere along the way, hatch marks—using the grill grates to make a diamond pattern on the outside of a steak or chop—became the symbol of true grill mastery. And while I don't argue that these marks look cool, I suggest avoiding them for the relatively thin, quick-cooking steaks and chops in this book. If you were to leave many of these cuts on the grill for the time necessary to get these marks, the meat would overcook. So just focus on perfect doneness and even cooking and let that be what truly impresses your guests.

Grilled Boneless Chicken

(Boneless, Skinless Breasts, Thighs)

If I were stuck on that proverbial desert island with only one ingredient to sear over my open fire (and if—stick with me here—I were too dense to craft a fishing pole), chances are I would go with chicken breasts. Yes, I know that chicken breasts can be a little bland, but they are easy and go well with so many sauces and flavors that they can stay exciting night after night. There would be some mangoes and papayas there and I would make spicy salsas and relishes and the whole thing would be like a sunny, seared-chicken version of *Lost*.

The Cut and the Prep

Boneless, skinless chicken breasts:

- *pounded to even out their thickness*
- *butterflied (see Pound or Butterfly Before Grilling technique on page 72)*
- *cut into paillards (cut in half horizontally and lightly pounded)*

Boneless, skinless chicken thighs: *Trimmed of excess fat and lightly pounded flat.* Because boneless chicken thighs are almost completely butterflied to start with, it's best to just spread them out and grill them whole.

YIELD: 4 SERVINGS

PREP TIME: 2 minutes
COOK TIME: 5 to 8 minutes

1½ pounds boneless, skinless chicken, cut as you like
    (see The Cut and the Prep)
About 1 teaspoon kosher salt
About ½ teaspoon freshly ground black pepper
1 teaspoon chopped fresh thyme or rosemary (optional)
2 tablespoons olive oil

1. SEAR: Season the chicken generously with salt and pepper and the thyme or rosemary, if using. (Or coat the chicken with a couple of tablespoons of a spice rub—see pages 14 to 15.) Drizzle with olive oil.

Light a medium charcoal fire or heat a gas grill to medium-high. Set the chicken on the grill and cook, untouched (and covered on a gas grill), until it starts to brown at the edges and easily releases from the grill grates when you gently lift up an edge, 2 to 3 minutes. Flip and cook the other side until the chicken breasts firm up to the touch and are just cooked through (slice into a thicker piece—it should be opaque but juicy and register 165°F on an instant-read thermometer), about 2 to 5 more minutes. Grill chicken thighs toward the higher end of this time range to sear off some of the fatty patches or until they register 170°F on an instant-read thermometer.

2. SAUCE: Brush with an SWS sauce (pages 86–150) and cook, basting and flipping another 1 to 2 minutes, so the sauce browns. Or, serve with an SAS sauce (pages 152–231).

3. SERVE: Basting chicken breasts with the Scorched Habanero and Mango Glaze (page 87) or Chinese Sweet and Sour Orange Glaze (page 90) makes up for any fun that you lose without the skin. Serve with Bulgur with Cherry Tomatoes, Mint, and Mozzarella (page 236) and some grilled corn on the cob (page 82). Thinly slice grilled chicken breasts and drizzle with the "House" Thyme-Dijon Vinaigrette (page 176) or the Lemon Caesar (page 179), set atop a bed of local greens, and serve with warm pita. Or pair grilled chicken thighs with the Spicy Hoisin Glaze (page 89) and wrap with thinly sliced cabbage, scallions, and red pepper in a spring roll skin or flour tortilla for a fresh take on Mu Shu Chicken.

TIP: If you're going to add a glaze, undercook chicken breasts a bit as they will continue cooking with the sauce for another couple of minutes. This isn't necessary for the thighs as they won't dry out.

CHICKEN

Options: Chicken Kebabs

Whether you call them skewers, kebabs, brochettes, or yakitori, grilled chicken on a stick is good eating and a nice way to cook vegetables and chicken at the same time. Thread some cherry tomatoes, peppers, onion, and zucchini on skewers (make sure to soak them if they're wooden) along with chunks of chicken and then cook over a moderate fire so big pieces cook through without drying out. Serve drizzled with a tangy vinaigrette or a yogurt sauce (see index) for dipping.

TIP: Advantages of Bone-in Chicken

Part of this has nothing to do with the bones themselves: bone-in chicken generally comes with its skin on which crisps up and makes it far more dynamic (if a little less healthy) than your standard boneless, skinless breast. Also, meat near the bone is generally less cooked than the rest of the chicken, which makes it more tender and juicy. As Harold McGee explains in *On Food and Cooking*, bones have a hollow structure that inhibits the transfer of heat and slows down the cooking of the meat around it. This is also why it's important to slice open a thicker piece of chicken to make sure it's cooked through all the way to the bone.

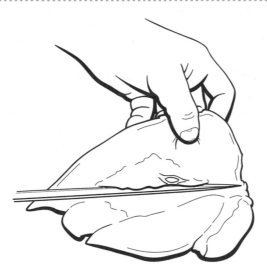

TIP: Pound or Butterfly Before Grilling

Chicken breasts have an uneven shape—their top is thick and wide while the bottom tapers to a thin point—which makes grilling them evenly difficult. Gently pound the breasts to even out their thickness so they cook more quickly and uniformly. It's also not a bad idea to pound boneless chicken thighs to smooth out their knobby pieces.

Grilled Bone-in Chicken Parts

(Split Breasts, Drumsticks, Thighs)

Though it's all chicken, this technique for grilling bone-in pieces varies considerably from the one for boneless chicken on the preceding pages. Bone-in chicken takes longer to cook so you need to build a more gentle, two-zone fire. Sear the chicken over the hot zone and then transfer to the cooler zone to finish cooking. You can also use the cooler zone during the searing stage for flare ups (which the fat from the skin can create).

Though I like to sprinkle a spice or herb rub on most anything grilled, I find it a near-must for bone-in chicken. Rubs give the skin some extra zip to go with its crisp texture and balance out the pleasant gaminess of dark meat thighs or drumsticks.

The Cut and the Prep

Bone-in split breasts: *Cut in half widthwise* (you'll need to use a little force to cut through the breast bone); cutting in half helps the fatter part of the upper breast and the thinner lower part of the breast each cook to a proper doneness on their own.

Drumsticks: Using a paring knife, cut off the piece of cartilage toward the bottom of the drumstick if you like.

Bone-in thighs: *Trimmed of excess fatty patches* (these will flare up on the grill).

Wings: *Trimmed of wing tip and halved at the joint* (use a chef's knife for this).

YIELD: 4 SERVINGS

PREP TIME: up to 2 minutes (or up to 5 minutes for a whole chicken)

COOK TIME: 10 to 15 minutes

3 pounds bone-in chicken parts, cut as you like (see Advantages of Bone-in Chicken on page 72)

About 1¾ teaspoons kosher salt

About ¾ teaspoon freshly ground black pepper

Fresh herbs if you have (1 teaspoon chopped fresh thyme or rosemary)

1 tablespoon olive oil

1. SEAR: Prepare a two-zone fire: heat half of the burners on a gas grill to medium-high and the other half to medium-low or light a medium charcoal fire with two-thirds of the coals banked to one side and the remainder on the other side (see How to Build a Charcoal Fire on page 69). Sprinkle the chicken generously with salt, pepper, and the herbs, if using, and drizzle with olive oil. Or coat the chicken with a couple of tablespoons of a spice rub (pages 14–15).

Set the chicken over the hotter part of the grill and cook, untouched, until it starts to brown at the edges and easily releases from the grill grates when you pick up an edge, 2 to 3 minutes; if the fire is too hot and the chicken starts to flare up, transfer it to the cooler zone until the flames die down a bit. Flip and cook the other side until browned, too, 2 to 3 minutes. Transfer to a cooler zone, cover (with the vents open on a charcoal grill), and cook, flipping every couple of minutes, until the chicken is firm to the touch and cooked through (check by slicing into a thicker piece—the meat should be completely opaque right to the bone—or an instant-read thermometer should register 165°F for white meat or 170°F for dark), 8 to 10 more minutes.

2. SAUCE: Brush with an SWS sauce (pages 86–150) and cook, basting and flipping another 1 to 2 minutes, so the sauce browns. Or, serve with an SAS sauce (pages 152–231).

3. SERVE: Make a double pairing with grilled chicken and both a rub and sauce. Build on the intense flavor of the Tex-Mex Spice Rub (page 15) with a slathering of the Spiced Pineapple-Rum Glaze (page 86) and serve with Spiced Grilled Vegetable Couscous (page 237). Or keep things closer to home with the Sweet Southern Spice Rub (page 14), a basting of the Quick Homemade BBQ Sauce (page 95), and sides of corn bread and coleslaw.

TECHNIQUE: How to Cut Up a Whole Chicken (into Eight Pieces)

This prep technique may push you past this book's desired 30-minute cooking window (it will take you a good 5 minutes to cut up a bird), but it's worth learning: nice way to save a couple of bucks and get a good mix of white and dark meat.

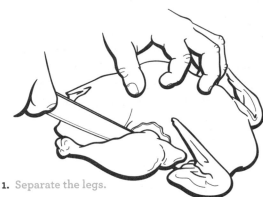

1. Separate the legs.

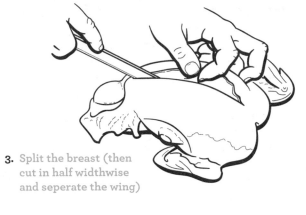

3. Split the breast (then cut in half widthwise and seperate the wing)

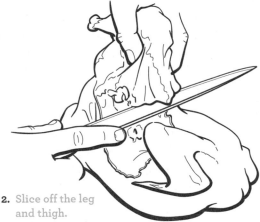

2. Slice off the leg and thigh.

4. Separate the leg and thigh.

TECHNIQUE: Slicing Against the Grain

Meat is comprised of long strands of muscle fibers. The longer these fibers are, the more chewy the meat. So by slicing down through (or "against the grain" of) these fibers, in a sense, you shorten the strands, making the cut more tender at the dinner table. If you look at a tough cut like flank or skirt steak, you can see these fibers running the length of the cut. To slice against the grain, cut straight down through these long fibers (in effect, making a plus sign with your knife and the long strands).

Grilled Steaks and Chops

(Bone-in or Boneless Pork, Beef, Lamb)

If you have an expense account, steakhouses are great. If you're paying, it's hard to swallow the a la carte approach that most steakhouses impose on diners (ten bucks for a baked potato?!!). It's far more satisfying to pick up a couple of good steaks or chops, prepare them perfectly, top with a dressy sauce, and serve with a nice bottle of red. Not only will you be more comfortable at home, but you will save loads of money. Slip your kids a couple bucks for doing the dishes, give the scraps to the dog, and retire to the couch to savor the wine.

· ·

The Cut and the Prep

Beef: Try grilling some of the same cuts that you might saute (page 38) or broil (page 64). Or break out and try something different (and affordable) like a top sirloin or chuck steak (see the chart on page 24); look for 1-inch thick steaks of either cut.

Pork: A whole tenderloin grills quickly and easily, though chops, particularly bone-in center-cut, are the perfect match for grilling. Drop them in a brine for 30 minutes (see Marinades and Pastes, page 16) for really juicy results.

Veal: Look for thinner (about 1¼-inch-thick) chops, which will cook through evenly over high heat.

Lamb: Look for rib or loin chops about 1 inch thick. Rib chops are cheaper, fattier, and more flavorful, too.

· ·

YIELD: 4 SERVINGS

PREP TIME: up to 2 minutes
COOK TIME: 5 to 10 minutes

1¾ pounds boneless or 2¾ pounds bone-in steaks or
    chops (see The Cut and the Prep)
About 1½ teaspoons kosher salt
About ½ teaspoon freshly ground black pepper
1 teaspoon chopped fresh thyme or rosemary (optional)
1½ tablespoons olive oil

1. SEAR: Light a medium charcoal fire or heat a gas grill to medium-high. Sprinkle the steaks generously with salt and pepper, the herbs, if using, and the olive oil. While the grill heats, let the steaks come to room temperature for 20 or 30 minutes if you have the time.

Set the meat on the grill and cook, untouched, covered on a gas grill, until it starts to brown at the edges and easily releases from the grill grates when you lift up an edge with tongs or a spatula, 2 to 3 minutes. Flip and cook the other sides until the meat is somewhat firm to the touch (press down with your index finger) and cooked through to the desired doneness, 2 to 5 minutes. Check by slicing into a thicker piece to see its level of pinkness or insert an instant-read thermometer into the center of a thicker cut to register its internal temperature: 130°F for a medium-rare steak or 145°F for medium well pork chops. See the meat doneness chart on page 24. If a thicker steak or chop is starting to burn before properly cooking through, move it to a cooler zone of the fire or reduce the heat on a gas grill to medium low and continue to cook, flipping occasionally, until done to your liking.

2. SAUCE: Brush with an SWS sauce (pages 86–150) and cook, basting for 1 to 2 minutes, so the sauce browns. Or, serve with an SAS sauce.

3. SERVE: I generally only use glazes with reasonably priced, chewy steaks where the coating enhances (as opposed to overpowers) the meat. Try brushing a flank steak with the Bulgogi Sauce (Korean BBQ) (page 93) and serve it with grilled scallions (page 80), stir-fried bok choy, and steamed rice. Read Slicing Against the Grain on page 74 before cooking. Toss together grilled beef fajitas with grilled peppers, onions, and the Avocado and Corn Salsa (page 158). Make steak frites with a pricier steak like a strip or rib eye, a generous pat of an infused butter like the Chive and Black Truffle Butter (page 198), some homemade fries, and a green salad. Spoon the Mango, Roasted Red Pepper, and Habanero Salsa (page 161) over some bone-in grilled pork chops and serve with rice and beans.

Grilled Burgers

(Beef, Lamb)

I've learned more about burgers than I ever would have imagined when I first started cooking for a living. Back then, I saw myself toiling in fancy restaurants for years to come. But a couple of years later, a college buddy asked me to help start up a healthier, homemade burger chain. I loved the idea (and the concept of improving one of the more neglected forms of dining), and now a couple of years later we have eight stores and make a whole lot of burgers. And, ironically, in the intervening years, burgers have become high-end fare with most every fancy chef offering up his own take.

As with many simple preparations, burgers are easy to make, but also easy to screw up. Follow a couple of tips below and you'll be just fine. My method is straightforward—choose meat with a little bit of fat, light a moderate fire so the exterior browns while the inside gently cooks through, and then go crazy with your sauce pairings.

. . . .

The Cut and the Prep

I only like to grill beef and lamb burgers; most everything else tends to fall apart on the grill and is better seared on the stove top (see the Sauté Nonbeef [or Lamb] Burgers tip page 77). Before grinding, cut steaks into 1-inch cubes and then chill in the freezer for 10 minutes so they firm up and grind easily.

. . . .

Beef: I prefer beef 85 percent lean—enough fat that there's flavor, but not so much you feel guilty. Look for meat from the chuck, which is the shoulder area of the animal and tends to be the most flavorful. If you want to grind your own (see page 41), try a chuck steak or a blend of something exotic and fatty like brisket and something lean like sirloin.

Lamb: Because many markets don't grind lamb, you can grind your own (see How to Grind Your Own, page 41) using most any boneless steak; trim off any fatty patches, which can give the burgers an overly gamey flavor.

YIELD: 4 SERVINGS
PREP TIME: up to 3 minutes
COOK TIME: 5 to 8 minutes

1½ pounds ground meat, formed into patties (see Little Burger Tricks tip on page 77)
About 1¼ teaspoons kosher salt
About ½ teaspoon freshly ground black pepper

1. **SEAR:** Light a medium charcoal fire or heat the burners on a gas grill to medium. Sprinkle the burgers generously with salt and pepper. Let sit at room temperature for 10 minutes while the grill heats.

Set the burgers on the grill and cook without touching (resist the urge to fiddle with them for the first couple of minutes, which could cause them to break up) until they start to brown at the edges, juices rise to the tops of the patties, and they easily release from the grill grates when you pick up an edge, 2 to 3 minutes. Flip and cook the other sides until browned and just firm to the touch for medium, 2 to 3 more minutes; make a nick with a paring knife into a thicker burger to check the level of pinkness. Or continue cooking and flipping until done to your liking.

2. **SAUCE:** Brush with an SWS glaze (pages 86–96), move to a cooler part of the fire and cook, flipping and brushing for 1 to 2 minutes, until the glaze starts to caramelize. Or, serve with an SAS sauce (pages 152–231).

3. **SERVE:** Sure, you can just make a plain cheeseburger, but if you're looking for a little inspiration, top-grilled beef patties with Ancho Chile Ketchup (page 172), Grilled Balsamic Onions (page 229), and Herb-Marinated Chopped Summer Tomatoes (page 219) and set on a sourdough bun. Or mix a sprinkling of curry powder into lamb patties, top with Cucumber-Mint Raita (page 203) and Pickled Red Onions (page 220), and serve on warm naan.

TIP: Little Burger Tricks

Gently cook over medium heat: Perhaps the biggest mistake cooks make when grilling burgers is lighting up a roaring fire. High flames char a burger's exterior before the inside can cook through. Moderate heat is the key for grilling burgers.

- Pack the burgers gently so they have a soft texture. The more you handle meat, the more likely it is to become dense and tough, instead of light and crumbly. I like to pack the burgers about ½-inch thick so they cook through quickly and evenly.

- Pick out the right meat: See The Cut and the Prep on page 31 for the best cuts for grinding (or what type of ground beef to buy).

- Don't press down the burgers on the grill! Sure this may help them cook more quickly, but it smashes the juices right out of the meat!

TIP: Burger Safety

If the beef wasn't ground by you or your local butcher, it's best you cook the burgers to well done (160°F, or until its pinkness is cooked off) because anything that's not been ground from a single muscle of a specific origin could have been contaminated during processing at the packing plant.

TIP: Sauté Nonbeef (or Lamb) Burgers

The idea of grilling a chicken, tuna, or turkey burger sounds great, but is impractical in reality. Each has a loose or soft texture that doesn't hold up well on the grill. You can bind these ingredients with eggs, bread crumbs or all sorts of other fillers, but your best bet for nonbeef (or lamb) burgers is to form them into patties and then sear them in a nonstick skillet (follow the delicate fish technique on page 44). You may miss a little smokiness, but the patties will still get a nice browned crust and will hold together perfectly.

OPTIONS: "Stuffed" Burgers

The focus when making burgers usually is on how to dress and top the patties. But one way to make a burger extra special is to stuff it with something rich—either cheese or a flavored butter—so that it stays moist and picks up flavor during cooking, kind of like an internal basting. To do this, make a little divot in the center of a patty and stuff with a pat of Chipotle-Lime Butter (page 199) or goat cheese mashed with fresh herbs. Then patty the burger so that it encloses the butter or cheese and grill it as you would any other burger. The surprise comes at the dinner table: when you bite into the burger, the meat will be coated with a warm mix of juices and butter or cheese. It might not be cardiologist approved, but it will be tasty.

Grilled Fish/Seafood

(Calamari, Halibut, Salmon, Shrimp, Swordfish, Tuna, Trout)

Of all the techniques in this book, this may be the most feared. When fish is not properly grilled, it goes very wrong. It sticks, it flakes, it breaks, it batters the morale of a cook. I know because I was left alone on the grill station at a fancy Roman seafood restaurant for six months (see Italian Grilling on page 79) and the first couple of weeks were among the most terrifying of my life (grilling while Roman waiters yell at you is the culinary equivalent of Pamplona's running with the bulls). But eventually I learned how to grill fish just right—all the searing tricks we've already talked about, only more because fish is delicate and grilling it can be demanding. And it's really that simple: just focus on the little things and you'll be fine.

The Fish and the Prep

Flaky fish (like cod) aren't included in this technique because they won't hold up on the grill. Use firm-fleshed filets and steaks. *Rinse them well to wash off any funk and then pat dry all over so they won't stick. Then rub the fish with oil before grilling to help avoid sticking.*

Calamari:*Butterfly the bodies* and lay them flat on the grill.

Halibut:Either steaks or filets are fine. Leave the skin on to help the fish hold together on the grill.

Salmon:Either steaks or filets are fine. Leave the skin on to help the fish hold together on the grill.

Shrimp:21–26 count, *peeled and deveined.* There is a debate as to whether you should peel shrimp before grilling. I peel it, because what you lose in texture (the shell protects shrimp giving it a softer, less rubbery consistency), you make up for with added smoky flavor.

Skewers:Cut filets—like swordfish or salmon—uniformly into 1- to 1½-inch pieces and thread on skewers along with vegetables.

Swordfish:You can remove any dark discolorations (these are just the blood lines, which tend to be stronger flavored).

Trout:Whole small fish are good for the grill. Snapper or red mullet are also good options if you can find them.

Tuna:You can remove any dark discolorations (these are just the blood lines, which tend to be stronger flavored).

YIELD: 4 SERVINGS

PREP TIME: up to 2 minutes

COOK TIME: 5 to 10 minutes

1½ pounds firm filets and steaks

2 tablespoons olive oil

About ¾ teaspoon kosher salt

About ½ teaspoon freshly ground black pepper

1. SEAR: Light a medium-high charcoal fire or heat the burners on a gas grill to high. Get the grill grates hot and clean (see tip on page 68) before cooking. Season the fish with salt and pepper.

Set the fish on the grill and cook until it starts to brown at the edges and easily releases from the grates when you lift up a corner, 2 to 3 minutes. Flip using a fish spatula and a pair of tongs to gently guide it on. Cook the other side until it has good grill marks and just starts to become firm to the touch, 2 to 3 minutes. Make a nick with a paring knife to check that the fish is still a little pink inside; see the chart on page 26 for more specific fish doneness. If the fish is starting to burn before it cooks through, transfer it to a cooler zone of the fire or reduce the heat to medium low on a gas grill and continue cooking until done.

2. SAUCE: Brush with an SWS glaze, move to a cooler part of the fire, and cook, brushing occasionally, for 1 to 2 minutes, until the glaze starts to caramelize. Or, serve with an SAS sauce.

3. SERVE:A briny vinaigrette like the Sun-Dried Tomato and Caper Vinaigrette (page 180) would present a perfect Mediterranean foil to grilled swordfish. Serve with Quinoa with Fennel and Feta (page 236). Or go Asian and pair the Soy and Wasabi Mayonnaise (page 191) with medium-rare tuna or salmon for a home-style take on seared sashimi; serve with steamed sushi rice and a fresh cucumber salad. Or try pairing grilled halibut or trout with the Grilled Sweet Corn and Pepper Relish (page 222) and serve with boiled new potatoes.

STORY: Italian Grilling

If you want to know the truth, they left me alone on the grill station way before they should have. I was relatively far along in my culinary education by the time I started cooking at Bastianelli al Molo, a fancy fish restaurant about 20 minutes outside of Rome. But I'd had very little experience with Mediterranean fish (like red mullet, sea bass, or sea bream) and my Italian was only passable, not good enough to deal with an onslaught of frustrated Italian waiters. And we're not just talking Italian waiters, but Roman waiters, bow-tied impresarios with the temperament, if not the vocabulary, of a New York cabby.

What I had going for me (besides not understanding when people were calling me a moron) was that I started in July and I was the guy who was going to fill in while each cook took their two-week summer vacations. So everybody looked at me rather hopefully and as I started to give off a faint air of competency, the waiters accepted that I was going to be around for a while. They began to work with me and I slowly found my way on the grill.

And I learned a lot about grilling fish. Most of it was the basics—how to get a nice, browned crust and avoid sticking—rather than any great Benihana's spatula trick. I did learn them in an Italian setting, though, so that by the end of six months, I had a sort of bravado that you can only pick up in Rome. Perhaps the best trick I learned was how to tell when a large grilled fish is done: gently pull at its backbone at the top of the spine—it should easily pull free. If not, keep on cooking. Use this as a party trick at your next big cookout and tell your guests you learned it in Rome. Works every time.

Grilled Quick-Cooking Vegetables

(Asparagus, Bell Peppers, Cherry Tomatoes, Chiles, Eggplant, Scallions, Zucchini)

My first culinary epiphany took place at a country club in the summer between my junior and senior years in college. It was one of my first cooking jobs and I was sent outside to grill a platter (OK, more like a 7-foot stainless steel charger) of vegetables for a wedding of 250 people. It could have been the heat (mid 90s), the fumes (I was working over charcoal), or the pressure (I hadn't been left on my own in that kitchen much before then), but I found my inner cook, grilling hundreds of vegetables. My take home that day: I learned that grilling vegetables demands finesse. A grill is unpredictable and each vegetable reacts a little differently to fire. Keep flipping and testing until each is just there.

. . . .

The Vegetable and the Prep

Asparagus: *Woody ends snapped off and stalks peeled if large.*

Bell peppers: *Quartered and cored.*

Cherry/grape tomatoes: *Stemmed, rinsed and threaded onto skewers.*

Chiles (jalapeños, Anaheims, poblanos): *Cut in half lengthwise, cored and seeded.*

Eggplant: *Sliced ¼-inch thick (either lengthwise or widthwise are fine).*

Plum tomatoes: *Halved (and seeded if you like).*

Scallions: *Trimmed, rinsed, but not dried (see tip on page 81).*

Zucchini/summer squash: *Cut lengthwise into ¼-inch slices or into thin disks on the diagonal.*

. . . .

YIELD: 4 SIDE DISH SERVINGS
PREP TIME: up to 4 minutes
COOK TIME: 4 to 8 minutes

Up to 1½ pounds vegetables
About 1 teaspoon kosher salt
About ½ teaspoon freshly ground black pepper
2 tablespoons olive oil

1. **SEAR:** Sprinkle the vegetables generously with salt and pepper and drizzle with the oil. Heat the burners on a gas grill to medium-high or light a medium charcoal fire. Set the vegetables on the grill and cook, without touching, until they start to get good grill marks, 2 to 3 minutes. Flip using tongs and cook the other side until it has good grill marks and just starts to soften, 2 to 3 minutes. Use your index finger to probe and press for doneness (see Doneness Tests for Grilled Vegetables on page 81 for how each vegetable should feel); if they're browned but still not cooked to your liking transfer to a cooler zone of the fire or reduce the heat on a gas grill to medium and continue cooking.

2. **SAUCE:** Brush with an SWS glaze and cook for 1 to 2 minutes so the glaze caramelizes but does not burn. Or, serve with an SAS sauce.

3. **SERVE:** Make a grilled vegetable ratatouille with peppers, eggplant and zucchini; after grilling, toss with the Salamanca Sherry-Thyme Vinaigrette (page 179) or Lemon-Basil Vinaigrette (page 178), set atop plain cooked couscous and sprinkle with fresh parsley and crumbled feta cheese. Grilled asparagus go nicely with an infused butter like the Shallot-Herb Butter (page 197) or with the Asian flavors in the Spicy Szechuan Chile and Black Bean Oil (page 209). Serve with rice and a grilled flank steak (page 75). Or make a first course starter with layers of grilled eggplant, herbed goat cheese, and a drizzle of the "House" Thyme-Dijon Vinaigrette (page 176).

. . . .

Doneness Tests for Grilled Vegetables

Because this technique covers so many different vegetables, it helps to organize the doneness of each (or how far you should cook them) into two basic groups.

1. Cooked all the way through (soft inside): Eggplant is the poster vegetable for this grouping. It must be cooked until completely soft or it's tough and unpleasant. Similarly, I like my zucchini and peppers nice and tender.

2. A little toothy: You want to give these vegetables a good grilled sear on the outside, but still maintain some firmness to their texture on the inside. Asparagus, tomatoes, and hot chiles are examples of vegetables that are best when their meaty texture is left mostly intact, and not overcooked into submission. I like tomatoes and cherry tomatoes blistered on the outside with a little bite on the inside.

Salting Eggplant (and Zucchini)

Though presalting eggplant may not rid it of its bitterness (as some cooks suggest), it does improve its texture (and zucchini, too) by pulling moisture out, which helps it brown more easily and gives it a firmer, more concentrated texture.

When a Sear Is a Sauce and a Sauce Is a Sear

This technique is an instance where the worlds of searing and sauces collide since it covers vegetables like grilled onions, which can be either or both. Just consider this a lot of a good thing, then, and use this method to help guide you whether you're preparing onions as a side or as a seared vegetable topping on pages 225 to 231.

No More Lost Vegetables!

We've all mourned the loss of an asparagus spear, red pepper wedge, or onion ring to the fire below. You can curse the grill gods, but there are a couple of other ways to battle back against this unwanted sacrifice. The first is obsessive, but highly effective: skewer everything. Thread cherry tomatoes, asparagus, or onions onto skewers (metal or soaked wooden ones). Not only will you hold on to all of your vegetables, but the flipping will be that much easier. The second method is more commonsensical: when you set the vegetables on the grill, make sure that they run perpendicular to the grates and try to keep them that way after flipping. You may still lose an onion every now and then, but your losses will be greatly reduced.

Don't Dry Scallions after Rinsing

Scallions grill exceedingly quickly, but like an onion, they can char on the grill (or under the broiler). One trick to combat burning is to leave them a little moist after rinsing. The water that clings to the scallions will protect them over the hot flames, creating some steam that helps to cook them more gently.

Grilled Hearty Vegetables

(Corn, Onions, Portobello Mushrooms)

The vegetables in this grouping can't be grilled over high heat from start to finish. They would burn before they cooked through. So you need to use a little finesse—in the form of a two-zone fire—to ensure that these veggies become both browned and tender. Use the hotter side of the fire to sear the vegetables. Then push to the cooler side and cover the grill to finish cooking them.

The Vegetable and the Prep

Corn:*Semi-shucked* (see the technique and illustration on page 83).

Onions:*Peeled and cut into ¼-inch disks*—you can thread them onto thin metal skewers to prevent these disks from breaking up on the grill (and falling through the grates)—me, I like to live dangerously.

Portobello mushrooms:*Stemmed* (peel and use these in a sauté if you like) *and gills scraped off using a spoon.*

YIELD: 4 SIDE DISH SERVINGS
PREP TIME: up to 4 minutes
COOK TIME: 8 to 12 minutes

1 to 2 pounds vegetables (or 4 portobellos)
About ¾ teaspoon kosher salt
About ½ teaspoon freshly ground black pepper
2 tablespoons olive oil

1. SEAR: Light a two-zone charcoal fire with a medium and a medium-low zone or heat half of the burners on a gas grill to medium high and the rest to medium low. Sprinkle the vegetables generously with salt and pepper and drizzle with the oil; pull back the husks of the corn to season each ear (see the technique on page 83).

Set the vegetables on the grill (the mushrooms cap-side down) and cook, covered on the gas grill, until they start to get good grill marks, 2 to 3 minutes. Flip the onions or mushrooms, roll over the corn, and continue cooking until this side gets good grill marks, too, 2 to 3 minutes. Transfer the vegetables to the cooler zone of the fire and continue cooking until the mushrooms are tender and cooked through (they should be completely soft when pressed), the corn kernels are bright yellow (or just bright for sweet corn) and tender when pressed, and the onions are starting to soften (see the tip on page 83 for how to get them more tender), 4 to 6 more minutes.

2. SAUCE: Brush with an SWS glaze (pages 86–94) and cook for 1 to 2 minutes over the hotter zone of the fire so the glaze caramelizes but does not burn. Or serve with an SAS sauce (pages 152–231).

3. SERVE: Unless you serve them as a package deal with some bright grain salads like those on page 236 to 237, most of these vegetables are wonderful summery sides with a grilled steak or fish filet. Melt generous pats of the Chipotle-Lime Butter (page 199) or Sun-Dried Tomato and Rosemary Butter (page 199) on grilled corn. Brush the onions with the Rosemary-Balsamic Glaze (page 88) or top with the Sherry-Ginger Butter (page 198). Brush meaty grilled portobellos with the Toasted Sesame Teriyaki Sauce (page 90) and serve with grilled zucchini and peppers, and steamed rice or set them in a sandwich with the Spanish Roasted Red Pepper Aioli (page 194), smoked gouda, and some baby spinach.

TIP: Grill-Steam Onions

I love grilled onions, but they represent a culinary riddle of sorts: how to get them tender without charring. After browning the onions, you can move them to a cooler part of the fire and cook for 15 to 20 minutes, but that's an unwanted expense of time. My weeknight compromise is to put the onions in a bowl the moment they're off the grill, cover with plastic wrap, and let sit for a couple of minutes (maybe while you finish your sauce). The steam of the onions will finish softening them, but still leave their smoky flavor intact. Also, pick the right onion for grilling. The higher its sugar content, the more apt it will be to burn. For this reason, you need to take extra care when grilling a sweet onion like a Vidalia. I like to grill large red onions, which have a nice sweet flavor, but don't burn easily.

TECHNIQUE: Semi-Husking Grilled Corn

Fresh picked summer corn (I'm talking about the stuff that's harvested that very morning) is sweet and tender enough to eat raw. Grilling corn, though, can add a layer of pleasant smoky flavor without taking much time. There are bunch of different methods for grilling corn, from wrapping the ears completely in foil and slowly grilling to setting shucked ears right over the flame and cooking for a couple of minutes. I follow a method I learned from *Fine Cooking* friend Jennifer Armentrout, one that's somewhere in between. I snap open the husks and pull down the leaves so the corn and its silk are completely exposed. Then I pull off and discard all of the silk and pull the husk back up to cover the corn. The husk acts like a more natural form of the aluminum foil, protecting the corn as it cooks, allowing it to brown in places and almost steam as it picks up smokiness from the flames.

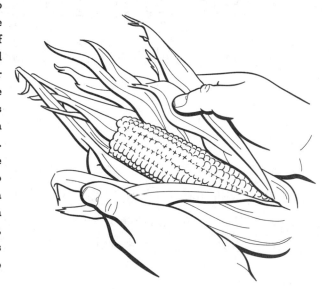

INFORMATION: Grilled Spuds?

Potatoes on the grill are tasty, but cooking them properly can be demanding; either you have to gently grill-roast them in foil over indirect heat or simmer them on the stove top until tender, cut into planks, and grill directly over moderate heat. Either manner simply doesn't fit within the constraints of our quick-cooking formula.

CHAPTER: 3

SAUCES WHILE YOU SEAR

BASTE, SCRAPE, TOSS, OR WHISK THESE BRIGHT, SPICED SAUCES WITH THE SEARED INGREDIENTS DURING THE FINAL STAGE OF COOKING

THE SAUCES IN THIS CHAPTER ARE ALL ADDED TO THE SEARED INGREDIENTS TOWARD THE END OF COOKING, WHETHER IT'S A GLAZE BASTED ONTO GRILLED OR BROILED FARE, A SAUTÉ OR STIR-FRY SAUCE SIMMERED WITH MEAT AND VEGETABLES, OR A PAN SAUCE GENTLY TOSSED WITH A STEAK OR CUTLET. COOKING A SAUCE WITH THE SEARED INGREDIENT ALLOWS THEIR FLAVORS TO MARRY, ULTIMATELY CREATING A MORE COMPLEX DISH. IT DOES MAKE THE LAST STAGE OF COOKING A LITTLE MORE COMPLICATED, BUT IT'S NOTHING THAT YOU CAN'T HANDLE.

ABOUT THE SAUCE RECIPES

YEILD: Sauces in this book shoot for four servings. If the yield is larger, it's because either the sauce will keep for a while (like a glaze or a vinaigrette) or it's the kind of thing for which you might as well make a large batch (like a marinara or barbecue sauce). Each sauce has an approximate volume yield so you know more or less how much you'll have and in what size dish to make it.

INGREDIENT LIST: I usually lean toward ease of use over exact measurements in the ingredient lists for each recipe. For instance, I will call for "1 garlic clove, minced (about 1 teaspoon)" as opposed to "1 teaspoon minced garlic." My reasoning is simple: in savory recipes, the importance of measuring ingredients is all relative. I don't want you stressing about mincing and measuring a perfect teaspoon of garlic when it really won't matter if it's a touch over or a touch under. Just think of my measurements as the amounts that worked for me in my tests, and then adjust them to suit your tastes.

SHELF LIFE: I include this information to help you decide whether you want to make a large batch or make a sauce ahead. Of course, in the best of all worlds, you'd make every sauce fresh, but we live in a busy world and compromise is better than takeout.

I. GLAZES/BBQ SAUCES

Food snobs will tell you that refined palettes should be above sweet stuff. And while I'm not one for cloying, you're-going-to-pay-for-this-at-the-dentist fare, I do love the way sticky glazes and barbecue sauces caramelize over a hot flame (or under the broiler), giving seared meat or vegetables another level of flavor and complexity.

Most of the glazes and barbecue sauces in this section also offer a healthy hit of heat or spice (to balance out the sweet) and a thick texture so they stick to whatever you're grilling or broiling. I suggest applying these sauces in a two-pronged attack: first, baste the seared ingredient with half of the sauce for 1 or 2 minutes to get some caramelization and then set the remainder out on the table for drizzling or dipping (see Avoid Cross-Contamination tip below).

And the best aspect of these sauces is that they're easy—most just need to be whisked together or quickly simmered on the stove top to smooth out their flavors and thicken.

BASIC TECHNIQUE

Most of the sauces in this section rely on some level of viscosity (I know, it's a word normally only used in motor oil commercials) so they coat whatever you're grilling or broiling and, accordingly, form a sticky, browned crust. There are a number of ways to thicken a glaze. You can rely on a base of something that's already thick, like maple syrup, honey, or jelly. Or you can reduce a liquid until it thickens—a process that's generally too time consuming for this book. And then there's a final option of using a cornstarch slurry to thicken the sauce just after it comes to a boil. Usually I take the first and third options in this section.

TIP: Avoid Cross-Contamination
I like to use glazes for both basting on the grill and for drizzling at the table. To keep things above board from a food safety perspective, I separate the glaze into two containers before searing: one for basting and basting only, as it will be contaminated by coming into contact with raw ingredients, and the other for drizzling or dipping the seared fare at the table.

Spiced Pineapple-Rum Glaze

This is what I make when I feel the Jimmy-Buffet, Hawaiian-shirt mood coming on. The rum adds sharpness without having an overly boozy effect and the spices offer a little depth to fill out the sweetness. It's a large batch, but this makes sense once you cut up a fresh pineapple or open up a can of pineapple.

YIELD: 2 CUPS, ABOUT 8 SERVINGS
PREP TIME: 2 minutes
COOK TIME: 5 minutes

2 tablespoons unsalted butter

¼ teaspoon allspice

⅛ to ¼ teaspoon cinnamon

1 (8-ounce) can crushed pineapple, drained, or 1 cup chopped fresh pineapple, pulsed in a food processor

¾ cup light brown sugar

2 tablespoons rum

1 tablespoon soy sauce

¼ teaspoon kosher salt

1 teaspoon cornstarch

Melt the butter in a small saucepan. Add the allspice and cinnamon and cook, stirring, until it becomes very fragrant, about 30 seconds. Add the remaining ingredients with the exception of the cornstarch, bring to a boil, and then simmer for a couple of minutes so the mixture starts to thicken and the alcohol from the rum mellows.

Whisk the cornstarch with 2 teaspoons water and stir into the glaze. Return to a boil so the mixture thickens. Remove from the heat and let cool for a couple of minutes.

OPTIONS: Add sautéed fresh ginger to fill out the spices in this glaze, or thinly sliced scallions or red bell pepper for color.

PAIRINGS: The sweetness and spice of this glaze pairs nicely with grilled pork chops (page 75) or broiled shrimp (page 66). Serve with steamed brown rice and warm black beans.

SHELF LIFE: Up to three days in the refrigerator.

SPICES: The allspice and cinnamon should offer just a mild hit, so this is one of those times to measure rather than eye these amounts.

TIP: Versatile BBQ Sauces

We all tend to cook more spontaneously in the summer—warm weather breeds activity, and by the time you're done with the gym, garden, or beach, it's nice to be able to just throw something on the grill and head to the table. These glazes and bbq sauces vibe with that set-up. Make a couple of these glazes on a Sunday—most of them will keep for at least a couple of days in the fridge—and then pair with grilled steak, fish, or vegetables throughout the week. The meal will feel planned out and complete even if it's anything but.

Mandarin Orange and Mint Glaze

The sweetness of this glaze, from equal parts honey and brown sugar, helps smooth out the somewhat unorthodox pairing of mint and orange. The result is a sauce that is bright enough to cut through fatty, full-flavored cuts.

YIELD: 1 CUP, ABOUT 6 SERVINGS

PREP TIME: 3 minutes
COOK TIME: 6 minutes

1 (8-ounce) can mandarin oranges and the juices, coarsely chopped
¼ cup honey
¼ cup light brown sugar
1 tablespoon rice vinegar
About ¼ teaspoon kosher salt
About ¼ teaspoon freshly ground black pepper
1 teaspoon cornstarch
2 tablespoons chopped fresh mint

Heat the oranges (and their juices), honey, brown sugar, vinegar, and a light sprinkling of salt and pepper in a small saucepan over high heat, whisking occasionally, until the mixture reduces by about half, about 5 minutes. Whisk the cornstarch with 1 tablespoon water and stir into the glaze. Return to a boil so the mixture thickens. Remove the glaze from the heat, stir in the mint, and let cool for a couple of minutes.

OPTIONS: When they're available (in the winter months), use diced fresh mandarins (along with a splash of their juices).

PAIRINGS: Brush on grilled lamb chops (page 75) or broiled chicken parts (page 63); serve with grilled pita or warmed store-bought naan and a garbanzo salad.

SHELF LIFE: Up to two days in the refrigerator; the mint starts to dull after this time.

Scorched Habanero and Mango Glaze

Food-science types gauge a chile's spiciness in Scoville units, a measurement of capsaicin. Tiny habaneros, full of sweet and citrus notes, top the charts with over 100,000 Scoville units; compare that to the jalapeño's 2,500. Seeding the chiles makes this glaze more palatable for non-chile heads; leave them in for really fiery fare.

YIELD: 1¼ CUPS, ABOUT 6 SERVINGS

PREP TIME: 8 minutes
COOK TIME: 5 minutes

2 tablespoons canola oil
1 habanero or scotch bonnet pepper, cored, seeded, and chopped, using gloves (see Handling Habaneros tip on page 88) (about 1 tablespoon)
1 small red onion, finely diced (about ½ cup)
About ½ teaspoon kosher salt
About ½ teaspoon freshly ground black pepper
½ cup diced fresh mango
¼ cup orange juice (preferably freshly squeezed)
¼ cup honey
2 tablespoons chopped cilantro (optional)

Heat the oil in a skillet over medium-high heat until shimmering hot, about 1½ minutes. Add the habanero and onion, sprinkle generously with salt and pepper, and cook, stirring, until the onion starts to soften and brown in places, about 3 minutes. Remove from the heat.

Set the mango, orange juice, honey, and habanero mixture in a food processor and pulse to coarsely chop and combine. Stir in the cilantro, if using, and season with salt and pepper to taste.

PAIRINGS: Brush this glaze on spice-rubbed bone-in pork chops (page 75) or chicken wings (page 73). Serve with buttered Uncle Ben's rice and grilled corn (page 82).

SHELF LIFE: Up to two days in the refrigerator.

> **TIP: Handling Habaneros**
>
> You only have to burn your eyes once (after accidentally rubbing them post–chile chopping) to develop a deep regard for what the oils from these chiles can do to sensitive parts of the body. It may seem a little extreme, but it's a good idea to use gloves when seeding or chopping habaneros. If not, make sure to wash your hands well thereafter and, even then, be careful with what you touch.

Sweet Apricot Glaze

Here, orange, both its juice and zest, perks up the relatively mellow flavor of apricot without overpowering it.

YIELD: 1¼ CUPS, 6 SERVINGS
PREP TIME: 3 minutes
COOK TIME: N/A

1 navel orange, zested (about 2 teaspoons) and juiced (about ½ cup)
½ cup apricot preserves
¼ cup honey
1 tablespoon soy sauce
2 teaspoons tomato paste
2 teaspoons chopped fresh thyme (optional)

Set half of the orange juice (about ¼ cup) with the zest and the remaining ingredients in a medium bowl and whisk well to combine. Add more of the orange juice to taste.

OPTIONS: If you're smack dab in the middle of apricot season, dice up a ripe fruit, sauté with a little butter, and fold into this glaze.

PAIRINGS: This mild sauce goes well with grilled pork chops (page 75) or broiled beef flank steak (page 64). Serve with Cold Peanut Noodles with Mint and Thai Chiles (page 233) and stir-fried snow peas (page 50).

SHELF LIFE: Up to three days in the refrigerator.

Rosemary–Balsamic Glaze

The better the balsamic, the more refined this glaze; the really cheap stuff has a way of tasting like cough medicine when it's mixed with something sweet like honey. Make sure to mash the garlic in this sauce so it melds with the other flavors.

YIELD: ¾ CUP, 4 SERVINGS
PREP TIME: 2 minutes
COOK TIME: N/A

½ cup honey
2 tablespoons balsamic vinegar, more to taste
1 teaspoon chopped fresh rosemary
1 garlic clove, minced and mashed to a paste on a cutting board (see page 153)
About ½ teaspoon kosher salt
About ½ teaspoon freshly ground black pepper

In a medium bowl, whisk together the ingredients with a generous sprinkling of salt and pepper. Add more vinegar, salt, and pepper to taste.

PAIRINGS: This mild glaze goes well with everything, though I especially like it on grilled asparagus (page 80) or broiled scallops (page 66). Make a meal out of the latter by pairing with Roasted Rosemary Fingerling Potatoes (page 235) and a green salad.

SHELF LIFE: Up to five days in the refrigerator.

Lemon-Rosemary Glaze

The sharp acidity of lemon makes it an unorthodox player in glazes. A healthy sprinkling of sugar smoothes out the citrus's rough edges and the toasted garlic and rosemary helps pair this sauce with all sorts of fish or seafood.

YIELD: 1 CUP; 4 SERVINGS
PREP TIME: 5 minutes
COOK TIME: 10 minutes

1 tablespoon olive oil
1 large garlic clove, halved
2 teaspoons chopped fresh rosemary
¼ teaspoon crushed red pepper flakes
¼ cup freshly squeezed lemon juice (about 1 lemon)
¼ cup granulated sugar
2 teaspoons cornstarch
About ½ teaspoon kosher salt, or to taste
About ½ teaspoon freshly ground black pepper, or to taste

Heat the oil with the garlic in a medium saucepan over medium heat until it starts to sizzle and become fragrant, about 2 minutes. Add the rosemary and red pepper flakes and cook, stirring, for 30 seconds so they sizzle and become very fragrant. Raise the heat to high, add the lemon juice, sugar, and ½ cup water and bring to a boil. Whisk the cornstarch with 1 tablespoon water and then stir into the lemon mixture. Let the mixture return to a boil so it thickens, then remove from the heat. Season with salt and pepper to taste.

SHELF LIFE: Up to three days in the refrigerator.

PAIRINGS: Brush this sharp glaze on broiled scallops (page 66) or grilled salmon (page 78) and serve with a white bean salad and a baguette.

EMBELLISHMENTS: Meyer lemons, smaller than regular lemons and more intensely flavored, are a nice upgrade if you can find them in the winter months—just use about half the amount of juice.

Spicy Hoisin Glaze

Hoisin sauce is like the Chinese equivalent of ketchup, a spiced condiment whose versatility plays well in all kinds of preparations like this simple glaze. This sauce keeps for a while so make a double batch if you feel so inclined.

YIELD: SCANT ¾ CUP, 4 SERVINGS
PREP TIME: 2 minutes
COOK TIME: N/A

⅓ cup honey
3 tablespoons hoisin sauce
1 tablespoon toasted sesame oil
1 tablespoon rice vinegar
1 tablespoon toasted sesame seeds
1 teaspoon Thai chile paste (like Sriracha)

In a medium bowl, mix all of the ingredients to combine.

OPTIONS: Add a little more depth to this sauce by stirring in sliced scallions or sautéed ginger or garlic.

PAIRINGS: Brush on grilled halibut (page 78) or broiled flank steak (page 64) and serve on a bed of summery greens. Or try this glaze drizzled on grilled asparagus (page 80) or eggplant (page 80).

SHELF LIFE: Up to two weeks in the refrigerator (there's not much in here that will go bad).

TIP: Hoisin brands: I like Koon Chun (thick and intensely flavored) or Lee Kum Kee (loose, sweet, and spiced) hoisin sauces and don't trust much else.

Chinese Sweet and Sour Orange Glaze

I'm always amazed how prominent a role citrus plays in the savory side of Chinese cuisine, adding nuanced acidity to sauces like this glaze.

YIELD: 1¼ CUPS, ABOUT 4 SERVINGS
PREP TIME: 4 minutes
COOK TIME: 4 minutes

1 navel orange, zested (about 2 teaspoons) and juiced
    (about ½ cup)
¼ cup honey
2 tablespoons soy sauce
1 tablespoon ketchup
1 teaspoon Thai chile paste (like Sriracha)
3 scallions (both white and green parts), trimmed and
    thinly sliced
2 teaspoons cornstarch

Combine all the ingredients except the cornstarch with ½ cup water in a medium saucepan. Bring to a simmer. Mix the cornstarch with 1 tablespoon water and whisk into the orange mixture. Return to a simmer so the sauce thickens and then remove from the heat.

OPTIONS: Fold in diced fresh orange to add freshness and texture.

PAIRINGS: I particularly like this versatile sauce brushed on grilled pork tenderloin (page 75) or broiled salmon filets (page 66); serve with Cold Peanut Noodles with Mint and Thai Chiles (page 233) and grilled scallions (page 80).

SHELF LIFE: Up to five days in the refrigerator.

Toasted Sesame Teriyaki Sauce

I was that get-a-lifer in college with the hibachi and jar of teriyaki sauce. If there was a game and a flat bed, I was ready to grill. My admiration for this preparation only grew after visiting Japan a couple of years back. A little heat (from Thai chile paste) and toasted sesame seeds round out this version.

YIELD: 1¼ CUPS, 4 SERVINGS
PREP TIME: 4 minutes
COOK TIME: 6 minutes

2 tablespoons chopped ginger
2 tablespoons canola oil
2 garlic cloves, coarsely chopped (about 2 teaspoons)
½ cup honey
2 tablespoons soy sauce
1 tablespoon toasted sesame seeds
1 tablespoon white vinegar
1 teaspoon Thai chile paste (like Sriracha)
2 teaspoons cornstarch

Set the ginger and garlic in a mini-chop or food processor and pulse to finely chop. Heat the oil, ginger, and garlic in a medium saucepan over medium-high heat until they sizzle steadily and just begin to brown at the edges, about 2 minutes. Whisk in the honey, soy sauce, sesame seeds, vinegar, and chile paste with ½ cup water and bring to a simmer, about 2 minutes.

In a small bowl, whisk the cornstarch with 1 tablespoon water and then stir into the sauce. Continue cooking, stirring, until the sauce thickens, about 1 minute.

PAIRINGS: No doubt you know teriyaki goes well with shellfish, meat, chicken, or vegetables. I particularly like brushing it on grilled flank steak (page 75) and zucchini (page 80) and serving with Thai Coconut Rice (steamed Jasmine Rice with coconut milk and sautéed ginger).

SHELF LIFE: Up to one week in the refrigerator.

Maple and Crushed Cumin Glaze

The pairing may sound strange—there aren't any cumin plants growing next to maple trees in Vermont—but the seeds add earthy depth to the maple's caramel-like sweetness.

YIELD: ¾ CUP, 4 SERVINGS
PREP TIME: 3 minutes
COOK TIME: 3 minutes

2 teaspoons cumin seeds, crushed with a mortar and
    pestle or a spoon in a small bowl (you don't have to
    crush them all—just enough to activate their oils)
¼ teaspoon crushed red pepper flakes
¾ cup maple syrup
1 tablespoon cider vinegar
1 teaspoon chopped fresh thyme
About ½ teaspoon kosher salt
About ½ teaspoon freshly ground black pepper

Heat the cumin and red pepper flakes in a large skillet over medium heat, tossing occasionally, until the seeds become fragrant, about 2 minutes. Remove from the heat and let cool for a minute or two. Stir in the remaining ingredients along with a generous sprinkling of salt and pepper.

PAIRINGS: Brush this earthy glaze on grilled, bone-in pork chops (page 75) and serve with Spiced Grilled Vegetable Couscous (page 237).

SHELF LIFE: Up to one week in the refrigerator.

Brown Mustard and Dried Cherry Glaze

My love for brown mustard started as a little guy during visits to Fenway Park. I loved the Red Sox, but the real game was seeing how many hot dogs I could squeeze out of my dad. The Fenway Franks always came accompanied by large packets of Gulden's and even though I was young, I appreciated its sharp, slightly spicy flavor. Use your preferred brand of brown mustard for this glaze. I'm still partial to Gulden's.

YIELD: 1 CUP, 6 SERVINGS
PREP TIME: 5 minutes
COOK TIME: N/A

½ cup maple syrup
⅓ cup spicy brown mustard
2 tablespoons finely chopped dried cherries
1 tablespoon cider vinegar
1 teaspoon chopped fresh thyme
About ½ teaspoon freshly ground black pepper
Kosher salt

In a medium bowl, mix to combine all of the ingredients with a generous sprinkling of pepper. Season with salt and more pepper to taste.

PAIRINGS: Slather this mustard on grilled salmon filets (page 78) or even a broiled ham steak (page 64). Pair with a warm spinach salad.

SHELF LIFE: Up to two weeks in the refrigerator, perfect for keeping on hand in the summer.

Chipotle Honey Glaze

This glaze, quick and full of smoky flavor, is a staple in my kitchen. It's ridiculously simple, holds for a while in the fridge, and goes great with everything from grilled chicken to broiled shrimp skewers.

YIELD: 1 CUP, 4 SERVINGS
PREP TIME: 3 minutes
COOK TIME: N/A

1 canned chipotle, minced, plus 2 tablespoons adobo sauce
½ cup honey
2 tablespoons cider vinegar
1 tablespoon tomato paste
2 teaspoons Dijon mustard
Kosher salt and freshly ground black pepper

In a medium bowl, mix to combine all of the ingredients; season with salt and pepper to taste.

PAIRINGS: Brush on grilled chicken parts (page 73), pork chops (page 75), or even pork ribs if you're doing some low and slow grilling. Serve with corn bread (make it out of a box, nobody will know the difference) and sautéed collard greens (page 53).

SHELF LIFE: Up to two weeks in the refrigerator; make a double batch to have on hand.

Spiced Fuji Apple Glaze

For my money, Fujis are as good as apples get: sweet and crisp with a firm texture. Here, the diced apple is paired with a mix of apple butter (kind of like a creamy, concentrated applesauce), honey, and spices.

YIELD: 1¼ CUPS, 6 SERVINGS
PREP TIME: 5 minutes
COOK TIME: 5 minutes

1 tablespoon unsalted butter
¼ teaspoon chile powder
¼ teaspoon ground cinnamon
½ cup peeled and finely diced Fuji or other firm-fleshed apple (½ apple)
½ cup apple butter or apple jelly
¼ cup honey
1 tablespoon freshly squeezed lemon juice
Kosher salt and freshly ground black pepper

Melt the butter in a medium saucepan over medium-high heat, about 1½ minutes. Add the chile powder and cinnamon and cook, stirring, until they sizzle and become fragrant, about 30 seconds.

Add the apples and cook, stirring, until they start to brown and soften, about 2 minutes. Add the remaining ingredients and bring to a steady simmer. Remove from the heat and let cool for a couple of minutes. Season with salt and pepper to taste.

PAIRINGS: Brush this glaze on broiled or grilled pork chops (page 175) or broiled butterflied turkey breasts (page 63) and serve with Wild Rice with Dried Cherries and Toasted Walnuts (page 236) and sautéed cauliflower (page 52).

SHELF LIFE: Up to three days in the refrigerator.

Bulgogi Sauce (Korean BBQ)

The steak (or chicken or pork) in Korean barbecue sizzles with a wonderful combination of heat, garlic and soy. A soy ginger marinade (like the one on page 17) is traditionally the key, but if you don't have time, this after-grilling sauce is the next best thing.

YIELD: 1¼ CUPS, 4 SERVINGS
PREP TIME: 4 minutes
COOK TIME: 6 minutes

1 garlic clove, minced (about 1 teaspoon)
1 tablespoon canola oil
2 tablespoons soy sauce
1 tablespoon sesame oil
1 tablespoon white vinegar
1 tablespoon light brown sugar
2 teaspoons Thai chile paste (like Sriracha)
2 teaspoons cornstarch
2 scallions (both white and green parts), trimmed and
  thinly sliced

Heat the garlic with the canola oil in a medium saucepan over medium heat until it sizzles steadily and just starts to turn light brown at the edges, about 2 minutes. Stir in the soy sauce, sesame oil, vinegar, brown sugar, chile paste, and ½ cup water and bring to a boil.

Whisk the cornstarch with 1 tablespoon water and then stir into the soy mixture along with the scallions. Let the mixture return to a boil so it thickens, then remove from the heat.

PAIRINGS: Match this intense sauce with a full-flavored steak like flank, skirt, or even a chuck eye (page 24). Thinly slice and serve with steamed jasmine rice and jarred kimchi.

SHELF LIFE: Up to three days in the refrigerator.

Maple Cranberry Glaze

This sauce has a tart complexity, which, in the finished dish, reads less of its primary ingredients than as a pleasant sweet and sour crust.

YIELD: 1¼ CUPS, ABOUT 4 SERVINGS
PREP TIME: 3 minutes
COOK TIME: N/A

½ cup maple syrup
½ cup cranberry sauce
1 tablespoon cider vinegar
2 teaspoons Dijon mustard
2 teaspoons chopped fresh thyme
About ½ teaspoon kosher salt
About ½ teaspoon freshly ground black pepper

In a medium bowl, mix to combine all of the ingredients with salt and pepper to taste.

PAIRINGS: Brush on grilled pork tenderloin (page 75) or sautéed turkey cutlets (page 36). Pair with Rosemary-Parmesan Mashed Yukon Potatoes (page 235) and some sautéed greens (page 53) and you've got a holiday meal.

SHELF LIFE: Up to one week in the refrigerator.

Root Beer Glaze

Sure, this sauce might sound like something that goes better on a sundae than a pork chop, but the spice of root beer melds nicely with the other strong flavors in here (ketchup, mustard, and Worcestershire), turning this into a fun, slightly exotic BBQ sauce.

YIELD: SCANT 1 CUP; 4 SERVINGS
PREP TIME: 3 minutes
COOK TIME: 6 minutes

1 tablespoon olive oil
1 small garlic clove, minced (about ½ teaspoon)
1¼ cups root beer
¼ cup orange juice (preferably freshly squeezed)
2 teaspoons ketchup
2 teaspoons Dijon mustard
1 teaspoon Worcestershire sauce
2 teaspoons cornstarch

Heat the oil and garlic in a medium saucepan over medium-high heat until the garlic starts to sizzle steadily, about 1 minute. Whisk in the root beer, orange juice, ketchup, mustard, and Worcestershire sauce and bring to a boil. Cook at a rapid simmer for 5 minutes so the liquid reduces by a little more than half. Whisk the cornstarch with 1 tablespoon water and then stir into the root beer mixture. Let the mixture return to a boil so it thickens, then remove from the heat.

PAIRINGS: It would be truly Southern to brush this glaze on a grilled or broiled ham steak (page 75 and 64) and serve with sautéed collard greens (page 53) and warm corn bread. Grilled boneless pork chops would be a little more upscale (page 75).

SHELF LIFE: Up to four days in the refrigerator.

Chinese BBQ Sauce

Known as *char siu*, this sauce gives spareribs and duck (the ones you see hanging in storefronts in Chinatown) a wonderful lacquered crust and sticky sweet flavor. There's no red food coloring in this version, but everything else is traditional.

YIELD: ¾ CUP, 4 SERVINGS
PREP TIME: 4 minutes
COOK TIME: N/A

¼ cup honey
2 tablespoons shaoxing rice wine or dry sherry
2 tablespoons soy sauce
1 tablespoon hoisin sauce
1 garlic clove, minced (about ¾ teaspoon)
½ teaspoon 5-spice powder

Combine all of the ingredients in a bowl and mix well.

PAIRINGS: Spareribs take far too long to cook for inclusion in this book, but this sauce would be just the thing. In its place, try grilled pork chops (page 75) or broiled chicken wings (page 63). Serve with Cold Peanut Noodles with Mint and Thai Chiles (page 233) and stir-fried bok choy.

SHELF LIFE: Up to two weeks in the refrigerator.

Quick Homemade BBQ Sauce

There's nothing wrong with the barbecue sauces lining supermarket shelves, save for all those multi-syllable preservatives. But you can make a decent sauce in about 15 minutes and its freshness and spice beats most anything you can get out of a jar. The chipotle powder (or pimentón) in this version offers up a little smokiness (along with liquid smoke, if you like—see below) to go with the familiar flavors of ketchup and honey.

YIELD: 1¼ CUPS; 4 SERVINGS

PREP TIME: 4 minutes

COOK TIME: 11 minutes

2 tablespoons olive oil

1 small yellow onion, finely diced (about ¾ cup)

About ¾ teaspoon kosher salt

About ½ teaspoon freshly ground black pepper

¼ to ½ teaspoon chipotle powder or pimentón de la Vera

½ cup ketchup

¼ cup honey

1 tablespoon soy sauce

1 tablespoon cider vinegar

2 teaspoons Worcestershire sauce

1 teaspoon liquid smoke (optional)

Heat the oil and onion in a medium saucepan over medium-high heat until the onion starts to sizzle steadily, about 1 minute. Reduce the heat to medium, sprinkle generously with salt and pepper, and cook, stirring, until the onion softens and becomes translucent, about 4 more minutes. Sprinkle in the chipotle powder or pimentón and cook, stirring, until it starts to become fragrant, about 30 seconds. Stir in the remaining ingredients, including the liquid smoke if you like, and simmer for 5 minutes so the flavors mix and meld and the onion becomes tender.

Using an immersion blender (or by transferring the sauce to a blender), purée the sauce until smooth.

PAIRINGS: You really shouldn't need my help figuring out what to do with a good BBQ sauce. I'm partial to this sauce on grilled chicken parts (page 73). Serve with slaw and buttered Uncle Ben's rice.

SHELF LIFE: Up to five days in the refrigerator.

What Is Liquid Smoke?

I know. It sounds like something you drank at that bar last night with that girl you only vaguely remember (and whose digits are magically still Sharpied on your wrist). But, no worries, it's not. The good kinds of liquid smoke (that is, those made by natural methods) are produced by heating wood (like mesquite or hickory) in a contained oven until they start to smoke. This resulting smoke is then chilled so it creates vapor, which, after being purified, becomes liquid smoke. It's not necessary for any of the barbecue sauces here, but it does add that familiar smoky flavor you may be seeking.

Coffee BBQ Sauce

With the growing popularity of barbecue contests, there always seem to be new sauces and techniques merging into the grilling mainstream. This is my contribution. Coffee is often used for marinades and rubs, though I like it in sauces, too, my homage to red-eye gravy. This sauce, though quick, gets a double hit of smoke from diced chipotle pepper as well as the roasted coffee essence.

YIELD: 1½ CUPS, 6 SERVINGS
PREP TIME: 3 minutes
COOK TIME: 10 minutes

1 large garlic clove, minced (about 1 teaspoon)
1 tablespoon olive oil
1 teaspoon chile powder
¾ cup tomato purée
½ cup brewed coffee
¼ cup light brown sugar
3 tablespoons ketchup
1 tablespoon Dijon mustard
1 canned chipotle, minced (about 1 tablespoon)
About ¼ teaspoon kosher salt
About ¼ teaspoon freshly ground black pepper

Heat the garlic with the oil in a medium saucepan over medium heat until it sizzles steadily, about 1 minute. Add the chile powder and cook, stirring, for 30 seconds. Stir in the remaining ingredients with a light sprinkling of salt and pepper and cook at a steady simmer, stirring occasionally, so the mixture thickens slightly and the flavors meld, about 8 minutes.

PAIRINGS: A tough, full-flavored steak, like a chuck eye (page 75) is the perfect pairing for this sauce. Brush the steak while it grills, thinly slice after cooking, and serve with grilled corn (page 82) and stewed black-eyed peas.

SHELF LIFE: Up to five days in the refrigerator.

Crushed Peach BBQ Sauce

This rustic sauce has the thick texture of applesauce, but the sweet, spiced punch of good barbecue. To refine things a bit, you can peel the peaches, though you won't notice them much after puréeing the sauce anyway.

YIELD: 2 CUPS, ABOUT 8 SERVINGS
PREP TIME: 5 minutes
COOK TIME: 10 minutes

2 tablespoons canola oil
1 small Vidalia or sweet onion (about ½ pound), thinly sliced
About ¾ teaspoon kosher salt
½ teaspoon chile powder
¼ teaspoon chipotle powder
2 ripe peaches (about ¾ pound), pitted and cut into ½-inch slices or 2 cups canned peaches, drained and sliced
2 tablespoons honey
1 tablespoon cider vinegar
1 teaspoon Worcestershire sauce

Heat the oil and onion in a medium saucepan over high heat until the onion starts to sizzle steadily, about 1 minute. Reduce the heat to medium, sprinkle generously with salt and cook, stirring occasionally, until the onion softens and becomes translucent, about 4 more minutes. Stir in the chile powder and chipotle powder and cook, stirring, for 30 seconds so they become fragrant.

Stir in the remaining ingredients and cook at steady simmer so the peaches completely soften and the flavors meld, about 5 minutes. Using an immersion blender (or by transferring to a blender), purée until smooth.

PAIRINGS: Pair this sauce with barbecued pork (grilled bone-in chops or tenderloin—page 75) and serve with potato salad and sautéed green beans (page 50).

SHELF LIFE: Up to three days in the refrigerator.

II. PAN SAUCES

Even though pan sauces don't require much more than a quick whisk and a little scraping, they have a boiled-down intensity that's reminiscent of a fancy French jus. They mimic true reductions by incorporating the caramelized brown crust that forms on the surface of a pan after searing meat, what the French refer to as a fond. These concentrated meat proteins become like a homemade bouillon cube (without the MSG), giving these quick sauces an umami-like depth.

The method for making these sauces is rather simple. After searing meat, chicken, or fish, set it aside on a plate, tent with foil (so it stays warm), add some broth and some sort of acidic liquid (generally booze, wine, or vinegar), and whisk together while scraping the bottom of the pan with a wooden spoon (see page 98) to incorporate the caramelized crust that developed during searing. The acid is important as it adds a little bounce to the mixture. Cook until the sauce reduces to a thick texture and then drizzle over the seared steak, chicken breast, or chop. You've got fancy food that feels nothing like your normal weeknight fare.

BASIC TECHNIQUE

1. Wipe the pan dry with a wad of paper towels, unless sautéing aromatics. Sopping up any grease left over from the sear ensures that these sauces don't acquire a greasy slick. For those pan sauces where an aromatic like garlic, shallots, or onions is sautéed, I prefer to leave in the searing grease as it will offer good flavor and the oil will mostly get soaked up by the aromatic.

2. Return the pan to high heat. Most of these sauces rely on reduction, the culinary equivalent of evaporation, to intensify their flavor and thicken to a saucy consistency. High heat helps expedite both.

3. Deglaze boozy/acidic liquids first. Add these to the pan and cook, scraping the bottom of the pan to incorporate the browned crust (or bits), until it almost completely reduces, cooking off most of the alcohol and the sharpness of the acidity.

4. Reduce brothy liquids (like chicken or beef broth) so the sauce acquires a thick texture.

5. Finish with a touch of richness (see information on page 98), be it butter, cream, or even coconut milk.

AVOID FISHY OR BURNT PAN SAUCES

Because the caramelized crust that is left behind in a pan after searing forms the base for a pan sauce, strong-flavored fishy fish like salmon or tuna or gamey cuts of meat like lamb chops generally don't make for good pan sauces. The sauce will take on an overly funky flavor. The same goes for a sauté that's burned. Even if the seared ingredient is recoverable, there's a good chance you might want to skip the pan sauce. That's because what makes pan sauces so great—that caramelized crust—can make them inedible if burned—think campfire marshmallow. If you do burn the sauté, call an audible and make up some sort of quick dipping sauce or vinaigrette instead.

AS RICH AS YOU LIKE IT

If calories are not a concern (and God bless you if that's the case), it's nice to whisk something rich (like butter or heavy cream) into a pan sauce toward the end of cooking to smooth out all of the disparate flavors and give the sauce a glossy texture. I leave this step optional so you can decide based on who you're serving and whether you've been to the gym on that particular day.

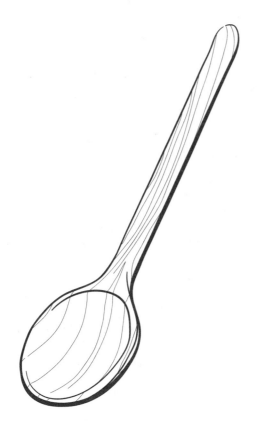

TIP: A Wooden Spoon's Worth

Wooden spoons are still around for a reason, as anachronistic as they may seem. Their soft, rounded edges are perfect for pan sauces, gently incorporating the caramelized crust without scraping up the pan. Silicone whisks or spatulas can also do the job, but I'm partial to my wooden spoon.

WHAT "SIMMERING" REALLY MEANS

"Simmer" is a vague term, describing the zone in which a liquid bubbles along just below a boil (about 200°F)—a "smile" as some chefs like to describe it, which doesn't reduce a sauce too much, but is still hot enough to allow the flavors and textures to marry. For most sauces, I will direct you to bring the sauce to a boil and then cook it at a steady simmer. To do this, lower the heat to medium or medium-low so it lightly bubbles. After a couple of times, you'll get the feel for simmering.

USE THE FAT IF SAUTÉING AROMATICS

Flavor, not appearance, is my primary goal when I make a pan sauce. For this reason, I generally don't wipe out the grease before sautéing any aromatics (shallots, garlic, ginger, or onions) because this remaining fat has good flavor. I like to sprinkle these aromatics with a light sprinkling of salt so they start to leach off some liquid. This liquid, in turn, helps incorporate the caramelized crust on the bottom of the pan. If for some reason the grease and caramelized crust on the bottom of the pan is burnt, ditch it and go in a different sauce direction.

TIP: Careful with Booze and a Hot Pan

This cryptic advice sounds like something you'd say to friends before they go to a party, but it's pertinent information for pan sauces. When you add any liquid, particularly alcohol, which is extremely flammable, to a pan over high heat on a gas range, there is the possibility of a flare-up. In a restaurant kitchen, pan flare-ups are ambiance, part of the environment. But in the home kitchen, where there's no Ansul system or nearby fire extinguishers, they can be a little scary. To avoid flare-ups, simply pull the pan off the heat when adding liquids.

TIP: More "Caramelized Crust" Than Browned Bits

Many recipes refer to the fond, the wonderful browned stuff left in the pan after searing, as "browned bits." And while, indeed, there are sometimes little bits of meat, fish, or vegetables, the larger part of what's left behind after sautéing is a browned crust from where the seared ingredients came in contact with the pan. So for the sake of accuracy, I refer to this as the "caramelized crust" and all those other recipes be damned.

Red Wine Pan Sauce

Though the butter is optional here depending on your diet and mood, it gives this sauce a rich, glossy finish.

YIELD: ⅓ CUP, 4 SERVINGS
PREP TIME: 4 minutes
COOK TIME: 6 minutes

1 large shallot, finely diced (about ¼ cup)
About ¼ teaspoon kosher salt
⅔ cup dry red wine
½ cup low-sodium chicken broth
2 teaspoons chopped fresh thyme
2 tablespoons unsalted butter, cut into pieces (optional)
About ½ teaspoon freshly ground black pepper

TIP: Why So Many Shallots?

Because they strike the right aromatic balance in these pan sauces, somewhere between the intensity of garlic and the sweetness of onions. Also, shallots cook quickly with less fear of burning or turning acrid.

Set the shallot in the empty pan over medium heat with any remaining fat from the sear, sprinkle gently with salt, and cook, stirring, until the shallot softens and starts to brown at the edges, about 2 minutes. Add the red wine, raise the heat to high, and cook, scraping the bottom of the pan with a wooden spoon to incorporate the caramelized crust, until it reduces to a glazy consistency of about 1 or 2 tablespoons, about 2 minutes. Add the chicken broth and thyme and cook, stirring, until it reduces by about half, about 2 minutes.

Remove from the heat, swirl in the butter, if using, until melted, sprinkle with black pepper, and season with more salt and pepper to taste.

OPTIONS: Sauté some oyster or shiitake mushrooms after the shallot starts to soften and before adding the red wine.

PAIRINGS: This sauce, rich and sharp, is just the thing for a good sautéed steak (page 38); try a strip or a filet mignon if you're feeling really flush. Serve with Horseradish Mashed Potatoes (page 35) and sautéed asparagus or broccolini (page 50).

Chunky Tomato and Red Wine Pan Sauce

This is one of those sauces that can be a lot of things depending on your mood. Purée it and the sauce becomes smooth and dressy. Add some crisp bacon or sautéed mushrooms and you get a hearty, Burgundy-like sauce. Serve it as is and it's a full-flavored rustic sauce.

YIELD: ¾ CUP, 4 SERVINGS
PREP TIME: 5 minutes
COOK TIME: 6 minutes

1 garlic clove, smashed
½ cup dry red wine
1 teaspoon chopped fresh rosemary or thyme or 1 tablespoon fresh oregano
1¼ cups canned tomatoes and their juices, smashed with a fork into small pieces
Kosher salt and freshly ground black pepper

Set the garlic in the empty pan over medium heat (with any remaining fat from the sear) and cook, stirring, until it starts to sizzle and become fragrant, about 1 minute.

Add the red wine and the fresh herbs, raise the heat to high, and cook, scraping the bottom of the pan with a wooden spoon to incorporate any of the caramelized crust, until it reduces to a glazy consistency of about 1 or 2 tablespoons, about 2 minutes. Add the tomatoes and cook, stirring, until their juices mostly reduce, about 2 minutes.

Season generously with salt and pepper to taste.

OPTIONS: Sauté some sliced white mushrooms right after the garlic starts to soften and before adding the red wine. Or fold in some crisp bacon or freshly grated Parmigiano.

PAIRINGS : The tomatoes in this sauce go nicely with seared lamb shoulder chops (page 38) or sautéed chicken breasts (page 31). Serve with Couscous with Zucchini, Sun-Dried Tomatoes, and Black Olives (page 237).

Maple Cranberry Pan Sauce

Maple syrup balances out the tartness of the cranberries and the fragrance of the ginger in this elegant, autumnal sauce.

YIELD: 1 CUP, 4 SERVINGS
PREP TIME: 6 minutes
COOK TIME: 6 minutes

1 tablespoon minced fresh ginger
1 cup low-sodium chicken broth
¼ cup maple syrup
¼ cup canned cranberry sauce
1 tablespoon cider vinegar
2 teaspoons chopped fresh thyme
2 tablespoons heavy cream (optional)
Kosher salt and freshly ground black pepper

Set the ginger in the empty pan (with any fat remaining from the sear) over medium-high heat until it sizzles and becomes fragrant, about 1 minute. Pour in the chicken broth, maple syrup, cranberry sauce, vinegar, and thyme and cook, scraping the bottom of the pan with a wooden spoon to incorporate any caramelized crust, until the liquid reduces by about half, about 4 minutes. Stir in the cream, if using, and bring to a boil. Season with salt and pepper to taste.

PAIRINGS: This sauce is another winner with sautéed pork chops or tenderloin medallions (page 38). Accompany with a baguette and some dressed baby arugula.

Brandy and Dried Cherry Pan Sauce

I don't drink brandy, but like everybody else, I have a couple of dusty bottles kicking around in the liquor cabinet. It usually goes into pan sauces like these for steaks or chops. Dried cherries give this sauce a tart twist and heavy cream (if you decide to use it) imparts richness. If you're working over a gas range, pull the pan from the heat before adding the brandy to avoid jumping stove-top flames (and singed eyebrows).

YIELD: ½ CUP, 4 SERVINGS
PREP TIME: 5 minutes
COOK TIME: 8 minutes

⅓ cup brandy
¼ cup dried cherries, coarsely chopped
1 tablespoon unsalted butter
1 large shallot, finely diced (about ¼ cup)
About ¼ teaspoon kosher salt
½ cup low-sodium chicken broth
2 teaspoons chopped fresh thyme
2 tablespoons heavy cream (optional)
About ½ teaspoon freshly ground black pepper

Set the brandy and cherries in a small bowl so the cherries start to plump up. Heat the butter and shallot in the empty pan (with any fat remaining from the sear) over medium heat, sprinkle lightly with salt, and cook, stirring, until the shallot softens and starts to brown at the edges, about 2 minutes.

Add the brandy and cherries, raise the heat to high, and cook, scraping the bottom of the pan with a wooden spoon, until it almost completely reduces, about 2 minutes. Add the chicken broth and thyme and cook, stirring, until it reduces by about half, about 2 minutes. Add the cream, if using, and pepper and cook until the sauce returns to a boil, 1 minute. Season with more salt and pepper to taste.

PAIRINGS: The fruit in this sauce directs it toward pork or beef. Drizzle it over center-cut pork chops or a dressy cut of beef like filet mignon (page 38). Pair with Herbed Goat Cheese Polenta (page 237) and some sautéed greens (page 53).

Apple Cider and Crisp Sage Pan Sauce

This sauce shouts fall and all the things you want to make once the leaves start to turn—pork, root vegetables, and hearty greens. Here, sage serves as both a flavor base and a crisp garnish.

YIELD: ½ CUP, 4 SERVINGS
PREP TIME: 2 minutes
COOK TIME: 7 minutes

1 tablespoon unsalted butter
12 medium sage leaves
¾ cup apple cider or apple juice
½ cup low-sodium chicken broth
1 tablespoon cider vinegar
Kosher salt and freshly ground pepper

Heat the butter and sage in the pan (with any drippings remaining from the sear) over medium-high heat, stirring, until the sage starts to brown and become fragrant, 2 minutes. Transfer the sage leaves to small plate lined with paper towels.

Add the cider, chicken broth, and cider vinegar and cook, stirring and scraping the bottom of the pan with a wooden spoon, until it reduces to about ⅓ cup, about 3 minutes. Season with salt and pepper to taste and serve, drizzled over the seared ingredient and topped with the crisp sage leaves.

PAIRINGS: This is as true a pairing for seared pork chops (page 38) as it gets. Serve with sautéed cauliflower (page 52) and Cheddar Cheese Grits (page 237).

Crisp Caper and Lemon Sauce

This is a dressy take on a standard piccata sauce. Searing the capers at the start of cooking gives them a crisp texture—like a briny version of bacon—and lemon zest adds another layer of citrus.

YIELD: ½ CUP, 4 SERVINGS
PREP TIME: 5 minutes
COOK TIME: 7 minutes

2 tablespoons unsalted butter
3 tablespoons nonpareil capers, rinsed and patted dry
1 lemon, the zest shaved into 6 (1-inch wide) strips (with a peeler) and the lemon juiced
1 tablespoon all-purpose flour
¾ cup low-sodium chicken broth
2 tablespoons chopped fresh parsley (optional)
Kosher salt and freshly ground pepper

Heat 1 tablespoon of the butter with the capers in the pan (with any fat remaining from the sear) over medium heat, stirring, until the capers brown and become fragrant, 2 to 3 minutes. Add the lemon zest and cook for 30 seconds so it becomes fragrant. Transfer both the capers and zest to a small plate lined with paper towels.

Add the remaining 1 tablespoon butter and the flour and cook, stirring, so the mixture acquires a light brown hue and smells slightly toasted, about 1 minute. Whisk in the chicken broth and 2 tablespoons of the lemon juice and cook, stirring and scraping the bottom of the pan with a wooden spoon, until the liquid reduces by about half and thickens, about 3 minutes.

Stir in the parsley, if using, season with salt, pepper, and more lemon juice to taste. Serve, drizzled over the seared ingredient and topped with the capers and lemon zest (the latter is more for garnish than for eating).

OPTIONS: Infuse this sauce with some toasted garlic: add a few smashed cloves at the same time as the capers and then discard them just before serving.

PAIRINGS: This sauce is perfect for seared chicken, pork, or veal cutlets (page 36). Serve with Penne with Broccoli and Sun-Dried Tomatoes (page 233).

Season Pan Sauces at the End

Good cooks advise seasoning a dish throughout its different stages of preparation. I generally agree with this counsel with the exception of pan sauces. For starters, the steak or chop which will go with the sauce will already be seasoned and some of this seasoning will leach out into the browned bits on the bottom of the pan. Couple that with the reduction of these sauces (which causes a sauce to become twice as salty or peppery at its end as at its start) and you're best off seasoning these sauces only once they're done cooking.

Whole-Grain Mustard and Thyme Pan Sauce

Whole-grain mustard makes this sauce a little special. Like all mustards, it's made from mustard seeds, spices, and wine or vinegar, but the grains are mostly left intact (instead of puréed), so it has a milder flavor and more interesting texture.

YIELD: ½ CUP, 4 SERVINGS
PREP TIME: 3 minutes
COOK TIME: 5 minutes

1 cup low-sodium chicken broth
2 tablespoons whole-grain mustard
1 tablespoon cider vinegar
1 teaspoon chopped fresh thyme
2 tablespoons heavy cream (optional)
Kosher salt and freshly ground black pepper

Gently blot any fat from the pan using a wad of paper towels. Set the pan over medium-high heat, add the chicken broth, mustard, vinegar, and thyme and cook, stirring to scrape up any caramelized crust, until the liquid reduces by about half, about 4 minutes. Stir in the cream, if using, and return to a boil, about 1 minute. Season with salt and pepper to taste.

OPTION: If you don't have whole-grain mustard, use regular Dijon mustard but halve the amount.

PAIRINGS: This is one of my favorite sauces to pair with pork chops (page 75). The mustard and cider vinegar sharpen out the pork's sweet profile. Serve with Garlicky Smashed Red Potatoes (page 235) and sautéed Brussels sprouts (page 52).

White Wine and Tarragon Pan Sauce

Tarragon, sweet with a measured punch of anise flavor, is one of those fresh herbs popular in French cuisine that you may not have kicking around in the fridge. Do seek it out, or grow it if you have an herb garden. The addition of the butter at the end of cooking is important as it smoothes out the sharpness of the herb and wine.

YIELD: ½ CUP, 4 SERVINGS
PREP TIME: 4 minutes
COOK TIME: 7 minutes

1 medium shallot, finely diced (about 3 tablespoons)
2 tablespoons unsalted butter
About ¼ teaspoon kosher salt
½ cup dry white wine
¾ cup low-sodium chicken broth
2 tablespoons chopped fresh tarragon
Freshly ground black pepper

Set the shallot with 1 tablespoon of the butter in the pan (with any drippings remaining from the sear) over medium heat, sprinkle with salt, and cook, stirring, until it starts to soften and become translucent, about 2 minutes.

Add the wine, raise the heat to high, and cook, scraping the bottom of the pan to incorporate any of the caramelized crust, until the wine almost completely reduces, about 2 minutes. Add the chicken broth and cook until it reduces by a little more than half, about 3 minutes. Swirl in the remaining 1 tablespoon butter and the tarragon and season with salt and pepper to taste.

PAIRINGS: Pair this dressy sauce with a seared strip steak (page 38) or sautéed shrimp (page 46); serve with an herb risotto and sautéed asparagus (page 50).

BROTH AND CREAM PAN SAUCES

The formula for the sauces in this section is simpler than the rest. Add the liquid (either canned chicken broth or heavy cream), scrape with a wooden spoon to pick up any of the caramelized crust, and then infuse with some fresh herbs or pantry ingredients.

Tomato-Rosemary Pan Sauce

I'd strongly encourage you to go with the butter in this recipe. It swerves this sauce in a dressy direction beyond your basic marinara.

YIELD: ¾ CUP, 4 SERVINGS
PREP TIME: 4 minutes
COOK TIME: 5 minutes

1 cup canned diced tomatoes (and their juices), puréed
½ cup low-sodium chicken broth
1 tablespoon balsamic vinegar
2 teaspoons chopped fresh rosemary
2 tablespoons unsalted butter (optional)
Kosher salt and freshly ground pepper

Blot any fat from the pan using a wad of paper towels. Set the pan over medium-high heat, add the puréed tomato, chicken broth, vinegar, and rosemary and cook, stirring to scrape up any of the caramelized crust, until the liquid reduces by a little more than half, about 4 minutes. Whisk in the butter, if using, and season with salt and pepper to taste.

OPTIONS: Sprinkle in chopped capers or black olives at the end of cooking for a hit of brininess. Add a teaspoon or so of sugar if you want to smooth out the sauce's acidity.

PAIRINGS: This sauce goes well with mild fish filets like cod or halibut (page 26). Serve with Israeli Couscous with Lemon Cream and Fresh Oregano (page 234) and sautéed broccoli rabe.

Spanish Tomato Saffron Broth

Tomatoes and saffron are a wonderful pairing—the nutty depth of the saffron fills out the fruits' sweetness, giving this sauce an earthy edge reminiscent of paella.

YIELD: 1 CUP, 4 SERVINGS
PREP TIME: 3 minutes
COOK TIME: 4 minutes

1 cup canned diced tomatoes (and their juices), puréed
½ cup low-sodium chicken broth
1 tablespoon sherry vinegar
2 teaspoons chopped fresh thyme
¼ to ½ teaspoon saffron threads
Kosher salt and freshly ground black pepper

Blot any fat from the pan using a wad of paper towels. Set the pan over high heat, add all the ingredients and cook, stirring to scrape up the caramelized crust on the pan's bottom, until the liquid reduces by about half, about 4 minutes. Season with salt and pepper to taste.

OPTIONS: Add a little more substance (and keep with the Spanish theme), by stirring some garbanzos or chorizo into the broth. If you're pairing this sauce with shellfish or fish, substitute clam juice for the chicken broth.

PAIRINGS: Try this intense broth with a mild fish like cod or halibut (page 26) or even scallops (page 26). Pair with sautéed kale (page 53) and Traditional Rice Pilaf (page 234).

Orange and Caramelized Fennel Pan Sauce

In this pan sauce, strips of fennel wilt and form a sweet, aromatic base for fresh orange juice and tarragon.

YIELD: ¾ CUP, 4 SERVINGS
PREP TIME: 5 minutes
COOK TIME: 7 minutes

1 tablespoon unsalted butter
1 medium fennel bulb (about ¾ pound), trimmed, halved, and thinly sliced
About ½ teaspoon kosher salt
About ½ teaspoon freshly ground black pepper
¾ cup low-sodium chicken broth
1 navel orange, juiced (about ⅓ cup), plus 1 teaspoon freshly grated zest
2 tablespoons chopped fresh tarragon (optional)

Set the butter and fennel in the empty pan (with any drippings remaining from the sear) over medium heat, sprinkle with salt and pepper, and cook, stirring, until it starts to soften and brown lightly, about 3 minutes. Add the chicken broth, orange juice, and orange zest and raise the heat to high. Cook, stirring to scrape up the caramelized crust on the bottom of the pan, until the liquid reduces by about half, about 4 minutes. Stir in the tarragon, if using, and season with salt and pepper to taste.

OPTIONS: Pernod, an anise-flavored liqueur, nicely reinforces the flavor of the fennel in this sauce. Add ¼ cup or so before the chicken broth, cook until almost completely reduced, and then continue on with the recipe.

PAIRINGS: Try this fragrant sauce with seared shrimp or scallops (page 46) and transform into a warm salad with lightly dressed butter lettuce. Serve with a warm baguette.

Caramelized Onion, Fennel, and Cider Broth

This chunky, fall sauce is perfect for a hearty cut of pork, like bone-in chops. The strips of fennel and onion wilt and create an intense broth with the apple cider and fresh thyme.

YIELD: 1½ CUPS, ABOUT 4 SERVINGS
PREP TIME: 6 minutes
COOK TIME: 7 minutes

2 tablespoons unsalted butter
1 small red onion (about 6 ounces), halved and thinly sliced (about 1¼ cups)
1 small fennel bulb (about ½ pound), halved and thinly sliced
About ½ teaspoon kosher salt
About ½ teaspoon freshly ground black pepper
1 cup apple cider or apple juice
2 teaspoons chopped fresh thyme (optional)

Melt the butter in the empty pan (with any drippings remaining from the sear) over medium-high heat, about 30 seconds. Add the onion and fennel, sprinkle with salt and pepper, and cook, stirring, until the vegetables mostly soften and brown in places, about 3 minutes. Add the cider and thyme, if using, raise the heat to high, and cook, stirring to scrape up any caramelized crust on the bottom of the pan, until the liquid reduces by about half, about 3 minutes. Season with salt and pepper to taste.

OPTIONS: Refine this sauce a bit by puréeing it with a splash of heavy cream. You can add a pinch of cinnamon for a little spice.

PAIRINGS: Try this fragrant sauce with seared pork chops (page 38) or sautéed turkey cutlets (page 36). Serve with Cheddar Cheese Grits (page 105) and roasted butternut squash.

Pomegranate and Apple Pan Sauce

Pomegranate juice is available in the juice aisle at most supermarkets. Though it's somewhat pricey, it has seemingly every antioxidant around and a tart, raisinlike flavor that makes for a fine pan sauce.

YIELD: ¾ CUP, 4 SERVINGS
PREP TIME: 7 minutes
COOK TIME: 7 minutes

2 tablespoons unsalted butter
½ crisp apple (like Fuji or Gala), peeled and cut in ¼-inch dice (about 1 cup)
1 medium shallot, finely diced (about 3 tablespoons)
About ¼ teaspoon kosher salt
About ¼ teaspoon freshly ground black pepper
¾ cup pomegranate juice
2 teaspoons cider vinegar
1 teaspoon granulated sugar
1 teaspoon chopped fresh thyme (optional)

Melt 1 tablespoon of the butter in the empty pan (with any drippings remaining from the sear) over medium-high heat. Add the apple and shallot, sprinkle with salt and pepper, and cook, stirring, until they start to soften and brown in places, 3 minutes.

Add the juice, vinegar, sugar, and thyme, if using, and cook, stirring to scrape up any caramelized crust on the bottom of the pan, until the liquid reduces by about half, about 3 minutes. Season with salt and pepper to taste and purée if you like.

OPTIONS: If you happen to have a pomegranate kicking around the kitchen, stir ¼ cup of the seeds into this sauce.

PAIRINGS: The tangy fruitiness of this sauce goes best with sautéed pork chops (page 38) or chicken breast (page 31). Serve with a nutty grain like quinoa and a green salad.

Piquillo Pepper, Toasted Garlic, and Thyme Broth

Piquillo peppers, grown in the north of Spain (near Rioja wine country), have an edge of heat and smoke that make them more dynamic than your basic roasted red pepper. Jarred piquillos are increasingly available at supermarkets, though you can use regular roasted peppers for this sauce.

YIELD: ABOUT ¾ CUP, 4 SERVINGS
PREP TIME: 4 minutes
COOK TIME: 5 minutes

1 tablespoon olive oil
2 medium garlic cloves, chopped (about 1¼ teaspoons)
1 cup low-sodium chicken broth
3 jarred piquillo peppers or 1 jarred roasted red pepper, drained and thinly sliced (about ½ cup)
1 tablespoon sherry vinegar
2 teaspoons chopped fresh thyme
Kosher salt and freshly ground black pepper

Set the oil and garlic in the empty pan (with any drippings remaining from the sear) over medium heat and cook, stirring, until the garlic starts to sizzle and become fragrant, about 1 minute. Add the remaining ingredients, raise the heat to high, and cook, stirring to scrape up any caramelized crust on the bottom of the pan, until the liquid reduces by about half, about 4 minutes. Season with salt and pepper to taste.

PAIRINGS: If you want to really go full-bore Iberian, pair this sauce with sautéed hake (page 44), a mild white fish popular in Spain and similar to cod. Serve with pan-roasted potatoes and sautéed spinach (page 53).

Aged Balsamic and Fig Pan Sauce

The vinegar here doesn't have to be aged, but it gives this sauce a more intense flavor and makes it sound fancy. Be careful chopping the figs. They tend to stick to the side of the chef's knife. Avoid the temptation to push them off while you're chopping or you could end up in the ER.

YIELD: ½ CUP, 4 SERVINGS
PREP TIME: 3 minutes
COOK TIME: 4 minutes

¾ cup low-sodium chicken broth
¼ cup chopped dried figs (about 6)
3 tablespoons balsamic vinegar
2 teaspoons chopped fresh thyme
2 tablespoons unsalted butter, cut into small pieces (optional)
Kosher salt and freshly ground black pepper

Blot any fat from the pan using a wad of paper towels. Set the pan over high heat, add the chicken broth, figs, vinegar, and thyme and cook at a rapid simmer, scraping the bottom of the pan to incorporate any of the caramelized crust, until the liquid reduces to a little more than ¼ cup (it should have a slightly glazy consistency), about 4 minutes. Remove from the heat and whisk in the butter, if using, swirling the pan so it melts. Season with salt and pepper to taste.

OPTIONS: For a little more depth, sauté some finely diced shallot before adding the liquids. If you have the time and inclination, macerate the figs in ¼ cup red wine for 30 minutes prior to cooking.

PAIRINGS: The balsamic pairs nicely with pork chops or a dressy steak like a strip steak (page 24). Accompany either with Roasted Rosemary Fingerling Potatoes (page 235) and sautéed Brussels sprouts (page 52). My recipe-testing brother Peter suggests that if you have any left-over steak or pork, make a sandwich with asiago cheese, baby arugula, and a squirt of Thai chile paste.

Fresh Grape and Balsamic Pan Sauce

I've tried to avoid repeating sauce ingredients throughout this book, but I make an exception with balsamic vinegar because of its convenience and versatality.

YIELD: ¾ CUP, 4 SERVINGS
PREP TIME: 5 minutes
COOK TIME: 6 minutes

1 tablespoon olive oil
1 medium shallot, finely diced (about 3 tablespoons)
About ¼ teaspoon kosher salt
About ¼ teaspoon freshly ground black pepper
¾ cup low-sodium chicken broth
2 tablespoons balsamic vinegar
1 teaspoon chopped fresh rosemary (optional)
12 seedless grapes (green or red are fine), halved and peeled if you're feeling fussy and fancy
1 tablespoon unsalted butter, cut into small pieces (optional)

Set the oil and shallot in the empty pan (with any drippings remaining from the sear) over medium heat, sprinkle with salt and pepper and cook, stirring, until it starts to sizzle and becomes fragrant, about 1 minute. Add the chicken broth, vinegar, and rosemary, if using, raise the heat to high, and cook, scraping the bottom of the pan to incorporate any of the caramelized crust, until the liquid reduces to a little more than ¼ cup (it should have a slightly glazy consistency), about 3 minutes.

Add the grapes and cook, shaking the pan, so they just heat through, about 1 minute. Whisk in the butter, if using, swirling the pan so it melts, and season with salt and pepper to taste.

PAIRINGS: In addition to the predictable pairing of pork chops (page 25), this sauce gives a simple, full-flavored cut of beef like skirt steak (page 24) a dressy edge. Serve with a salad of frisée and fresh tarragon leaves.

Basil and Sun-Dried Tomato Cream

Blending this sauce gives it a smooth texture and a pretty red hue. Use an immersion blender (one of those sticklike, handheld contraptions—see page 22) so you can buzz the broth and tomatoes in the same cup that you use for measuring them.

YIELD: ½ CUP, 4 SERVINGS
PREP TIME: 3 minutes
COOK TIME: 5 minutes

¾ cup low-sodium chicken broth
3 oil-packed sun-dried tomatoes, drained well and chopped
1 teaspoon balsamic vinegar
2 tablespoons to ¼ cup heavy cream
4 basil leaves, torn into large pieces
Kosher salt and freshly ground black pepper

Purée the chicken broth and sun-dried tomatoes in a blender. Blot any fat from the pan using a wad of paper towels. Set the pan over medium-high heat, add the puréed tomato mixture and balsamic vinegar and cook, stirring to scrape up any of the caramelized crust, until the liquid reduces to about ⅓ cup, about 4 minutes. Stir in the cream (use the higher end of the range for a richer sauce) and bring to a simmer. Stir in the basil and season with salt and pepper to taste.

PAIRINGS: This sauce goes particularly well with chicken. Thinly slice sautéed chicken breasts (page 31), sprinkle with this sauce and some Parmigiano, and serve over Buttered Egg Noodles with Chives (page 233) with seared broccoli rabe (page 50).

Chipotle and Cilantro Cream

This is my homage to the wonderful sauces drizzled on enchiladas at Café Azteca in Lawrence, MA, my favorite local Mexican spot. Make no mistake—this sauce is spicy. But the cream smoothes it out a bit and the chile's smokiness and the tang of the lime juice balance out the heat.

YIELD: ½ CUP, 4 SERVINGS
PREP TIME: 4 minutes
COOK TIME: 5 minutes

¾ cup low-sodium chicken broth
1 canned chipotle, minced (about 1 tablespoon), plus 2 tablespoons adobo sauce
2 teaspoons freshly squeezed lime juice
¼ cup heavy cream
2 tablespoons chopped fresh cilantro
Kosher salt and freshly ground black pepper

Blot any fat from the pan using a wad of paper towels. Heat the chicken broth, chipotle, adobo sauce, and lime juice over medium-high heat, stirring to scrape up any of the caramelized crust, until the liquid thickens to a little less than ½ cup, about 3 minutes.

Whisk in the cream and half of the cilantro, cook for a minute or two so it thickens slightly, and then season to taste with salt, pepper, and more lime juice. Serve sprinkled with the remaining cilantro.

OPTIONS: Purée this sauce with an immersion blender to make it more dressy. Add sautéed fresh corn kernels and peppers to give it a little more heft.

PAIRINGS: Make this sauce with sautéed spice-rubbed chicken breasts (page 31) or pork chops (page 38) and serve with Spanish Yellow Rice (page 234) and stewed pinto beans.

Warm Mint Pan Sauce

I know it might seem like common sense that a pan sauce be warm, but so many mint sauces are served cold that it's worth noting. The sharp punch of this sauce, from white wine vinegar and garlic, is meant to cut through and freshen lamb's rich, gamey flavor.

YIELD: ½ CUP, 4 SERVINGS
PREP TIME: 4 minutes
COOK TIME: 7 minutes

1 tablespoon olive oil
1 garlic clove, minced (about ¾ teaspoon)
About ¼ teaspoon kosher salt
¾ cup low-sodium chicken broth
2 tablespoons white wine vinegar
2 teaspoons granulated sugar
¼ cup chopped fresh mint
About ½ teaspoon freshly ground black pepper

Set the pan over medium heat (with any drippings remaining from the sear), add the oil and garlic, sprinkle with salt, and cook, stirring, so the garlic becomes fragrant and starts to turn just a very light brown at its edges, about 1 minute.

Raise the heat to high, whisk in the chicken broth, vinegar, and sugar and cook, stirring to scrape up any of the caramelized crust, until the liquid reduces to a little less than ½ cup, about 3 minutes. Stir in the mint and pepper and season with more salt, pepper, or vinegar to taste.

PAIRINGS: I've already shown my hand: this is the perfect sauce to go with lamb chops or steaks (pages 24–25). Serve with Couscous with Cinnamon and Oranges (page 237) and sautéed asparagus (page 50).

Soy Ginger Pan Sauce

Even though the flavors in this sauce might scream stir-fry, the drippings and caramelized crust from the sear give it a balanced richness altogether different.

YIELD: ½ CUP, 4 SERVINGS
PREP TIME: 4 minutes
COOK TIME: 7 minutes

1 tablespoon minced fresh ginger
¼ cup mirin or dry sherry
½ cup low-sodium chicken broth
2 tablespoons low-sodium soy sauce
2 tablespoons honey
1 tablespoon balsamic vinegar
1 scallion (both white and green parts), trimmed and
    thinly sliced
1 tablespoon unsalted butter (optional)

Heat the ginger in the pan (with any drippings remaining from the sear) over medium heat, stirring, until it starts to sizzle steadily and turn light brown, about 1 minute. Add the mirin or sherry, raise the heat to high, and cook, stirring to scrape up any caramelized crust on the bottom of the pan, until it almost completely reduces, about 1½ minutes.

Add the chicken broth, soy sauce, honey, and balsamic vinegar and cook, stirring, until it reduces by a little more than half and starts to get a glazy consistency, about 3 minutes. Stir in the scallions and butter, if using, and cook, stirring, for 1 minute so the butter melts.

OPTIONS: Sauté sliced shiitake or oyster mushrooms with the ginger (add 1 tablespoon cooking oil so the pan doesn't get too dry).

PAIRINGS: Drizzle on top of sautéed cod (page 44) or chicken breasts (page 31) and serve with sautéed Napa cabbage (page 53) and steamed brown rice.

Morel and Chive Pan Sauce

A couple of years ago after a long rain, I discovered a patch of morels sprouting up in my backyard. Some new mulch along with the weather had somehow combined into my good fortune. After checking to make sure that the fungi weren't those pesky, poisonous "false" morels, I made this sauce and paired it with veal chops, and it was good. I do call for dried morels in this sauce because chances are there are no fresh ones in your backyard and those at the market are obscenely expensive.

YIELD: ABOUT ½ CUP, 4 SERVINGS
PREP TIME: 5 minutes
COOK TIME: 8 minutes

½ ounce dried morels
1 tablespoon unsalted butter
1 large shallot, finely diced (about ¼ cup)
About ¼ teaspoon kosher salt
1 teaspoon chopped fresh thyme (optional)
¼ cup dry sherry
3 tablespoons thinly sliced fresh chives
2 tablespoons heavy cream (optional)
Freshly ground black pepper

Set the mushrooms and 1 cup water in a microwave-proof bowl and cook for 1 minute so the water just comes to a simmer. Set another bowl on top so the mushrooms are completely submerged and soak for 5 minutes so they soften. Coarsely chop the mushrooms and drain the soaking liquid through a coffee filter or paper towels to remove any sediment, reserving the strained liquid.

Meanwhile, heat the butter and shallot in the pan (with any fat remaining from the sear) over medium heat, sprinkle lightly with salt, and cook, stirring, until the shallot softens and starts to become translucent, about 2 minutes. Add the mushrooms, thyme, if using, sprinkle with salt, and cook, until the mushrooms sizzle steadily and acquire a nutty fragrance, about 2 minutes.

Raise the heat to high, add the sherry, and cook, stirring, until it almost completely reduces, about 2 minutes. Add the mushroom soaking liquid and cook until it reduces by about half, about 2 minutes. Stir in the chives and the cream, if using, and season with salt and pepper to taste.

PAIRINGS: Pair this fancy sauce with a good, expensive steak, like a strip or tenderloin (page 24). If you have the time, serve with a creamy saffron risotto and sautéed greens (page 53).

Wild Mushroom and Marsala Sauce

Marsala is the Italian equivalent of sherry, a fortified wine that is at once sweet and nuanced. It serves as the perfect base for a sauce with herbs or mushrooms or both as is the case here. Anything goes for "wild" mushrooms. They can be as conventional as shiitake or oyster mushrooms or as exotic as chanterelles or morels.

YIELD: ½ CUP, 4 SERVINGS
PREP TIME: 4 minutes
COOK TIME: 7 minutes

1 tablespoon olive oil
2 garlic cloves, smashed
3½ ounces fresh wild mushrooms, stemmed and
    thinly sliced
1 teaspoon chopped fresh rosemary or thyme
About ½ teaspoon kosher salt
¼ cup marsala or dry sherry
½ cup low-sodium chicken broth
2 tablespoons heavy cream (optional)
Freshly ground black pepper

Heat the oil and garlic in the pan (with any drippings remaining from the sear) over medium-high heat until the garlic starts to sizzle, about 30 seconds. Add the mushrooms and fresh herbs, sprinkle with salt, and cook, until softened and browned in places, about 2 minutes.

Raise the heat to high, add the marsala, and cook, stirring, until it almost completely reduces, about 2 minutes. Add the chicken broth and cook until it reduces by about half, about 2 minutes. Swirl in the cream, if using, discard the garlic cloves, and season with salt and pepper to taste.

PAIRINGS: Pair this sauce with thin cutlets to make chicken or veal marsala (page 36); serve over Buttered Egg Noodles with Chives (page 233).

Rosemary and Wild Mushroom Gravy

There may be no giblets in here, but the flavorful drippings from the sear (especially if they're from skin-on chicken breasts) give this sauce a nice flavor base that will remind you of Thanksgiving gravy.

YIELD: 1¼ CUPS, 6 SERVINGS
PREP TIME: 7 minutes
COOK TIME: 8 minutes

2 tablespoons unsalted butter
1 large shallot, finely diced (about ¼ cup)
About ¾ teaspoon kosher salt
3½ ounces oyster or shiitake mushrooms, stemmed
    and thinly sliced
About ½ teaspoon freshly ground black pepper
2 tablespoons all-purpose flour
1 cup low-sodium chicken broth
1 teaspoon cider vinegar
1 teaspoon chopped fresh rosemary

Melt the butter in the pan (with any drippings remaining from the sear) over medium heat. Add the shallot, sprinkle lightly with some of the salt, and cook, stirring, until it softens and starts to become translucent, 1 to 2 minutes. Add the mushrooms, sprinkle with the remaining salt and the pepper and cook, stirring, until they brown and soften, about 2 minutes.

Add the flour and cook, stirring, so it coats the mushrooms and starts to turn light brown, about 1 minute. Whisk in the chicken broth, vinegar, and rosemary and bring to a boil. Reduce to a steady simmer and cook, stirring, until the mixture thickens to a gravylike consistency, about 2 minutes. Season with more salt, pepper, and vinegar to taste.

PAIRINGS: This gravy goes particularly well with seared poultry, like chicken breasts (page 31) or turkey cutlets (page 36). Build on the holiday feel with Garlicky Smashed Red Potatoes (page 233) and sautéed green beans (page 50) topped with a pat of Shallot-Herb Butter (page 197).

Toasted Garlic, Sherry, and Thyme Gravy

The garlic and sherry vinegar in this sauce make it a little sharper than the preceding gravy, better to go with a rich cut like a pork chop.

YIELD: 1¼ CUPS, 4 SERVINGS
PREP TIME: 4 minutes
COOK TIME: 7 minutes

3 garlic cloves, halved
2 tablespoons unsalted butter
2 tablespoons all-purpose flour
1 cup low-sodium chicken broth
2 teaspoons chopped fresh thyme
1½ teaspoons sherry vinegar
Kosher salt and freshly ground black pepper

Cook the garlic with the butter in the pan (with any drippings remaining from the sear) over medium heat until the garlic browns lightly and becomes very fragrant, about 2 minutes. Add the flour and cook, whisking, so it starts to turn light brown and acquires a nutty fragrance, about 1 minute.

Whisk in the chicken broth, thyme, and vinegar and bring to a boil. Reduce to a steady simmer and cook over medium heat, stirring, until the mixture thickens to a gravylike consistency, about 2 minutes. Discard the garlic cloves and season the gravy with salt, pepper, and more vinegar to taste.

PAIRINGS: This gravy goes well with sautéed bone-in pork chops or tenderloin medallions (page 38). Serve with Rosemary-Parmesan Mashed Yukon Potatoes (page 235) and sautéed snap peas (page 50).

Caramelized Shallot and Herb Jus

Shallots can be quite sweet if you gently sauté them. Here they star in a light sauce whose brothy, loose texture is somewhere between a sauce and a soup; serve it in shallow bowls.

YIELD: 1 CUP, 4 SERVINGS
PREP TIME: 4 minutes
COOK TIME: 8 minutes

1 tablespoon olive oil
2 large shallots (about 5 ounces), cut into thin disks
    (about ¾ cup)
About ½ teaspoon kosher salt
About ¼ teaspoon freshly ground black pepper
1¼ cups low-sodium chicken broth
1 tablespoon cider vinegar, more to taste
2 teaspoons tomato paste
2 teaspoons chopped fresh thyme
¼ cup freshly grated Parmigiano Reggiano

Set the pan over medium heat (with any fat remaining from the sear), add the oil and the shallot, sprinkle with salt and pepper, and cook, stirring, until it wilts and starts to brown, about 4 minutes.

Add the chicken broth, vinegar, tomato paste, and thyme, raise the heat to high, and cook, scraping the bottom of the pan to incorporate any of the caramelized crust, until the liquid reduces by about half and the shallot becomes completely tender, about 3 minutes. Stir in the Parmigiano and season with more vinegar, salt, and pepper to taste.

PAIRINGS: Try this broth with seared chicken breasts (page 31) or a mild fish like cod or halibut (pages 42 and 44); serve with sautéed kale (page 53) and a crusty sourdough baguette.

INFUSED CREAM SAUCES

Now these aren't the sauces you're going to make on the first day of a new diet (unless it's an all-cream regimen), but they are quick and simple and wonderfully flavorful. The method is straightforward. Sauté aromatics, then add in the cream, chicken broth, and fresh herbs, gently simmer, and reduce.

Sherry and Thyme Cream Sauce

One of the simpler preparations in this section, this sauce has a clean, dressy feel that is greater than the sum of its parts.

YIELD: ⅓ CUP, ABOUT 4 SERVINGS
PREP TIME: 2 minutes
COOK TIME: 6 minutes

½ cup dry sherry
2 teaspoons chopped fresh thyme
½ cup low-sodium chicken broth
3 tablespoons heavy cream
Kosher salt and freshly ground pepper

Gently blot any fat from the pan using a wad of paper towels. Add the sherry and thyme to the pan, set over high heat, and cook, scraping the bottom of the pan with a wooden spoon to incorporate any caramelized crust, until it almost completely reduces, about 2 minutes.

Add the chicken broth and cook, stirring, until it reduces to about ¼ cup, about 3 minutes. Add the cream and cook until the sauce acquires the desired thickness, 1 to 2 minutes. Season with salt and pepper to taste.

OPTIONS: Mushrooms, like oysters or cremini, are a perfect fit for this sauce; sauté them before adding the sherry.

PAIRINGS: Like many in this book, this sauce goes especially well with seared chicken breasts (page 31); serve over Roasted Red Pepper and Thyme Polenta (page 237) and sprinkle with chopped fresh chives.

TIP: What to Do with a Zested Lemon
Once a lemon has been stripped of its protective coating, it doesn't hold very long in the fridge (about a week). Of course leftover lemon is great in tea and cold beverages or try adding a squirt to some of the vinaigrettes (pages 176–185) for an extra layer of acidity. Or sprinkle on grilled fish or chicken the moment it's off the grill and before hitting it with a salsa or dipping sauce.

Rosemary Lemon Cream

The lemon in this sauce comes from freshly grated zest, which infuses the cream with a pleasant, citrus warmth, as opposed to lemon juice, which would get lost in the heaviness of the sauce.

YIELD: ⅓ CUP, ABOUT 4 SERVINGS
PREP TIME: 3 minutes
COOK TIME: 5 minutes

½ cup low-sodium chicken broth
¼ cup heavy cream
1 teaspoon chopped fresh rosemary
1 teaspoon freshly grated lemon zest (from about 1 lemon)
About ½ teaspoon freshly ground pepper
Kosher salt

Gently blot any fat from the pan using a wad of paper towels. Set the pan over medium-high heat, add the chicken broth, cream, rosemary, lemon zest, and a generous sprinkling of pepper, and cook at a steady simmer, stirring to scrape up any caramelized crust on the bottom of the pan, until it reduces by about half, about 4 minutes. Season with salt and pepper to taste.

OPTIONS: Add some chopped parsley to build on the freshness of the rosemary or a couple of smashed garlic cloves to infuse the cream.

PAIRINGS: Scallops or shrimp (page 26) go nicely with the richness of this sauce. Sprinkle with plenty of black pepper and pair with sautéed carrots (page 52) and Traditional Rice Pilaf (page 234).

White Truffle and Parmesan Cream

There was a brief period in the mid-'90s when American chefs discovered white truffle oil and, like teenagers who've found a new band or style of clothing, completely lost their minds. Every mashed potato, pasta, or polenta dish that left a restaurant kitchen oozed with the stuff. While this might have been a little much (in excess, truffle oil can taste like burnt rubber), a restrained drizzle can add a pleasant richness to a sauce.

YIELD: ½ CUP, ABOUT 4 SERVINGS
PREP TIME: 5 minutes
COOK TIME: 5 minutes

½ cup low-sodium chicken broth
¼ cup heavy cream
About ½ teaspoon freshly ground pepper
⅓ cup freshly grated Parmigiano Reggiano
3 tablespoons thinly sliced fresh chives
½ teaspoon white truffle oil
Kosher salt

Gently blot any fat from the pan using a wad of paper towels. Pour in the chicken broth and cream, sprinkle generously with pepper, set over medium-high heat, and cook at a steady simmer, stirring to scrape up any caramelized crust on the bottom of the pan, until the broth reduces by about half, about 3 minutes. Stir in the Parmigiano, chives, and white truffle oil and season with salt and more pepper to taste (remember the Parmigiano is salty).

OPTIONS: Sauté smashed garlic cloves or thinly sliced mushrooms before adding the broth and cream. Or add fresh herbs—like rosemary or thyme—for depth.

PAIRINGS: This sauce can make boneless chicken breasts (page 24) taste like a whole lot more. Or drizzle on seared filet mignon (page 38). Pair either with a risotto with peas and sautéed green beans (page 50).

III. STIR-FRY SAUCES

I've never had the good fortune to work in an Asian restaurant, so my knowledge of those cuisines comes from a lot of eating, reading, travel, and practice. It's what I like to cook. If I'm not testing recipes, chances are I'm playing around with a stir-fry, trying to understand and replicate Asian cuisine's harmony of strong sweet, sour, and spicy notes.

The following stir-fry sauces do depart somewhat from tradition to fit our sear-and-sauce method. Most stir-fry sauces are prepared in the same pan as the stir-fry itself: you stir-fry some meat, chicken, or vegetables, set them aside, and then use the same pan to make a quick sauce and toss the whole thing together. That formula works, of course, but the goal of this book is to streamline things a bit (avoiding having to transfer ingredients to and from the pan). By preparing these stir-fry sauces in a separate pan (or by whisking them together in a bowl), you can move things along (though it might mean you have an extra pan to wash). It also allows you to concentrate your focus on searing the meat just right before tossing it with the sauce (doneness can be more complicated during a back-and-forth transfer).

FINDING A BALANCE

Any good cook will advise you never to oversauce a dish. This especially holds true for stir-fries, a method that should be light and full of bright textures. Still, sauces are integral to stir-fries; Asian cuisine tends to be less meat-heavy than Western cooking. The recipes in this section should strike a balance between the light, fresh, mixtures from the new wave of Asian cooking and the familiar but sometimes gloppy sauces of old-school Chinese-American restaurants. They have bright, fresh flavors, but they are saucy sauces, substantial enough to amply dress whatever you sear.

TO THICKEN OR NOT

Chinese greasy spoons often thicken sauces into gluey, gelatinous messes. Cornstarch, the preeminent thickener, is partly to blame. In excess, it can both dull and overwhelm a stir-fry. But if you use just a little bit (1 or 2 teaspoons mixed with 1 tablespoon water), cornstarch helps a sauce cling to stir-fried meat or vegetables. For this reason, cornstarch is optional in most of these recipes, so you can decide whether you want a sauce thick or thin.

Spicy Black Bean Sauce

I almost always order something with black beans at Chinese restaurants. It's my litmus test. There are a bunch of decent jarred black bean sauces available at the supermarket (you can mix a couple of table-spoons with ½ cup chicken broth), though they don't match the complexity or freshness of this sauce.

YIELD: 1 CUP, 4 SERVINGS
PREP TIME: 6 minutes
COOK TIME: 6 minutes

2 tablespoons coarsely chopped fermented black
    beans (below)
2 tablespoons coarsely chopped minced ginger
    (from about a 1½-inch knob)
1 medium garlic clove, coarsely chopped
    (about ¾ teaspoon)
¼ teaspoon crushed red pepper flakes
1 tablespoon canola oil
2 tablespoons low-sodium soy sauce
2 tablespoons dry sherry
2 teaspoons toasted sesame oil
1½ teaspoons granulated sugar

Set the black beans, ginger, garlic, and red pepper flakes in a mini-chop or food processor and pulse to mince; you may need to scrape down the sides of the work bowl a couple of times.

Heat the oil with this black bean mixture in a skillet over medium heat until it sizzles steadily and the garlic starts to brown ever so lightly at the edges, about 2 minutes.

Raise the heat to high, whisk in the soy sauce, sherry, sesame oil, sugar, and ½ cup water (or chicken broth if you have) and bring to a steady simmer. Reduce the heat to medium and cook, stirring, for 2 minutes so the flavors meld. Thicken with cornstarch (2 teaspoons with 1 tablespoon water) if you like by whisking it in and returning to a boil.

PAIRINGS: I love this sauce with stir-fried chicken (page 56) or beef (page 60); toss in some blanched broccoli. The black beans also pair well with shellfish (page 60) like clams, shrimp, or scallops. Serve with steamed rice.

TIP: Though some cooks advocate rinsing black beans to mellow their saltiness, I think it's an unnecessary step and can leach them of some of their flavor. Just make sure not to overseason whatever you're searing with this sauce.

Use a Food Processor for Mincing

With this recipe for Spicy Black Bean Sauce and those that follow, you can speed up your prep by using a mini-chop or food processor to mince ginger or garlic quickly. A couple of pulses and one or two times scraping down the sides should do the job.

Spicy Szechuan Garlic and Double Chile Sauce

In this quick sauce, the dried chiles play the good cop (smooth, toasted flavor) while sliced Thai chiles play bad cop (sharp, tongue-numbing heat).

YIELD: 1 CUP, ABOUT 4 SERVINGS
PREP TIME: 5 minutes
COOK TIME: 6 minutes

3 tablespoon canola oil
4 dried chiles
1 Thai chile (or 1 jalapeño), sliced into thin rings
About ½ teaspoon kosher salt
2 garlic cloves, minced (about 2 teaspoons)
½ cup low-sodium chicken broth
2 teaspoons oyster sauce
1 teaspoon white vinegar
1 teaspoon toasted sesame oil
2 scallions (both white and green parts), trimmed and thinly sliced

Heat the oil and chiles (both dried and fresh) in a large skillet over medium heat, sprinkle with salt, and cook, stirring, until they start to sizzle steadily and become fragrant, about 2 minutes. Add the garlic and cook, stirring, until it sizzles steadily and just starts to turn light brown at the edges, about 30 seconds.

Stir in the chicken broth, oyster sauce, vinegar, and sesame oil. Bring to a boil, and then cook until the mixture reduces slightly and the flavors meld, about 2 minutes. Stir in the scallions.

OPTIONS: Toast some Szechuan peppercorns or fermented black beans with the chiles; either are available at an Asian grocer. Or sauté a sprinkling of 5-spice powder at the same time as the garlic.

PAIRINGS: This is one of those sauces that is big enough to match the full flavor of stir-fried lamb (page 60). Pork or beef (page 60) are also good choices, or pair with a green vegetable like spinach or bok choy (page 53). Serve with brown rice.

Spicy Chile and Cilantro Sauce

Cilantro polarizes folks into love-it or hate-it camps. Although now I'm a convert, I wouldn't go near Thai food as a kid because of it. This fresh herb has a way of growing on you, though, and if you can learn to like it, it opens up so many cuisines and dishes. Here, it adds a bright, citrus kick.

YIELD: 1½ CUPS, 4 SERVINGS
PREP TIME: 7 minutes
COOK TIME: 6 minutes

1 tablespoon canola oil
2 Thai chiles or 1 jalapeño, cored, seeded if you like, and chopped (about 3 tablespoons)
1 medium Spanish onion (about ½ pound), thinly sliced (about 1½ cups)
½ cup low-sodium chicken broth
2 tablespoons low-sodium soy sauce
1 tablespoon white vinegar
2 teaspoons tomato paste
1 teaspoon granulated sugar
¼ cup chopped fresh cilantro

Heat the oil and chiles in a large skillet over high heat until they start to sizzle, about 1 minute. Add the onion and cook, stirring, until it just starts to soften and brown in places, about 2 minutes.

In a small bowl, mix the chicken broth, soy sauce, vinegar, tomato paste, and sugar. Add to the skillet and bring to a boil. Reduce the heat to medium and cook, stirring, until the onion become crisp tender and the sauce thickens slightly, about 2 minutes. Stir in the cilantro.

OPTIONS: Sauté minced ginger and garlic with the chiles to give this sauce a little more fragrance.

PAIRINGS: Pair with thin strips of chicken (page 56) or pork (page 60), accompany with some sautéed garlicky spinach (page 53), and Thai Coconut Rice.

Homestyle XO Sauce

Traditionally dried shrimp, dried scallops, and Chinese ham power this Hong Kong–style sauce. I'm guessing that none of those ingredients are kicking around your pantry. So instead pulse some fresh shrimp and prosciutto in a food processor and stir-fry with chiles and garlic.

YIELD: 1 CUP, ABOUT 4 SERVINGS
PREP TIME: 6 minutes
COOK TIME: 6 minutes

3 slices prosciutto (about 1 ounce), coarsely chopped
2 ounces shrimp (about 3), peeled, deveined, rinsed, and patted dry
2 teaspoons toasted sesame oil
3 tablespoons canola oil
2 garlic cloves, minced (about 2 teaspoons)
¼ teaspoon crushed red pepper flakes
2 tablespoons dry sherry
1 tablespoon soy sauce
¼ cup low-sodium chicken broth

Pulse the prosciutto in a mini-chop or food processor to finely chop, then transfer to a small bowl. Pulse the shrimp with 1 teaspoon of the sesame oil until finely chopped.

Cook the prosciutto with the canola oil in a large skillet over medium-high heat, stirring, until it sizzles steadily and just starts to brown, 2 to 3 minutes.

Stir in the garlic and red pepper flakes and cook, stirring, so the garlic starts to sizzle and just turns light brown at the edges, about 1 minute. Add the shrimp mixture and cook, stirring, until it turns opaque, about 1 minute.

Add the sherry and soy sauce and cook, stirring to pick up any of the caramelized crust, for 1 minute. Add the chicken broth and the remaining 1 teaspoon sesame oil, bring to a simmer, and then remove from the heat.

OPTIONS: If you can find dried scallops or shrimp at a local Asian grocer, rehydrate a couple of tablespoons of either in ¼ cup boiling water and then sub them in for the fresh shrimp.

PAIRINGS: Toss this sauce with tofu or stir-fried shrimp (page 60) and accompany with stir-fried Chinese broccoli (page 58) and white rice.

Caramelized Ginger Sauce with Straw Mushrooms and Bamboo Shoots

Though Asian cuisines celebrate fresh ingredients, the pantry can serve as a base for a sauce, too. I'm a sucker for canned straw mushrooms and bamboo shoots. They're both relatively mild so they blend with whatever you pair them; in this case, that's ginger that's been seared gently for a couple of minutes so it almost caramelizes.

YIELD: 2 CUPS, 4 SERVINGS
PREP TIME: 5 minutes
COOK TIME: 8 minutes

1 tablespoon canola oil
2 tablespoons minced ginger
5 scallions (both white and green parts), trimmed, thinly sliced, and white and green parts kept separate
About ¼ teaspoon kosher salt
1 (15½-ounce) can straw mushrooms, drained
1 (8-ounce) can bamboo shoots, drained
¾ cup low-sodium chicken broth
1 tablespoon toasted sesame oil
2 teaspoons white vinegar
1 teaspoon granulated sugar

Heat the oil and ginger in a small skillet over medium heat, stirring, so the ginger sizzles steadily and just starts to brown at the edges, 2 to 3 minutes. Add the white parts of the scallions, raise the heat to medium high, sprinkle with salt, and cook, stirring, until the scallion softens and starts to brown, about 2 minutes.

Add the remaining ingredients (with the exception of the scallion greens) and bring to a boil. Simmer for a couple of minutes so the flavors meld and the sauce thickens slightly, then stir in the scallion greens. Thicken with cornstarch (2 teaspoons with 1 tablespoon water) if you like; stir it in and return to a boil.

OPTIONS: Sauté some minced garlic or diced chiles (jalapeños or Thai chiles) with the scallions.

PAIRINGS: Pair with thinly sliced stir-fried chicken (page 56) or diced tofu (see page 121) and serve atop egg noodles tossed with sesame oil.

Spicy Hunan Stir-Fry Sauce

Green peppers get a bad rap. They may not be as sweet or refined as their red brethren, but their bitter flavor balances out the sweetness in this Chinese restaurant staple.

YIELD: 1½ CUPS, 4 SERVINGS
PREP TIME: 5 minutes
COOK TIME: 8 minutes

2 tablespoons canola oil
1 green bell pepper, cut in ½-inch dice (about 1½ cups)
About ¼ teaspoon kosher salt
1 garlic clove, minced (about 1 teaspoon)
¾ cup low-sodium chicken broth
2 tablespoons low-sodium soy sauce
2 teaspoons white vinegar
2 teaspoons Thai chile paste (like Sriracha)
1 teaspoon toasted sesame oil
1 teaspoon granulated sugar
About ½ teaspoon freshly ground black pepper
1 teaspoon cornstarch

Heat the oil in a medium skillet over medium-high heat until it's shimmering hot, about 1½ minutes. Add the green pepper, sprinkle lightly with salt, and cook,

tossing, until it starts to brown and soften lightly, 2 to 3 minutes. Add the garlic and cook, stirring, for 30 seconds so it becomes fragrant but doesn't burn.

Add the chicken broth, soy sauce, vinegar, chile paste, sesame oil, sugar, and a generous sprinkling of black pepper. Bring to a boil, then cook, stirring, until the peppers become crisp-tender, 1 to 2 minutes.

Whisk the cornstarch with 1 tablespoon water, stir into the sauce, and cook until the sauce returns to a simmer and thickens, about 30 seconds.

OPTIONS: I often make this sauce like my childhood favorite restaurant, Seven Star Mandarin, with minced ginger and thinly sliced bamboo shoots (jarred are fine).

PAIRINGS: This sauce is a winner with broccoli and chicken (page 58), beef (page 60), or tofu. Serve with steamed white rice.

Toasted Sesame–Ginger Stir-Fry Sauce

The trick to cooking with sesame oil is to surround it with other strong flavors—sweet (tomato paste), sour (vinegar), and spicy (chile paste)—so that it blends in and doesn't overpower.

YIELD: ¾ CUP, 4 SERVINGS
PREP TIME: 4 minutes
COOK TIME: 5 minutes

1 tablespoon canola oil
3 tablespoons minced ginger
1 garlic clove, minced (about 1 teaspoon)
1 tablespoon low-sodium soy sauce
1 tablespoon tomato paste
1 tablespoon toasted sesame oil
2 teaspoons white vinegar
1 teaspoon Thai chile paste (like Sriracha)
1 teaspoon cornstarch

Heat the oil, ginger, and garlic in a small skillet over medium heat, stirring, so they sizzle steadily and just start to turn light brown at the edges, about 2 minutes.

In a small bowl, mix the soy sauce, tomato paste, sesame oil, vinegar, and chile paste with ½ cup water. Add to the pan, raise the heat to high, and bring to a steady simmer. Whisk the cornstarch with 1 tablespoon water and then stir into the sauce. Return to a simmer so the sauce thickens, and then remove from the heat.

PAIRINGS: Beef (page 60) and blanched snap peas (or snow peas) go great with this sauce's nuanced sweetness, as does shrimp (page 60). Pair with Chinese Egg Noodles with Scallions and Shiitakes (page 233).

Kung Pao Sauce

Half of the fun of making this sauce is its name. Say it "POW!!" with a flourish and punch the hell out of whomever's shoulder is closest to you at the dinner table. It's juvenile, of course—the stir-fry equivalent of the punch buggy game—but it feels good after a long day.

YIELD: ¾ CUP, 4 SERVINGS
PREP TIME: 6 minutes
COOK TIME: 7 minutes

4 dried chiles

2 tablespoons canola oil

½ red bell pepper, cored, seeded, and cut in ½-inch dice (about ¾ cup)

¼ cup coarsely chopped peanuts

1 garlic clove, minced (about 1 teaspoon)

2 tablespoons low-sodium soy sauce

1 tablespoon balsamic vinegar

2 teaspoons toasted sesame oil

2 teaspoons granulated sugar

Heat the chiles with the oil in a large skillet over medium-high heat, until they start to sizzle steadily, about 1½ minutes. Add the pepper and peanuts and cook, stirring, until the pepper starts to brown and soften, about 2 minutes. Add the garlic and cook for 30 seconds, stirring, so it becomes fragrant.

In a bowl mix the soy sauce, vinegar, sesame oil, sugar, and ¼ cup water. Add to the skillet and cook, stirring, until the sauce reduces by about half, about 3 minutes.

OPTIONS: Toss in some diced celery along with the bell pepper.

PAIRINGS: Stir-fried chicken (page 56) or shrimp (page 60) or both together are classic partners with this sauce. Serve with steamed rice and sautéed snow peas (page 50).

Old-School Sweet and Sour Sauce

OK, if I were ever invited to the James Beard House in New York City to present a fancy dinner, this would probably be the last thing that I'd make. But, it is tasty and comforting and something that everyone will like.

YIELD: 1¼ CUPS, ABOUT 4 SERVINGS
PREP TIME: 3 minutes
COOK TIME: 5 minutes

¼ cup rice vinegar

¼ cup honey

1 tablespoon ketchup

1 tablespoon soy sauce

½ teaspoon Thai chile paste (optional)

1 teaspoon cornstarch

½ cup diced canned or fresh pineapple

2 scallions (both white and green parts), trimmed and thinly sliced

Heat the vinegar, honey, ketchup, soy sauce, and chile paste in a small saucepan over medium heat, whisking occasionally, until the mixture just comes to a simmer, about 3 minutes.

Mix the cornstarch with 1 tablespoon water, whisk into the sauce, and return to a simmer so the sauce thickens, about 30 seconds. Stir in the pineapple and scallions and remove from the heat.

PAIRINGS: Toss with stir-fried pork (page 60) or chicken and serve with steamed broccoli and brown rice.

Ma Po Tofu Sauce

This ground pork and chile sauce is based on the spicy Szechuan dish. Though it is traditionally paired with tofu, I love how this sauce goes with all types of fish and seafood.

YIELD: ABOUT 2 CUPS, 4 SERVINGS
PREP TIME: 6 minutes
COOK TIME: 8 minutes

3 scallions (both white and green parts), thinly sliced, whites and green parts separated
2 tablespoons fermented black beans, chopped
2 tablespoons minced ginger
2 tablespoons canola oil
½ pound ground pork (see Fatty Ground Pork Makes the Difference on page 122)
1 tablespoon toasted sesame oil
About ½ teaspoon kosher salt
About ½ teaspoon freshly ground black pepper
Heaping ½ teaspoon crushed red pepper flakes
2 tablespoons soy sauce
1 tablespoon black vinegar or balsamic vinegar

Cook the white parts of the scallions with the black beans, ginger, and canola oil in a large skillet or wok over high heat until they start to sizzle steadily and the ginger just starts to brown at its edges, about 2 minutes.

Meanwhile, mix the pork with 1 teaspoon sesame oil and sprinkle generously with salt and pepper. Stir the red pepper flakes into the pan and once they start to sizzle steadily, about 15 seconds, add the pork. Cook, breaking up with a wooden spoon, until the pork loses its raw color, about 3 minutes.

In a cup measure, mix ⅓ cup water with the soy sauce, vinegar, and the remaining 2 teaspoons sesame oil. Add to the sauce, bring to a boil, and then remove from the heat.

OPTIONS: This is one of those sauces that could easily have twenty ingredients. Szechuan peppercorns (available in most Asian groceries) with their exotic, tingling spiciness would be my first addition. Try stir-frying some minced garlic or dried chiles with the ginger during the initial cooking stage or lightly sprinkle the pork with some 5-spice powder for a little depth.

PAIRINGS: Of course, this sauce goes perfectly with cubes of fresh tofu—just stir them into the sauce at the end and then continue cooking until warmed through. But it also goes nicely with stir-fried shrimp (page 60) or even sautéed cod (page 44). Serve with steamed long-grain rice.

> **TIP: Ketchup in My Chinese Food?!?**
> Admittedly, America's favorite condiment would seem to have little place in refined Chinese stir-fries. But a tablespoon or two adds an unidentifiable sweetness and spice, similar to 5-spice powder, which makes sense because ketchup has many of the same spices in it.

TIP: Balsamic Vinegar and Chinese Food?
Chinese black vinegar has a dark hue and aged intensity reminiscent of Italian balsamic vinegar. Traditionally made from sweet black rice, this vinegar has a sharp and slightly sweet flavor that balances out the prominent spice and heat in authentic Szechuan cooking. You can find it at an Asian grocer or just sub in balsamic vinegar.

TIP: Fatty Ground Pork Makes the Difference
Try to pick out ground pork that has a little fat to it for the two recipes on page 121 (Ma Po Tofu Sauce) and below (Lobster Sauce), preferably from the animal's shoulder (also known as pork butt). See if your butcher will comply—he might just give you one of those stares (the "buddy, it's already ground!" stare), but nicely marbled pork will add good flavor and won't dry out.

Lobster Sauce

Those who are familiar with the Chinese-American restaurant classic Shrimp in Lobster Sauce will know that despite its name, there's no lobster in here. Rather this is a lobster-style sauce that's richened with ribbons of beaten eggs (kind of like egg drop soup) and sautéed ground pork.

YIELD: 1¾ CUPS, 4 SERVINGS
PREP TIME: 5 minutes
COOK TIME: 7 minutes

2 tablespoons canola oil

3 scallions, thinly sliced with white and green parts
   separated

1 tablespoon chopped fermented black beans

½ pound ground pork (preferably from the shoulder—see
   Fatty Ground Pork Makes the Difference above)

2 teaspoons toasted sesame oil

About ½ teaspoon kosher salt

About ½ teaspoon freshly ground black pepper

¾ cup low-sodium chicken broth

1 tablespoon oyster sauce

1 tablespoon dry sherry

2 eggs, beaten

Heat the canola oil with the whites of the scallions and the black beans in a large skillet over medium-high heat, stirring, until the scallions brown lightly and soften, about 2 minutes.

Meanwhile, mix the pork with 1 teaspoon sesame oil and a generous sprinkling of salt and pepper. Add the pork and cook, breaking up with a wooden spoon, until it loses its raw color, about 2 minutes.

In a small bowl, mix the broth with the oyster sauce, sherry, and the remaining 1 teaspoon sesame oil, add to the pan, and bring to a simmer, 2 minutes. Remove the sauce from the heat and whisk the egg into the sauce so it forms thick yellow ribbons. Cook for another minute or so to heat through.

OPTIONS: Peas are a traditional player in this sauce; defrost a cup of frozen peas and add to the sauce just before the eggs. Or stir-fry minced garlic and minced ginger along with the black beans and scallions.

PAIRINGS: Stir-fried shrimp (page 60) is the obvious pairing here, though I also like this sauce with diced tofu; stir the latter into the sauce and cook until it heats through. Serve with Curried Rice Noodles (page 234).

Oyster Stir-Fry Sauce

Oyster sauce is like the Chinese equivalent of fish sauce, adding a gentle hit of brininess to a stir-fry or sauce. This thick, dark sauce also appears in Thai and Cambodian cuisines and has a measure of sweetness (generally from sugar) to go with its fishy flavor from oyster extract; the latter is a heavily reduced liquid from oysters.

YIELD: 1 CUP, ABOUT 4 SERVINGS
PREP TIME: 2 minutes
COOK TIME: N/A

½ cup chicken broth or water
2 scallions (both white and greens), trimmed and thinly sliced
2 tablespoons oyster sauce (I prefer Lee Kum Kee brand)
1 tablespoon rice vinegar
1 tablespoon soy sauce
2 teaspoons toasted sesame oil
1 teaspoon Thai chile paste (like Sriracha)

Mix all the ingredients in a cup measure.

PAIRINGS: The light fishiness of this sauce plays perfectly with a beef (page 60) or chicken (page 56) stir-fry; stir in some blanched Chinese broccoli or just plain broccoli and serve with the Chinese Egg Noodles with Scallions and Shiitakes (page 233).

SHELF LIFE: Up to five days in the refrigerator.

Orange and Scallion Sauce

Scallions, soy sauce, and a drizzle of sesame oil give fresh orange juice a savory Asian twist

YIELD: 1 CUP, ABOUT 4 SERVINGS
PREP TIME: 5 minutes
COOK TIME: N/A

3 scallions (both white and green parts), trimmed and thinly sliced
¼ cup freshly squeezed orange juice (about ½ medium orange)
1 tablespoon soy sauce
1 tablespoon tomato paste
2 teaspoons toasted sesame oil
1 teaspoon light brown sugar

Whisk to combine all of the ingredients in a medium bowl.

PAIRINGS: This sauce goes well with stir-fried beef (page 60) and broccoli or shrimp (page 60) and asparagus. Blanch either vegetable first before adding to the stir-fry and serve with Cold Peanut Noodles with Mint and Thai Chiles (page 233).

SHELF LIFE: Up to two days in the refrigerator.

Hoisin Stir-Fry Sauce

Admittedly, this sauce doesn't scream authentic Chinese cooking, but it's tasty and colorful (particularly if you pair it with something green like broccoli or asparagus) and perfect for a quick weeknight stir-fry. The onions and red peppers are meant to be crisp-tender as is traditional in stir-fries.

YIELD: 1½ CUPS, 4 SERVINGS
PREP TIME: 6 minutes
COOK TIME: 5 minutes

1½ tablespoons canola oil
1 yellow onion, thinly sliced (about 1 cup)
½ red bell pepper, thinly sliced (about ½ cup)
⅓ cup low-sodium chicken broth or water
2 tablespoons hoisin sauce
1 tablespoon soy sauce
1 tablespoon rice vinegar
2 teaspoons toasted sesame oil
½ teaspoon Thai chile paste (like Sriracha)

Heat the oil in a medium skillet over medium-high heat until shimmering hot, about 1½ minutes. Add the onion and pepper and cook, stirring occasionally, until they start to soften and brown, about 3 minutes. In a small bowl, mix the remaining ingredients, add to the pan, and cook, stirring, until the mixture just comes to a boil.

PAIRINGS: I like tossing this sauce with broccoli or snap peas (page 50); or pair with stir-fried beef or chicken (page 56) and serve atop Japanese soba noodles.

SHELF LIFE: Up to three days in the refrigerator.

Spicy Thai Peanut and Mint Sauce

This sauce plays on Thai cuisine's wonderful penchant for mixing sweet, spicy, and sour flavors all in one dish.

YIELD: 1 CUP, 4 SERVINGS
PREP TIME: 5 minutes
COOK TIME: 6 minutes

⅓ cup roasted shelled peanuts, coarsely chopped
1 large shallot, coarsely chopped (about ¼ cup)
2 Thai chiles or 1 jalapeño, stemmed and coarsely chopped (2 to 3 tablespoons)
2 tablespoons canola oil
About ½ teaspoon kosher salt
½ cup low-sodium chicken broth
1 tablespoon freshly squeezed lime juice (about ½ lime), more to taste
2 teaspoons fish sauce
2 teaspoons granulated sugar
2 tablespoons chopped fresh mint

Set the peanuts, shallot, and chiles in a mini-chop or food processor and pulse to finely chop (you may need to scrape down the sides of the work bowl once or twice).

Heat the oil in a large skillet or wok over medium-high heat until shimmering hot, about 1½ minutes. Add the peanut mixture, sprinkle generously with salt, and cook, stirring, until the shallot starts to soften and become translucent, about 2 minutes.

In a cup measure, whisk together the chicken broth, lime juice, fish sauce, and sugar and then pour into the skillet. Cook, stirring, until the sauce comes to a boil and then reduces slightly, about 2 minutes. Stir in the mint and add more lime juice to taste.

PAIRINGS: The light fishiness of this sauce plays perfectly with thinly sliced stir-fried flank steak (page 60) or chicken (page 56). Add blanched broccoli or Chinese broccoli to round out the dish and serve with jasmine rice.

SHELF LIFE: N/A

Thai Black Pepper Sauce

This sauce was one of the revelations of a recent trip to Thailand. There's not much more to it than black pepper and soy sauce, but they form a surprisingly complex flavor pairing for a light stir-fry. Don't skimp on the black pepper.

YIELD: HEAPING ¼ CUP, 4 SERVINGS
PREP TIME: 3 minutes
COOK TIME: N/A

2 tablespoons low-sodium chicken broth or water

2 tablespoons soy sauce

2 teaspoons oyster sauce

1 teaspoon freshly ground black pepper

1 small garlic clove, minced (about ½ teaspoon)

In a small bowl, mix to combine all of the ingredients.

PAIRINGS: The black pepper in this sauce is a natural fit with stir-fried beef (page 60) or shrimp. Serve atop sliced jalapeños and shredded iceberg lettuce with steamed white rice.

SHELF LIFE: Up to three days in the refrigerator.

Seared Mango and Chile Sauce

You don't see mango much in savory cooking, save for a salsa here or there. But it fits rather nicely in this stir-fry sauce. Sear it over high heat to brown lightly and then toss it with Thai chiles, lime juice, and a touch of fish sauce.

YIELD: 1½ CUPS, 4 SERVINGS
PREP TIME: 9 minutes
COOK TIME: 5 minutes

1 large shallot, coarsely chopped (about ¼ cup)

2 Thai chiles or 1 jalapeño, cored, seeded, and coarsely chopped (2 to 3 tablespoons)

2 tablespoons canola oil

1 large mango (about ¾ pound), cut in ½-inch dice (about 1½ cups)

1 tablespoon freshly squeezed lime juice (about ½ lime)

1 teaspoon fish sauce

1 teaspoon granulated sugar

½ teaspoon Sriracha or other chile paste

2 tablespoons chopped fresh cilantro

Set the shallot and chiles in a mini-chop or food processor and pulse to finely chop (you may need to scrape down the sides of the work bowl once or twice).

Heat the oil in a 12-inch, heavy-based skillet over medium-high heat until it's shimmering hot. Add the shallot mixture and cook, stirring, until it becomes fragrant and starts to soften, about 1 minute. Stir in the mango and cook until it heats through and softens, 2 minutes. Add the lime juice, fish sauce, sugar, and Sriracha and cook, stirring, until it heats through, about 2 minutes. Remove from the heat and stir in the cilantro.

PAIRINGS: Toss with stir-fried beef or pork (page 60) and serve with lightly dressed rice noodles and some sautéed Napa cabbage (page 53).

SHELF LIFE: N/A. This sauce is best made right before stir-frying as the fresh mango will start to pickle from the surrounding acidic flavors.

Vietnamese Caramel Sauce

A quick caramel serves as the base for this sweet but savory sauce, known as *nuoc mau* in the Vietnamese kitchen. If you've never made caramel before, don't stress it. You're basically just melting sugar in a saucepan until it takes on a rich, caramel color and then whisking with a splash of chicken broth, fish sauce, and vinegar.

YIELD: ¾ CUP, 4 SERVINGS
PREP TIME: 3 minutes
COOK TIME: 8 minutes

⅓ cup light brown sugar

½ cup low-sodium chicken broth

1 tablespoon fish sauce

2 teaspoons white vinegar

2 scallions (both white and green parts), trimmed and thinly sliced

½ teaspoon Thai chile paste (like Sriracha)

¼ teaspoon crushed red pepper flakes

Heat the brown sugar in a medium saucepan over medium-high heat, swirling the pan occasionally, until it melts and starts to turn a slightly darker brown at the edges, about 2 minutes. Reduce the heat to medium and cook, whisking, until the caramel turns a uniform medium brown, about 2 minutes.

Remove from the heat and carefully whisk in the remaining ingredients. Return to the heat and cook, stirring at a gentle simmer for a couple of minutes so the flavors meld. Season with more vinegar and fish sauce to taste.

PAIRINGS: This light, brothy sauce is great with stir-fried scallops or shrimp (page 60). Accompany with stir-fried bok choy (page 58) and steamed jasmine rice.

SHELF LIFE: Up to three days in the refrigerator.

TIP: Browned, Not Burnt Sugar
Don't stray while the caramel is heating—it can go from brown to black in the time it takes to open an e-mail. Also, whisk the liquid into the caramel carefully as it will be extremely hot and create a quick flash of steam.

NOT STIR-FRIES, BUT CLOSE ENOUGH

In reality, traditional Indian and Thai curries are more gentle braises than quick stir-fries. But for the sake of our high-heat method, these spiced sauces fit just fine with the stir-fry or sauté techniques in this book. Use tender, quick-cooking cuts so these dishes come together quickly.

Indian Curry

True curries are homemade mixtures of freshly toasted and freshly ground spices. And they're great, in large part because of this spicing, but they're not necessarily weeknight-friendly. Using preground spices is a perfectly acceptable shortcut. Simmer them with onions, fresh ginger, and coconut milk, and your dining companions will think the sauce was dropped in from Mumbai.

YIELD: 1 ½ CUPS, 4 SERVINGS
PREP TIME: 5 minutes
COOK TIME: 10 minutes

1 yellow onion, cut in ½-inch dice (about 1¼ cups)
2 tablespoons coarsely chopped fresh ginger
2 tablespoons canola oil
About ½ teaspoon kosher salt
About ½ teaspoon freshly ground black pepper
1 tablespoon tomato paste
1 tablespoon curry powder
¼ teaspoon chipotle powder or cayenne
1 cup coconut milk
Freshly squeezed juice of ½ lime (about 1 tablespoon)
3 tablespoons chopped fresh cilantro

Pulse the onion and ginger in a mini-chop or food processor until finely chopped (you may need to scrape down the sides).

Heat the oil in a large skillet over medium-high heat until shimmering hot, about 1 ½ minutes. Add the onion and ginger, sprinkle generously with salt and pepper, and cook, stirring, until the onion softens and starts to brown lightly, 3 minutes. Add the tomato paste, curry powder, and chipotle powder and cook stirring for 30 seconds so they become fragrant.

Stir in the coconut milk and lime juice and bring to a boil. Simmer, stirring, until the onions become tender and the sauce thickens slightly, about 5 minutes. Stir in the cilantro and season with more salt, pepper, and lime juice to taste.

PAIRINGS: Curried lamb (page 38) and chicken (page 36) are both great or try a vegetarian curry with sautéed cauliflower and carrots (page 52) and frozen peas. Serve with steamed basmati rice.

SHELF LIFE: Up to four days in the refrigerator; reseason with lime juice before serving.

Indian Tikka Masala

This sauce streamlines the traditional masala, which is made by slowly simmering oven-baked tandoori meat in a spiced tomato sauce. Browned onions, spices, and a heavy splash of coconut milk replicate the traditional version's slow-cooked flavor.

YIELD: 2 CUPS, 6 SERVINGS
PREP TIME: 5 minutes
COOK TIME: 10 minutes

2 tablespoons canola oil
1 yellow onion, thinly sliced (about 1 cup)
1 tablespoon minced fresh ginger
About ½ teaspoon kosher salt
About ½ teaspoon freshly ground black pepper
2 teaspoons curry powder
¼ teaspoon ground cayenne
1 (15½-ounce) can diced tomatoes, drained and puréed
   (about 1¼ cups)
½ cup coconut milk
3 tablespoons chopped fresh cilantro

Heat the oil in a large skillet over medium-high heat until shimmering hot, about 1½ minutes. Add the onion and ginger, sprinkle generously with salt and pepper and cook, stirring, until the onion softens and starts to brown lightly, 3 to 4 minutes. Add the curry powder and cayenne and cook, stirring, for 30 seconds so they become fragrant.

Stir in the puréed tomato and coconut milk and bring to a boil. Simmer, stirring, until the onion becomes tender and the sauce thickens slightly, about 5 minutes. Stir in the cilantro and season with salt and pepper to taste.

PAIRINGS: Stir-fried chicken (page 56) or shrimp (page 60) go nicely with this spiced tomato sauce, or go vegetarian with cauliflower (page 52) and boiled potatoes.

SHELF LIFE: Up to four days in the refrigerator.

5-Spice and Caramelized Leek Sauce

Five-spice powder can vary according to the brand, though it generally consists of cinnamon, fennel seed, star anise, cloves, and a wildcard spice like cassia or Szechuan peppercorns. A little goes a long way, so use it sparingly.

YIELD: ¾ CUP, 4 SERVINGS
PREP TIME: 7 minutes
COOK TIME: 7 minutes

1 tablespoon canola oil
1 large leek, trimmed, outer leaves removed, cut in
   ¼-inch dice, soaked and patted dry (about 1 cup)
1 tablespoon minced ginger
About ½ teaspoon kosher salt
About ½ teaspoon freshly ground black pepper
1 teaspoon 5-spice powder
½ cup low-sodium chicken broth
1 tablespoon soy sauce
1 tablespoon rice vinegar, more to taste
2 teaspoons tomato paste
2 scallions (both white and green parts), trimmed and
   thinly sliced

Heat the oil in a large skillet over medium-high heat until shimmering hot, about 1½ minutes. Add the leek and ginger, reduce the heat to medium, sprinkle generously with salt and pepper, and cook, stirring, until the leek starts to wilt and brown in places, about 2 minutes. Add the 5-spice powder and cook, stirring, until it becomes very fragrant, about 30 seconds.

Stir in the broth, soy sauce, vinegar, and tomato paste and bring to a boil. Reduce to a simmer and cook, stirring, until the leek just becomes tender and the sauce thickens slightly, about 3 minutes. Stir in the scallions and season with more salt and pepper to taste.

PAIRINGS: This sauce is a perfect fit with stir-fried beef (page 60); accompany with steamed brown rice and stir-fried snap peas (page 50).

SHELF LIFE: Up to three days in the refrigerator.

Fragrant Ginger and Lemongrass Coconut Broth

This sauce is like a curry, only instead of spices powering a coconut milk broth, fresh aromatics like lemongrass and shallots do the trick. Lemongrass has an unmistakable citrus flavor that gives many Thai and Vietnamese sauces a fragrant base. Because it has a fibrous texture, I like to cut it into large pieces, and then fish them out and discard before serving.

YIELD: 1½ CUPS, 4 SERVINGS
PREP TIME: 6 minutes
COOK TIME: 9 minutes

2 tablespoons canola oil
2 stalks lemongrass, tops trimmed, outer leaves discarded, halved lengthwise, cut into 2-inch pieces, and smashed with the side of chef's knife
1 large shallot, finely diced (about ¼ cup)
2 Thai chiles or 1 jalapeño, stemmed, and thinly sliced
About ¼ teaspoon kosher salt
1 cup low-sodium chicken broth
½ cup coconut milk
2 teaspoons freshly squeezed lime juice
2 teaspoons light brown sugar
1 teaspoon fish sauce

Heat the oil with the lemongrass, shallot, and chiles in a medium sauté pan over high heat until they just start to sizzle steadily, about 1 minute. Reduce the heat to medium, sprinkle lightly with salt, and cook, stirring, until the shallot starts to soften and brown in places, 2 to 3 minutes.

Stir in the remaining ingredients and bring to a boil. Reduce to a simmer, cover, and cook, stirring occasionally, until the shallots are completely tender and the lemongrass infuses the broth, about 5 minutes. Discard the lemongrass if you like and season with more lime juice and fish sauce to taste.

PAIRINGS: Simmer this broth with sautéed mussels or clams (page 48) and serve with steamed brown rice. Sprinkle with fresh cilantro.

SHELF LIFE: N/A. This sauce is best made fresh.

Thai Green Curry

A combination of kaffir lime leaves and Thai basil form the traditional base for this curry. But because neither is readily available in your local supermarket, I've made this more user-friendly with regular basil and an aromatic base of ginger, garlic, and chiles.

YIELD: 1¼ CUPS, 4 SERVINGS
PREP TIME: 7 minutes
COOK TIME: 8 minutes

1 to 2 Thai chiles or 1 jalapeño, stemmed and coarsely chopped
2 tablespoons chopped fresh ginger
1 large shallot, cut in ¼-inch dice (about ¼ cup)
2 tablespoons canola oil
About ¾ teaspoon kosher salt
About ½ teaspoon freshly ground black pepper
1 teaspoon ground cumin
1 cup unsweetened coconut milk
8 basil (or Thai basil) leaves, coarsely chopped
1 tablespoon freshly squeezed lime juice (about ½ lime)
1 teaspoon granulated sugar

Add the chiles, ginger, and shallot to a food processor and pulse to finely chop. Heat the oil in a sauté pan over medium-high heat until shimmering hot, about 1½ minutes. Add the chile mixture, reduce the heat to medium, sprinkle generously with salt and pepper, and cook, stirring, so the shallot starts to soften and become translucent, about 3 minutes.

Add the cumin and cook, stirring, for 30 seconds so it becomes fragrant. Stir in the coconut milk, basil, lime juice, and sugar and bring to a boil. Cook, stirring, for another minute or two so the broth thickens slightly. Purée using an immersion blender (or an upright blender) and then add more lime juice to taste.

PAIRINGS: This fragrant sauce goes wonderfully with stir-fried shrimp (page 60) or chicken (page 56). Pair with steamed jasmine rice and sautéed Napa cabbage (page 53).

SHELF LIFE: Up to three days in the refrigerator; the green hue of this mixture fades over time.

Thai Red Curry

Red chiles traditionally color this curry, but I've cheated and added some tomato paste. This not only helps ensure the proper pigmentation, but also adds a little sweetness to go with the heat of the peppers and the acidity of the lime juice.

YIELD: 1¼ CUPS, 4 SERVINGS
PREP TIME: 6 minutes
COOK TIME: 8 minutes

1 large shallot, cut in ¼-inch dice (about ¼ cup)
2 tablespoons chopped fresh ginger
1 to 2 Thai red chiles or 1 jalapeño, stemmed and
    coarsely chopped
1½ tablespoons canola or peanut oil
About ¾ teaspoon kosher salt
About ½ teaspoon freshly ground black pepper
1 teaspoon ground coriander
2 teaspoons tomato paste
1 cup unsweetened coconut milk
1 tablespoon fish sauce
1 tablespoon freshly squeezed lime juice, more to taste

Add the shallot, ginger, and chiles to a food processor and pulse to finely chop. Heat the oil in a sauté pan over medium-high heat until shimmering hot, about 1½ minutes. Add the chile mixture, reduce the heat to medium, sprinkle generously with salt and pepper, and cook, stirring, so the shallot starts to soften and become translucent, about 3 minutes.

Add the coriander and cook, stirring, for 30 seconds so it becomes fragrant. Add the tomato paste and cook, stirring, so it coats the shallot mixture, about 30 seconds. Stir in the coconut milk, fish sauce, and lime juice and bring to a boil. Gently simmer, stirring, for a couple of minutes so the broth thickens slightly and the flavors evenly infuse the broth. Add more fish sauce or lime juice to taste.

OPTIONS: Sauté some smashed pieces of lemongrass with the shallot or whisk a teaspoon of shrimp paste (available at Asian markets) in with the coconut milk.

PAIRINGS: I like the funkiness of this sauce (hello, fish sauce!) with stir-fried beef (page 60) or something simple like tofu. Serve with steamed jasmine rice.

SHELF LIFE: Up to three days in the refrigerator.

Floating Rock's Chile-Basil Sauce

Floating Rock is a tiny mom-and-pop Cambodian restaurant formerly of Revere, Massachusetts, and soon to open in Cambridge, where assorted members of the family make, serve, and clean up the meals. The food is traditional Cambodian with warming, homey touches. This is a riff on my favorite sauce there. It bursts with spicy (Thai chiles), sweet (sugar), sour (lime), and salty (fish sauce) notes and pairs well with stir-fried ground chicken or beef.

YIELD: 1 CUP, 4 SERVINGS
PREP TIME: 7 minutes
COOK TIME: 7 minutes

1 large shallot, cut in ¼-inch dice (about ¼ cup)
1 to 2 Thai chiles or 1 jalapeño, stemmed and coarsely
    chopped
1 tablespoon chopped fresh ginger
2 tablespoons canola oil
About ¼ teaspoon kosher salt
½ cup chicken broth
1 tablespoon freshly squeezed lime juice
2 teaspoons fish sauce
1½ teaspoons granulated sugar
8 basil or Thai basil leaves, ripped into pieces

Pulse the shallot, chiles, and ginger in a mini-chop or food processor until finely chopped (you may need to scrape down the sides). Heat the oil in a medium saucepan over medium-high heat until shimmering hot, about 1½ minutes. Reduce the heat to medium, add the ginger mixture, sprinkle lightly with salt, and cook, stirring, until the shallot just starts to turn translucent and soften, about 3 minutes.

Add the chicken broth, lime juice, fish sauce, and sugar and bring to a boil. Reduce to a simmer and cook for 3 minutes so the aromatics infuse the broth. Remove from the heat and stir in the basil.

OPTIONS: Sprinkle with chopped, roasted peanuts and fresh cilantro leaves.

PAIRINGS: Follow Floating Rock's lead and pair this with sautéed ground beef or chicken (page 40) and serve with lightly-dressed rice noodles and stir-fried broccoli (page 58).

SHELF LIFE: N/A

Taiwanese 3-Cup Sauce

This intense broth gets its name from the equal measurements of its 3 main ingredients—soy sauce, rice wine or sherry, and water (or chicken broth if you prefer). Though traditionally meats, chicken, or seafood are simmered in the broth (from start to finish), I like stir-frying them first so they stay moist and then braising them for a minute or two in this sauce.

YIELD: 1¼ CUPS, 4 SERVINGS
PREP TIME: 6 minutes
COOK TIME: 7 minutes

¼ cup soy sauce
¼ cup Shaoxing rice wine or dry sherry
2 tablespoons toasted sesame oil
1 tablespoon granulated sugar
2 garlic cloves, smashed
2 Thai chiles or 1 jalapeño, thinly sliced crosswise
2-inch knob ginger, peeled and thinly sliced
4 basil leaves (or Thai basil if you have), torn into pieces
2 scallions (both white and green parts), trimmed and
     thinly sliced

Whisk ¼ cup water with all of the ingredients with the exception of the basil and scallion in a medium saucepan and bring to a boil. Gently simmer for 5 minutes so the flavors mix and meld. Discard the garlic and ginger, if you like, and then stir in the basil and scallions.

PAIRINGS: This sauce is perfect for stir-fried calamari or shrimp (page 60); serve with Cold Peanut Noodles with Mint and Thai Chiles (page 233) and stir-fried bok choy (page 58).

TIP: There are nine ingredients in this sauce, but I'm not cheating. I've allowed myself cooking oil in each recipe and in this sauce, the sesame oil acts as the cooking oil. That's cool, right?

IV. SAUTÉ SAUCES

The sauces in this grouping are prepared in a separate pan from the sear before the two are simmered together. The primary reason for preparing the sear and the sauté sauce separately (as opposed to making them in the same pan like a pan sauce) is that these sauces involve more intensive or prolonged cooking. Also, this allows you to make both the sauce and the sear simultaneously, which ultimately speeds up your preparations.

BASIC SAUTÉ SAUCE TECHNIQUE

Sauté aromatics and quick-cooking vegetables, add broth (such as chicken broth, mushroom soaking liquid, or canned tomatoes), and simmer until tender and the sauce thickens slightly.

KEEP ON SIMMERING

To keep things on the quick side (and stay within our self-imposed time constraints), many of these sautéed sauces are pulled from the flame after a brief simmer, just enough time for the different flavors to meld. If you are in a slow-cooking state of mind, keep simmering them to your liking; just add a splash of chicken broth or water if they reduce too much.

TOMATO SAUCES FROM AROUND THE GLOBE

The first part of this section contains tomato sauces, both fresh and canned. Red sauces became passé years ago as folks started to discover the full breadth of Italian cuisine. But tomato-based sauces can still be plenty nuanced and tasty, whether it's a basic marinara or a fresh tomato and fennel mixture. And these sauces go with most anything you can sear.

Fresh Tomato and Basil Sauce

I might endorse plenty of shortcuts in this book, but I don't condone buying tomatoes out of season (or getting gouged for roses on Valentine's Day, but that's a whole other story). Wait until the time is right (early August where I live) and then, like a squirrel before the frost, get busy stocking away this sauce. Use a wide sauté pan—the large surface area cooks the tomatoes quickly, keeping their flavor and texture fresh.

YIELD: 1½ CUPS, 4 SERVINGS
PREP TIME: 5 minutes
COOK TIME: 9 minutes

2 tablespoons olive oil
2 garlic cloves, smashed
¼ teaspoon crushed red pepper flakes
1½ pounds ripe plum tomatoes (about 8 medium),
    cored and cut in ½-inch dice (about 3 cups)
About ¾ teaspoon kosher salt
About ½ teaspoon freshly ground black pepper
6 basil leaves, torn into pieces

Heat the oil and garlic in a large sauté pan or skillet over medium heat until the garlic starts to brown lightly and becomes very fragrant, about 3 minutes. Stir in the red pepper flakes and cook for 15 seconds so they sizzle steadily.

Raise the heat to medium-high, add the tomatoes, sprinkle generously with salt and pepper, and cook, stirring, until they start to soften and melt into a sauce, 4 to 6 minutes. Discard the garlic cloves and purée the sauce, if you like, using an immersion blender (or a regular blender). Stir in the basil and season with more salt and pepper to taste.

OPTIONS: Add a layer of flavor by stirring in a teaspoon of balsamic vinegar or a pinch of sugar if the tomatoes are overly acidic.

PAIRINGS: I like tucking a sautéed mild fish like cod (page 44) into this sauce, or tossing with seared green beans (page 50). Serve either with a mushroom risotto.

SHELF LIFE: Up to three days in the refrigerator.

Fresh Tomato and Fennel Sauce

Yes, fennel tastes like black licorice and maybe you don't like black licorice, but I don't either and I still love the way this aromatic root vegetable adds subtle sweetness and complexity to the tomatoes in this sauce. Try it.

YIELD: 2 CUPS, 4 SERVINGS
PREP TIME: 6 minutes
COOK TIME: 10 minutes

3 tablespoons olive oil
1 medium fennel bulb (about ¾ pound), outer layers discarded, cored, and cut in ½-inch dice (about 1½ cups)
About 1¼ teaspoons kosher salt
About ½ teaspoon freshly ground black pepper
1½ pounds ripe plum tomatoes (about 8), cored and cut in ½-inch dice (about 3 cups)
¼ teaspoon crushed red pepper flakes
6 basil leaves, torn into pieces, or 2 tablespoons chopped fresh tarragon

Heat the oil in a large sauté pan or skillet over medium-high heat until shimmering hot, about 1½ minutes. Add the fennel, sprinkle with salt and pepper, and cook, stirring, until it starts to soften and brown in places, about 3 minutes.

Add the tomatoes and red pepper flakes, sprinkle generously with salt and pepper, and cook, stirring, until the fennel becomes tender and the tomatoes melt into a sauce, about 5 minutes. Stir in the basil and season with more salt or pepper to taste.

OPTIONS: Wherever fennel goes, sausage can most certainly follow. Sauté chunks of Italian sausage before adding the fennel to this sauce.

PAIRINGS: I like how the fresh fennel in this sauce goes with sautéed mussels or clams (page 48). A baguette is all you'll need to make it a meal.

SHELF LIFE: Up to three days in the refrigerator.

. . . .

TIP: Go with What You Got for Fresh Herbs
There is no rule for what fresh herb goes best with which sauce (rather, it's mostly a question of personal taste). If you're like me, you usually have one or two herbs kicking around in the fridge, but not the whole spectrum. Don't be shy to allow your own personal tastes to guide you when subbing one in for another.

. . . .

Black Olive and Cherry Tomato Sauce

Cherry tomatoes can be exceedingly sweet. Here, olives, crushed pepper flakes, and fresh rosemary help ground that sweetness.

YIELD: 1½ CUPS, 4 SERVINGS
PREP TIME: 6 minutes
COOK TIME: 9 minutes

3 tablespoons olive oil
2 scallions, trimmed and thinly sliced (white and green
    parts kept separate)
1 teaspoon chopped fresh thyme
¼ teaspoon crushed red pepper flakes
1 pint cherry or grape tomatoes, halved (about 2½ cups)
About ¾ teaspoon kosher salt
About ½ teaspoon freshly ground black pepper
½ cup pitted Kalamata olives, coarsely chopped

Heat the oil, the white parts of the scallions, the thyme, and red pepper flakes in a large sauté pan or skillet over medium-high heat until the scallion starts to soften and brown in places, about 3 minutes.

Add the tomatoes, sprinkle generously with salt and pepper, and cook, stirring, until the tomatoes soften into a sauce, about 6 minutes. Stir in the green parts of the scallion and the olives and season with more salt and pepper to taste.

OPTIONS: Add chopped capers and anchovies and this sauce becomes a fresh puttanesca. Or sprinkle with crumbled feta for a touch of richness.

PAIRINGS: The brininess of the olives pairs well with sautéed swordfish (page 42) or cod (page 44). Serve with sautéed broccoli rabe (page 50) and Buttery Herbed Couscous (page 237) for a vegetarian side dish, try simmering this sauce with sautéed green beans (page 50).

SHELF LIFE: Up to three days in the refrigerator.

Quick Marinara

Everybody should have a simple marinara in their repertoire. That there is a whole aisle devoted to jarred pasta sauces in most supermarkets simply makes no sense. It's just as easy to make your own marinara as it is to heat up the jarred stuff, and the homemade is far cheaper and tastier. Infuse a splash of olive oil with garlic, red pepper flakes, and rosemary, simmer with good canned tomatoes, and you're there.

YIELD: 1½ CUPS, ABOUT 4 SERVINGS
PREP TIME: 4 minutes
COOK TIME: 10 minutes

2 tablespoons olive oil

3 garlic cloves, smashed

2 teaspoons chopped fresh rosemary or 1 teaspoon
    dried oregano

Heaping ¼ teaspoon crushed red pepper flakes

1 (15½-ounce) can diced tomatoes, puréed (about 1½ cups)

About ¾ teaspoon kosher salt

About ½ teaspoon freshly ground black pepper

Heat the oil and the garlic in a medium saucepan over medium heat until the garlic starts to brown lightly and becomes very fragrant, about 3 minutes. Add the rosemary and red pepper flakes and cook, stirring, for 30 seconds so they become fragrant and sizzle steadily.

Add the puréed tomato, sprinkle with salt and pepper, and bring to a boil. Cover and simmer, stirring occasionally, until the garlic evenly infuses its flavor, about 6 minutes. Fish out and discard the garlic cloves and season with salt and pepper to taste.

OPTIONS: In August or July when there are good local tomatoes, use fresh plum tomatoes—just purée them or pass them through a food mill before adding to the sauce.

PAIRINGS: Ladle this sauce over sautéed steaks (page 38) or chicken breasts (page 31), sprinkle with mozzarella, and set under the broiler to melt the cheese; in Italy, this technique is known as *pizzaiola* (or, made like a pizza). Serve with a salad of arugula and shaved Parmesan and a crusty loaf of bread.

SHELF LIFE: Up to five days in the refrigerator or two months in the freezer.

Spicy Tomato Vodka Sauce

What's vodka doing in a tomato sauce? Acting as a relatively mild flavoring: think wine with a bit more zip. This sauce might not cure a hangover, but it's a perfect weeknight accompaniment for seared cutlets or steaks.

YIELD: 1½ CUPS, ABOUT 4 SERVINGS
PREP TIME: 4 minutes
COOK TIME: 10 minutes

2 tablespoons olive oil

1 garlic clove, minced (about ¾ teaspoon)

Heaping ½ teaspoon crushed red pepper flakes

1 teaspoon chopped fresh rosemary or 1 teaspoon dried oregano

1 (15½-ounce) can diced tomatoes (and their juices), puréed (about 1½ cups)

3 tablespoons vodka

About ¾ teaspoon kosher salt

About ½ teaspoon freshly ground black pepper

2 to 3 tablespoons heavy cream

2 tablespoons chopped fresh parsley (optional)

Heat the oil and the garlic in a medium saucepan over medium heat until the garlic starts to brown lightly at its edges and becomes very fragrant, about 2½ minutes. Stir in the red pepper flakes and rosemary and cook for 30 seconds so they become fragrant and sizzle steadily.

Add the puréed tomato and vodka, sprinkle generously with salt and pepper, and bring to a boil. Reduce to a steady simmer, whisk in the cream, and cook, stirring occasionally, until the sauce thickens slightly and the flavors meld, about 5 minutes.

Stir in the parsley, if using, and season with salt and pepper to taste.

PAIRINGS: Yes, this rich sauce goes great with spaghetti, but I also like it with sautéed veal cutlets (page 36) or pork chops (page 38); serve with Penne with Broccoli and Sun-Dried Tomatoes (page 233).

SHELF LIFE: Up to four days in the refrigerator or two months in the freezer.

Cacciatore Sauce

A traditional cacciatore involves slowly simmering browned chicken parts (or rabbit or veal) with peppers, tomatoes, and onions in the style of the hunter's wife ("a la cacciatora"), so they meld together and intensify. You can't necessarily replicate that slow-cooked flavor in 15 minutes or so but this sauce comes close.

YIELD: 3 CUPS, 4 SERVINGS
PREP TIME: 5 minutes
COOK TIME: 11 minutes

2 tablespoons olive oil

1 red bell pepper, cut in ¼-inch dice (1½ cups)

About 1 teaspoon kosher salt

1 large garlic clove, minced (about 1 teaspoon)

8 ounces thinly sliced white mushrooms

About ½ teaspoon freshly ground black pepper

½ cup dry white wine

1 (15½-ounce) can diced tomatoes, puréed (about 1½ cups)

1 teaspoon chopped fresh rosemary or 1 teaspoon dried oregano

Heaping ¼ teaspoon crushed red pepper flakes

Heat the oil in a large saucepan over high heat until shimmering hot, about 1 minute. Add the red pepper, sprinkle with salt, and cook, stirring until it starts to brown and soften, about 2 minutes. Add the garlic and cook, stirring, until it sizzles steadily and becomes fragrant, about 30 seconds.

Add the mushrooms, sprinkle with salt and pepper, and cook, stirring, until they start to brown in places and become tender, about 2 minutes. Add the wine and cook, scraping the bottom of the pan with a wooden spoon to pick up any of the caramelized crust, until almost completely reduced, about 2 minutes.

Stir in the puréed tomato, rosemary, and pepper flakes and bring to a boil. Reduce to a steady simmer, cover, and cook, stirring occasionally, until the peppers soften and the flavors start to meld, about 4 minutes.

PAIRINGS: Dredge chunks of boneless chicken thighs or breasts in flour before sautéing (page 31) so they stay moist and then simmer with this sauce until the chicken just cooks through. Serve with pasta tossed with lemon and asparagus.

SHELF LIFE: Up to three days in the refrigerator.

TIP: It's fine to go with the supermarket presliced mushrooms to save a little time.

Salsa Capricciosa

Many pizzerias have a capricciosa pie, literally one made according to the whim of the chef. Generally, it includes a mixture of cured ham, garlic, and hot peppers. This sauce, emulating the pizza, is at once spicy, acidic, and sharp, a perfect topping for pork chops.

YIELD: 2¼ CUPS, ABOUT 4 SERVINGS
PREP TIME: 6 minutes
COOK TIME: 8 minutes

2 ounces thinly sliced prosciutto (domestic is fine), cut into strips
2 tablespoons olive oil
3 tablespoons chopped jarred hot cherry peppers or sliced jalapeños
2 teaspoons chopped fresh rosemary
1 garlic clove, minced (about ¾ teaspoon)
1 (15½-ounce) can diced tomatoes (and their juices), puréed (about 1½ cups)
About ½ teaspoon kosher salt
About ½ teaspoon freshly ground black pepper
¾ cup grated pecorino Romano

Cook the prosciutto with the oil in a nonstick skillet over medium heat, stirring occasionally, until the prosciutto starts to crisp and brown, 2 to 3 minutes. Using a slotted spoon, transfer the prosciutto to a plate lined with paper towel.

Add the cherry peppers, rosemary, and garlic and cook, stirring, until the garlic becomes fragrant and starts to color lightly at the edges and the rosemary becomes fragrant, about 1 minute.

Stir in the puréed tomato, sprinkle generously with salt and pepper, and cook until it simmers steadily and reduces a bit, about 3 minutes. Serve sprinkled with the crisp prosciutto and pecorino.

PAIRINGS: Just the kind of sauce to punch up veal cutlets (page 36) or bone-in pork chops (page 38). Serve with sautéed asparagus (page 50) and a fresh ciabatta.

SHELF LIFE: Three days in the fridge; one month in the freezer.

Puttanesca Sauce

This origin of this sauce is purportedly intertwined with the prostitutes of Italy. It was said that this sauce was so easy to make, its preparation would vibe with most anyone's work schedule, no matter how busy.

YIELD: 2 CUPS, 4 SERVINGS
PREP TIME: 4 minutes
COOK TIME: 7 minutes

½ cup pitted Kalamata or Gaeta olives
3 tablespoons nonpareil capers, rinsed and patted dry
2 anchovy filets, rinsed and patted dry (optional)
2 tablespoons olive oil
1 garlic clove, minced (about ¾ teaspoon)
1 teaspoon chopped fresh thyme
½ teaspoon crushed red pepper flakes
1 (15½-ounce) can diced tomatoes (and their juices), puréed (about 1½ cups)
Kosher salt and freshly ground black pepper

Add the olives, capers, and anchovies (if using) to a food processor or mini-chop and pulse to coarsely chop.

Heat the oil and garlic in a large saucepan over medium-high heat, stirring, until the garlic becomes fragrant and starts to color lightly at the edges, about 1½ minutes. Stir in the thyme and red pepper flakes and cook so they become fragrant and sizzle steadily, about 15 seconds. Stir in the olive mixture and cook, stirring, for 15 seconds so it, too, sizzles steadily.

Add the puréed tomato and bring to a boil. Reduce to a steady simmer and cook until it reduces a bit and the flavors of the olive mixture become evenly infused, about 4 minutes. Season with salt and pepper to taste; remember the olives and capers are salty.

PAIRINGS: Pair this sauce with sautéed boneless, skinless chicken thighs (page 31) or sautéed shrimp (page 46) and toss with a small, sturdy pasta like penne or ziti.

SHELF LIFE: Up to three days in the refrigerator or indefinitely in the freezer.

Seared Mushroom and Zucchini Sauce

Though zucchini is available year-round, it's at its sweetest in the summer months. Follow this seasonal pull and sub a couple cups of diced fresh tomatoes in for the canned.

YIELD: 2½ CUPS, ABOUT 4 SERVINGS
PREP TIME: 6 minutes
COOK TIME: 9 minutes

2 tablespoons olive oil

2 large garlic cloves, smashed

1 medium zucchini (about 6 ounces), cut in ½-inch dice (about 1¼ cups)

6 ounces thinly sliced mushrooms

1 teaspoon chopped fresh thyme or rosemary or 1 tablespoon chopped fresh oregano

¼ teaspoon crushed red pepper flakes

About 1 teaspoon kosher salt

About ½ teaspoon freshly ground black pepper

1 (15½-ounce) can diced tomatoes, drained

Heat the oil and garlic in a large sauté pan over medium-high heat, stirring occasionally, until the garlic starts to brown lightly and becomes very fragrant, about 2 minutes. Add the zucchini, mushrooms, fresh herbs, and red pepper flakes and sprinkle generously with salt and pepper. Cook, stirring, until both the mushrooms and zucchini start to soften and brown in places, about 3 minutes.

Add the tomato and bring to a rapid simmer. Lower the heat to medium, cover, and cook, stirring occasionally, until the zucchini and mushrooms cook through but are still toothy, about 4 minutes. Season with more salt and pepper to taste.

PAIRINGS: Toss with sautéed boneless skinless thighs (page 31) for a quick, but hearty chicken stew or nap on top of sautéed cod (page 44). Serve with Israeli Couscous with Lemon Cream and Fresh Oregano (page 234).

SHELF LIFE: N/A. Best made fresh as the zucchini and mushrooms lose their light, toothy texture.

Amatriciana Sauce

This hopped-up red sauce holds special memories for me of Rome where I cooked for eight months at a fancy seafood restaurant. On Mondays (my off day), I would wander the city in search of small neighborhood trattorias, nose my way into a small corner table, and quietly feast while I studied my Italian verbs. Of all the traditional Roman dishes, this sauce was my favorite. It's traditionally made with guanciale, a cured cut of pork jowls similar in flavor to pancetta. You can use pancetta or even bacon, though make sure the strips are thick so they add texture to the sauce.

YIELD: 2¼ CUPS, 4 SERVINGS

PREP TIME: 5 minutes

COOK TIME: 11 minutes

3 ounces thickly sliced guanciale, pancetta, or bacon, cut into ¼-inch strips

1 tablespoon olive oil

½ teaspoon crushed red pepper flakes

1 large red onion (about 8 ounces), thinly sliced

About 1 teaspoon kosher salt

About ½ teaspoon freshly ground black pepper

1 (15½-ounce) can diced tomatoes (and their juices), puréed

1 teaspoon chopped fresh rosemary

¾ cup grated pecorino Romano (optional)

Cook the guanciale (or pancetta or bacon) with the oil in a large skillet over high heat until it starts to sizzle steadily, 1 minute. Reduce the heat to medium and cook, stirring occasionally, until it starts to crisp and brown, about 4 minutes. Using a slotted spoon, transfer to a plate lined with paper towel.

Add the red pepper flakes and cook, stirring, for 15 seconds so they sizzle steadily. Add the onion, sprinkle with salt and pepper, and cook, stirring, until it wilts and starts to brown at the edges, about 3 minutes.

Add the puréed tomato and rosemary, sprinkle with salt, and cook until the sauce simmers steadily and reduces a little bit, about 3 minutes. Stir in the reserved guanciale and serve sprinkled with the pecorino.

PAIRINGS: Traditionally, this sauce goes with bucatini (a cross between spaghetti and ziti), though I like pairing it with a mild, plain fish like cod (page 44) or halibut (page 42). Serve with steamed artichokes and a loaf of sourdough.

SHELF LIFE: Three to four days refrigerated; up to three months in the freezer.

Spanish Stewed Chorizo and Garbanzos

Roasted red peppers are an essential player in Spanish cuisine and, of them all, the small, slightly spicy piquillos from the northern region of Navarra (not far from where Rioja wines are produced) are the most prized. Jarred piquillos are increasingly available in supermarkets in the United States though you can use any old roasted red peppers. The same goes for the chorizo, though look for the Spanish brand Palacios.

YIELD: 2½ CUPS, 4 SERVINGS

PREP TIME: 4 minutes

COOK TIME: 12 minutes

1 tablespoon olive oil

6 ounces chorizo, cut in ½-inch pieces (about 1 cup)

2 garlic cloves, smashed

⅓ cup dry sherry

1 cup low-sodium chicken broth

1 cup canned garbanzos, rinsed well

3 jarred piquillo peppers (or 1 large jarred roasted red pepper), drained and diced

2 teaspoons chopped fresh thyme

Kosher salt and freshly ground black pepper

Heat the oil in a large sauté pan over medium-high heat until shimmering hot, about 1½ minutes. Add the chorizo and cook, stirring, until it starts to brown, about 2 minutes. Add the garlic and cook, stirring, until it sizzles steadily and becomes fragrant, about 30 seconds.

Add the sherry and cook, scraping the bottom of the pan with a wooden spoon to pick up any browned crust, until it almost completely reduces, about 1 minute. Add the remaining ingredients, bring to a boil, and then simmer for 5 minutes so the flavors mix and meld. Discard the garlic and season with salt and pepper to taste.

PAIRINGS: Ladle this hardy broth over sautéed cod (page 44) or simmer with sautéed clams (page 48) and serve with a rustic loaf of bread and and escarole salad.

SHELF LIFE: Up to four days in the refrigerator or indefinitely in the freezer.

Cajun Creole Sauce

This aromatic sauce is one of those regional specialties that people from Louisiana might not find completely authentic but the rest of us should like just fine.

YIELD: 2½ CUPS, ABOUT 4 SERVINGS
PREP TIME: 7 minutes
COOK TIME: 9 minutes

2 tablespoons olive oil
1 small yellow onion, diced (about ¾ cup)
½ green bell pepper, cut in ¼-inch dice (about ¾ cup)
About 1 teaspoon kosher salt
About ½ teaspoon freshly ground black pepper
1 garlic clove, minced (about 1 teaspoon)
1 bay leaf, broken into pieces
¾ teaspoon pimentón de la Vera or chipotle powder
1 (15½-ounce) can diced tomatoes (and their juices), puréed
4 basil leaves, chopped (optional)

Set the oil, onion, and bell pepper in a large sauté pan over medium-high heat, sprinkle generously with salt and pepper and cook, stirring occasionally, until the onion wilts and starts to brown at its edges, about 4 minutes.

Add the garlic, bay leaf, and pimentón and cook, stirring, for 30 seconds so they become fragrant. Add the tomato, bring to a simmer, and then cook, covered and stirring, for 4 minutes so the flavors mix and meld.

Stir in basil, if using, and season with salt and pepper to taste.

OPTIONS: Toss in some chorizo or sliced okra during the initial sautéing stage.

PAIRINGS: This sauce goes wonderfully with seared shrimp (page 46) or sautéed chicken thighs (page 31); serve over buttered Uncle Ben's rice.

SHELF LIFE: Up to three days in the refrigerator.

Stewed Cannellini Beans with Rosemary and Crisp Bacon

Here, a host of flavorings give canned white beans some bounce. A little bacon fat adds richness, jarred roasted red peppers offer some sweetness, and lemon (both the juice and the zest) brightens up the dish.

YIELD: 2 CUPS, ABOUT 4 SERVINGS
PREP TIME: 4 minutes
COOK TIME: 11 minutes

2 ounces thick bacon (about 2 slices), cut into thin strips
1 tablespoon olive oil
2 teaspoons chopped fresh rosemary
1 large garlic clove, minced (about 1 teaspoon)
Scant ¼ teaspoon crushed red pepper flakes
1 (15½-ounce) can cannellini beans, rinsed and drained well
1 cup low-sodium chicken broth
1 jarred roasted red pepper, drained and thinly sliced
    (about ½ cup)
½ lemon, zested and juiced
¾ teaspoon freshly ground black pepper
Kosher salt

Cook the bacon with the oil in a medium skillet over medium-high heat, stirring occasionally, until it renders most of its fat and starts to brown, about 4 minutes. Using a slotted spoon, transfer it to a plate lined with paper towels.

Add the rosemary, garlic, and red pepper flakes and cook, swirling around the pan, until they sizzle steadily and become fragrant, about 30 seconds. Add the beans, chicken broth, roasted red pepper, and lemon zest, bring to a boil, and then reduce to a steady simmer. Cook, stirring, until the broth thickens a little and the flavors meld, about 4 minutes.

Stir in 1 tablespoon of the lemon juice and the black pepper and season with more lemon juice, salt, and pepper to taste (remember the bacon is salty). Serve sprinkled with the bacon.

PAIRINGS: Ladle this soupy sauce into a shallow bowl and top with sautéed salmon or halibut (page 42) and accompany with a baguette and sautéed spinach (page 53). Or turn this sauce into a vegetarian main course by omitting the bacon, stirring in some grated Parmigiano, and simmering with a sautéed hearty green (page 53) like Dinosaur kale or Swiss chard.

SHELF LIFE: Two to three days in the refrigerator.

TIP: Rinse Canned Beans
Most canned beans have a doggy smell upon opening that is not very appetizing, but if you give the beans a quick rinse, they quickly freshen up and also lose that slightly slimy texture that from the canning process.

Venetian Agradolce Sauce with Raisins and Pine Nuts

I learned this sauce from Italian cooking master Giuliano Bugialli. It's one of the sweet and sour mixtures that evolved during the sieges of Venice as a manner of preserving fish. Like many food techniques borne out of necessity, it proves to be tasty, too.

YIELD: 1 CUP, ABOUT 4 SERVINGS
PREP TIME: 6 minutes
COOK TIME: 6 minutes

2 tablespoons olive oil
1 garlic clove, minced (about 1 teaspoon)
½ cup low-sodium chicken broth
¼ cup pine nuts, toasted
¼ cup raisins
2 tablespoons red wine vinegar
1 tablespoon granulated sugar
2 tablespoons chopped fresh parsley
Kosher salt and freshly ground black pepper

Heat the oil with the garlic in a medium saucepan over medium-high heat, stirring, until it sizzles steadily and just starts to turn light brown at its edges, about 2 minutes. Whisk in all the remaining ingredients with the exception of the parsley and bring to a boil. Simmer for a couple of minutes so the raisins plump. Stir in the parsley and season with salt and pepper to taste.

OPTIONS: Sprinkle with coarse toasted bread crumbs (see bread crumbs tip on page 231).

PAIRINGS: This intense broth adds zip to mild fish like sautéed cod or sole (page 44) or stands up to the assertiveness of sautéed tuna or swordfish (page 42). Keep the Italian theme going by pairing with sautéed broccoli rabe (page 50).

SHELF LIFE: Four days in the refrigerator.

Lemon Artichoke Sauce

Bright, acidic ingredients like lemon and sun-dried tomatoes compliment artichokes' slightly astringent flavor. Fresh artichokes are wonderful, but labor-intensive. If they are in season (early spring) and you have the time, boil some artichokes, peel to the hearts, and thinly slice.

YIELD: 1¾ CUPS, 4 SERVINGS
PREP TIME: 5 minutes
COOK TIME: 8 minutes

2 tablespoons unsalted butter
2 garlic cloves, smashed
1 (15-ounce) can artichoke hearts, drained and thinly sliced (about 1¼ cups)
¾ cup low-sodium chicken broth
2 sun-dried tomatoes, coarsely chopped (about 3 tablespoons)
1 tablespoon freshly squeezed lemon juice, more to taste
2 tablespoons chopped fresh parsley
Kosher salt and freshly ground black pepper

Heat the butter and garlic in a medium sauté pan over medium-high heat, stirring, until the butter melts and the garlic starts to sizzle steadily and become fragrant, about 1½ minutes. Add the artichokes and cook, stirring, until they heat through and start to brown lightly, about 2 minutes.

Add the chicken broth and sun-dried tomatoes and bring to a boil. Lower to a gentle simmer and cook, stirring occasionally, until the sun-dried tomatoes color the broth and the artichokes soften completely, about 4 minutes. Stir in the lemon juice and parsley and season with salt and pepper to taste. Discard the garlic cloves before serving.

PAIRINGS: Ladle this broth over a mild fish like cod (page 44) or halibut (page 42) and serve with boiled potatoes or Pesto Mashed Potatoes (page 235) if you have the time.

SHELF LIFE: Up to three days in the refrigerator.

Sautéed Bacon and Browned Apples

Try to pick up thick slices of bacon and dice them into large cubes, about the same size as the apple, so you get a nice contrast in textures and flavor between the two.

YIELD: 1½ CUPS, 4 SERVINGS
PREP TIME: 6 minutes
COOK TIME: 9 minutes

2 ounces thick bacon (about 2 slices), cut into ½-inch dice
1 tablespoon olive oil
1 firm, medium-sweet apple (like Fuji or Gala), peeled, cored, and cut in 1-inch pieces (about 1¼ cups)
About ¼ teaspoon kosher salt
About ¼ teaspoon freshly ground black pepper
½ teaspoon ground cumin
¼ cup apple juice or cider
1 teaspoon cider vinegar
1 teaspoon chopped fresh thyme

Cook the bacon with the oil in a medium skillet over high heat until it starts to sizzle steadily, about 1 minute. Reduce the heat to medium and cook, stirring occasionally, until the bacon renders most of its fat and starts to brown, about 4 minutes. Using a slotted spoon, transfer it to a plate lined with paper towels.

Add the apple, sprinkle lightly with salt and pepper and the cumin and cook, stirring, until it starts to brown and soften, about 3 minutes. Add the apple juice, vinegar, and thyme and bring to a boil, stirring. Season with salt and pepper to taste and stir in the bacon.

PAIRINGS: Pair this rustic sauce with sautéed medallions of pork tenderloin (page 36). Serve with sautéed Brussels sprouts (page 52) and a warm baguette for a nice autumn meal.

SHELF LIFE: N/A. The apple will suffer when you try to reheat this sauce.

Brown Butter and Rosemary Sauce

The milk solids in butter give it depth of flavor, but also can cause it to burn. In a brown butter, these milk solids walk a delicate tightrope between gathering toasted flavor and crossing over to the dark, burnt side. It's not nearly as ominous as I'm making it sound if you stick close during cooking.

YIELD: ½ CUP, ABOUT 4 SERVINGS
PREP TIME: 3 minutes
COOK TIME: 7 minutes

4 tablespoons unsalted butter
1 teaspoon chopped fresh rosemary
¼ cup low-sodium chicken broth
1 tablespoon freshly squeezed lemon juice
Kosher salt and freshly ground black pepper

Heat the butter in a large skillet over medium-high heat, swirling the pan, until it melts and its bubbling foam starts to cook off, about 1½ minutes. Reduce the heat to medium, and continue cooking and swirling the pan so the butter starts to turn light brown and acquires a fragrant, nutty essence, about 2 to 4 more minutes. Add the rosemary and cook, stirring, for 15 seconds so it sizzles and becomes fragrant. Add the chicken broth and lemon juice and bring to a boil. Season with salt and pepper to taste.

OPTIONS: Sub fresh sage leaves in for the rosemary—add them a minute or two earlier so the sage becomes crisp.

PAIRINGS: This butter goes best with lean, mildly flavored ingredients. Sautéed chicken breasts (page 31) fit that description, though even better might be a thin filet of sole (page 44) for a preparation that's almost like sole meunière. Serve with Pesto Mashed Potatoes (page 235).

SHELF LIFE: NA.

SOUTH OF THE BORDER CORNER

Here starts a little Tex–Mex, New Mexican, and Mexican section of hearty, spiced mixtures that form quick braises when briefly simmered with ground beef, sautéed chicken, or pork.

New Mexican Green Chile Sauce

There are a couple of glorious weeks in the late summer when I can find fresh New Mexican Hatch chiles here in the Northeast. These peppers have a wonderful flavor, slightly spicy, concentrated, and intense, which goes great in sautés, soups, and braises. Because canned green chiles may be all that's available, I list them as the primary option here.

YIELD: 1½ CUPS, 4 SERVINGS
PREP TIME: 5 minutes (longer if you use fresh chiles)
COOK TIME: 7 minutes

2 tablespoons olive oil
2 medium garlic cloves, minced (about 1½ teaspoons)
2 (4½-ounce) cans diced green chiles, drained, or 3
    Hatch chiles or Anaheim peppers, broiled until
    browned, skinned, seeded, and coarsely chopped
About ½ teaspoon kosher salt
½ teaspoon ground cumin
½ teaspoon chile powder
½ cup low-sodium chicken broth
2 teaspoons cider vinegar
1 tablespoon chopped fresh oregano (optional)

Heat the oil and garlic in a medium sauté pan over medium-high heat until the garlic starts to sizzle steadily, about 1½ minutes. Add the chiles, sprinkle with salt, and cook, stirring, so they start to sizzle steadily and brown in places, about 2 minutes. Add the cumin and chile powder and cook, stirring, for 30 seconds so the spices become fragrant.

Stir in the chicken broth, cider vinegar, and oregano, if using, and bring to a boil. Simmer for a couple of minutes so the chiles infuse the broth. Purée using an immersion blender or a regular blender and season with salt and pepper to taste.

OPTIONS: A splash of cream smoothes out the texture and flavor of this sauce.

PAIRINGS: Turn into a quick braise with sautéed chicken (page 31) or pork tenderloin (page 34). Serve with cilantro and lime rice and pinto beans.

SHELF LIFE: Two to three days in the refrigerator.

Spicy Chipotle White Bean Chili

Yes, you'd be hard-pressed to find many chili recipes that take only fifteen minutes. But this one works—its measured spice and thick texture (the latter created by puréeing canned beans and tomatoes) will fool most anyone into thinking it was slow-cooked.

YIELD: 2½ CUPS, ABOUT 4 SERVINGS
PREP TIME: 4 minutes
COOK TIME: 10 minutes

1 (15-ounce) can cannellini or navy beans, rinsed and drained well
1 cup canned diced tomatoes (and their juices)
1 tablespoon chopped canned chipotle pepper plus 1 tablespoon adobo sauce
2 teaspoons cider vinegar
2 tablespoons olive oil
2 garlic cloves, minced (about 2 teaspoons)
1 teaspoon chile powder
1 teaspoon ground cumin
About ½ teaspoon kosher salt
About ½ teaspoon freshly ground black pepper

In a blender or using an immersion blender, purée ½ cup of the beans (reserve the remainder) with the tomatoes (and their juices), chipotle, adobo sauce, and vinegar.

Heat the oil and garlic in a medium saucepan over medium-high heat until it starts to sizzle steadily, about 1½ minutes. Add the chile powder and cumin, sprinkle with salt and pepper, and cook for 15 seconds, stirring, so they become fragrant.

Add the puréed bean mixture as well as the reserved beans and bring to a boil, stirring. Reduce to a simmer, cover, and cook, stirring occasionally, until the mixture thickens slightly and the spices infuse the broth, about 6 minutes.

PAIRINGS: Simmer with sautéed chicken chunks (page 34) thighs are perfect—or ground beef (page 40), sprinkle with grated cheddar or Monterrey jack, some diced fresh tomatoes and red onion, and serve with Spanish Yellow Rice (page 234).

SHELF LIFE: Two to three days in the refrigerator.

Ancho, Black Bean, and Corn Chili

Ancho chiles are poblano peppers that have been ripened to a red hue and then dried. They pack mild heat and a measure of sweetness and spice. Ground ancho powder, convenient and increasingly available (McCormick's is good), is perfect for this quick chili.

YIELD: 2½ CUPS, ABOUT 4 SERVINGS
PREP TIME: 6 minutes
COOK TIME: 10 minutes

1 (15-ounce) can black beans, rinsed and drained well
1 (15-ounce) can corn, drained well
½ cup low-sodium chicken broth
2 teaspoons cider vinegar
2 tablespoons olive oil
1 small yellow onion, finely diced (about ¾ cup)
About 1 teaspoon kosher salt
About ½ teaspoon freshly ground black pepper
2 teaspoons ancho chile powder
½ cup crumbled queso fresco or feta
1 scallion (both white and green parts), trimmed and thinly sliced

In a blender or using an immersion blender, purée ½ cup of the beans and ½ cup corn (reserve the remainder of each) with the chicken broth and cider vinegar.

Set the oil and onion in a medium saucepan over high heat, sprinkle generously with salt and pepper, and cook, stirring, until the onion starts to soften and become translucent, about 4 minutes (it's OK if it browns in places). Add the ancho powder and cook for 30 seconds, stirring, so it becomes fragrant.

Add the puréed bean mixture as well as the reserved beans and corn and bring to a boil, stirring.

Reduce to a simmer, cover, and cook, stirring occasionally, until the mixture heats through and the ancho infuses its flavor, about 4 minutes. Season with more salt, pepper, and vinegar to taste and serve sprinkled with the queso fresco and scallion.

OPTIONS: In the summer, substitute fresh corn (the kernels of 2 ears) for the canned—there's no need to cook them first.

PAIRINGS: Pair with sautéed chunks of pork loin or beef chuck steak (page 34) and serve with warm corn tortillas.

SHELF LIFE: Two to three days in the refrigerator.

Sizzling Stove-Top Spiced Fajita Broth

The "sizzling" in this recipe is optional, a nod to those restaurants like Chili's that execute the dramatic tableside sizzle. The onions and peppers in this broth are meant to be toothy to add texture to the fajitas.

YIELD: 1¾ CUPS, 4 SERVINGS
PREP TIME: 6 minutes
COOK TIME: 9 minutes

2 tablespoons olive oil
1 medium Spanish onion (about ½ pound), thinly sliced
   (about 1 cup)
1 green bell pepper, cored and thinly sliced (about 1¼ cups)
About 1 teaspoon kosher salt
About ½ teaspoon freshly ground black pepper
1 teaspoon tomato paste
1 teaspoon chile powder
1 teaspoon ground cumin
⅛ to ¼ teaspoon chipotle powder (optional)
½ cup low-sodium canned chicken broth
2 teaspoons cider vinegar

Heat the oil in a large sauté pan or skillet over medium-high heat until shimmering hot, about 1½ minutes. Add the onion and bell pepper, sprinkle generously with salt and pepper, and cook, stirring, until the onion starts to soften and brown in places, about 3 minutes.

Add the tomato paste, chile powder, cumin, and chipotle powder, if using, and cook for 30 seconds, stirring, so the tomato paste coats the onions and peppers and the spices become fragrant.

Add the chicken broth and vinegar, bring to a boil, and simmer steadily so it mostly reduces and the peppers and onions become tender, but slightly toothy, about 2 minutes. Season with more salt and pepper to taste.

OPTIONS: If you want to do the sizzling thing, heat a cast-iron pan over medium heat for a couple of minutes (a droplet of water should evaporate instantly), add the fajita mixture, and bring out to the table with potholders.

PAIRINGS: Simmer with sautéed shrimp (page 46) or skirt steak (page 38)—toss either with a light dusting of the Tex-Mex Spice Rub (page 15) before sautéing—and wrap in warm flour tortillas with grated cheese and Chunky Homestyle Guacamole (page 159).

SHELF LIFE: Two to three days in the refrigerator.

Poblana Spiced Taco Sauce

This is my fresh take on the Ortega taco mix that dominated many weeknights in our house growing up. Back then, tortilla chips were slightly exotic and salsa was something that came strictly out of a jar.

YIELD: ½ CUP, 4 SERVINGS
PREP TIME: 5 minutes
COOK TIME: 8 minutes

2 tablespoons olive oil

1 small yellow onion, finely diced (about ¾ cup)

2 garlic cloves, minced (about 2 teaspoons)

About 1 teaspoon kosher salt

2 teaspoons chile powder

2 teaspoons ground cumin

1 teaspoon tomato paste

Pinch of cinnamon

1 teaspoon dried oregano

¼ teaspoon chipotle powder

Heat the oil in a large skillet over high heat until shimmering hot, about 1½ minutes. Add the onion and garlic, sprinkle generously with salt, reduce the heat to medium, and cook, stirring, until the onion starts to soften and brown lightly, about 4 minutes.

Add the spices, tomato paste, and oregano and cook, stirring, so they become fragrant and sizzle steadily, 30 seconds. Add ¼ cup water and bring to a boil. Simmer for a couple of minutes so the onion becomes tender.

PAIRINGS: Pair with sautéed ground beef or turkey (page 40), sprinkle with sharp grated cheddar, diced tomatoes, and lettuce and wrap in warm flour tortillas.

SHELF LIFE: Two to three days in the refrigerator. Reheat in the microwave and then simmer with sautéed meat.

Spiced Moroccan Olive and Orange Sauce

The southern Mediterranean (or North African coast) doesn't get enough credit for the complexity and versatility of its cuisine. This quick sauce reflects that region's trademark balance of sweet and spice.

YIELD: 1¼ CUPS, 4 SERVINGS

PREP TIME: 5 minutes

COOK TIME: 10 minutes

3 tablespoons olive oil

1 small yellow onion, finely diced (about ¾ cup)

1 garlic clove, minced

¼ teaspoon saffron threads (optional)

About 1 teaspoon kosher salt

1 teaspoon ground cumin

Pinch of ground cinnamon

½ cup low-sodium chicken broth

½ large navel orange, juiced (about ¼ cup)

½ cup pitted olives (like Gaeta, Kalamata, or picholine), coarsely chopped

Freshly ground black pepper

Heat the oil in a large skillet over medium-high heat until shimmering hot, about 1½ minutes. Add the onion, garlic, and saffron if using, sprinkle generously with salt, reduce the heat to medium, and cook, stirring, until the onion starts to soften and brown lightly, about 4 minutes. Add the cumin and cinnamon and cook, stirring, for 30 seconds so they become fragrant.

Add the chicken broth and orange juice and bring to a boil. Cook at a steady simmer so the sauce reduces slightly and the spices infuse the broth, about 3 minutes. Stir in the olives and season with more salt and pepper to taste.

OPTIONS: Sprinkle with chopped fresh cilantro and orange segments.

PAIRINGS: This sauce makes a fine quick braise with sautéed boneless, skinless chicken thighs (page 31) or sautéed chunks of lamb (page 34). Fold in some canned garbanzos and serve over Couscous with Zucchini, Sun-Dried Tomatoes, and Black Olives (page 237).

SHELF LIFE: N/A. Try to make this sauce fresh. The strong flavors in here will clash upon sitting.

Porcini and Pea Sauce

Porcini are the Italian version of French cèpes, large wild mushrooms shaped like a bullet with a deep, woodsy essence. Because fresh porcini can be hard to come by (unless you're comfortable foraging in the woods after a rainy spell), dried are a better bet. You can store dried porcini in the cupboard indefinitely and then pull them out at a moment's notice (along with the frozen peas) for this dressy sauce.

YIELD: 1½ CUPS, 4 SERVINGS
PREP TIME: 5 minutes
COOK TIME: 10 minutes

1 ounce dried porcini mushrooms

1 tablespoon unsalted butter

1 medium shallot, finely diced (about 3 tablespoons)

About ¼ teaspoon kosher salt

¼ cup dry sherry

1 cup frozen peas

2 teaspoons sherry vinegar

2 tablespoons heavy cream (optional)

1 tablespoon chopped fresh mint (optional)

Freshly ground black pepper

Set the mushrooms and 1 cup boiling water in a bowl, top with another bowl so the mushrooms are completely submerged, and soak for 5 minutes so they soften.

Coarsely chop the porcinis, drain the soaking liquid through a coffee filter or paper towels to remove any sediment, and reserve this mushroom broth.

Meanwhile, melt the butter in a medium saucepan over medium-high heat. Add the shallot, sprinkle lightly with salt, and cook, stirring, until it just becomes translucent and tender, about 2 minutes. Add the chopped porcini and cook, stirring, until they heat through and become fragrant, about 2 minutes. Add the sherry and cook, stirring, until it almost completely reduces, about 1 minute.

Stir in the mushroom-soaking liquid, peas, and vinegar and bring to a boil. Reduce to a simmer, stir in the cream and mint, if using, and cook, stirring occasionally until the sauce intensifies in flavor and thickens slightly, 2 minutes. Season with salt and pepper to taste

PAIRINGS: I like porcinis with beef. Toss with cubes of sautéed beef (page 34) for a light, fresh version of beef stroganoff. Serve atop Buttered Egg Noodles with Chives (page 233) and sautéed asparagus (page 250).

SHELF LIFE: Up to three days in the refrigerator.

TIP: Porcini at the Market
It's worth paying a little extra for good dried porcini. The cheaper stuff has a shriveled, curled-up appearance and overly pungent aroma that can overpower a dish. Look for slices of porcini that are full-looking and have a relatively mild scent.

Creamy Pea and Pancetta Sauce

This sauce is an upscale take on the classic pairing of ham and peas. Pancetta is like Italian bacon, only without the smoke and with a hit of garlic instead. Ask them to slice it thick at the deli counter; large pieces cook more evenly and add a pleasant meaty texture to this sauce.

YIELD: 1½ CUPS, 4 SERVINGS
PREP TIME: 4 minutes
COOK TIME: 11 minutes

1 tablespoon olive oil

3 ounces thickly sliced pancetta or bacon, cut into strips

1 medium shallot, finely diced (about 3 tablespoons)

1 teaspoon chopped fresh thyme (optional)

About ¼ teaspoon kosher salt

¼ cup dry sherry

1 cup frozen peas

½ cup low-sodium chicken broth

2 tablespoons heavy cream

About ¾ teaspoon freshly ground black pepper

Heat the oil and pancetta in a medium skillet or sauté pan over high heat until it starts to sizzle steadily, about 1 minute. Reduce the heat to medium and cook, stirring occasionally, until it renders most of its fat and becomes crisp and lightly browned, about 4 more minutes. Using a slotted spoon, transfer the pancetta to a plate lined with paper towels.

Add the shallot and thyme, if using, to the pan, sprinkle lightly with salt, and cook, stirring, until it just becomes translucent and tender, about 2 minutes. Raise the heat to high, add the sherry, and cook, stirring, until it almost completely reduces, about 1 minute.

Stir in the peas and chicken broth and bring to a boil. Reduce to a simmer, stir in the cream and a generous sprinkling of pepper, and cook, stirring occasionally so the sauce thickens slightly, about 2 minutes. Stir in the crisped pancetta or bacon and season with salt and pepper to taste.

PAIRINGS: This sauce goes nicely with bone-in pork or veal chops or a seared steak (page 38 dressy enough to match filet mignon, for instance. Accompany with Roasted Rosemary Fingerling Potatoes (page 235) and sautéed green beans (page 50).

SHELF LIFE: N/A. The peas don't reheat well so you're best off making this sauce fresh.

Garlicky White Wine and Butter Sauce

I like to thinly slice the garlic cloves in this sauce (as opposed to mincing or chopping them) so they infuse their flavor gently without burning or becoming acrid. Plus, this allows diners to push the slivers to the side if they like.

YIELD: SCANT ¾ CUP, 4 SERVINGS

PREP TIME: 3 minutes

COOK TIME: 7 minutes

3 tablespoons unsalted butter, cut into pieces

3 garlic cloves, peeled and thinly sliced

½ cup dry white wine

½ cup low-sodium chicken broth

2 tablespoons chopped fresh parsley, more for sprinkling on the finished dish

Kosher salt and freshly ground black pepper

Heat the butter and garlic in a medium skillet over medium heat, stirring occasionally, until the garlic turns a very light brown and becomes fragrant, about 3 minutes. Raise the heat to high, add the white wine, and cook, stirring, until it almost completely reduces, about 2 minutes. Add the chicken broth, bring to a boil, and then remove from the heat. Stir in the parsley and season with salt and pepper to taste.

PAIRINGS: Make a scampi with this sauce and sautéed shrimp (page 46) or clams (page 48); serve with Spaghetti with Garlic, Oil, and Hot Pepper Flakes (page 233) and sautéed broccoli rabe (page 50).

SHELF LIFE: N/A. You're best off making this sauce fresh as the garlic will overpower the broth upon sitting.

TIP: "Dry" Wine?

I generally call for "dry" white wines. What constitutes a dry wine might be easiest to define by what it's not, and that is fruity and sweet (like a Beaujolais or Riesling, for instance). Those wines would overwhelm a sauce, sticking out rather than blending in. But don't stress it. Because most of the alcohol gets cooked off in these sauces, you're left with little more than a mild hint of the original wine. If you'd drink it, it will be fine for cooking.

CHAPTER: 4

SAUCES AFTER SEARING

CHOP AND TOSS THESE SAUCES WHILE YOU SEAR, THEN DIP OR DRIZZLE THEM ON AT THE TABLE

THE ONE THEME THAT UNIFIES ALL OF THE DISPARATE SAUCES IN THIS CHAPTER—AND I'VE TRIED TO PACK THE WHOLE GLOBE IN HERE, FROM CREAMY ITALIAN BÉCHAMELS TO SPICED INDIAN CHUTNEYS—IS THAT THEY ARE MERGED WITH THE SEARED INGREDIENTS AFTER COOKING. THIS MAKES PREPARING THESE SAUCES SIMPLER. YOU CAN MAKE THEM SEPARATE FROM THE SEAR, EVEN AHEAD OF TIME IF YOU LIKE, AND THEN PAIR THE TWO TOGETHER AT THE DINNER TABLE.

HOW YOU SERVE THESE SAUCES IS UP TO YOU, THOUGH THE MAKEUP OF EACH SHOULD HELP GUIDE YOU. THICKER MIXTURES ARE BETTER FOR DIPPING AND DUNKING (FILL SMALL, INDIVIDUAL BOWLS FOR DINERS TO AVOID DOUBLE-DIPPING CONTROVERSIES, PAGE 163), WHILE THINNER SAUCES ARE EASIER TO DRIZZLE OR PASS AT THE TABLE.

VARIED SERVING SIZES

Most all of the sauces in chapter 3 yield four servings because they're paired with four-serving pan or grill techniques; any extra sauce would just saturate the dish. Conversely, the yield on the salsas, chutneys and dips in this chapter tend to vary, often serving between six and ten. The large yields are intentional, partly because the sauces in this chapter tend to have long shelf lives and partly because they're jazzy condiments that you'll be glad to have on hand to set out with whatever is for dinner tonight.

SALSAS

Though the word "salsa" has become part of the American lexicon, most of us still relate to it as one thing and one thing only—a chunky tomato mixture with jalapeño, onion, cilantro, and lime. And while this is a traditional Mexican sauce—*salsa Mexicana* or *pico de gallo*, depending on where you are in that country—it is only one of many in Central and South American cuisines. This section tries to cover many of the rest. Most of these salsas are vegetable- or fruit-based with big, intense flavors, which match the casual vibe of summer. Serve them in bowls for dipping or spoon over grilled or broiled fare.

BASIC SALSA METHOD

Chop and toss or purée. Sometimes the ingredients are seared on the grill or stove top first, though most are simply added in the raw state.

SPICY-METER

I try to ballpark each salsa's level of piquancy—mild, medium, hot, and very hot. Heat levels may vary from one chile to the next, but the basic goal of this feature is to help you choose what to make and what to stay away from.

Fresh Tomato–Jalapeño Salsa

(Pico de Gallo)

Everybody should have a good salsa recipe; this is mine. I generally only make it in the summer when there are good, local tomatoes available (you can find OK plum tomatoes year-round if you're feeling the itch). *Pico de gallo* (rooster's beak) is the traditional name for this finely diced salsa, a reference to the way in which the salsa was traditionally eaten, using the thumb and forefingers like a beak to pick at the chunky mixture.

YIELD: 2½ CUPS, 6 TO 8 SERVINGS
PREP TIME: 12 minutes
COOK TIME: N/A
LEVEL OF SPICINESS: Medium

1 pound ripe plum tomatoes (about 5 medium), cored and cut in ½-inch dice (about 2 cups)
1 small red onion, finely diced (about ½ cup)
¼ cup coarsely chopped fresh cilantro
1 jalapeño, cored, seeded (leave the seeds in if you want some real heat), and finely diced (about 3 tablespoons)
1 tablespoon freshly squeezed lime juice (from about ½ lime), more to taste
1 small garlic clove, minced (optional) about ½ teaspoon
About 1 teaspoon kosher salt
About ½ teaspoon freshly ground black pepper

In a medium bowl, mix to combine all of the ingredients with a generous sprinkling of salt and pepper; add more salt, pepper, and lime juice to taste.

PAIRINGS: This salsa will go with most anything though I like it with mild grilled ingredients like boneless chicken thighs (page 31) or shrimp (page 46). Serve either on top of rice and beans with some lime wedges for squeezing.

SHELF LIFE: Up to three days in the refrigerator, though this salsa is at its best shortly after being made when the textures and flavors are fresh.

TIP: Save time by using a food processor to chop the jalapeños and onions.

TIP: I call for plum tomatoes in salsa recipes because they have a meatier texture and less water content than most varieties. If you purchase the tomatoes a couple of days before making this salsa, try to store them at room temperature for the best flavor and texture.

Mincing and Mashing Garlic

In this book, I call for garlic in all shapes and sizes: smashed, sliced, chopped, or minced. Each form serves a purpose, infusing garlic's flavor to suit the preparation. I generally prefer garlic cooked—gentle heat tends to mellow and smooth out its flavor. In vinaigrettes and salsas, though, I will include a raw clove here or there. When I do, I like for the garlic's texture to be as smooth and its flavor as evenly incorporated as possible. So I take it a level past minced where it's like a smooth paste. Here's how:

1. **SMASH** with the side of a chef's knife: give it a good thump as the more the garlic splinters, the less chopping you'll have to do.
2. **CHOP** and sprinkle with salt: the coarse texture of the salt helps break down the garlic.
3. **MASH** to a paste using the side of a chef's knife: scrape the knife back and forth, pressing the garlic against the cutting board until it becomes a loose paste.

1. Smash with the side of the knife.

2. Chop and sprinkle with salt

3. Mash to a paste.

Char-Grilled Tomato Salsa

Grilling the main components in this salsa gives them a touch of smokiness and intensifies their texture (searing off the wateriness that plagues some salsas). To speed things up, pulse this mixture in a food processor once it's off the grill (instead of hand-chopping it).

YIELD: 1½ CUPS, 8 SERVINGS
PREP TIME: 6 minutes
COOK TIME: 6 minutes
LEVEL OF SPICINESS: Medium

1 pound ripe plum tomatoes (about 5 medium),
    cored and halved lengthwise
4 scallions, trimmed and rinsed (don't pat dry—see
    Don't Dry Scallions After Rinsing tip on page 81)
1 jalapeño
1 tablespoon olive oil
¾ teaspoon kosher salt
½ teaspoon freshly ground black pepper
¼ cup coarsely chopped fresh cilantro
1 tablespoon freshly squeezed lime juice (from about
    ½ lime), more to taste

Heat the gas grill to high or prepare a medium-high charcoal fire. Drizzle the tomatoes, scallions, and jalapeño with the olive oil, salt, and pepper. Grill, flipping after a couple of minutes, until the vegetables have good grill marks and just start to soften, 3 to 4 minutes total for the scallions and 4 to 5 minutes for the tomatoes and jalapeños.

Transfer to a cutting board to cool for a couple of minutes and then coarsely chop. Add to a food processor along with the cilantro and lime juice and pulse so the mixture is chunky but uniform. Season generously with salt, pepper, and lime juice to taste.

PAIRINGS: Use this salsa as a garnish for grilled chicken (page 71) or beef (page 75) fajitas; use boneless thighs for the former or a flank or strip steak for the latter. Pair with cilantro-lime rice and grilled peppers and onions.

SHELF LIFE: Up to four days in the refrigerator.

Chipotle Salsa

It's nice to have a salsa you can turn to when there are no good, local tomatoes available, which is about nine months of the year where I live in the Northeast. Chipotle peppers and canned tomatoes are the leading players in this salsa, which springs strictly from the pantry.

YIELD: 1½ CUPS, 10 SERVINGS
PREP TIME: 4 minutes
COOK TIME: N/A
LEVEL OF SPICINESS: Medium

1 (14½-ounce) can diced tomatoes, drained well
1 canned chipotle, minced, plus 2 tablespoons adobo
    sauce
2 teaspoons cider vinegar
1 teaspoon light brown sugar
½ teaspoon kosher salt
½ teaspoon dried oregano
¼ teaspoon ground cumin
¼ teaspoon freshly ground black pepper

Add all the ingredients to a food processor and purée until smooth. Add more vinegar, salt, or pepper to taste.

SHELF LIFE: Up to five days in the refrigerator.

PAIRINGS: Spread this salsa on grilled burgers (page 76) or chicken breast sandwiches as an alternative to ketchup or drizzle on grilled chicken tacos with boneless breasts (page 71) and sharp cheddar cheese.

OPTIONS: If you want to take this salsa in a fresher route, add fresh corn or substitute chopped fresh cilantro for the oregano.

Tomatillo Salsa Verde

Tomatillos look and, of course, sound like tomatoes. They're even part of the same nightshade family. But they're more tart than sweet. Here, they form a tangy base for this staple green salsa. Though tomatillos are often roasted before puréeing, I skip this step to vibe with our weeknight aspirations.

YIELD: 1¾ CUPS, 10 SERVINGS
PREP TIME: 10 minutes
COOK TIME: N/A
LEVEL OF SPICINESS: Medium

¾ pound tomatillos, (about 6) husked, rinsed, and cut in 1-inch pieces
1 small yellow onion, finely diced (about ½ cup)
1 jalapeño, cored (seeded if you like) and coarsely chopped (about 3 tablespoons)
1 garlic clove, minced and mashed to a paste using the side of a chef's knife and working against a cutting board (see page 153)
3 tablespoons chopped fresh cilantro
1 tablespoon freshly squeezed lime juice (from about ½ lime), more to taste
1 teaspoon kosher salt

Add all of the ingredients to a food processor and pulse to chop and combine. Season with more salt and lime juice to taste.

PAIRINGS: This mild salsa goes nicely with spice-rubbed grilled shrimp (page 78) or boneless chicken thighs (page 71). Serve with Spanish Yellow Rice (page 234) and refried beans.

SHELF LIFE: Refrigerate up to four days.

Spicy Tomato–Habanero Salsa

Because of its intense heat, you'll want to drizzle this salsa delicately rather than dip it with a chip—habaneros are one of the spiciest chiles around (see discussion of Scoville units on page 87). I purée this salsa to spread out the heat (so you don't get any unpleasant bites). I also include jalapeños to give the sauce some grounded, earthy heat.

YIELD: 1¼ CUPS, 8 SERVINGS
PREP TIME: 10 minutes
COOK TIME: N/A
LEVEL OF SPICINESS: Very hot

1 cup diced plum tomatoes (about 2 large)
½ cup diced Spanish onion (about ⅓ onion)
1 jalapeño, cored, seeded, and finely diced (about 3 tablespoons)
1 habanero, cored, seeded, and finely diced, using gloves (about 1 tablespoon)
2 tablespoons chopped fresh cilantro
1 tablespoon freshly squeezed lime juice
About 1 teaspoon kosher salt

Add all the ingredients and a generous sprinkling of salt to a food processor and pulse to finely chop. Season with more salt and lime juice to taste.

PAIRINGS: This heat may test your taste buds, so go down-home (and not delicate) with the pairings. Try it with a rough, tough chuck steak on the grill (page 75) or grilled country-style pork ribs (page 75) and serve with Traditional Rice Pilaf (page 234) and grilled peppers (page 80).

SHELF LIFE: Up to four days in the refrigerator.

TECHNIQUE: How to Dice an Avocado

Cutting avocados is a bit of a riddle. They've got a tough, leathery skin on the outside and a hard pit on the inside. So how to slice the soft, buttery flesh in between?

1. Using a chef's knife, slice the avocado lengthwise, pivoting around the core when you get to it so that you evenly halve the avacado.
2. Set one hand on the bottom half and the other hand on the top half and twist (like an Oreo) to break apart the two sides.

3. One side will have a pit. Set this half in your left (or noncutting) hand (hold a dishtowel beneath it to avoid cutting yourself), and using a chef's knife and a flick of the wrist, cut into the pit (a gentle tap should do) and twist. The pit should easily slide free. To remove the pit from the knife, brush it against the side of a waste basket so it easily falls off; this is a lot safer than using your hands.
4. Using a paring knife, slice or dice each half of avocado flesh all the way to, but not through, the skin.
5. Use a spoon to scoop out the sliced or diced flesh.

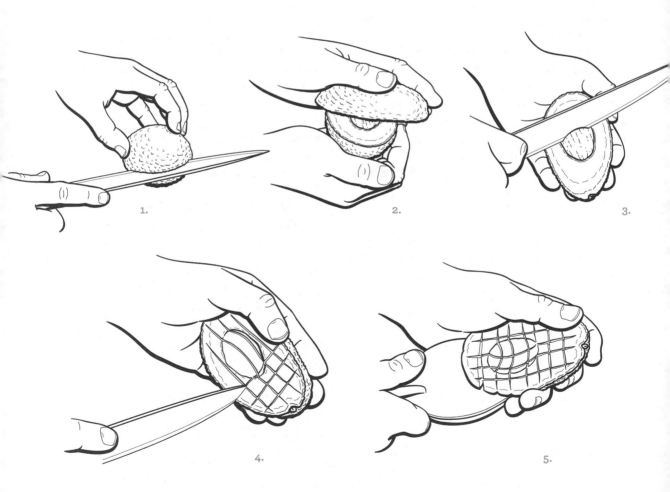

Roasted Chile Salsa Verde

Fresh Anaheim and poblano peppers are interchangeable in this salsa. They're different—Anaheims are a little spicier while poblanos have more depth of flavor—but each is relatively mild with a firm, meaty texture. Slide the chiles under the broiler (or on the grill if you prefer) for a couple of minutes to brown and soften slightly. Then chop and purée with minced garlic and freshly squeezed lime juice.

YIELD: ¾ CUP, 4 SERVINGS

PREP TIME: 8 minutes

COOK TIME: 3 minutes

LEVEL OF SPICINESS: Hot for Anaheim chiles, medium for poblanos

2 Anaheim chiles or poblano peppers

1 tablespoon olive oil

1 teaspoon kosher salt

1 tablespoon freshly squeezed lime juice (about ½ lime)

2 teaspoons chopped fresh oregano or ½ teaspoon dried oregano

1 large garlic clove, minced and mashed to a paste using the side of a chef's knife, about 1 teaspoon (see page 153)

½ teaspoon freshly ground black pepper

Heat the broiler to high and set a rack 4 inches away from the element. Toss the chiles with the oil and half of the salt. Broil, flipping every minute or so, until the chiles are browned and softened, 3 to 4 minutes. Let cool for a couple of minutes, then core, remove the loose skin, and, if you like, the seeds.

Set the chiles and the remaining ingredients in a food processor along with the remaining salt and the pepper and purée until uniform and smooth. Add more salt, pepper, or lime juice to taste.

OPTIONS: Use fresh New Mexican Hatch chiles (see page 144) to give this salsa an extra layer of complexity.

PAIRINGS: This spicy salsa pairs well with hardy ingredients that won't be bowled over by its heat. That rules out most fish, but does make it a good fit for grilled chicken thighs (page 71) or flank steak (page 75). Serve with sautéed corn and warm tortillas.

SHELF LIFE: Up to two days in the refrigerator.

TIP: Substitute two 4-ounce cans roasted green chiles for the fresh if you're on the go.

Seared Jalapeño and Garlic Salsa

Searing the garlic and fresh jalapeño on the stove top mellows their flavor while a splash of cider vinegar gives this salsa a punch of acidity to balance the heat. Doubling up the jalapeño with jarred slices ensures that the pepper's flavor is assertive.

YIELD: ½ CUP, 4 SERVINGS
PREP TIME: 8 minutes
COOK TIME: 3 minutes
LEVEL OF SPICINESS: Hot

3 tablespoons olive oil
2 jalapeños, sliced into thin rings (about ½ cup)
2 garlic cloves, smashed
1 teaspoon kosher salt
2 tablespoons chopped fresh cilantro
1 tablespoon cider vinegar
1 tablespoon chopped jarred jalapeños
½ teaspoon freshly ground black pepper

Heat the oil in a large skillet over high heat until shimmering hot, about 1 minute. Add the fresh jalapeños and garlic, sprinkle with half of the salt, and cook, stirring, until the garlic starts to brown lightly at its edges, about 2 minutes.

Remove from the heat and let cool for a couple of minutes. Transfer to a food processor with ¼ cup water, the cilantro, vinegar, jarred jalapeños and the remaining salt, and the pepper. Pulse until chopped or purée into a paste. Add more vinegar, salt, and pepper to taste.

PAIRINGS: This spicy sauce is meant more as a light spoonful than a full-on dollop. Serve with grilled shrimp (page 78) or chicken thighs (page 71) and Traditional Rice Pilaf (page 234).

SHELF LIFE: Up to two days in the refrigerator.

TIP: Use cooked garlic. I try to avoid raw garlic in sauces as it has a tendency to stay with you long after a meal is done. Lightly sautéing it, as in this salsa, smoothes out its flavor so it complements the ingredients around it.

Avocado and Corn Salsa

Avocado is often typecast in a mashed-up role in guacamole. But it can also be diced and tossed into a salsa, so its rich, buttery texture balances spicy and acidic ingredients. Look for medium-ripe avocados for this salsa—if they're too soft, they'll turn to mush. The corn can be cooked or raw if it's the middle of the summer when it's fresh and sweet.

YIELD: 2 CUPS, 8 SERVINGS
PREP TIME: 10 minutes
COOK TIME: N/A
LEVEL OF SPICINESS: Mild

1 medium ripe avocado, cut in ½-inch dice (see How to Dice an Avocado, page 156)
1 cup corn kernels (canned, grilled, sautéed, or raw)
¼ cup finely diced red onion (from ½ small red onion)
1 plum tomato, cored and cut in ¼-inch dice (about ⅓ cup)
2 tablespoons chopped fresh cilantro
1 jalapeño, cored, seeded, and finely diced (about 2 tablespoons)
1 tablespoon freshly squeezed lime juice (about ½ lime)
About 1 teaspoon kosher salt
About ½ teaspoon freshly ground black pepper

Gently toss the avocado, corn, onion, tomato, cilantro, jalapeño, and lime juice with a generous sprinkling of salt and pepper. Season with more salt, pepper, and lime juice to taste.

PAIRINGS: I like making soft tacos with this salsa, grilled red onions (page 82), and chopped, spice-rubbed grilled chicken thighs (page 71) or thinly sliced skirt steak (page 75).

SHELF LIFE: Up to two days in the refrigerator (see How to Keep Avocado from Browning tip on page 159).

Chunky Homestyle Guacamole

I like everything big in this sauce—the avocado, chopped cilantro, and tomatoes. Their coarseness adds a level of texture to each bite. Of course, you can mash this salsa up with a fork if you want it to be more of a dip.

YIELD: 2 CUPS, 8 SERVINGS

PREP TIME: 10 minutes

COOK TIME: N/A

LEVEL OF SPICINESS: Mild

2 ripe avocados, cut into ½-inch dice (see illustration on page 156) (about 1½ cups)

1 small red onion (or ½ large), finely diced (about ½ cup)

1 large plum tomato, cored and cut in ¼-inch dice (about ⅓ cup)

3 tablespoons coarsely chopped fresh cilantro

2 tablespoons freshly squeezed lime juice (from about 1 lime)

½ teaspoon crushed red pepper flakes

About 1 teaspoon kosher salt

Gently toss the avocado, onion, tomato, cilantro, lime juice, red pepper flakes, and a generous sprinkling of salt. Season with more salt and lime juice to taste.

PAIRINGS: I like pairing this relatively mild guacamole with other mild ingredients like grilled pork tenderloin (page 75) or sautéed shrimp (page 46). Dust either with the Tex-Mex Spice Rub (page 15) before searing and serve with warm flour tortillas and diced tomatoes.

SHELF LIFE: Up to two days in the refrigerator, though best eaten right away; see How to Keep Avocado from Browning tip below.

TIP: How to Keep Avocado from Browning

Like apples or potatoes, avocados' one major flaw is that they are quick to oxidize or discolor. The way to avoid this is to prevent exposure: cover guacamole so that the plastic wrap is completely flush with the top skin so air won't get at it and so it will stay bright green indefinitely.

Mashed Guacamole with Lemon and Toasted Garlic

Subbing lemon for the more traditional and assertive lime allows an avocado's mild creaminess to come to the fore. Along those lines, this is one of those times where I like to mellow garlic a bit by gently sautéing it instead of throwing it in raw.

YIELD: 2 CUPS, 8 SERVINGS
PREP TIME: 8 minutes
COOK TIME: 3 minutes
LEVEL OF SPICINESS: Mild

2 medium garlic cloves, minced (about 1½ teaspoons)
1 tablespoon olive oil or canola oil
2 ripe avocados, cut into ½-inch dice, about 1½ cups (see How to Dice an Avocado, page 156)
3 tablespoons freshly squeezed lemon juice
2 tablespoons chopped fresh cilantro
⅛ to ¼ teaspoon crushed red pepper flakes
About 1 teaspoon kosher salt

Cook the garlic with the oil in a medium saucepan over medium heat, stirring, until it becomes very fragrant and sizzles steadily, about 1½ minutes. Remove from the heat and let cool for a couple of minutes.

Using a fork in a medium bowl, gently mash the avocado with the lemon juice, cilantro, red pepper flakes, a generous sprinkling of salt, and the garlic mixture. Season with more salt and lemon juice to taste.

PAIRINGS: Use this lemony guacamole as an accompaniment for fish tacos—try with sautéed cod (page 44) or broiled shrimp (page 66) along with thinly sliced cabbage and chopped tomato.

SHELF LIFE: Up to two days in the refrigerator, see How to Keep Avocado from Browning on page 159.

Corn and Black Bean Salsa

This hearty sauce is a cross between a salsa and a salad. Sun-dried tomatoes and fresh oregano help concentrate the flavors around the beans and corn.

YIELD: 2 CUPS, 8 SERVINGS
PREP TIME: 10 minutes
COOK TIME: N/A
LEVEL OF SPICINESS: Mild

¾ cup canned black beans, rinsed and drained well
½ cup corn kernels (canned, grilled, sautéed, or raw)
1 medium ripe avocado, cut into ½-inch dice (about ¾ cup, see How to Dice an Avocado, page 156)
2 scallions (both white and green parts), trimmed and thinly sliced (about ¼ cup)
1 jalapeño, cored, seeded, and finely diced (about 3 tablespoons)
1 tablespoon chopped fresh oregano
1 tablespoon chopped sun-dried tomato
1 tablespoon freshly squeezed lime juice
About 1 teaspoon kosher salt
About ½ teaspoon freshly ground black pepper

Gently toss all of the ingredients with the lime juice and a generous sprinkling of salt and pepper. Season with more salt, pepper, and lime juice to taste.

PAIRINGS: Chop up a broiled flank or grilled 64 or page 75) and make tacos with this salsa, grated jack cheese, and fresh cilantro.

SHELF LIFE: Up to three days in the refrigerator.

Peach and Vidalia Onion Salsa

It's not that large a leap to take a ripe summer peach and use it as the base for a salsa. After all, tomatoes are fruit and on the sweet side, too. Though peach and Vidalia onion seasons don't overlap for long, I like the idea of mixing two of Georgia's sweet culinary resources.

YIELD: 1½ CUPS, 8 SERVINGS
PREP TIME: 10 minutes
COOK TIME: N/A
LEVEL OF SPICINESS: Medium

1 large medium-ripe peach, cut in ¼-inch pieces (about 1 cup)
¼ cup finely diced red bell pepper (about ¼ pepper)
¼ cup finely diced sweet onion (like Vidalia)
1 canned chipotle, finely chopped (about 1 tablespoon)
1 tablespoon freshly squeezed lime juice (about ½ lime)
About ¾ teaspoon kosher salt
About ½ teaspoon freshly ground black pepper

Set all of the ingredients in a medium bowl and toss with a generous sprinkling of salt and pepper. Season with more salt and lime juice to taste.

PAIRINGS: Pork and peaches are a natural pairing, so try this salsa with grilled pork chops (page 75) or spice-rubbed broiled pork tenderloin (page 64). Serve with brown rice.

SHELF LIFE: Up to two days in the refrigerator.

TIP: Look for slightly firm peaches. As with tomatoes in salsas, you don't want to use overly ripe peaches or they'll turn to mush.

Mango, Roasted Red Pepper, and Habanero Salsa

Mangoes, roasted red peppers, and fresh oregano may appear to be a clash of culinary cultures, but the fruit's tropical flavor melds seamlessly with the earthy notes from the peppers and fresh herbs.

YIELD: 1½ CUPS, 8 SERVINGS
PREP TIME: 12 minutes
COOK TIME: N/A
LEVEL OF SPICINESS: Hot

1 large ripe mango, cut in ¼-inch dice (about 1¼ cups)
1 jarred roasted red pepper, cut in ¼-inch dice (about ½ cup)
½ small red onion, finely diced (about ¼ cup)
2 tablespoons chopped fresh mint
1 habanero or scotch bonnet chile, cored, seeded, and finely diced, using gloves (about 1 tablespoon)
1 tablespoon chopped fresh oregano
1 lime, juiced (about 2 tablespoons)
About ¾ teaspoon kosher salt
About ½ teaspoon freshly ground black pepper

Set all of the ingredients in a medium bowl and toss well with a generous sprinkling of salt and pepper. Season with more lime juice, salt, and pepper to taste.

PAIRINGS: I like the sweetness of mangos with grilled shrimp skewers (page 78) or broiled scallops (page 66). Serve with toasted naan (available at the supermarket) or Traditional Rice Pilaf (page 234) and some grilled zucchini (page 80).

SHELF LIFE: Up to two days in the refrigerator.

Toasted Chile Salsa Roja

One of my favorite eating holidays came wandering the food stalls of Mexico City. There, in the early morning hours, street vendors set up carts with small grills and griddles for tacos and quesadillas. Crowds on the way to work stop to grab something, drizzle it with one of the staple red or green salsas, and head on their way. The green salsa is usually tomatillo-based while the red is made with dried guajillo chiles. Any red chile will do for this recipe. Toast the chiles to activate their oils and intensify their flavor before simmering with tomatoes and a little water.

YIELD: 1 CUP, 6 SERVINGS
PREP TIME: 7 minutes
COOK TIME: 5 minutes
LEVEL OF SPICINESS: Hot (medium if using the ancho)

1 ounce dried chiles (like 2 guajillo, 5 long arbol chiles
    or 1 ancho)
2 large garlic cloves, chopped (about 1 tablespoon)
1 tablespoon olive oil
1 cup diced plum tomatoes (about 2 medium) or 1 cup
    canned tomatoes, drained well
About ¾ teaspoon kosher salt
½ cup diced Spanish onion
1 tablespoon lime juice

Toast the chiles and garlic with the oil in a large skillet over medium heat, tossing occasionally, until they heat through and become fragrant, about 2 minutes. Add ½ cup water, the tomatoes, and a generous sprinkling of salt, and bring to a boil. Cook at a steady simmer until much of the water cooks off, about 3 minutes.

Transfer to a blender along with the onion and lime juice and purée. Season with more salt and lime juice to taste.

PAIRINGS: Drizzle this sauce over ground beef or turkey (page 40) tacos with thinly sliced radish and fresh cilantro leaves.

SHELF LIFE: Up to four days in the refrigerator.

Caribbean Pineapple and Black Bean Salsa

At face value, the pairing of black beans and pineapples may seem strange, but it works. The sweet acidity of the pineapple perks up the plainness of the beans while the heat of the habanero pulls it all together.

YIELD: 1½ CUPS, 10 SERVINGS
PREP TIME: 10 minutes
COOK TIME: N/A
LEVEL OF SPICINESS: Hot

1 cup diced fresh or canned pineapple
¾ cup canned black beans, rinsed well and drained
¼ cup finely diced red onion (from ½ onion)
3 tablespoons chopped fresh cilantro
2 tablespoons freshly squeezed lime juice (from about 1
    lime)
1 habanero or Scotch bonnet pepper, cored, seeded,
    and finely diced, using gloves (about 1 tablespoon)
1 tablespoon fresh mint
About ¾ teaspoon kosher salt

Toss all the ingredients in a medium bowl with a generous sprinkling of salt to taste.

PAIRINGS: Because this spicy salsa is on the heavy side, pair it with something sturdy. Try grilled spice-rubbed boneless chicken thighs (page 71) or breasts (page 71) and serve with Thai coconut rice.

SHELF LIFE: Up to two days in the refrigerator.

DIPPING AND DRIZZLING SAUCES

This catch-all group of sauces is for drizzling or dunking at the table. They don't need to be strictly for dinner tonight, either. Many of these versatile condiments have long shelf lives and their casual compositions make them the kinds of things you can keep in the fridge for a couple of days and then pull out to provide a finishing flourish to seared food.

TIP: Thick or Thin

The general rule with these sauces is that the thinner ones are easier to drizzle (or toss) with seared ingredients while the thicker sauces are better for dipping or spooning over.

BASIC DIPS AND DRIZZLING SAUCES METHOD

Whisk together these loose oil, broth, and vinegar mixtures.

REVERSE MARINADES

Most everyone is familiar with the concept of a marinade—soak meats or fish in a flavor bath prior to cooking to add flavor. I like to reverse this process. Instead of marinating meats before cooking, I sear them first and then toss them in an intense sauce. It works wonders. The icon of this flavoring technique might be buffalo wings—first you fry or grill them and then toss with a hot sauce so the crisp skin sponges up the sauce, but this "reverse" marinade works perfectly with other cuts and with the vinaigrettes and thin dipping sauces in this chapter.

DIPPING ETIQUETTE

Ever since George Costanza on *Seinfeld* almost started a brawl with a double-dipping mourner at a wake, I've been fascinated with what's socially acceptable when it comes to dipping. I like to put most of the sauces in this section into small bowls or ramekins for each diner, more out of convenience than etiquette. It simply avoids a lot of passing around the table, though it can also promote harmony. If your family is extra tight, go with one, communal bowl.

Smashed Garlic and Rosemary Chimichurri

This is an Argentine cross between a steak sauce and a vinaigrette. The rosemary in this version adds a little woodsy depth while there's enough garlic to give it punch without repulsing your significant other.

YIELD: 1 CUP, 8 SERVINGS
PREP TIME: 7 minutes
COOK TIME: N/A

2 medium garlic cloves, minced and mashed to a paste
    using the side of a chef's knife (see page 153)
1 teaspoon chopped fresh rosemary
1 teaspoon salt
About 1 teaspoon kosher salt
About ½ teaspoon freshly ground black pepper
2 tablespoons white wine vinegar
3 tablespoons olive oil
¼ cup chopped fresh parsley

Set the garlic in a medium bowl and, using the side of a spoon (or, even better, in a mortar using a pestle), smash the garlic with the rosemary and a sprinkling of salt and pepper. While still smashing, drizzle in first the vinegar and then the oil.

Whisk in the parsley and ½ cup water and season with salt and pepper to taste (each should be plenty assertive).

SHELF LIFE: Up to three days in the refrigerator.

PAIRINGS: In traditional Argentine barbecue, this sharp sauce is paired with that country's wonderful beef, like grilled strip steaks or T-bones (page 75). It also goes nicely with full-flavored grilled fish (page 78) like salmon or swordfish. Serve with a simple green salad and a crusty baguette.

TIP: Mashing the garlic both on the cutting board and in a bowl melds its flavor more evenly with the other ingredients in this sauce and prevents there from being big pieces floating around waiting to be crunched on).

Salsa Criolla

This chunky, sweet and sour sauce is the lesser known but equally tasty sibling of chimichurri in Argentine barbecue (or parrillada).

YIELD: 1½ CUPS, 8 SERVINGS
PREP TIME: 6 minutes
COOK TIME: N/A

1 small yellow onion, finely diced (about ½ cup)
½ red bell pepper, finely diced (about ½ cup)
¼ cup olive oil
¼ cup white wine vinegar
1 tablespoon chopped fresh oregano (or 1 teaspoon
    dried oregano)
About 1¼ teaspoons kosher salt
About 1 teaspoon freshly ground black pepper

In a medium bowl, mix to combine all of the ingredients with a generous sprinkling of salt and pepper. Whisk well before serving.

SHELF LIFE: Up to three days in the refrigerator.

PAIRINGS: Though this sweet and sour sauce is very different than acidic and garlicky chimichurri, it can be applied to the same sort of grilled fare: steaks (page 75), sausages (page 75), and chicken—try boneless thighs (page 71). Serve with a fresh tomato salad and steamed long-grain rice.

Garlicky Lime Mojo

This Latin salsa is like a chimichurri with citrus. The lime gives it a slightly sweeter edge that pairs nicely with spice-rubbed chicken or pork.

YIELD: ½ CUP, 4 SERVINGS
PREP TIME: 6 minutes
COOK TIME: N/A

1 large garlic clove, minced and mashed to a paste using the
    side of a chef's knife, about 1 teaspoon (see page 153)
2 tablespoons olive oil
2 tablespoons chopped fresh cilantro
2 tablespoons freshly squeezed lime juice (from about 1 lime)
About ¾ teaspoon kosher salt
About ¾ teaspoon freshly ground black pepper

In a medium bowl, mix to combine all of the ingredients with ¼ cup water and a generous sprinkling of salt and pepper to taste. Mix well again before serving.

PAIRINGS: Make grilled cubano sandwiches with sliced grilled pork tenderloin (page 75), thinly sliced deli ham, dill pickle, Swiss cheese, and a generous drizzle of this sauce on a pressed bulky roll. Or serve this sauce with spiced-rubbed steak (page 75) or shrimp (page 78) and an avocado and tomato salad.

SHELF LIFE: Up to three days in the refrigerator.

Edgar's Ceviche Sauce

Ceviche is the South American technique of marinating (or "cooking") raw fish or shellfish in citrus juices (normally lime). The acid doesn't actually cook the fish but rather denatures its protein strands so they have a grayish cooked appearance, but a soft, raw, delicate texture. I like pairing this technique (and sauce) with grilled fare, too. The acidity of this sauce stands up nicely to the smoky flavor.

YIELD: 1½ CUPS, UP TO 8 SERVINGS
PREP TIME: 12 minutes
COOK TIME: N/A

1 medium-ripe avocado, diced (about ¾ cup)
¼ cup finely diced radish (about 2)
¼ cup finely diced red onion (about ½ small onion)
¼ cup chopped fresh cilantro
2 limes, juiced (about ¼ cup)
2 tablespoons olive oil
About 1 teaspoon kosher salt

In a medium bowl, mix to combine all of the ingredients with a generous sprinkling of salt to taste.

PAIRINGS: Toss with grilled (and diced) shrimp (page 78) or broiled scallops (page 68). Undercook either a bit, let cool, and then toss with this sauce. Serve at room temperature with tortilla chips and a drizzle of ketchup and Thai chile paste.

SHELF LIFE: N/A

Rosemary-Buffalo Sauce

Chopped fresh rosemary and a squirt of lemon juice elevate this sauce beyond basic pub grub. Heck, you could even serve it for company!

YIELD: ⅔ CUP, 6 SERVINGS
PREP TIME: 4 minutes
COOK TIME: N/A

¼ cup Frank's Red Hot sauce or your favorite hot sauce
¼ cup olive oil or melted butter
2 tablespoons freshly squeezed lemon juice
1½ teaspoons chopped fresh rosemary
¼ teaspoon coarsely cracked black pepper

In a medium bowl, combine all of the ingredients and mix well.

PAIRINGS: Toss with grilled or broiled chicken wings or drumsticks (page 73 or page 63) for a healthier take on the bar classic. Hit the chicken parts with the Lemon-Herb Rub (page 15) to add a little complexity or go all out and serve with blue cheese dressing (page 190) and celery and carrot sticks.

SHELF LIFE: Up to three days in the refrigerator; the rosemary starts to fade after this.

Hoisin and Toasted Sesame Dipping Sauce

On its own, hoisin sauce can be a little overwhelming, not the kind of thing you want to just slather on grilled fish or a sautéed steak. But when you pair it with complementary flavors like sesame oil, rice vinegar, and chile paste, it mellows.

YIELD: ½ CUP, 4 SERVINGS
PREP TIME: 4 minutes
COOK TIME: N/A

3 tablespoons hoisin sauce (I like Lee Kum Kee or Koon Chun brands)
1 tablespoon soy sauce
1 tablespoon rice vinegar
1 tablespoon toasted sesame oil
1 tablespoon honey
2 teaspoons toasted sesame seeds
1 teaspoon Thai chile paste (like Sriracha)
1 scallion (both white and green part), trimmed and thinly sliced (optional)

In a medium bowl, mix to combine all of the ingredients.

PAIRINGS: Drizzle this sauce onto grilled salmon (page 78) or broiled scallops (page 66). Serve with Chinese Egg Noodles with Scallions and Shiitakes (page 233) and stir-fried Chinese broccoli (page 50).

SHELF LIFE: Up to two weeks in the refrigerator.

Thai Sweet and Sour Dipping Sauce

This is my simple take on the light chile sauce served with spring rolls and other crispy appetizers in Thai restaurants. Though it packs some heat (from crushed red pepper flakes), the sweet (honey) and sour (vinegar) flavorings lead the way.

YIELD: ⅔ CUP, 4 SERVINGS
PREP TIME: 4 minutes
COOK TIME: N/A

¼ cup rice vinegar
1 medium shallot, finely diced (about 3 tablespoons)
2 tablespoons honey
2 tablespoons chopped fresh mint
1 teaspoon fish sauce
½ teaspoon crushed red pepper flakes

In a medium bowl, mix to combine all of the ingredients with 2 tablespoons water.

PAIRINGS: Prior to cooking, dust grilled shrimp (page 78) or chicken skewers (page 71) with the Sweet Southern Rub (page 14) and then serve with this sauce for dipping.

SHELF LIFE: Up to one week in the refrigerator.

Thai Peanut Dipping Sauce

This mild sauce is a traditional accompaniment to spiced Thai fare. I like to juice it up with some heat and fresh herbs, which you can omit if you prefer.

YIELD: 1 CUP, 4 SERVINGS
PREP TIME: 10 minutes
COOK TIME: N/A

½ cup peanut butter (either chunky or smooth is fine)
2 tablespoons canola or peanut oil
1 tablespoon minced (or finely grated) ginger
1 tablespoon freshly squeezed lime juice, more to taste
1 to 2 teaspoons Thai chile paste (like Sriracha)
2 scallions (both white and green parts), trimmed and
    thinly sliced (optional)
2 tablespoons chopped fresh cilantro

Puree the peanut butter, oil, ginger, lime juice, and chile paste in a food processor until smooth. As needed, add 2 or 3 tablespoons water while puréeing so the mixture loosens to a saucy consistency. Transfer to a medium bowl and stir in the scallions, if using, and cilantro and season with more lime juice to taste.

PAIRINGS: Serve this dipping sauce with grilled beef or chicken satays (page 75 or 71); rub these thin pieces of meat with a little garlic, ginger, and ground coriander before grilling. Serve with steamed jasmine rice and grilled Japanese eggplant (page 80).

SHELF LIFE: Up to three days in the refrigerator.

Soy-Ginger Dipping Sauce

This is the kind of sauce that Chinese restaurants serve with dumplings, but it's also versatile enough to drizzle over grilled or broiled meat and fish. The salty soy sauce, sweet brown sugar, and fragrant punch of ginger and scallions all meld into a balanced whole.

YIELD: ½ CUP, 4 SERVINGS
PREP TIME: 5 minutes
COOK TIME: N/A

3 tablespoons soy sauce
1 scallion (both white and green part), trimmed and thinly sliced
1 tablespoon minced ginger
2 teaspoons rice vinegar
2 teaspoons light brown sugar
1 teaspoon toasted sesame oil
¼ teaspoon crushed red pepper flakes

In a medium bowl, mix to combine all of the ingredients with 3 tablespoons water. Whisk to make sure the sugar dissolves.

PAIRINGS: Though this is a "dipping" sauce, you can drizzle it on a grilled salmon filet (page 78) or broiled cod (page 66). Serve with Cold Peanut Noodles with Mint and Thai Chiles (page 233) and some lightly dressed mesclun.

SHELF LIFE: Up to five days in the refrigerator.

Ponzu Dipping Sauce

This loose Japanese dipping sauce is made with soy sauce and some sort of citrus juice. Traditionally it's yuzu, a small fruit whose flavor is a cross between lemon, lime, and orange. Because yuzu is hard to come by in the United States, I call for a mix of freshly squeezed lime and orange juice.

YIELD: 1 CUP, 4 SERVINGS
PREP TIME: 6 minutes
COOK TIME: N/A

¼ cup low-sodium soy sauce
2 tablespoons freshly squeezed orange juice
2 tablespoons freshly squeezed lime juice
1 tablespoon granulated sugar
1 tablespoon minced ginger
Pinch of crushed red pepper flakes

In a medium bowl, mix to combine all of the ingredients with ¼ cup water.

PAIRINGS: This is a nice summery sauce to go with grilled shrimp (page 78) or broiled scallops (page 66). Serve with grilled or broiled vegetable skewers and soba noodles tossed with sesame oil and scallions.

SHELF LIFE: Up to one week in the refrigerator.

Japanese Tonkatsu Sauce

Katsu is Japan's take on fried cutlets. This sauce, a sharp mix of ketchup, Worcestershire sauce, and soy sauce, is the traditional accompaniment for the pork (which is the *ton* in the *tonkatsu*) or chicken cutlets. My version goes lighter on the Worcestershire than most.

YIELD: ⅔ CUP, 4 SERVINGS
PREP TIME: 2 minutes
COOK TIME: N/A

¼ cup ketchup
2 tablespoons soy sauce
2 tablespoons Worcestershire sauce
2 tablespoons honey
1 teaspoon Dijon mustard
About ¾ teaspoon freshly ground black pepper

In a small bowl, mix to combine all the ingredients with a generous sprinkling of pepper.

PAIRINGS: Pair this sauce with breaded and pan-fried cutlets (page 36) or turn it into a spiced Japanese steak sauce with grilled flank steak (page 75); serve with thinly sliced green cabbage, and steamed white rice.

SHELF LIFE: Up to two weeks in the refrigerator.

Korean Steak Sauce

A garlicky marinade, one like the Soy Ginger Marinade on page 17, traditionally flavors *bulgogi*, or Korean barbecue. But when you don't have the luxury to conduct a lengthy marinade, this sauce is the next best thing.

YIELD: 1¼ CUPS, 6 SERVINGS
PREP TIME: 6 minutes
COOK TIME: 6 minutes

2 tablespoons canola oil
2 garlic cloves, minced (about 2 teaspoons)
¼ cup soy sauce
2 tablespoons light brown sugar
1 tablespoon ketchup
1 tablespoon white vinegar
1 tablespoon toasted sesame oil
2 teaspoons Thai chile paste (like Sriracha)
2 teaspoons cornstarch
3 scallions (both white and green parts), trimmed and
   thinly sliced

Heat the oil and garlic in a medium saucepan over medium heat until the garlic sizzles steadily and becomes very fragrant, 2 minutes. Add the soy sauce, sugar, ketchup, vinegar, sesame oil, chile paste, and ½ cup water and bring to a boil. Whisk the cornstarch with 1 tablespoon water and stir into the sauce. Return to a boil so the sauce thickens, then stir in the scallions.

OPTIONS: Stir in some toasted sesame seeds and minced ginger.

PAIRINGS: Drizzle over thinly sliced grilled skirt steak (page 75) or boneless pork chops (page 75) and serve with steamed medium-grain rice and an Asian slaw.

SHELF LIFE: Up to four days in the refrigerator.

Spanish Garlic and Thyme Dipping Sauce

Bambu is a barbecue spot near the majestic Plaza Mayor in Salamanca, Spain. In this warm, well-lit basement space, the locals drink beers and big Spanish red wines and nosh on grilled tapas. This is my take on the ubiquitous sauce Bambu serves with pork spare ribs, a garlicky mixture of vinegar and fresh thyme that's kind of like a Spanish chimichurri.

YIELD: 1 CUP, 6 SERVINGS
PREP TIME: 5 minutes
COOK TIME: N/A

2 large garlic cloves, minced and mashed to a paste
    using the side of a chef's knife, about 2 teaspoons
    (see page 153)
2 teaspoons chopped fresh thyme or 1 teaspoon dried
    oregano
About 1 teaspoon kosher salt
About ½ teaspoon freshly ground black pepper
2 tablespoons white wine vinegar
2 tablespoons olive oil

In a medium bowl, using the back of a spoon (or a mortar and pestle) and working against the sides of the bowl, smash the garlic with the thyme, salt, and pepper. Add the vinegar and smash some more. Whisk in the olive oil and ½ cup water and season with more salt and pepper to taste.

PAIRINGS: Though the long cook time for spareribs doesn't fit the constraints of this book, this sauce goes just as nicely with grilled bone-in pork chops (page 75) or broiled chicken parts (page 163). Serve with Roasted Rosemary Fingerling Potatoes (page 235) and a baby arugula salad.

SHELF LIFE: Up to five days in the refrigerator.

Aunt Debbie's Bajan Scotch Bonnet Hot Sauce

Everyone should have an aunt who lives in Barbados. I'm lucky—I do. This is my version of that small island's traditional hot sauce, a spicy mix of habaneros, mustard, and vinegar. I seed the hot chiles, though leave them in if you're feeling crazy.

YIELD: 1 CUP, ABOUT 4 SERVINGS
PREP TIME: 6 minutes
COOK TIME: 6 minutes

1 ½ tablespoons olive oil
1 yellow onion, finely diced (about 1 cup)
2 to 3 scotch bonnet peppers or habaneros, cored,
    seeded, and chopped, using gloves (about 1 table-
    spoon)
1 tablespoon minced ginger
About ½ teaspoon kosher salt
1 teaspoon turmeric
¼ cup yellow mustard
1 tablespoon white vinegar
1 teaspoon granulated sugar

Heat the oil, chiles, and ginger in a medium saucepan over medium-high heat, sprinkle with salt, and cook, stirring, until the onion softens and starts to brown in places, 4 to 5 minutes. Stir in the turmeric and cook for 30 seconds, stirring, so it becomes fragrant.

Remove from the heat, add ¼ cup water along with the mustard, vinegar, and sugar. Transfer to a blender and puree. Serve immediately and refrigerate.

PAIRINGS: In Barbados, this sauce often accompanies crisp flying fish filets. I like pairing it with other mild white fish like sautéed cod (page 44) or broiled sole (page 66) or even with something assertive like grilled swordfish (page 78). Serve with Curried Basmati Rice with Currants and Almonds (page 234) and sautéed green beans (page 50).

SHELF LIFE: Up to one week in the refrigerator.

Quick Steak Sauce

It's hard to make something at home that tastes exactly like A1. So don't try. Instead, go in a different direction with this sauce, a sharp mix of sweet and sour flavorings.

YIELD: 1 CUP, 6 SERVINGS
PREP TIME: 6 minutes
COOK TIME: 10 minutes

2 tablespoons olive oil
1 medium Spanish onion (about ½ pound), finely diced (about 1½ cups)
About 1 teaspoon kosher salt
About ½ teaspoon freshly ground black pepper
1 medium garlic clove, chopped (about ¾ teaspoon)
2 tablespoons chopped raisins
2 teaspoons Dijon mustard
2 teaspoons Worcestershire sauce
2 teaspoons red wine vinegar
1 teaspoon soy sauce
1 teaspoon granulated sugar

Heat the oil in a medium saucepan over medium-high heat until shimmering hot, about 1 minute. Add the onion, sprinkle generously with salt and pepper, and cook, stirring, until it starts to soften and become translucent, about 3 minutes. Add the garlic and cook, stirring, until it becomes fragrant, about 30 seconds.

Stir in the remaining ingredients and ⅓ cup water, and bring to a simmer. Cook, stirring occasionally, until the onions become tender, about 5 minutes. Purée using an immersion blender or a regular blender. Serve immediately or refrigerate.

PAIRINGS: My ideal pairing for this sauce would be a sautéed strip steak (page 38). Serve with a baked potato and some sautéed spinach (page 53), the latter to assuage a carnivore's guilt.

SHELF LIFE: Up to one week in the refrigerator.

Cider Gastrique

A gastrique is a fancy French name for a sweet and sour reduction. This sauce starts with a quick caramel base, which is then sharpened with a splash of cider vinegar.

YIELD: ½ CUP, ABOUT 4 SERVINGS
PREP TIME: 2 minutes
COOK TIME: 6 minutes

¼ cup granulated sugar
⅓ cup apple cider vinegar
1 teaspoon chopped fresh thyme
About ¼ teaspoon kosher salt
About ¼ teaspoon freshly ground black pepper

Cook the sugar with 3 tablespoons water in a medium saucepan over medium heat, stirring, until it dissolves, about 2 minutes. Raise the heat to high and cook until the mixture turns a light golden brown, about 4 minutes. Remove from the heat and carefully add the vinegar (it will bubble and steam) and then stir in the thyme and a sprinkling of salt and pepper to taste.

OPTIONS: Upgrade this sauce by using an unfiltered, artisan cider vinegar like Bragg's.

PAIRINGS: Drizzle this sauce over a sautéed pork chop (page 38) or sautéed salmon (page 42) and serve either with Horseradish Mashed Potatoes (page 235) and sautéed Swiss chard (page 53).

SHELF LIFE: Up to two weeks in the refrigerator.

Ancho Chile Ketchup

If you've read Malcolm Gladwell's wonderful piece on ketchup in the *New Yorker*, you understand why it may be near impossible to beat the flavor of Heinz. So when I make homemade ketchup, I like to swerve it in an assertive flavor direction—here ancho chile is the thing—so it's more an intensely spiced condiment than a Heinz imposter.

YIELD: 1½ CUPS, 6 SERVINGS
PREP TIME: 5 minutes
COOK TIME: 10 minutes

½ cup finely diced yellow onion (about 1 medium)
2 tablespoons olive oil
2 teaspoons ground ancho chile powder
¼ teaspoon allspice
⅛ teaspoon mace (optional—don't make a special trip
    to the market if you don't have it!)
About ¾ teaspoon kosher salt
About ¾ teaspoon freshly ground black pepper
1 cup tomato purée
2 tablespoons light corn syrup
2 tablespoons light brown sugar
1 tablespoon cider vinegar

Cook the onion with the oil in a large saucepan over medium-high heat, stirring occasionally, until it starts to soften and become translucent, about 4 minutes. Add the spices and generous sprinklings of salt and pepper, and cook, stirring for 30 seconds so they become fragrant. Stir in the remaining ingredients, bring to a simmer, cover, and cook, stirring occasionally, until the onions become tender, 5 minutes. Purée and let cool to room temperature before serving.

PAIRINGS: Pair with the same sorts of things to which you'd normally add ketchup like a grilled burger (page 76) or grilled chuck steak (page 75). Serve either with French fries and a vinegary slaw.

SHELF LIFE: Up to one week in the refrigerator.

Herbed Honey Whole-Grain Mustard

This sauce doesn't redline the creativity meter, but it's tasty and sophisticated enough for a seared chop or cutlet.

YIELD: ¾ CUP, 4 SERVINGS
PREP TIME: 4 minutes
COOK TIME: N/A

½ cup whole-grain mustard
¼ cup honey
2 teaspoons chopped fresh tarragon
1 teaspoon chopped fresh thyme
About ½ teaspoon freshly ground black pepper

Stir together all the ingredients in a medium bowl and season with more pepper to taste.

PAIRINGS: Make a colorful meal with this sauce, sautéed pork chops (page 38), sautéed carrots (page 52), and Wild Rice with Dried Cherries and Toasted Walnuts (page 172).

SHELF LIFE: Up to one week in the refrigerator.

Cranberry Mustard Sauce

I'm that guy who keeps on passing the cranberry sauce at Thanksgiving. Its tangy bite just isn't my thing. I do like cranberries as a supporting player in sauces like this one, though, where it adds a measured sweet and sour punch.

YIELD: ¾ CUP, 4 SERVINGS
PREP TIME: 4 minutes
COOK TIME: N/A
¼ cup brown mustard
¼ cup canned cranberry jelly
2 tablespoons maple syrup
2 teaspoons cider vinegar
1 teaspoon chopped fresh thyme
About ½ teaspoon freshly ground black pepper

Stir together all the ingredients in a medium bowl and season with pepper to taste.

PAIRINGS: Spread on sautéed boneless pork chops (page 38) or turkey cutlets (page 36) and serve with sautéed Brussels sprouts (page 52) and Couscous with Cinnamon and Oranges (page 237).

SHELF LIFE: Up to one week in the refrigerator.

Carolina BBQ Sauce

This sauce is my take on the vinegary mixtures that North Carolinians pair with slow-cooked barbecue. Because this sauce is both spicy and highly acidic, serve it with full-flavored, even fatty cuts.

YIELD: 1¼ CUPS, 8 SERVINGS
PREP TIME: 2 minutes
COOK TIME: 3 minutes

¼ cup Frank's Red Hot sauce
¼ cup white vinegar
¼ cup light brown sugar
1 teaspoon Dijon mustard
½ teaspoon freshly ground black pepper

Combine all the ingredients with ½ cup water in a medium saucepan. Bring to a simmer so the mixture heats through. Season with more pepper to taste.

PAIRINGS: Partner with hardy cuts for which the acidity and heat of the sauce will act as a welcome foil. Pull (or shred) grilled, boneless chicken thighs (page 71) or grilled country–style ribs (page 75), toss with this sauce, and stuff into a bulky roll with thinly sliced cabbage and dill pickle.

SHELF LIFE: Up to two weeks in the refrigerator.

Homemade Hummus

This is another example of a sauce that's easy enough to make yourself (and make well), so why buy it at the supermarket?

YIELD: 1½ CUPS, 6 TO 8 SERVINGS
PREP TIME: 6 minutes
COOK TIME: N/A

1 (15½-ounce) can garbanzos, rinsed and drained well
2 tablespoons tahini, stirred well (look in the supermarket international aisle)
2 tablespoons freshly squeezed lemon juice
1 small garlic clove, chopped (about ½ teaspoon)
½ teaspoon ground cumin
⅛ to ¼ teaspoon hot pimentón de la Vera or cayenne, more for sprinkling
About ¾ teaspoon kosher salt
About ½ teaspoon freshly ground black pepper
¼ cup olive oil, more for drizzling

In a food processor or blender, pulse the garbanzos, tahini, lemon juice, garlic, cumin, and pimentón with a generous sprinkling of salt and pepper and purée until chopped. While still processing, add the oil in a thin, steady stream and then a couple of tablespoons of water so the mixture is smooth. Season with more salt, pepper, and lemon juice to taste and serve drizzled with olive oil and sprinkled with a pinch of pimentón.

OPTIONS: Add a couple of teaspoons of chopped fresh thyme or rosemary or 1 jarred roasted red pepper before puréeing.

PAIRINGS: I like to spread hummus into sandwiches and burgers as a healthier alternative to butter or cheese. Make a grilled pita sandwich with this sauce, diced grilled chicken breasts (page 71), or thinly sliced grilled flank steak (page 75), chopped cucumber, tomatoes, and pickles.

SHELF LIFE: Up to five days in the refrigerator.

Lemony Tahini Sauce

Tahini, or ground sesame paste, is what gives hummus its nutty, toasted flavor. But if you leave the garbanzos out of the mix and instead purée a large spoonful of this paste (available in the international aisle at most supermarkets) with lemon juice and fresh cilantro, you get a loose drizzling sauce that goes nicely with Mediterranean-inspired dishes.

YIELD: 1 CUP, 6 TO 8 SERVINGS
PREP TIME: 5 minutes
COOK TIME: N/A

½ cup tahini, stirred well
¼ cup freshly squeezed lemon juice plus 1 teaspoon zest
2 tablespoons chopped fresh cilantro
1 garlic clove, chopped (about 1 teaspoon)
½ teaspoon ground cumin
¼ teaspoon Tabasco
About ¾ teaspoon kosher salt
About ½ teaspoon freshly ground black pepper

In a food processor or blender, purée all of the ingredients and then, with the motor still running, drizzle in up to ¼ cup water so the mixture becomes smooth and saucy. Add more lemon juice, salt, and pepper to taste.

PAIRINGS: Drizzle this sauce on spice-rubbed grilled or broiled lamb chops (page 74 or 65) and serve with Couscous with Cinnamon and Oranges (page 237).

SHELF LIFE: Up to five days in the refrigerator.

Mint Sauce with Shallot and Green Olives

This is a slightly dressy take on your basic mint sauce. The shallot is more delicate than garlic and the salty punch from the olives balances out the sweetness of the mint.

YIELD: 1 CUP, 6 SERVINGS
PREP TIME: 6 minutes
COOK TIME: N/A

2 tablespoons red wine vinegar
1 tablespoon granulated sugar
¼ cup coarsely chopped pitted green olives (I like picholine)
3 tablespoons chopped fresh mint
1 medium shallot, finely diced (about 3 tablespoons)
About ¾ teaspoon kosher salt
About ½ teaspoon freshly ground black pepper

In a medium bowl mix all the ingredients with ¼ cup water and season with more salt and pepper to taste.

PAIRINGS: This is one of those sauces intended almost exclusively for a specific pairing. Yes, you could drizzle it on seared chicken breasts or a steak, but the most natural pairing is grilled or broiled lamb chops (page 75 or page 64). Make it a spring menu with grilled asparagus (page 80) and boiled buttery new potatoes.

SHELF LIFE: Up to three days in the refrigerator.

VINAIGRETTES

Vinaigrettes are not just for salads. They're for searing, too: for drizzling on sautéed pork chops or broiled asparagus spears or grilled swordfish steaks. Their composition tends to be simple: a little vinegar, a heavy splash of oil, and a base of some sort of aromatic allium (like shallots or garlic) and fresh herb. But the resulting balance of acidic, sweet, and rich elements helps vinaigrettes punch up bland fare (like a cod filet or a chicken breast) or stand up to full-flavored seared ingredients (like lamb chops or salmon steaks). Whether you decide to set seared ingredients that have been dressed with a vinaigrette over a bed of greens is your call.

Though I love fresh herbs in vinaigrettes, I try to list options for dried herbs just in case you're working straight from the pantry. Likewise, I give you the choice to whisk these vinaigrettes by hand or pulse them in a blender. Finally, you'll notice a dearth of creamy dressings in this section. That's because all of the mayonnaise-based vinaigrettes are listed in the following section on page 189.

BASIC VINAIGRETTE TECHNIQUE

Whisk together vinegar, mustard, and oil in a bowl or buzz using an immersion blender (or upright blender). I prefer an immersion blender (or an Aerolatte milk-frothing whisk) because it's quick and great for pulling these mixtures into uniform, creamy emulsions. Then, fold in fresh herbs, aromatics like garlic and shallot, and, in some cases, seared ingredients like bacon or mushrooms.

EMULSIFYING ISN'T NECESSARY

The primary goal when preparing a vinaigrette is to bring oil and vinegar together into a happy coexistence (scientifically known as an emulsion). Like a pair of Patriots and Jets fans, though, these two want nothing to do with each other. So some artifice is needed to make this love connection. One way is through mustard or egg yolks, which act as emulsifiers. The other is timely whisking at the start of the process so that fat globules from the oil chain together with the water molecules from the vinegar into a stable link.

OIL-VINEGAR RATIO

The traditional vinaigrette ratio, three parts oil to one part vinegar, produces a sauce with a proper balance of acidity and richness. And while I do appreciate this balance, I generally lean toward a slightly more acidic makeup for the vinaigrettes in this book because they're meant to accompany not just salad greens, but full-flavored seared ingredients like chicken, meat, or fish where a little extra acidity adds a pleasing kick.

"House" Thyme–Dijon Vinaigrette

This is my "house" vinaigrette. It's simple and balanced and would be the one sauce I'd urge you to make each week—if you only had time to make one—because it goes with so many things: a quick salad with grilled chicken, plain sautéed pork chops or steaks, or broiled fish or vegetables.

YIELD: ¾ CUP, 4 SERVINGS
PREP TIME: 5 minutes
COOK TIME: N/A

3 tablespoons red wine vinegar
2 teaspoons Dijon mustard
About ½ teaspoon kosher salt
About ½ teaspoon freshly ground black pepper
½ cup olive oil
1 medium shallot, finely diced (about 3 tablespoons)
2 teaspoons finely chopped fresh thyme or ½ teaspoon
   dried oregano

In a medium bowl (or in a blender for a quicker, thicker emulsion), whisk (or purée) the vinegar with the mustard, salt, and pepper. Still whisking (or puréeing) slowly drizzle in the oil so it thickens with the mustard mixture and then the shallot and thyme or oregano. Season with more salt or pepper to taste.

OPTIONS: Whisk in ¼ cup chopped black olives, sun-dried tomatoes, or grated parmesan.

PAIRINGS: Drizzle this vinaigrette over grilled chicken breasts (page 71) or a relatively mild fish like halibut (page 78) or swordfish (page 78).

SHELF LIFE: Up to five days in the refrigerator (even longer if you go without the shallot or add it right before serving).

North End Rosemary Vinaigrette

Many of the Sunday nights of my youth were spent huddled around a wooden booth at the European, the oldest of old-school Boston pizzerias where there were mini jukeboxes at each table and a seemingly endless line of families waiting to order a massive pie. Before the pizza, there would always be a large platter of antipasto tossed with a tangy vinaigrette that I've tried to replicate here.

YIELD: ABOUT ¾ CUP, 4 SERVINGS
PREP TIME: 5 minutes
COOK TIME: N/A

3 tablespoons red wine vinegar
1 teaspoon Dijon mustard
About ½ teaspoon kosher salt
About ½ teaspoon freshly ground black pepper
½ cup extra-virgin olive oil
1½ teaspoons chopped fresh rosemary
1 small garlic clove, minced and mashed to a paste using the
   side of a chef's knife, about ½ teaspoon (see page 153)

In a medium bowl (or in a blender for a quicker, thicker emulsion), whisk (or purée) the vinegar with the mustard, salt, and pepper. Still whisking (or puréeing) slowly drizzle in the oil so it thickens with the mustard mixture. Whisk in the rosemary and garlic and season with more salt or pepper to taste.

PAIRINGS: Make a fresh antipasto with this vinaigrette, sliced grilled chicken breasts (page 71) or grilled tuna (page 78), shaved pecorino, jarred pepperoncini peppers, and good olives.

SHELF LIFE: Up to five days in the refrigerator.

Balsamic Vinaigrette

To this day, my mom always has some version of this vinaigrette on hand in the fridge in a glass jar. She gives it a quick shake to re-emulsify and then drizzles it over Romaine leaves and sliced grilled chicken breasts.

YIELD: ABOUT ¾ CUP, 4 SERVINGS
PREP TIME: 6 minutes
COOK TIME: N/A

2½ tablespoons balsamic vinegar

1 teaspoon Dijon mustard

About ½ teaspoon kosher salt

About ½ teaspoon freshly ground black pepper

½ cup extra-virgin olive oil

1 medium shallot, finely diced (about 3 tablespoons) (optional)

1 teaspoon chopped fresh thyme or ½ teaspoon dried oregano

In a medium bowl (or in a blender for a quicker, thicker emulsion), whisk (or purée) the vinegar with the mustard, salt, and pepper. Still whisking (or purée-ing) slowly drizzle in the oil so it thickens with the mustard mixture. Whisk in the shallot, if using, and thyme and season with more salt and pepper to taste.

PAIRINGS: Balsamic vinegar goes great with most anything though I particularly like it on grilled pork chops (page 75) or broiled scallops (page 66). Serve with Roasted Rosemary Fingerling Potatoes (page 235) and sautéed asparagus (page 50).

SHELF LIFE: Up to one week in the refrigerator (even longer if you go without the shallot or add it right before serving).

Grainy Maple Mustard Vinaigrette

Though the basic ingredients in a whole-grain mustard and a Dijon mustard are the same—wine, mustard seeds, and seasonings—the seeds in the whole-grain are left intact, not puréed, so they impart texture and a slightly milder flavor to a vinaigrette like this one.

YIELD: ¾ CUP, 4 SERVINGS
PREP TIME: 6 minutes
COOK TIME: N/A

2 tablespoons cider vinegar

1 tablespoon whole-grain Dijon mustard

About ½ teaspoon kosher salt

About ½ teaspoon freshly ground black pepper

½ cup extra-virgin olive oil

2 tablespoons maple syrup

1 medium shallot, finely diced (about 3 tablespoons) (optional)

1 teaspoon chopped fresh thyme

In a medium bowl (or in a blender for a quicker, thicker emulsion), whisk (or purée) the vinegar with the mustard, salt, and pepper. Still whisking (or purée-ing) slowly drizzle in the oil so it thickens with the mustard mixture. Whisk in the maple syrup, shallot, if using, and thyme and season with more salt and pepper to taste.

PAIRINGS: Drizzle this sweet and sour vinaigrette over sautéed or grilled pork chops (page 38 or 75) and serve over Cheddar Cheese Grits (page 237) with sautéed carrots (page 52) for a meal that screams autumn.

SHELF LIFE: Up to one week in the refrigerator (even longer if you go without the shallot or add it right before serving).

Philly Hot Cherry Pepper Vinaigrette

You know those "My parents went to _____, and all I got was this crappy T-shirt!" T-shirts? Well, my midsummer guys' trip to Philadelphia a couple of years back (to watch the Red Sox take on the Phillies) went something like that. Mostly all I got was an unhealthy appreciation for cheese steaks. This vinaigrette works the classic cheesesteak's toppings—onions, peppers, cheese, hot cherry peppers— into a tangy, spicy sauce.

YIELD: ABOUT 1 CUP, 4 TO 6 SERVINGS
PREP TIME: 8 minutes
COOK TIME: N/A

3 tablespoons red wine vinegar
1½ teaspoons spicy brown mustard (like Gulden's)
About ¾ teaspoon kosher salt
About ½ teaspoon freshly ground black pepper
½ cup canola oil
¼ cup freshly grated Parmesan
¼ cup chopped jarred hot cherry peppers
1 small garlic clove, minced and mashed to a paste using the side of a chef's knife, about ½ teaspoon (see page 153)
½ teaspoon dried oregano

In a medium bowl (or in a blender for a quicker, thicker emulsion), whisk (or purée) the vinegar with the mustard, salt, and pepper. Still whisking (or puréeing) slowly drizzle in the oil so it thickens with the mustard mixture. Whisk in the remaining ingredients and season with more salt and pepper to taste.

PAIRINGS: In the sporting spirit of this sauce, drizzle it on a sliced grilled steak (page 75) sandwich or on broiled pork chops (page 64). Serve with potato chips or something else bad for you.

SHELF LIFE: Up to three days in the refrigerator.

Lemon–Basil Vinaigrette

This is meant to be a loose (i.e., broken) vinaigrette, so there's no need for mustard here (besides, its flavor would clash with the fresh lemon juice). Follow my mom's vinaigrette method and put all the ingredients in a jar and give them a good shake to momentarily thicken right before serving.

YIELD: ABOUT ¾ CUP, 4 SERVINGS
PREP TIME: 7 minutes
COOK TIME: N/A

3 tablespoons freshly squeezed lemon juice (from about ½ lemon) plus 1 teaspoon freshly grated lemon zest
½ teaspoon granulated sugar
½ cup canola oil
2 tablespoons chopped fresh basil
1 scallion (both white and green part), trimmed and thinly sliced
About ¾ teaspoon kosher salt
About ¾ teaspoon freshly ground black pepper

Set all the ingredients in a jar or sealable container. Shake well just before serving.

PAIRINGS: This vinaigrette goes particularly well with grilled seafood (page 78) or fish (page 78). Or stir a couple of tablespoons into a pot of sautéed clams or mussels (page 48) and serve with grilled corn on the cob (page 82).

SHELF LIFE: Up to two days in the refrigerator.

Lemon Caesar

I've got a couple of different takes on Caesar in this book, because one is simply not enough. This is the lighter, vinaigrette version. Lemon plays the lead, bridging the intense flavors of Worcestershire sauce, Parmigiano, and anchovies. I usually omit the anchovies (unless it's with a creamy dressing like page 187 where their flavor melds in a little better), though if they're your thing, go for it.

YIELD: 1 CUP, 4 TO 6 SERVINGS
PREP TIME: 6 minutes
COOK TIME: N/A

3 tablespoons freshly squeezed lemon juice (from about ½ lemon)
1 teaspoon red wine vinegar
½ teaspoon Dijon mustard
½ teaspoon Worcestershire sauce
1 garlic clove, minced and mashed to a paste using the side of chef's knife (see page 153)
About ½ teaspoon kosher salt
About ½ teaspoon freshly ground black pepper
½ cup extra-virgin olive oil
½ cup freshly grated Parmigiano Reggiano

In a medium bowl (or in a blender for a quicker, thicker emulsion), whisk (or purée) the lemon juice with the vinegar, mustard, Worcestershire sauce, garlic, salt, and pepper. Still whisking (or puréeing) slowly drizzle in the oil so it thickens with the mustard mixture. Whisk in the Parmigiano and season with more salt or pepper to taste.

PAIRINGS: Use this dressing as the base for a Caesar salad with grilled chicken (page 71), broiled shrimp (page 66), or grilled vegetables (page 80). Toss half of the dressing with Romaine hearts, shaved Parmigiano, and bread crisps or croutons, top with the seared ingredients, and then drizzle with the remaining vinaigrette.

SHELF LIFE: Up to one week in the refrigerator.

Salamanca Sherry-Thyme Vinaigrette

I spent a year in college studying in the Spanish university town of Salamanca. Beyond improving my Spanish, I learned the beauty of the Spanish way of life and how to live on my own and make a proper mess of a kitchen with my slacker Spanish flatmates. This vinaigrette was a staple of my roommate Juan Murillo, habitually unshaven and unkempt but adept in the kitchen.

YIELD: ¾ CUP, 4 SERVINGS
PREP TIME: 4 minutes
COOK TIME: N/A

2 tablespoons sherry vinegar
1 teaspoon Dijon mustard
About ½ teaspoon kosher salt
About ½ teaspoon freshly ground black pepper
½ cup extra-virgin olive oil
2 tablespoons finely diced jarred piquillo pepper or roasted red pepper (optional)
2 teaspoons chopped fresh thyme
1 small garlic clove, minced and mashed to a paste using the side of a chef's knife, about ½ teaspoon (see page 153)

In a medium bowl (or in a blender for a quicker, thicker emulsion), whisk (or purée) the vinegar with the mustard, salt, and pepper. Still whisking (or puréeing) slowly drizzle in the oil so it thickens with the mustard mixture. Whisk in the pepper (if using), thyme, and garlic and season with more salt or pepper to taste.

PAIRINGS: This dressing is perfect for a composed grilled salad of shrimp (page 78), zucchini, red peppers (page 80), and canned chick peas.

SHELF LIFE: Up to one week in the refrigerator.

Sun-Dried Tomato and Caper Vinaigrette

The intensity of sun-dried tomatoes and capers make this vinaigrette a better fit for our sear-and-sauce applications than for your everyday green salad. Use a blender to ensure that the sun-dried tomatoes get evenly incorporated into the sauce.

YIELD: 1 CUP, 4 TO 6 SERVINGS
PREP TIME: 8 minutes
COOK TIME: N/A

3 tablespoons red wine vinegar
1 teaspoon Dijon mustard
2 oil-packed sun-dried tomatoes, chopped (about 3 tablespoons)
1 clove garlic, minced and mashed to a paste using the side of a chef's knife (see page 153)
About ¼ teaspoon kosher salt
About ¾ teaspoon freshly ground black pepper
½ cup extra-virgin olive oil
1 tablespoon nonpareil capers, drained well and chopped
1 teaspoon chopped fresh rosemary

Using an immersion blender or a regular blender, purée the vinegar and mustard with the sun-dried tomatoes, garlic, salt, and pepper and while still puréeing, slowly add the oil so the mixture thickens. Stir in the capers and rosemary, and season with salt and pepper to taste.

PAIRINGS: I like sticking with the Mediterranean vibe of this vinaigrette by drizzling it over grilled tuna (page 78) or broiled swordfish (page 66) and serving with grilled eggplant and peppers (page 80).

SHELF LIFE: Up to five days in the refrigerator.

Champagne Vinaigrette

Champagne vinegar is, indeed, produced from champagne, so it's a little more expensive than your basic red or white wine vinegar, and also has a sweetness and lightness that makes this vinaigrette a little elegant.

YIELD: ABOUT ¾ CUP, 4 SERVINGS
PREP TIME: 6 minutes
COOK TIME: N/A

2½ tablespoons champagne vinegar
½ teaspoon Dijon mustard
About ¾ teaspoon kosher salt
About ½ teaspoon freshly ground black pepper
½ cup extra-virgin olive oil
1 medium shallot, finely diced (about 3 tablespoons)
1 teaspoon chopped fresh thyme

In a medium bowl (or in a blender for a quicker, thicker emulsion), whisk the vinegar with the mustard, salt, and pepper. Still whisking (or puréeing) slowly drizzle in the oil so it thickens with the mustard mixture. Whisk in the shallot and thyme and season with more salt and pepper to taste.

PAIRINGS: Match this vinaigrette with delicate ingredients that showcase the sauce's nuanced flavors. Sautéed scallops (page 46) are just the thing. Toss mesclun greens with some of this vinaigrette, set in the middle of dinner plates, and drizzle with the remaining vinaigrette. Top the scallops with little dollops of American caviar if you're serving company.

SHELF LIFE: Up to three days.

Greek Dressing

This vinaigrette incorporates the basic elements of a Greek salad—cucumbers, onions, and olives—into a chunky saladlike sauce.

YIELD: ABOUT 1¼ CUPS, 4 TO 6 SERVINGS
PREP TIME: 10 minutes
COOK TIME: N/A

2 tablespoons freshly squeezed lemon juice
1 tablespoon red wine vinegar
1 teaspoon Dijon mustard
About ½ teaspoon kosher salt
About ¾ teaspoon freshly ground black pepper
½ cup extra-virgin olive oil
¼ cup finely diced red onion (about ½ onion)
¼ cup chopped English seedless cucumber
¼ cup chopped pitted Kalamata olives
½ teaspoon dried oregano

In a medium bowl (or in a blender for a quicker, thicker emulsion), whisk (or purée) the lemon juice and vinegar with the mustard, salt, and pepper. Still whisking (or puréeing) slowly drizzle in the oil so it thickens with the mustard mixture. Stir in the remaining ingredients and season with more salt and pepper to taste.

PAIRINGS: Pair this dressing with summery grilled fare. Sandwich sliced grilled lamb steaks (page 75) or steak (page 75) into a pita with chopped Romaine, crumbled feta, cherry tomatoes, and a generous drizzle of this vinaigrette.

SHELF LIFE: Up to three days in the refrigerator.

Orange Soy Vinaigrette

This is one of the first salad dressings I put on the menu at b.good. The orange juice knocks the salty edge off the soy, giving this sauce a pleasant creamy/tangy balance.

YIELD: ABOUT ¾ CUP, 4 TO 6 SERVINGS
PREP TIME: 4 minutes
COOK TIME: N/A

2 teaspoons Dijon mustard
2 tablespoons soy sauce
½ cup canola oil or grapeseed oil
⅓ cup orange juice (preferably freshly squeezed)
1 tablespoon rice vinegar
1 scallion (both white and green parts), trimmed and
   thinly sliced

In a medium bowl (or in a blender for a quicker, thicker emulsion), whisk the mustard with the soy sauce. Still whisking (or puréeing) slowly drizzle in the oil so it thickens with the mustard mixture. Stir in the remaining ingredients and add more soy sauce or orange juice to taste.

PAIRINGS: Make a grilled teriyaki beef salad with this dressing. Brush a grilled flank steak with the Toasted Sesame Teriyaki Sauce (page 90), and then let cool for a couple of minutes, thinly slice, and set atop mesclun greens and shredded carrots with this dressing.

SHELF LIFE: Up to three days in the refrigerator.

Sesame-Miso Dressing

You've probably had miso, or fermented soy bean paste, in Japanese miso soup. This intensely flavored paste also goes great in light vinaigrettes like this one. Its sweet, concentrated saltiness gives this dressing an infusion of umami depth.

YIELD: ¾ CUP, 4 SERVINGS
PREP TIME: 6 minutes
COOK TIME: N/A

1 tablespoon red or white miso

2 teaspoons Dijon mustard

2 tablespoons rice vinegar

½ cup canola oil or grapeseed oil

1 tablespoon soy sauce

2 teaspoons toasted sesame oil

1 teaspoon light brown sugar

1 scallion (both white and green parts), trimmed and thinly sliced

In a medium bowl (or in a blender for a quicker, thicker emulsion), whisk (or purée) the miso with the mustard and vinegar. Still whisking (or puréeing) slowly drizzle in the oil so it thickens with the mustard mixture. Stir in the remaining ingredients and add more soy sauce to taste.

PAIRINGS: In the winter months when I know I should be eating healthier, I'll make a composed salad with this dressing, thinly sliced green cabbage, carrots, scallions, and broiled chicken breasts (page 63) or shrimp (page 66).

SHELF LIFE: Up to three days in the refrigerator.

Seared Jalapeño and Lime Vinaigrette

This is another one of those sauces that is less mild-mannered salad partner and more kick-ass, fire-and-acid concoction, meant to hop up basic seared food.

YIELD: ¾ CUP, 4 SERVINGS
PREP TIME: 6 minutes
COOK TIME: 4 minutes

6 tablespoons olive oil or canola oil

2 jalapeños, cored, seeded, and finely diced (about ⅓ cup)

¾ teaspoon kosher salt

½ teaspoon freshly ground black pepper

1 medium garlic clove, minced (about ¾ teaspoon)

2 tablespoons chopped fresh cilantro

2 tablespoons freshly squeezed lime juice

½ teaspoon granulated sugar

Heat 2 tablespoons of the oil in a skillet over medium-high heat until shimmering hot, about 1½ minutes. Add the jalapeños, sprinkle with half of the salt and pepper and cook, stirring, until they start to turn light brown at the edges, about 2 minutes. Add the garlic and cook, stirring, until it becomes fragrant, about 30 seconds.

Remove from the heat and let cool for a couple of minutes then transfer to a jar or sealable container along with the remaining ingredients, the remaining oil, and the remaining salt and pepper. Shake well just before serving.

PAIRINGS: Toss this vinaigrette with grilled chicken parts (page 71) for a fresher, more tangy take on buffalo chicken. Serve with grilled corn (page 82) and vegetable salad.

SHELF LIFE: Up to three days in the refrigerator.

Pineapple Lime Vinaigrette

I like making this sauce in spring when pineapples are in season. Instead of emulsifying it, simply stir or shake it well before serving.

YIELD: ABOUT 1¼ CUPS, 4 SERVINGS
PREP TIME: 8 minutes
COOK TIME: N/A

1 cup diced fresh or canned pineapple, pulsed in a food
    processor to chop
6 tablespoons olive oil or canola oil
2 scallions (both white and green parts), trimmed and
    thinly sliced
1 jalapeño, cored, seeded, and finely diced (about 3
    tablespoons)
2 tablespoons freshly squeezed lime juice
1 tablespoon chopped fresh mint
2 teaspoons red wine vinegar
1 teaspoon light brown sugar
About ¾ teaspoon kosher salt
About ½ teaspoon freshly ground black pepper

In a large bowl, mix all the ingredients. Season with more salt and pepper to taste and transfer to a jar or sealable container. Shake well just before serving.

PAIRINGS: I like this vinaigrette with seafood: try it drizzled over grilled shrimp skewers (page 78) or broiled scallops (page 66).

SHELF LIFE: Up to two days in the refrigerator.

Shiitake-Ginger Vinaigrette

Shiitakes are one of those mushrooms that really add depth of flavor to a sauce. In this case, it's an umami-like richness, which is flanked by sautéed garlic and ginger.

YIELD: ¾ CUP, 4 SERVINGS
PREP TIME: 6 minutes
COOK TIME: 4 minutes

2 tablespoons minced ginger
6 tablespoons canola or peanut oil
2 ounces shiitake mushrooms (about 6), stemmed and
    cut in ¼-inch dice
1 medium garlic clove, minced (about ¾ teaspoon)
About ¼ teaspoon kosher salt
About ¼ teaspoon freshly ground black pepper
2 tablespoons rice vinegar
1 tablespoon soy sauce
1 teaspoon toasted sesame oil
½ teaspoon light brown sugar

Heat the ginger with 2 tablespoons of the canola oil in a skillet over medium-high heat until it sizzles steadily and just starts to turn light brown at its edges, about 2 minutes. Add the shiitakes and garlic, sprinkle lightly with salt and pepper, and cook, stirring often, until the mushrooms soften completely, about 2 minutes. Remove from the heat and let cool for a couple of minutes.

Transfer the seared shiitake mixture with the remaining oil and the remaining ingredients to a jar or sealable container. Shake well just before serving.

PAIRINGS: Drizzle this vinaigrette over sautéed cod (page 44), stir-fried bok choy or Chinese broccoli (page 50), and serve with Chinese egg noodles tossed with some of this vinaigrette as well.

SHELF LIFE: Up to three days in the refrigerator.

Lemongrass-Chile Vinaigrette

Lemongrass has a vibrant citrus flavor that will remind you of your favorite Vietnamese or Thai dishes. It also has a tough, fibrous texture, so cut it into large pieces that will be easy to fish out of the sauce.

YIELD: ¾ CUP, 4 SERVINGS
PREP TIME: 7 minutes
COOK TIME: 4 minutes

6 tablespoons canola or peanut oil
1 lemongrass stalk, trimmed, outer leaves discarded, cut in half lengthwise and then cut into 2-inch pieces
1 large shallot, finely diced (about ¼ cup)
2 Thai chiles or 1 jalapeño, cored, seeded, and finely diced (about 2 tablespoons)
About ½ teaspoon kosher salt
2 tablespoons freshly squeezed lime juice
1 teaspoon fish sauce
1 teaspoon granulated sugar

Heat 2 tablespoons of the oil with the lemongrass in a skillet over medium-high heat until the lemongrass starts to sizzle steadily, about 1½ minutes.

Add the shallot and chiles, sprinkle with salt, reduce the heat to medium, and cook, stirring, until the shallot softens and becomes translucent, about 2 minutes. Remove from the heat and let cool for a couple of minutes.

Transfer the seared lemongrass mixture with the remaining oil and the remaining ingredients to a jar or sealable container. Whisk well and season with more sugar and salt to taste. Shake again (and discard the lemongrass) just before serving.

PAIRINGS: The sweet and heat in this sauce go perfectly with grilled or sautéed pork chops or tenderloin (page 75 or 38). Thinly slice the meat, drizzle with this vinaigrette and serve alongside sautéed Napa cabbage (page 53) and steamed jasmine rice.

SHELF LIFE: Up to three days in the refrigerator.

Chipotle-Balsamic Vinaigrette

I know smoked jalapeños from Mexico and vinegar from Italy may sound like a funny match, but the two form a perfect pairing. The smokiness of the chipotles cuts the sweetness of the balsamic. Do make this vinaigrette with a blender so it properly purées the chipotle, spreading the heat around evenly.

YIELD: ¾ CUP, 4 SERVINGS
PREP TIME: 4 minutes
COOK TIME: N/A

2 tablespoons balsamic vinegar
1 canned chipotle, minced plus 2 tablespoons adobo sauce
1 teaspoon Dijon mustard
About ¾ teaspoon kosher salt
About ½ teaspoon freshly ground black pepper
½ cup extra-virgin olive oil
½ teaspoon dried oregano
¼ teaspoon dried cumin

Purée the vinegar, chipotle, adobo sauce, mustard, salt, and pepper in a blender or using an immersion blender and while still puréeing, slowly add the oil so the mixture thickens. Remove from the blender, stir in the remaining ingredients and season with salt and pepper to taste.

OPTION: Fold in some diced red onion or minced garlic after emulsifying this vinaigrette.

PAIRINGS: Drizzle this spicy vinaigrette over a grilled sliced steak (page 75) or toss with a grilled chicken salad (page 71) with grilled corn (page 82), sliced jicama, and diced avocado.

SHELF LIFE: Up to one week in the refrigerator.

Brazilian BBQ Vinaigrette

One of the little benefits of my work at b.good is that I've made a lot of Brazilian friends; that country is the birthplace of a number of leaders in our company. During our parties over the years, this sauce often pops up alongside grilled meats, a tangy mixture of bell pepper, tomatoes, and onions. Like a chimichurri (page 164) or a salsa criolla (page 164), this vinaigrette is meant to be unemulsified. Just give it a quick whisk before serving.

YIELD: 1 CUP, 6 SERVINGS
PREP TIME: 10 minutes
COOK TIME: N/A

1 garlic clove, minced
3 tablespoons white wine vinegar
About ¾ teaspoon kosher salt
About ¾ teaspoon freshly ground black pepper
¼ cup olive oil
1 large plum tomato, cored, seeded and finely diced (about ½ cup)
½ red pepper bell pepper, cored, seeded, and finely diced (about ½ cup)
1 teaspoon chopped fresh thyme (optional)

In a medium bowl, using the back of a spoon and working against the bottom of the bowl, mash the garlic with 1 tablespoon of the vinegar and a generous sprinkling of salt and pepper. Whisk in the oil, the remaining vinegar, the tomato, and bell pepper and season with more salt or pepper to taste. Rewhisk just before serving.

PAIRINGS: Drizzle this vinaigrette on broiled lamb chops (page 64) or grilled Italian sausage (page 75) and pair with rice and stewed black beans.

SHELF LIFE: Up to three days in the refrigerator.

Warm Bacon, Apple, and Sage Vinaigrette

I suppose your eagerness to try this cross between a pan sauce and a vinaigrette largely depends on how much you like bacon fat. There are only a couple of tablespoons of the rendered grease (as opposed to the ½ cup olive oil in most vinaigrettes in this section), as a little of bacon's smoky richness goes a long way.

YIELD: 1 CUP, 6 SERVINGS
PREP TIME: 7 minutes
COOK TIME: 8 minutes

3 ounces thick bacon (about 3 strips), cut in ½-inch pieces
2 tablespoons olive oil
½ cup peeled ¼-inch dice Granny Smith apple (about ½ apple)
1 large shallot, finely diced (about ¼ cup)
2 tablespoons chopped fresh sage
About ¼ teaspoon kosher salt
About ½ teaspoon freshly ground black pepper
3 tablespoons cider vinegar

Heat the bacon with the oil in a large skillet over high heat until it starts to sizzle, about 1 minute. Reduce the heat to medium and cook, stirring, until the bacon starts to brown and renders most of its fat, about 4 minutes. Using a slotted spoon, transfer the bacon to a plate lined with paper towel.

Add the apple, shallot, and sage to the pan, sprinkle lightly with salt and pepper, and cook, stirring, until the apple starts to soften, about 1 minute. Stir in the vinegar and crisp bacon, season with salt and pepper to taste, and give a quick whisk just before serving warm.

PAIRINGS: Drizzle this sauce over vegetables or lean cuts that could use a little meatiness, like sautéed cauliflower (page 52), roasted butternut squash, or a broiled pork tenderloin (page 64).

SHELF LIFE: N/A; this warm vinaigrette should be made fresh.

DRESSINGS AND EMULSIONS

I have a startling admission to make: I really don't like plain mayonnaise: I find it often adds more richness than flavor, which is something I can usually do without. My aversion to mayonnaise can be broken when flavor gets added into the mix, either when the mayo is homemade (see below) – which means it will have a little more zing to start with – or when the jarred stuff is doctored up with some bold flavors. This section covers all the ways in which plain, old mayonnaise can become dynamic, flavor-packed sauces.

BASIC DRESSINGS AND EMULSIONS TECHNIQUE

Because mayonnaise is already emulsified (or thickened), most of the sauces in this section don't demand a blender. A whisk should do just fine. Whisk, fold, or blend herbs, pantry ingredients, and citrus into jarred or homemade mayonnaise and then spread or drizzle as a condiment over seared steaks, fish filets, chicken breasts, or vegetables. Or make mayonnaise the base for creamy vinaigrettes or drizzling sauces.

Master Recipe:
Homemade Mayonnaise

Is it worth making mayonnaise when there are perfectly good jarred concoctions at the supermarket? Only you can answer that question, but it's easy enough to make and the flavor and texture will certainly be superior. For many cooks, one of the drawbacks to making homemade mayo is that the sauce's traditional base, raw eggs, can present a health risk. Get around this by purchasing pasteurized egg yolks at the market.

YIELD: ¾ CUP, 6 SERVINGS

PREP TIME: 4 minutes

COOK TIME: N/A

2 teaspoons Dijon mustard

1 teaspoon red wine vinegar

1 egg yolk or 2 tablespoons pasteurized egg yolks

About ½ teaspoon kosher salt

About ½ teaspoon freshly ground black pepper

½ cup canola oil

2 teaspoons freshly squeezed lemon juice

In a medium bowl (or in a food processor), whisk (or purée) the mustard and vinegar with the egg yolk and a sprinkling of salt and pepper. Still whisking (or puréeing), slowly drizzle in the oil so it thickens with the mustard mixture. Stir in the lemon juice and season with more salt or pepper to taste. You can add a tablespoon or so of water to loosen if you like.

OPTIONS: The recipes that follow in this section show some of the ways that this basic mayo can be jazzed up, though there are so many options it's hard to list them all. If you do want to build on this basic mayo, try whisking in a favorite herb, like rosemary or tarragon, or some minced garlic or finely diced ginger.

PAIRINGS: We often relate to mayonnaise much less as a sauce, than a sandwich condiment. When it's made fresh, though, a mayonnaise's vinaigrette roots are exposed. The lemony tang of this sauce goes great drizzled over a seared fish; we New Englanders love it over grilled bluefish (page 78), though tuna or swordfish would be good, too.

SHELF LIFE: Up to five days in the refrigerator.

Parmesan and Black Pepper Dressing

Use an immersion blender or a food processor for this dressing to smooth out the Parmesan so you get a loose, creamy texture.

YIELD: 1 CUP, 4 TO 6 SERVINGS
PREP TIME: 7 minutes
COOK TIME: N/A

½ cup mayonnaise
⅓ cup freshly grated Parmigiano Reggiano
2 tablespoons red wine vinegar
1 teaspoon chopped fresh thyme (optional)
1 small garlic clove, minced and mashed to a paste using the
    side of a chef's knife, about ½ teaspoon (see page 153)
About ½ teaspoon kosher salt
About 1 teaspoon coarsely ground black pepper

Using an immersion blender or in a blender, blend the mayonnaise with the Parmigiano, vinegar, thyme (if using), garlic, 2 tablespoons of water, and a sprinkling of salt and pepper. Add more water to thin the sauce to the desired consistency and season with more vinegar, salt, and pepper to taste.

PAIRINGS: Beef and black pepper are a natural pairing (think *steak au poivre*). Drizzle this sauce on a thinly sliced grilled top sirloin (page 75) or make a steak salad with this dressing, grilled asparagus (page 80), baby spinach, and cherry tomatoes.

SHELF LIFE: Up to four days in the refrigerator.

TIP: Crack the black pepper coarsely so it adds a little crunch to this dressing.

Creamy Caesar

Whereas the Caesar dressing on page 179 is a loose vinaigrette, this one is creamy and darn near unctuous. This richness makes it the perfect vehicle for anchovies—you'll mostly only get their depth of flavor with just a pleasant hint of fishiness. Toss this dressing well with greens so the sauce gets evenly mixed—it's too thick to just drizzle.

YIELD: ABOUT 1 CUP, 4 TO 6 SERVINGS
PREP TIME: 5 minutes
COOK TIME: N/A

¾ cup jarred or homemade mayonnaise
⅓ cup freshly grated Parmigiano Reggiano
1 large garlic clove, minced and mashed to a paste using the
    side of a chef's knife, about 1 teaspoon (see page 153)
1 tablespoon freshly squeezed lemon juice
1 tablespoon red wine vinegar
1 teaspoon Dijon mustard
½ teaspoon Worcestershire sauce
About ¾ teaspoon kosher salt
About ½ teaspoon freshly ground black pepper

Using an immersion blender or in a blender, blend the mayonnaise with the Parmigiano, garlic, lemon juice, vinegar, mustard, Worcestershire, 2 tablespoons of water, and a sprinkling of salt and pepper. Add more water to thin the sauce to the desired consistency and season with more lemon juice, salt, and pepper to taste.

PAIRINGS: I generally favor Romaine hearts for this preparation and a mild seared ingredient like grilled chicken breasts (page 71) or broiled shrimp (page 66). Or try topping a dressed caesar salad with grilled asparagus (page 80) and spring onions (page 80).

SHELF LIFE: Up to three days in the refrigerator; season with fresh lemon juice before serving.

Tex-Mex Caesar Dressing

Caesar salad was created in the Baja region of Mexico by Caesar Cardini, so it's only natural that this American restaurant classic gets a Tex-Mex makeover.

YIELD: ABOUT 1 CUP, 4 TO 6 SERVINGS
PREP TIME: 8 minutes
COOK TIME: N/A

½ cup homemade or jarred mayonnaise
¼ cup freshly grated Parmigiano
2 tablespoons freshly squeezed lime juice (from about 1 lime)
1 large garlic clove, minced and mashed to a paste using the side of a chef's knife, about 1 teaspoon (see page 153)
½ teaspoon Worcestershire sauce
¼ teaspoon chile powder
About ½ teaspoon kosher salt
About ½ teaspoon freshly ground black pepper
2 tablespoons chopped jarred jalapeño slices
2 tablespoons chopped fresh cilantro

Using an immersion blender or in a blender, blend the mayonnaise with the Parmigiano, lime juice, garlic, Worcestershire, chile powder, 2 tablespoons of water, and a sprinkling of salt and pepper. Stir in the jalapeño and cilantro, add more water to thin the sauce to the desired consistency, and season with more lime juice, salt, and pepper to taste.

PAIRINGS: Make a Tex-Mex chicken Caesar salad. Grill chicken breasts (page 71), top with this dressing, canned pinto beans, diced tomatoes, crumbled queso fresco, and tortilla strips.

SHELF LIFE: Up to three days in the refrigerator; season with lime juice before serving.

Thousand Island Sauce

I'm not one for tossing this dressing on standard salads (I find it too sweet for greens), but I do love it in sandwiches or on burgers.

YIELD: ABOUT 1 CUP, 4 TO 6 SERVINGS
PREP TIME: 5 minutes
COOK TIME: N/A

½ cup homemade or jarred mayonnaise
3 tablespoons finely diced red onion
3 tablespoons dill relish
2 tablespoons ketchup
1 tablespoon chopped fresh parsley
2 teaspoons cider vinegar
¼ teaspoon Tabasco sauce
About ¼ teaspoon kosher salt
About ½ teaspoon freshly ground black pepper

In a medium bowl, mix all of the ingredients with a light sprinkling of salt and pepper to taste.

OPTIONS: Substitute finely diced cornichon pickles for the relish for more nuanced flavor and texture. Add 1 tablespoon chopped jalapeño slices for a little more tang and heat.

PAIRINGS: Make an old-school burger (page 76) with this sauce, sharp cheddar, crisp Iceberg lettuce, sliced beefsteak tomatoes, and red onion. Or whip together a grilled chicken (page 71) salad by tossing diced pieces with this dressing, halved boiled new potatoes, and thinly sliced scallion.

SHELF LIFE: Up to five days in the refrigerator.

Tangy Buttermilk Ranch Dressing

Maybe because of its inclusion in so many salad bars, buttermilk dressing can have a down-market feel. Fresh chives and dill elevate this version while buttermilk, which is the liquid left over from churning milk into butter, gives this dressing a pleasant tang.

YIELD: ABOUT 1 CUP, 6 SERVINGS
PREP TIME: 5 minutes
COOK TIME: N/A

½ cup homemade or jarred mayonnaise
¼ cup buttermilk
¼ cup thinly sliced fresh chives
2 tablespoons sour cream
1 tablespoon red wine vinegar
1 small garlic clove, minced and mashed to a paste using
   the side of a chef's knife, about ½ teaspoon (page 153)
About ¾ teaspoon kosher salt
About ¾ teaspoon freshly ground black pepper

In a medium bowl, mix all of the ingredients with a generous sprinkling of salt and pepper to taste.

PAIRINGS: Make a composed grilled beef (page 75) salad: toss sliced cucumber, tomatoes, and baby arugula with half of the dressing, top with sliced steak and drizzle with the remaining dressing.

SHELF LIFE: Up to three days in the refrigerator.

Green Goddess Dressing

This is one of those iconic, old-school dressings of hotel origins that is still very much relevant in the modern kitchen. The only catch is that you're going to want to include as many of the fresh herbs as you can to give this sauce its proper essence. This is an easier task in the middle of the summer when your herb garden or vegetable crisper are both full.

YIELD: 1¼ CUPS, 4 TO 6 SERVINGS
PREP TIME: 10 minutes
COOK TIME: N/A

¾ cup homemade or jarred mayonnaise
¼ cup buttermilk
¼ cup thinly sliced fresh chives
1 tablespoon chopped fresh tarragon
1 tablespoon chopped fresh chervil or flat-leaf parsley
1 tablespoon freshly squeezed lemon juice
About ¾ teaspoon kosher salt
About ¾ teaspoon freshly ground black pepper

Using an immersion blender or in a blender, blend the mayonnaise with the remaining ingredients. Season with more lemon juice, salt, and pepper to taste.

PAIRINGS: Make a salad of grilled salmon or tuna (page 78) with diced avocado, grape tomatoes, diced red onion, and baby spinach with this dressing on the side for drizzling.

SHELF LIFE: Up to two days in the refrigerator.

Blue Cheese Dressing

This full-flavored sauce may not be ideal the night before a cholesterol test, but it goes great with grilled chicken (hit it with the buffalo sauce first), a sautéed steak, or a burger.

YIELD: 1 CUP; ABOUT 4 SERVINGS
PREP TIME: 6 minutes
COOK TIME: N/A

½ cup mayonnaise
½ cup crumbled blue cheese (about 3 ounces)
2 tablespoons buttermilk
1 teaspoon red wine vinegar
1 small garlic clove, minced and mashed to a paste using the
    side of a chef's knife, about ½ teaspoon (see page 153)
About ½ teaspoon kosher salt
About ½ teaspoon freshly ground black pepper
1 teaspoon chopped fresh thyme

Using an immersion blender or in a blender, blend the mayonnaise with the blue cheese, buttermilk, vinegar, garlic, and a generous sprinkling of salt and pepper. Add more buttermilk to thin the sauce to the desired consistency and season with more vinegar, salt, and pepper to taste.

PAIRINGS: Go old-school steakhouse and pair this dressing with a grilled strip steak or rib eye (page 75), a wedge of iceberg lettuce, and some sliced tomatoes. Drizzle over both the steak and salad and make yourself a promise to eat something heart-friendly like oatmeal in the morning.

SHELF LIFE: Up to three days in the refrigerator.

Curried Apple Mayonnaise

I could give you a culinary explanation for why apples and curry go so well together (the sweet and the spice and blah, blah, blah), but just trust me, they do. Throw together this lively condiment and see all the ways it will improve your searing life.

YIELD: 1¼ CUPS, 6 SERVINGS
PREP TIME: 7 minutes
COOK TIME: N/A

¾ cup homemade or jarred mayonnaise
¼ cup finely diced peeled Granny Smith apple or other
    crisp-tart apple
3 tablespoons coarsely chopped raisins
2 teaspoons freshly squeezed lime juice
1 teaspoon curry powder
⅛ to ¼ teaspoon cayenne powder
About ¼ teaspoon kosher salt
About ½ teaspoon freshly ground black pepper

In a medium bowl, mix the mayonnaise with the remaining ingredients. Season with more salt, pepper, and vinegar to taste.

OPTIONS: Fold in some Browned Sherry Onions (page 225) or grilled onions (page 82).

PAIRINGS: I like making a spontaneous grilled chicken salad (as opposed to those which chill in the fridge for a couple of hours). Let grilled chicken breasts (page 71) cool for 5 minutes, and then dice and toss with this mayo and some toasted slivered almonds; serve with toasted naan.

SHELF LIFE: Up to four days in the refrigerator.

Soy and Wasabi Mayonnaise

You can whisk together the wasabi yourself (just mix a little water with wasabi powder), though the prepared stuff is more convenient.

YIELD: 1 CUP, 6 SERVINGS
PREP TIME: 6 minutes
COOK TIME: N/A

¾ cup homemade or jarred mayonnaise
1 scallion (both white and green parts), trimmed and
    thinly sliced
1 tablespoon soy sauce
1 tablespoon minced fresh ginger
2 teaspoons prepared wasabi
1 teaspoon rice wine vinegar
About ½ teaspoon freshly ground black pepper

In a medium bowl, mix the mayonnaise with the remaining ingredients and a light sprinkling of pepper. Season with more soy sauce, pepper, and vinegar to taste.

PAIRINGS: This sauce goes nicely with the kinds of fish with which wasabi is normally paired. Try grilled tuna (page 78) or broiled salmon (page 66). Sear either quickly so the outside is browned but the inside is still pink and then serve with Orzo with Wild Mushrooms and Baby Spinach (page 233).

SHELF LIFE: Up to five days in the refrigerator.

Lemon-Saffron Mayonnaise

Steep the saffron in the lemon juice for a couple of minutes so it can "bloom," which is just a fancy way of saying that the citrus activates the fragrant orange strands so they become vibrant and colorful.

YIELD: SCANT ¾ CUP, 6 SERVINGS
PREP TIME: 4 minutes
COOK TIME: N/A

1 tablespoon freshly squeezed lemon juice plus
    1 teaspoon freshly grated zest
¼ to ½ teaspoon saffron threads
¾ cup homemade or jarred mayonnaise
2 tablespoons thinly sliced fresh chives (optional)
About ½ teaspoon kosher salt
About ½ teaspoon freshly ground black pepper

In a small bowl, mix the lemon juice, lemon zest, and saffron and let sit for 5 minutes so the mixture turns a bright yellow. In a medium bowl, mix the mayonnaise with this lemon juice mixture, the chives, if using, and a sprinkling of salt and pepper. Season with more salt, pepper, and lemon juice to taste.

PAIRINGS: Color scheme shouldn't be at the top of your searing priorities but this yellow mayo really pops with grilled asparagus (page 80) or sautéed salmon (page 42). Pair with Quinoa with Fennel, Roasted Red Peppers, and Feta (page 236).

SHELF LIFE: Up to one week in the refrigerator.

Half-Homemade Tartar Sauce

I have the same problem with jarred tartar sauce that I do with supermarket mayonnaise: it's rather bland, which can make its richness hard to justify. My relationship with tartar sauce changes when I make my own, even with jarred mayo and relish (hence the "half homemade"). Doctor the mixture with fresh lemon juice, parsley, and shallot.

YIELD: 1¼ CUPS, 6 SERVINGS
PREP TIME: 6 minutes
COOK TIME: N/A

¾ cup jarred or homemade mayonnaise
¼ cup dill or sweet pickle relish
1 small shallot, finely diced (about 2 tablespoons)
1 tablespoon chopped fresh parsley (optional)
2 teaspoons freshly squeezed lemon juice
1 teaspoon Dijon mustard
¼ teaspoon Tabasco
About ¼ teaspoon kosher salt
About ½ teaspoon freshly ground black pepper

In a medium bowl, mix all of the ingredients with a light sprinkling of salt and pepper and more lemon juice to taste.

PAIRINGS: Tartar sauce goes well with mild and assertive fish alike. Pair it with grilled swordfish (page 78) or broiled cod (page 66) and serve with French fries and a red leaf lettuce salad.

SHELF LIFE: Up to four days in the refrigerator.

Fresh Cucumber and Dill Tartar Sauce

This is a tartar sauce more in spirit. The fresh cucumber takes the place of jarred sweet relish, giving the sauce a softer edge to go with mild fish like sole or tilapia.

YIELD: ABOUT 1¼ CUPS, 6 SERVINGS
PREP TIME: 7 minutes
COOK TIME: N/A

¼ cup finely diced English cucumber or pickling cucumber
¼ cup finely diced red onion
About ¾ teaspoon kosher salt
About ½ teaspoon freshly ground black pepper
½ cup jarred or homemade mayonnaise
1 tablespoon chopped fresh dill
2 teaspoons white wine vinegar
1 teaspoon freshly grated lemon zest

Set the cucumber and onion on a large plate lined with paper towels. Sprinkle generously with salt and pepper, and let sit for a couple of minutes. Then pat dry to remove any juices. Transfer to a medium bowl and mix with the remaining ingredients and more salt, pepper, and vinegar to taste.

PAIRINGS: Make a lighter fish-and-chips type sandwich with sautéed cod filets (page 44), a healthy shmear of this sauce, and some lettuce and tomato. Make Roasted Yukon Wedges with Bacon and Thyme (page 236) for the chips part of the equation.

SHELF LIFE: Up to four days in the refrigerator.

French Cornichon and Tarragon Tartar Sauce

Cornichons are small French gherkins with a delicate flavor and texture. Coupled with the tarragon, they make this sauce dressy and a little special. If you're feeling moved to make homemade mayo, this would be a good place.

YIELD: 1 ¼ CUPS, 6 SERVINGS
PREP TIME: 8 minutes
COOK TIME: N/A

½ cup jarred or homemade mayonnaise
¼ cup finely diced dill cornichons
1 medium shallot, finely diced (about 3 tablespoons)
1 tablespoon chopped fresh tarragon
2 teaspoons white wine vinegar
About ¼ teaspoon kosher salt
About ½ teaspoon freshly ground black pepper

In a medium bowl, mix all of the ingredients with a light sprinkling of salt and pepper. Season with more salt, pepper, and vinegar to taste.

PAIRINGS: I like spreading this delicate sauce on a grilled burger (page 76) with just cheddar cheese, lettuce, and tomato. It's also perfect for dolloping on sautéed tuna steaks (page 42) or a sautéed tuna burger (page 40).

SHELF LIFE: Up to four days in the refrigerator.

Herb and Celery Root Remoulade

Remoulade is like a French tartar sauce, only instead of going with fried fish, it often accompanies shredded celery root—the knobby root has a clean, fragrant essence, reminiscent of gin. I like to include the celery root in this sauce along with the traditional pickle and herb base.

YIELD: 1 ¼ CUPS, 6 SERVINGS
PREP TIME: 10 minutes
COOK TIME: N/A

½ cup jarred or homemade mayonnaise
½ cup peeled and grated celery root
2 tablespoons finely diced dill cornichons
1 anchovy, finely diced to a paste (optional)
1 tablespoon chopped chervil or flat-leaf parsley
2 teaspoons freshly squeezed lemon juice
1 teaspoon Dijon mustard
1 teaspoon chopped fresh thyme
About ¼ teaspoon kosher salt
About ½ teaspoon freshly ground black pepper

In a medium bowl, mix all of the ingredients with a light sprinkling of salt, pepper, and more lemon juice to taste.

PAIRINGS: Celery root goes nicely with beef. Pair with something dressy like grilled beef tenderloin (page 75) or a sautéed rib eye (page 38). Slice the beef, top with this remoulade and serve with Horseradish Mashed Potatoes (page 235).

SHELF LIFE: Up to three days in the refrigerator.

Cajun Remoulade

The Cajun incarnation of this sauce usually has a healthy hit of spice (Tabasco and cayenne do the honors here) as well as tomato paste or ketchup.

YIELD: ABOUT 1¼ CUPS, ENOUGH FOR 6 SERVINGS
PREP TIME: 5 minutes
COOK TIME: N/A

½ cup jarred or homemade mayonnaise
¼ cup sour cream
¼ cup dill relish
¼ cup finely diced red onion
2 teaspoons tomato paste
1 tablespoon brown mustard
1 teaspoon Tabasco sauce (or your favorite hot sauce)
About ¼ teaspoon kosher salt
About ½ teaspoon freshly ground black pepper
Pinch cayenne

In a medium bowl, mix all of the ingredients with a light sprinkling of salt and pepper to taste.

PAIRINGS: Sauté some catfish, tilapia, or sole (page 44) and top with this sauce. Pair with Dirty Rice (page 234) and rock out the zydeco.

SHELF LIFE: Up to four days in the refrigerator.

Toasted Garlic Aioli

I like smoothing out aioli, the garlicky mayonnaise from the Western Mediterranean, by gently sautéing the garlic until it's just lightly browned before whisking with mayonnaise and a splash of vinegar.

YIELD: 1 CUP, 6 SERVINGS
PREP TIME: 5 minutes
COOK TIME: 3 minutes

2 tablespoons olive oil
3 medium cloves garlic, chopped (about 2 teaspoons)
¾ cup homemade or jarred mayonnaise
2 teaspoons sherry vinegar or red wine vinegar
About ¼ teaspoon kosher salt
About ¼ teaspoon freshly ground black pepper

Heat the oil with the garlic in a medium skillet over medium heat, stirring occasionally, until the garlic turns a very light golden hue, about 3 minutes.

Let cool for a couple of minutes and then stir this garlic mixture into the mayonnaise with the vinegar and a sprinkling of salt and pepper; whisk well so the oil becomes evenly incorporated.

PAIRINGS: Pair with a full-flavored seared fish like broiled halibut (page 66) or grilled tuna (page 78).

SHELF LIFE: Up to four days in the refrigerator.

Spanish Roasted Red Pepper Aioli

Using homemade roasted red peppers or even jarred Spanish piquillo peppers gives this flavored mayonnaise a tangy boost.

YIELD: ¾ CUP, 4 SERVINGS
PREP TIME: 5 minutes
COOK TIME: N/A

½ cup homemade or jarred mayonnaise
1 jarred roasted red pepper or 2 piquillo peppers, coarsely chopped (about ⅓ cup)
2 teaspoons sherry vinegar or red wine vinegar
1 teaspoon chopped fresh thyme or rosemary
1 large garlic clove, minced and mashed to a paste using the side of a chef's knife, about 1 teaspoon (see page 153)
¼ teaspoon pimentón de la Vera or chipotle powder
About ½ teaspoon kosher salt
About ½ teaspoon freshly ground black pepper

Using an immersion blender or in a blender, blend the mayonnaise with the red pepper, vinegar, thyme, garlic, pimentón, 2 tablespoons water, and a sprinkling of salt and pepper. Season with more vinegar, salt, and pepper to taste.

PAIRINGS: Pair this aioli with grilled portabellos (page 82) and make a sandwich of it on toasted ciabatta with baby arugula, chopped caper berries or green olives, and Browned Sherry Onions (page 235). Or make like a Spaniard and serve this sauce with French fries for dipping.

SHELF LIFE: Up to three days in the refrigerator.

Black Pepper, Tarragon, and Caper Aioli

Mayonnaise is rich so big flavors like capers and black pepper are just the thing to cut through its creaminess and add some complexity.

YIELD: 1 CUP; 6 SERVINGS
PREP TIME: 8 minutes
COOK TIME: N/A

¾ cup homemade or jarred mayonnaise
2 tablespoons chopped nonpareil capers
2 tablespoons chopped fresh tarragon
1 tablespoon freshly squeezed lemon juice, more to taste
1 medium garlic clove, minced and mashed to a paste with the side of a chef's knife, about ¾ teaspoon (see page 153)
About ¼ teaspoon kosher salt
About ¾ teaspoon freshly ground black pepper

In a medium bowl, mix all of the ingredients with salt, pepper, and more lemon juice to taste.

PAIRINGS: Capers often get typecast in a supporting role with salmon, but it's because the two work well together. Spoon this sauce over broiled salmon filets (page 66) or pair with a grilled steak (page 75) and serve with boiled potatoes and fresh summer corn.

SHELF LIFE: Up to four days in the refrigerator.

Spicy Sriracha and Lime Mayo

Just a few years ago, the only place you'd see Sriracha was at Asian restaurants. But since then, this chile paste with the green cap and rooster on the bottle has made a quick leap into the culinary mainstream and into most supermarkets, too. Its smooth heat and garlicky edge is perfect for boosting mayonnaise.

YIELD: 1 CUP, 6 SERVINGS
PREP TIME: 4 minutes
COOK TIME: N/A

¾ cup homemade or jarred mayonnaise (try Kewpie mayonnaise—see option on page below)
1 scallion (both white and green parts), trimmed and thinly sliced (about 2 tablespoons)
1 tablespoon soy sauce
2 teaspoons freshly squeezed lime juice
1 to 2 teaspoons Sriracha
About ¼ teaspoon freshly ground black pepper

In a medium bowl, mix the mayonnaise with all the ingredients and season with more soy, pepper, lime juice, or Sriracha to taste.

OPTION: Look for Kewpie at your local Asian grocer, the Japanese mayonnaise with a superbly creamy texture and marked depth of flavor (partly due to MSG); it comes in a small plastic squeeze bottle inside of a rose-colored plastic bag.

PAIRINGS: I like to serve this as a dipping sauce for large grilled shrimp (page 78) or drizzle it on grilled tuna or salmon (page 78) and serve with a lightly dressed watercress salad.

SHELF LIFE: Up to three days in the refrigerator.

INFUSED DAIRY AND OILS

All of the sauces in this section contain a rich ingredient—butter, sour cream, crème fraîche, yogurt, milk, or cooking oil—which gets a boost from fresh herbs, aromatics, and pantry ingredients. Compound, or flavored, butters have been a not-so-well-kept restaurant secret for years. Fold intense ingredients (everything from capers to chipotle peppers) into softened butter and you get a wonderful punch of concentrated flavor when it melts into action; kind of like culinary cryogenics.

Now, the real secret is that you can apply this same technique to all sorts of other dairy ingredients. Some, like sour cream or yogurt, you infuse while they're cold, while others, like béchamels (thickened milk mixtures) you can infuse while they're warm.

Flavored oils follow the same pattern: the uncooked ones are made by puréeing fresh herbs and aromatics with oil—anything from neutral-flavored canola oil to assertive olive oil—while the cooked ones made by gently heating the oil over low heat with these same sorts of flavorings until toasted and fragrant. The former tend to be prettier, though the latter are more complexly flavored.

What do you do with these flavored oils? Of course, you can set out a small bowl for dipping with bread, but there are other, more dynamic applications. I like to use these oils as a lighter, more concentrated version of an infused butter, to add moisture to lean chicken breasts or fish or to offer a touch of richness to a steak or chop; for the latter you can both brush the oil on the meat while grilling or drizzle it over the meat just before serving.

INFUSED DAIRY OR OIL TECHNIQUE

Fold, mash, purée, or heat chopped fresh herbs, pantry flavorings, aromatics, and citrus or vinegar with oil, sour cream, yogurt, softened butter, or thickened milk. Serve immediately or chill and melt onto hot, seared ingredients.

ALL ABOUT FLAVORED BUTTERS

You'll need soft butter to make these compound butters, but this may take a couple of hours depending on the weather and the temperature in your house. If you don't think to pull out a stick of butter before heading out the door to work, the microwave is the thing. I can't give you exact instructions for how to soften butter because the power on everybody's microwave is different. My advice is to use the defrost level and cook it for up to three minutes, checking every thirty seconds. After preparing the butter, you've got options.

Traditionally, flavored butters are prepared ahead of time and chilled in the refrigerator so they harden. This makes it easier to slice the butter into pats for melting on grilled, broiled, or sautéed fare. I have promised that you can both prepare and serve these sauces in around fifteen minutes, though. So, if you don't have time to make these butters ahead, just spoon the softened mixture over what you've seared.

If you do want to store a compound butter, spoon the softened butter onto the center of a large piece of plastic wrap and form into a log shape by folding over the plastic wrap and tightening the ends as if it were a sausage. Refrigerate until firm, about 2 hours. Then just slice the butter (through the plastic) into pats as needed.

LARGE SERVING SIZES FOR LONG STORAGE TIMES

Because most of these infusions can hold for at least a couple of days if not a week or two in the fridge, most of these recipes yield about eight servings. If you want to make just a small serving for dinner tonight, feel free to halve the amounts.

Shallot-Herb Butter

This is the quintessential infused butter: mild and fancy, with shallots and plenty of fresh herbs. The result is rich and wonderfully versatile, the kind of thing that's nice to have on hand in the refrigerator. Just grab a ¼ cup of whatever fresh herbs you've got kicking around in the crisper or herb garden—I don't care if it's lovage or purslane for God's sake!

YIELD: ¾ CUP, 6 TO 8 SERVINGS
PREP TIME: 10 minutes
COOK TIME: N/A

8 tablespoons (1 stick) unsalted butter, softened
1 large shallot, finely diced (about ¼ cup)
¼ cup thinly sliced chives
2 tablespoons chopped fresh parsley
2 teaspoons chopped fresh thyme
About ½ teaspoon kosher salt
About ½ teaspoon freshly ground black pepper

In a medium bowl, partly mash and partly fold the butter with the remaining ingredients and a generous sprinkling of salt and pepper to taste.

PAIRINGS: I particularly like this butter with simple, seared vegetables like grilled asparagus (page 80) or a fancy sautéed steak (page 38) like filet mignon; serve the latter with a baguette and a fresh tomato salad.

SHELF LIFE: Up to one week in the refrigerator or one month in the freezer (see the technique on page 196 for how to store).

Lemon-Caper Butter

Alone, capers are strong and almost overpoweringly briny—but chopped into butter, they behave, perking up the mixture with a measured punch.

YIELD: ¾ CUP, 6 TO 8 SERVINGS
PREP TIME: 7 minutes
COOK TIME: N/A

8 tablespoons (1 stick) unsalted butter, softened
2 tablespoons chopped jarred nonpareil capers
1 tablespoon freshly squeezed lemon juice plus 1 tea-
    spoon lemon zest
2 teaspoons chopped fresh thyme
1 small garlic clove, minced and mashed to a paste using the
    side of a chef's knife, about ½ teaspoon (see page 153)
6 drops Tabasco sauce
About ¼ teaspoon kosher salt
About ½ teaspoon freshly ground black pepper

In a medium bowl partly mash and partly fold the butter with the remaining ingredients and a light sprinkling of salt, pepper, and more lemon juice to taste.

PAIRINGS: Melt the butter onto sautéed or broiled scallops (page 46 or 66) and set atop a salad of lightly dressed frisée with some Roasted Rosemary Fingerling Potatoes (page 235).

SHELF LIFE: Up to one week in the refrigerator or one month in the freezer (see the technique on page 196 for how to store).

Chive and Black Truffle Butter

Upon melting, this butter reveals, tiny chunks of black truffles and mounds of pretty chive rings. The truffles may sound out of reach, but black truffles can be found in .5-ounce jars in most gourmet shops for about $15.

YIELD: ¾ CUP, 6 TO 8 SERVINGS
PREP TIME: 6 minutes
COOK TIME: N/A

8 tablespoons (1 stick) unsalted butter, softened
⅓ cup thinly sliced fresh chives
⅓ cup freshly grated Parmigiano
2 jarred black truffles, drained and finely diced (about 2
    tablespoons)
About ½ teaspoon kosher salt
About ½ teaspoon freshly ground black pepper

In a medium bowl, partly mash and partly fold the butter with the remaining ingredients and a generous sprinkling of salt and pepper to taste.

PAIRINGS: Melt a couple of pats of this butter onto a sautéed filet mignon (page 38) or grilled strip steak (page 75). Serve with a frisée and grape tomato salad and a crusty loaf of olive bread.

SHELF LIFE: Up to one week in the refrigerator or 1 month in the freezer (see the technique on page 196 for how to store).

Dill and Green Peppercorn Butter

Brined green peppercorns have a milder flavor and more tender texture than dried black peppercorns (which is the stuff you put in your pepper mill). They impart a gentle piquancy and crunch to this butter.

YIELD: ¾ CUP, 6 SERVINGS
PREP TIME: 6 minutes
COOK TIME: N/A

8 tablespoons (1 stick) unsalted butter, softened
1 large shallot, finely diced (about ¼ cup)
3 tablespoons brined green peppercorns, drained well
    and coarsely chopped
2 tablespoons chopped fresh dill
About ½ teaspoon kosher salt
About ½ teaspoon freshly ground black pepper

In a medium bowl, partly mash and partly fold the butter with the remaining ingredients and a generous sprinkling of salt, pepper, and more lemon juice to taste.

PAIRINGS: Melt this butter onto broiled salmon or halibut (page 66) or onto grilled steaks (page 75). Pair with Warm Farro Salad with Orange and Asparagus (page 236).

SHELF LIFE: Up to one week in the refrigerator or one month in the freezer (see the technique on page 196 for how to store).

Sherry–Ginger Butter

Though butter doesn't hold a prominent place in its cuisines, I like how Asian ingredients can give dairy a mildly exotic twist.

YIELD: ¾ CUP, 6 SERVINGS
PREP TIME: 5 minutes
COOK TIME: N/A

1½-inch knob ginger, peeled and coarsely chopped
8 tablespoons (1 stick) unsalted butter, softened
3 scallions (both white and green parts), trimmed and
    thinly sliced
1 tablespoon soy sauce
1 tablespoon dry sherry
½ teaspoon Thai chili paste (like Siracha)
About ¼ teaspoon freshly ground black pepper

Pulse the ginger in a mini-chop or food processor, scraping down the sides as needed, until minced (about 3 tablespoons).

In a medium bowl, partly mash and partly fold the butter with the ginger, the remaining ingredients, and a light sprinkling of pepper to taste.

PAIRINGS: Melt a pat of this butter onto stir-fried baby bok choy (page 50) or green beans (page 50) or grilled chicken breast (page 71) and serve with soba noodles tossed with soy sauce and scallions.

SHELF LIFE: Up to one week in the refrigerator or one month in the freezer (see the technique on page 196 for how to store).

Chipotle–Lime Butter

Use a food processor or mini-chop to ensure that the chipotle (and its adobo sauce) uniformly incorporates into this spicy butter.

YIELD: ¾ CUP, 8 SERVINGS
PREP TIME: 7 minutes
COOK TIME: N/A

8 tablespoons unsalted butter (1 stick), softened to
    room temperature
¼ cup chopped fresh cilantro
1 canned chipotle chile, minced, plus 1 tablespoon adobo sauce
1 tablespoon freshly squeezed lime juice
1 small garlic clove, minced and mashed to a paste using the
    side of a chef's knife, about ½ teaspoon (see page 153)
¼ teaspoon ground cumin
About ½ teaspoon kosher salt
About ½ teaspoon freshly ground black pepper

Pulse all of the ingredients together in a food processor until just combined; you may need to scrape down the sides with a spatula once or twice. Season with salt and pepper to taste.

PAIRINGS: This butter is a nice pick-me-up for lean, mildly flavored cuts like grilled chicken breasts (page 71) or broiled pork tenderloin (page 64); serve with an additional squirt of lime and Traditional Rice Pilaf (page 234).

SHELF LIFE: Up to one week in the refrigerator or one month in the freezer (see the technique on page 196 for how to store).

Sun-Dried Tomato and Rosemary Butter

The exotic hues of compound butters—this one takes the deep red of sun-dried tomatoes—happily hint at their flavors. They also look a heck of a lot more interesting on the plate than yellow butter.

YIELD: ¾ CUP, 8 SERVINGS
PREP TIME: 6 minutes
COOK TIME: N/A

8 tablespoons unsalted butter (1 stick), softened to
    room temperature
4 oil-packed sun-dried tomatoes, drained well and
    coarsely chopped (about ¼ cup)
2 teaspoons chopped fresh rosemary
1 teaspoon sherry vinegar or balsamic vinegar
1 small garlic clove, minced and mashed to a paste using the
    side of a chef's knife, about ½ teaspoon (see page 153)
About ½ teaspoon kosher salt
About ½ teaspoon freshly ground black pepper

Pulse all of the ingredients with a sprinkling of salt and pepper in a food processor until just combined; you may need to scrape down the sides with a spatula once or twice. Season with salt and pepper to taste.

PAIRINGS: I like sun-dried tomatoes with mild white fish like cod or halibut. Sauté either (page 44 or 42), then top with a pat of this butter and pair with boiled artichokes. Or toss with a sauté of shrimp (page 46), canned artichokes, black olives, and penne.

SHELF LIFE: Up to one week in the refrigerator or one month in the freezer (see the technique on page 196 for how to store).

....

The Difference Between Sour Cream and Crème Fraîche

Beginning with the recipe for Scallion and Black Pepper Cream, we launch a cadre of sauces that have a base of either sour cream or crème fraîche. I leave you the choice as to which one to use, though there are measurable differences between the two. Crème fraîche, the more expensive, tends to have a slightly thicker texture and richer flavor, while sour cream is slightly looser but more tangy.

....

Café de Paris Butter

This is one of those classic sauces whose exact origins are somewhat murky. It is thought to reference the Café de Paris in Geneva, Switzerland, and its famed rib eye dish. It's since evolved into a popular spiced butter containing up to twenty ingredients. In most restaurants where I've cooked, it simply goes by "CDP."

YIELD: 1 CUP, 8 SERVINGS
PREP TIME: 7 minutes
COOK TIME: N/A

8 tablespoons unsalted butter (1 stick), softened to room temperature
3 tablespoons chopped fresh parsley
1 tablespoon chopped nonpareil capers
1 tablespoon tomato paste
1 large garlic clove, minced and mashed to a paste using the side of a chef's knife, about 1 teaspoon (see page 153)
1 teaspoon Dijon mustard
1 teaspoon chopped fresh thyme
1 teaspoon Worcestershire sauce
½ teaspoon curry powder
About ½ teaspoon kosher salt
About ½ teaspoon freshly ground black pepper

Set all of the ingredients in a food processor and pulse together with a generous sprinkling of salt and pepper until just combined; you may need to scrape down the sides with a spatula once or twice. Season with more salt and pepper to taste.

PAIRINGS: Melt this rust-colored concoction onto a sautéed rib eye steak (page 38), and serve with some sort of fancy potato preparation (potatoes soufflé!) and sautéed haricots verts (page 50).

SHELF LIFE: Up to one week in the refrigerator or one month in the freezer (see the technique on page 196 for how to store).

Scallion and Black Pepper Cream

I like to grind the pepper for this sauce coarsely so it adds a little texture. You can go with chives instead of the scallions for a more delicate flavor and feel.

YIELD: 1 CUP, 4 TO 6 SERVINGS
PREP TIME: 4 minutes
COOK TIME: N/A

¾ cup crème fraîche or sour cream
4 scallions (both white and green parts), trimmed and thinly sliced (about ½ cup)
2 teaspoons freshly squeezed lemon juice plus 1 teaspoon freshly grated lemon zest
10 drops Tabasco
About ½ teaspoon kosher salt
About 1¼ teaspoons coarsely ground black pepper

In a small bowl, mix all the ingredients with a sprinkling of salt and a heavy punch of pepper to taste.

PAIRINGS: Yes, you could dollop this flavored cream on a baked potato, but it's also nice as a cooling touch for spice-rubbed grilled boneless chicken thighs (page 71) or skirt steak (page 75). Thinly slice either and wrap into tortillas with diced fresh tomato and jarred jalapeño slices.

SHELF LIFE: Up to three days in the refrigerator.

Horseradish Cream Sauce

Even if you're not a fan of horseradish, its mellow tang and measured heat will win you over in this creamy sauce.

YIELD: 1 CUP, 4 TO 6 SERVINGS
PREP TIME: 4 minutes
COOK TIME: N/A

¾ cup sour cream or crème fraîche
2 tablespoons heavy cream
2 tablespoons prepared horseradish
2 tablespoons thinly sliced fresh chives
About ¼ teaspoon kosher salt
About ½ teaspoon freshly ground black pepper

In a medium bowl, mix the sour cream with the remaining ingredients and a light sprinkling of salt and pepper to taste.

OPTIONS: Fold in some finely diced shallot or minced garlic to reinforce the chives.

PAIRINGS: Dollop on a broiled salmon filet (page 66) or make a warm grilled steak sandwich with thinly sliced broiled flank (page 64), Browned Sherry Onions (page 225), and baby arugula on toasted ciabatta.

SHELF LIFE: Up to one week in the refrigerator.

Jalapeño–Parmesan Cream

This pairing of Mexican (hot peppers) and Italian (cheese) ingredients is the second instance that I've merged these two very different cuisines together (balsamic vinegar and chipotle peppers are another favorite pairing of mine, page 184), proving that rich Italian cuisine can vibe with Mexican spice.

YIELD: 1 CUP, 4 TO 6 SERVINGS
PREP TIME: 6 minutes
COOK TIME: N/A

¾ cup sour cream
¼ cup freshly grated Parmigiano
¼ cup chopped jarred jalapeños
2 teaspoons freshly squeezed lime juice
1 teaspoon chopped fresh thyme or 1 tablespoon chopped fresh oregano
About ½ teaspoon kosher salt
About ½ teaspoon freshly ground black pepper

In a food processor or mini-chop, pulse all the ingredients with a sprinkling of salt and pepper. Season with more salt, pepper, and lime to taste.

PAIRINGS: This is a wonderful topping for a grilled burger (page 76) or try mixing it into a ground turkey or beef sauté (page 40). Sprinkle the meat with a tablespoon or so of the Tex-Mex Spice Rub (page 15) before sautéing and then once it's cooked through, stir in this cream.

SHELF LIFE: Up to three days in the refrigerator.

Cilantro-Lime Cream

Yogurt and sour cream each has their own unique tang. Together with fresh cilantro and lime they form the perfect cooling counterpoint to spiced Tex-Mex food.

YIELD: 1 CUP, 4 TO 6 SERVINGS
PREP TIME: 6 minutes
COOK TIME: N/A

½ cup plain yogurt (I like using a full-fat Greek yogurt like Fage)
¼ cup sour cream
¼ cup chopped fresh cilantro
2 teaspoons freshly squeezed lime juice plus 1 teaspoon freshly grated lime zest
1 tablespoon chopped fresh oregano (optional)
¼ teaspoon chile powder
About ½ teaspoon kosher salt
About ½ teaspoon freshly ground black pepper

In a food processor or mini-chop, pulse to chop and combine all the ingredients with a sprinkling of salt and pepper. Season with more salt, pepper, and lime to taste.

PAIRINGS: This is my topping of choice for tacos and fajitas. Layer sautéed spiced beef (page 34), or spice-rubbed grilled chicken thighs (page 71) into a tortilla and top with some diced Herb-Marinated Chopped Summer Tomato Sauce (page 219) and a dollop of this sauce.

SHELF LIFE: Up to three days in the refrigerator.

Lemon-Herb Crème Fraîche

I call exclusively for crème fraîche here (as opposed to sour cream) so this sauce has a particularly thick texture and rich flavor to go with the fresh herbs.

YIELD: ABOUT 1 CUP, 4 TO 6 SERVINGS
PREP TIME: 7 minutes
COOK TIME: N/A

¾ cup crème fraîche
¼ cup thinly sliced chives (optional)
2 tablespoons chopped fresh tarragon
1 teaspoon chopped fresh thyme or rosemary
1 teaspoon freshly squeezed lemon juice plus 1 teaspoon freshly grated lemon zest (from about ½ lemon)
About ½ teaspoon kosher salt
About ½ teaspoon freshly ground black pepper

In a medium bowl, mix the crème fraîche with remaining ingredients and a sprinkling of salt and pepper to taste.

PAIRINGS: Spoon this sauce into the center of dinner plates, top with a perfectly broiled salmon filet (page 66) or grilled tuna steak (page 78), and serve with Garlicky Smashed Red Potatoes (page 202) and sautéed asparagus (page 50).

SHELF LIFE: Up to three days in the refrigerator.

Greek Dill-Cucumber Tzatziki

I go a little light on the garlic in this yogurt sauce so you can venture out into social settings after dinner without feeling self-conscious. Add more if you're not going anywhere or don't care.

YIELD: 2 CUPS, 8 SERVINGS
PREP TIME: 8 minutes
COOK TIME: N/A

1¼ cups plain yogurt (preferably full-fat Greek yogurt like Fage)
⅓ English seedless cucumber, finely diced (about ½ cup)
1 tablespoon chopped fresh dill
2 teaspoons freshly squeezed lemon juice

1 medium garlic clove, minced and mashed to a paste using the side of a chef's knife, about ¾ teaspoon (see page 153)

¼ teaspoon Tabasco

About ¾ teaspoon kosher salt

About ½ teaspoon freshly ground black pepper

In a medium bowl, mix the yogurt with all the ingredients and a generous sprinkling of salt and pepper to taste.

PAIRINGS: Make a Greek sandwich with grilled chicken breasts (page 71) or flank steak (page 75), warm pita, sliced tomatoes, dressed Romaine, hot sauce, and a drizzle of this sauce.

SHELF LIFE: Up to four days in the refrigerator.

Cucumber–Mint Raita

Raita is a cooling counterpoint to spiced Indian cuisine. The mint gives this sauce a slightly sweeter edge than the tzatziki on page 202.

YIELD: ABOUT 2 CUPS, 8 SERVINGS
PREP TIME: 7 minutes
COOK TIME: N/A

1¼ cups plain yogurt (preferably full-fat Greek yogurt)

¼ English seedless cucumber, finely diced (about ⅓ cup)

½ small red onion (about ¼ cup)

1 tablespoon chopped fresh mint

1 tablespoon freshly squeezed lemon juice

About ½ teaspoon kosher salt

About ½ teaspoon freshly ground black pepper

In a medium bowl, mix the yogurt with all the ingredients and a sprinkling of salt and pepper to taste.

PAIRINGS: Serve with grilled shrimp or chicken skewers (page 78 or 71) for dipping. Marinate with Tandoori Yogurt Marinade (page 17) and serve with warm naan and grilled onions and peppers (page 80).

SHELF LIFE: Up to four days in the refrigerator.

Warm Blue Cheese Cream

Bob Calderone, a great mentor and one of the first chefs I ever worked for, used to pair this simple sauce with prosciutto-wrapped pears, though it goes equally well with seared steaks, chicken breasts, or grilled burgers. To make the sauce, just melt crumbled blue cheese into heavy cream. The cheese thickens the cream, giving it a texture similar to a béchamel without the roux base.

YIELD: 1 CUP, 6 SERVINGS
PREP TIME: 2 minutes
COOK TIME: 4 minutes

½ cup heavy cream

6 ounces crumbled blue cheese (about 1½ cups)

1 tablespoon freshly squeezed lemon juice

About ¾ teaspoon freshly ground black pepper

Set the cream and blue cheese in a small saucepan and cook over medium heat, stirring, until the blue cheese completely melts, about 4 minutes. Remove from the heat, stir in the lemon juice, and season generously with pepper to taste.

PAIRINGS: I love drizzling this sauce over a dressy sautéed steak (page 38) like a strip or filet mignon and serving with a wedge of iceberg lettuce and thick-cut tomatoes. Or drizzle this warm sauce over broiled asparagus (page 65).

SHELF LIFE: N/A; the sauce is difficult to reheat without it separating.

BEURRE BLANC

Whereas compound butters are made by mashing aromatic flavorings into softened butter and then chilling, beurre blanc more or less inverses this process by whisking melted butter with aromatic ingredients to create a warm, thick sauce. Both types of sauces splash butter's blank palette with big flavors and go well with lean cuts of meat or fish.

Beurre Blanc

The preparation of this sauce was one of the first nightly tasks I assumed when I first started cooking at L'Espalier in Boston. It's not a complicated sauce, but I whisked it together shakily; fearful that it would break. I quickly learned the trick to avoid the sauce from separating is to reduce the wine with the shallot so it forms a viscous, acidic base with which the butter can re-emulsify.

YIELD: ½ CUP, 4 SERVINGS
PREP TIME: 6 minutes
COOK TIME: 5 minutes

¾ cup dry white wine (like a Chardonnay)
1 large shallot, finely diced (about ¼ cup)
6 tablespoons unsalted butter, cut into small cubes
1 tablespoon chopped fresh parsley (optional)
1 teaspoon freshly squeezed lemon juice
About ¼ teaspoon kosher salt
About ¼ teaspoon freshly ground black pepper

Set the wine and shallot in a small saucepan over high heat and cook, stirring occasionally, until the wine almost completely reduces, about 4 minutes. Remove the pan from the heat and whisk in the butter a couple of cubes at a time until they all melt and the sauce becomes thick and creamy; return the pan to low heat if the butter takes a while to melt. Stir in the parsley (if using), lemon juice, and a sprinkling of salt, pepper, and more lemon juice to taste.

PAIRINGS: Pair this sauce with a sautéed mild fish like cod or tilapia (page 44) and serve with sautéed haricots verts (page 50) and pan-fried new potatoes.

SHELF LIFE: N/A: make this fresh as it would break while thawing and reheating.

Sun-Dried Tomato and Lemon Beurre Blanc

Adding sun-dried tomatoes and chopped fresh thyme to your basic beurre blanc gives the sauce a brighter, slightly sweeter disposition, which makes it a more dynamic partner for vegetables, chicken, or fish.

YIELD: ½ CUP, 4 SERVINGS
PREP TIME: 6 minutes
COOK TIME: 6 minutes

¾ cup dry white wine (like a Chardonnay)
2 cloves garlic, smashed
3 oil-packed sun-dried tomatoes, finely chopped (about 3 tablespoons)
1 teaspoon chopped fresh thyme
6 tablespoons unsalted butter, cut into small cubes
1 teaspoon freshly squeezed lemon juice
1 teaspoon freshly grated lemon zest
About ¼ teaspoon kosher salt
About ¼ teaspoon freshly ground black pepper

Set the wine, garlic, sun-dried tomatoes, and thyme in a small saucepan over high heat and cook, stirring occasionally, until the wine almost completely reduces, about 4 minutes. Remove the pan from the heat and whisk in the butter a couple cubes at a time until they all melt and the sauce becomes thick and creamy; return the pan to low heat if the butter takes a while to melt. Stir in the lemon juice, lemon zest, and a sprinkling of salt and pepper to taste. Fish out and discard the garlic cloves.

PAIRINGS: I like pairing the sun-dried tomatoes with chicken or beef. Drizzle on broiled chicken breasts (page 63) or flank steak (page 64) and pair with sautéed spinach (page 53) and Traditional Rice Pilaf (page 234).

SHELF LIFE: N/A: make this fresh as it would break while thawing and reheating.

Rosemary Beurre Rouge

Beurre rouge is similar to beurre blanc, only with red wine serving as the base for the reduction. This color change produces a sauce that's slightly deeper in flavor and a little less acidic. As much as I like rosemary, I use it sparingly here so its piney essence doesn't overwhelm.

YIELD: ½ CUP, 4 SERVINGS
PREP TIME: 6 minutes
COOK TIME: 6 minutes

¾ cup dry red wine
1 large shallot, finely diced (about ¼ cup)
1 teaspoon chopped fresh rosemary
6 tablespoons unsalted butter, cut into small cubes
1 tablespoon red wine vinegar
About ½ teaspoon kosher salt
About ½ teaspoon freshly ground black pepper

Set the wine, shallot, and rosemary in a small saucepan over high heat and cook, stirring occasionally, until the wine almost completely reduces, about 4 minutes. Remove the pan from the heat and whisk in the butter a couple of cubes at a time until they all melt and the sauce becomes thick and creamy; return the pan to low heat if the butter takes a while to melt. Stir in the vinegar and a generous sprinkling of salt and pepper to taste.

PAIRINGS: Pair the assertive rosemary with a full-flavored fish like sautéed halibut (page 42) or broiled salmon (page 66). Surround the fish and sauce, both buttery, with austere sides like boiled potatoes and steamed green beans.

SHELF LIFE: N/A: make this fresh as it would break while thawing and reheating.

Aged Cheddar Cheese Sauce with Caraway and Apple

I favor a sharp, aged cheddar cheese here so the sauce has a little bite to go with the sweetness of the apples and the aromatic caraway seeds.

YIELD: 1½ CUPS, 4 SERVINGS
PREP TIME: 7 minutes
COOK TIME: 9 minutes

1 shallot, finely diced (about ¼ cup)
2 tablespoons unsalted butter
1½ tablespoons all-purpose flour
1 cup whole milk, warmed in the microwave or on the stove top
1 cup freshly grated sharp cheddar cheese (about 4 ounces)
½ cup diced Granny Smith apple (about ½ apple)
1 teaspoon caraway seeds
About ½ teaspoon kosher salt
About ½ teaspoon freshly ground black pepper

Cook the shallot with the butter in a medium saucepan over medium-high heat, stirring until it just starts to soften and become translucent, about 3 minutes. Add the flour and cook, stirring, until it takes on a light golden hue and acquires a nutty fragrance, about 1 minute.

Whisk in the warm milk and cook, stirring occasionally, until it just comes to a simmer and starts to thicken, 5 minutes. Remove from the heat and stir in the cheddar, apple, and caraway seeds, and a sprinkling of salt and pepper, to taste.

PAIRINGS: Drizzle over sautéed boneless pork chops (page 38) or spoon over sautéed veal cutlets (page 36).

SHELF LIFE: Up to three days in the refrigerator; reheat gently on the stove top.

Wild Mushroom and Herb Béchamel

Though "béchamel" is in the title, this warm milk mixture is more of a creamy mushroom sauce than a plain, staid white sauce.

YIELD: 1½ CUPS, 4 SERVINGS
PREP TIME: 6 minutes
COOK TIME: 10 minutes

2 tablespoons unsalted butter
3½ ounces mixed wild mushrooms (like oysters, shiitakes, and cremini), stemmed and thinly sliced
About ½ teaspoon kosher salt
About ½ teaspoon freshly ground black pepper
2 tablespoons all-purpose flour
1 cup whole milk, warmed in the microwave or on the stove top
1 tablespoon dry sherry
¼ cup freshly grated Parmigiano Reggiano
3 tablespoons thinly sliced fresh chives (optional)
1 teaspoon chopped fresh thyme

Melt the butter in a medium saucepan over medium-high heat. Add the mushrooms, sprinkle with salt and pepper, and cook, stirring, until they start to soften and brown, about 2 minutes. Add the flour and cook, stirring, until it coats the mushrooms and acquires a nutty fragrance, about 1 minute.

Whisk in the warm milk and sherry and cook, stirring occasionally, until the sauce just comes to a simmer and starts to thicken, about 5 minutes. Remove from the heat and stir in the Parmigiano, chives, if using, and thyme and more salt and pepper to taste.

PAIRINGS: I like stirring this sauce into a beef (page 38) or chicken (page 31) sauté. Serve over Buttered Egg Noodles with Fresh Chives (page 233) and blanched broccoli.

SHELF LIFE: Up to three days in the refrigerator; reheat gently on the stove top.

Basil Oil

Restaurant chefs insist on blanching basil in boiling water before puréeing to set its bright green color (see the technique on page 210), though this isn't necessary. Similarly, you can strain the oil after puréeing to give it a green translucent hue, which looks cool, but strains off some flavor, too.

YIELD: ¾ CUP, 8 SERVINGS
PREP TIME: 5 minutes
COOK TIME: N/A

½ cup olive oil
2 cups lightly packed basil leaves, soaked and spun dry
About 1 teaspoon kosher salt

Purée the oil and basil in a blender with a generous sprinkling of salt. Strain through a fine mesh sieve if you like.

PAIRINGS: Drizzle this oil over mild seared ingredients, like sautéed shrimp (page 46); toss with snap peas and strips of prosciutto. Or stir into sautéed clams (page 48) along with some halved cherry tomatoes.

SHELF LIFE: Up to three days in the refrigerator.

Italian Garlic and Hot Chile Oil

This is my take on the exceedingly simple Italian pasta sauce *aglio, olio, e pepperoncino*. There are only three ingredients in here but like the Police (Sting's Police, not law enforcement) they each do their job and it ends up feeling like a whole lot more.

YIELD: ½ CUP, 6 SERVINGS
PREP TIME: 2 minutes
COOK TIME: 3 minutes

½ cup olive oil
2 garlic cloves, chopped (about 1½ teaspoons)
½ to ¾ teaspoon crushed red pepper flakes

Set the oil and garlic in a small skillet over medium heat and cook, swirling the pan occasionally, until the garlic starts to sizzle steadily and just starts to color ever slightly, 2 to 3 minutes. Add the red pepper flakes and remove the pan from the heat. Let cool for a couple of minutes.

PAIRINGS: Baste this oil on a lean grilled fish like halibut (page 78) or on herbed chicken breasts (page 71). Set either over dressed baby greens, sprinkle with chopped fresh rosemary, and serve with lemon wedges for squeezing. Or toss this oil with pasta, sautéed cauliflower (page 52), and a sprinkling of fresh parsley.

SHELF LIFE: Up to three days in the refrigerator.

Lemon-Rosemary Oil

Only add the rosemary to this oil once the garlic sizzles steadily for about thirty seconds; drop it in any earlier and the rosemary will overwhelm, taking on a menthol-like glow. Use a peeler to shave the lemon zest. Take care to press hard enough to make the strips, but not so hard that you get any bitter white pith.

YIELD: ½ CUP, 6 SERVINGS
PREP TIME: 2 minutes
COOK TIME: 3 minutes

½ cup olive oil
1 garlic clove, smashed
6 (1-inch) wide strips of lemon zest (use a peeler)
2 sprigs fresh rosemary

Set the oil and garlic in a small skillet over medium heat and cook, swirling the pan occasionally, until the garlic starts to sizzle steadily and just starts to color ever so slightly, 2 to 3 minutes. Add the lemon zest and rosemary and remove the pan from the heat. Let cool for about 5 minutes and then strain the oil if you like.

PAIRINGS: Drizzle on grilled fish or seafood kebabs (page 78). Thread shrimp, swordfish, or salmon chunks onto metal skewers with cherry tomatoes, red onion wedges, and zucchini pieces and drizzle with this oil after grilling.

SHELF LIFE: Up to three days in the refrigerator.

Orange-Cinnamon Oil

This infused oil has a decidedly Mediterranean flair. It is one of the few oils that I insist on straining to catch all the little pieces.

YIELD: ½ CUP, 6 SERVINGS
PREP TIME: 4 minutes
COOK TIME: 5 minutes

½ cup olive oil, canola oil, or grapeseed oil
1 cinnamon stick, broken into a couple of pieces
1 tablespoon crushed cumin seeds
1½-inch knob ginger, peeled and thinly sliced
1 shallot, thinly sliced
6 (1-inch) wide strips of orange zest (use a peeler)

Set the oil, cinnamon, and cumin in a medium saucepan over medium heat and cook, swirling the pan occasionally, until the cinnamon starts to sizzle steadily, about 2 minutes. Add the ginger and shallot and cook, stirring, until the shallot softens and becomes translucent, about 2 minutes. Add the orange zest, remove from the heat and let cool for a couple of minutes. Strain before serving.

PAIRINGS: Make a chickpea salad with grilled boneless, skinless chicken thighs (page 71) or broiled shrimp (page 66), grilled (or broiled) zucchini and peppers (page 80 or 65) and this infused oil; squirt with some freshly squeezed orange juice before serving.

SHELF LIFE: Up to five days in the refrigerator.

Spicy Szechuan Chile and Black Bean Oil

After being banned for years by the USDA for fear of Lord knows what, Szechuan peppercorns are now readily available in the United States (that is, if you have access to an Asian grocer), and fans of Chinese cooking and tingling taste buds should rejoice. The tiny rounds give Szechuan dishes its characteristic fragrant spice and tingle.

YIELD: ½ CUP, 6 SERVINGS
PREP TIME: 6 minutes
COOK TIME: 5 minutes

½ cup canola oil or peanut oil
3 garlic cloves, smashed
1½-inch knob ginger, peeled and thinly sliced
2 tablespoons chopped fermented black beans
½ teaspoon crushed red pepper flakes
1 tablespoon Szechuan peppercorns (optional)

Set the oil, garlic, ginger, black beans, and pepper flakes in a medium saucepan over medium heat and cook, swirling the pan occasionally, until the garlic starts to sizzle steadily and turns a very light brown in places, about 2 minutes. Add the peppercorns, remove from the heat, and let cool for a couple of minutes. Strain before serving.

PAIRINGS: This oil is spicy and sharply flavored so a little goes a long way. Drizzle a couple teaspoons into a beef (page 60) and broccoli stir-fry. Or make a warm slaw by tossing this oil with sautéed Napa cabbage (page 53), scallions, and grated carrots.

SHELF LIFE: Up to five days in the refrigerator.

PESTOS, PASTES, AND PURÉES

There are plenty of sauces in this book that are blended or puréed. What makes the ones in this grouping unique is that puréeing or blending is their central characteristic, what makes them what they are. It may be a nice option to give a pan sauce a little refinement by puréeing, but a basil pesto or an olive tapenade is not a pesto or tapenade if you don't mash them up.

There's also the matter of what blending does for these sauces, helping unify different flavors and textures. How to purée? I love mortar and pestles, but I usually use my blender or food processor because they're simply faster. If you're feeling nostalgic or want to burn some calories, have at it.

BASIC PESTOS, PASTES, AND PURÉES METHOD

Purée fresh herbs, greens, aromatics, and pantry ingredients (like nuts or olives) with oil until smooth and uniform.

TIP: How Sharp Are Your Blades?
Pesto is one of those things that will really tell you how sharp the blades on your blender or food processor are. Dull blades mash, instead of chop, turning green herbs like basil, parsley, or cilantro dark and unattractive. Replacement blades are readily available on the Web.

Basil Pesto

This sauce, *pesto Genovese*, is the most iconic pesto: aromatic and vibrant green from Italy's northern region of Liguria. This fresh take should cure pesto-phobics who OD'd on it during the pesto craze of the late '80s.

YIELD: 1 CUP, 6 SERVINGS
PREP TIME: 10 minutes
COOK TIME: 3 minutes (for the pine nuts)

3 cups lightly packed basil leaves (from about 1 bunch), washed and spun dry
⅓ cup freshly grated Parmigiano Reggiano
¼ cup lightly packed fresh parsley leaves (optional)
¼ cup toasted pine nuts
1 small garlic clove, minced and mashed to a paste using the side of a chef's knife, about ½ teaspoon (see page 153)
About ¼ teaspoon kosher salt
About ¼ teaspoon freshly ground black pepper
¼ cup olive oil

Set the basil, Parmigiano, parsley (if using), pine nuts, garlic, and a sprinkling of salt and pepper in a food processor or blender and pulse until uniformly chopped. While puréeing, add the oil in a thin, steady stream so the pesto becomes smooth and slightly loose. Add 1 or 2 tablespoons water to loosen the pesto's texture if you like and season with more salt and pepper to taste.

PAIRINGS: Though often thought of as simply a pairing for pasta, basil pesto is a great topping for grilled chicken breasts (page 71) or a mild sautéed fish like cod (page 44). Or toss with sautéed green beans (page 50), some thinly sliced sun-dried tomatoes, and Parmigiano.

SHELF LIFE: Up to four days in the refrigerator; see storage tip on this page.

TECHNIQUE: The greenest pesto: Set the green color of the basil leaves by dropping them in a couple of cups of boiling water and then immediately "shocking" the leaves in ice water to stop the cooking. Pat dry well with paper towels before puréeing.

TIP: When storing pesto, press plastic wrap down flush so it covers the top surface to avoid a darkened top skin.

Walnut-Parsley Pesto

The formula for this pesto is similar to the basil one on the left: toasted nuts, fresh herbs, and a little cheese. But whereas the basil pesto has an almost sweet glow, the parsley swings this sauce in a more earthy direction.

YIELD: 1 CUP, 6 TO 8 SERVINGS
PREP TIME: 8 minutes
COOK TIME: 4 minutes (for the walnuts)

1 cup lightly packed chopped fresh parsley (from about 1 bunch)
½ cup chopped and toasted walnuts
⅓ cup freshly grated Parmigiano Reggiano
2 scallions (both white and green parts), trimmed and thinly sliced (about ¼ cup)
About ¼ teaspoon kosher salt
About ¼ teaspoon freshly ground black pepper
¼ cup olive oil
1 teaspoon freshly squeezed lemon juice

Set the parsley, walnuts, Parmigiano, scallions, and a sprinkling of salt and pepper in a food processor or blender and pulse until uniformly chopped. While puréeing, add the oil in a thin, steady stream so the pesto becomes smooth and slightly loose. Purée with the lemon juice and 1 or 2 tablespoons water to loosen the pesto's texture if you like and season with more salt, pepper, and lemon juice to taste.

PAIRINGS: The assertiveness of the parsley is perfect for beef or chicken. Spoon on top of a thinly sliced grilled flank steak (page 75) or broiled chicken breasts (page 63) and serve with a fresh tomato salad and toasted pita.

SHELF LIFE: Up to four days in the refrigerator; press plastic wrap down so it touches the pesto to help avoid a darkened top skin.

Mint and Toasted Almond Pesto

Scallions and mint place this purée very much in the spirit of spring, perfect for the special occasions—Passover, Easter, graduations—that pop up during that time of year.

YIELD: ¾ CUP, 4 SERVINGS
PREP TIME: 10 minutes
COOK TIME: 4 minutes (for the almonds)

¾ cup lightly packed chopped fresh mint (from about 1 bunch)
¼ cup toasted slivered almonds, chopped
¼ cup freshly grated Pecorino Romano
2 scallions (both white and green parts), trimmed and thinly sliced (about ¼ cup)
About ¼ teaspoon kosher salt
About ¼ teaspoon freshly ground black pepper
3 tablespoons olive oil

Set the mint, almonds, Pecorino, scallions, and a sprinkling of salt and pepper in a food processor or blender and pulse until uniformly chopped. While puréeing, add the oil in a thin, steady stream so the pesto becomes smooth and slightly loose and then add 1 or 2 tablespoons water to loosen the pesto's texture if you like and season with more salt and pepper to taste.

PAIRINGS: Toss a couple generous spoonfuls of this sauce with sautéed snap peas (page 50) or carrots (page 52). Or serve with sautéed lamb chops (page 38) and Buttery Herbed Couscous (page 237).

SHELF LIFE: Up to two days in the refrigerator; press plastic wrap down so it touches the pesto to help avoid a darkened top skin.

Rosemary and Toasted Bread Crumb Pesto

Fresh rosemary, sun-dried tomatoes, and Pecorino Romano liven up the toasted bread crumbs and olive oil in this earthy paste.

YIELD: 1 CUP, 4 TO 6 SERVINGS
PREP TIME: 8 minutes
COOK TIME: 7 minutes

½ cup olive oil
4 ounces baguette or ciabatta, cut into 1-inch pieces and pulsed into coarse crumbs in a food processor (about 1 cup)
2 teaspoons chopped fresh rosemary
½ cup freshly grated Pecorino Romano
2 sun-dried tomatoes, coarsely chopped (about 2 tablespoons)
1 teaspoon freshly grated lemon zest
About ¼ teaspoon kosher salt
About ¼ teaspoon freshly ground black pepper

Heat half of the oil in a large skillet over medium-high heat until shimmering hot, about 1½ minutes. Add the bread crumbs and cook, stirring, until they start to turn light brown, about 3 minutes. Add the rosemary and cook, stirring, until it becomes fragrant, about 1 minute.

Remove this mixture from the heat and let cool for a minute or two. Transfer to a food processor or blender along with the Pecorino, sun-dried tomatoes, lemon zest, and a sprinkling of salt and pepper. Purée, adding the remaining ¼ oil and a couple of table-spoons of water if needed, so the pesto becomes smooth and slightly loose. Season with more salt and pepper to taste.

PAIRINGS: I like the rosemary in this pesto with a cheap but tasty grilled steak (page 75) like a top sir-loin or with grilled chicken breasts (page 71). Serve either with grilled asparagus (page 80) and Quinoa with Fennel and Feta (page 236).

SHELF LIFE: Up to four days in the refrigerator.

Orange Gremolata

Gremolata, a simple Italian purée of parsley, garlic, and lemon zest, traditionally adds a little zing to rich, braised cuts like osso bucco or oxtail. This version gives the citrus a twist by using orange instead of lemon. I like pulsing this mixture in a mini-chop or food processor to make sure it's uniform.

YIELD: ½ CUP, 4 SERVINGS
PREP TIME: 8 minutes
COOK TIME: N/A

½ cup lightly packed chopped fresh parsley
2 teaspoons freshly grated orange zest (from 1 navel orange)
2 medium cloves garlic, minced and mashed to a paste using the side of a chef's knife and a sprin-kling of salt, about 1½ teaspoons (see page 153)
About ¼ teaspoon kosher salt
About ¼ teaspoon freshly ground black pepper
3 tablespoons extra-virgin olive oil

Set the parsley, orange zest, garlic, and a sprin-kling of salt and pepper in a food processor or blender and pulse until uniformly chopped. While puréeing, add the oil in a thin, steady stream so the sauce becomes smooth and slightly loose. Season with more salt and pepper to taste.

PAIRINGS: Match with broiled lamb chops (page 64) or grilled chicken parts (page 73). If you have the time, soak either in the Red Wine and Rosemary Marinade (page 17).

SHELF LIFE: Up to two days in the refrigerator.

Italian Salsa Verde

Same name and same green color, but different lan-guage and flavors than the Mexican tomatillo salsa on page 155. Italians traditionally pair this zesty mix of herbs, pickles, and capers with boiled meats. If you have a hard-boiled egg kicking around the fridge, it will give this sauce a wonderful creaminess.

YIELD: ¾ CUP, 4 SERVINGS
PREP TIME: 8 minutes
COOK TIME: N/A

1 cup lightly-packed chopped fresh parsley
1 hard-boiled egg, coarsely chopped (optional)
¼ cup chopped cornichons or small gherkins
1 tablespoon freshly squeezed lemon juice, more to taste
1 tablespoon nonpareil capers, drained well
1 medium garlic clove, minced and mashed to a paste using the side of a chef's knife, about ¾ tea-spoon (see page 153)
About ¼ teaspoon kosher salt
About ½ teaspoon freshly ground black pepper
3 tablespoons olive oil

Set all of the ingredients in a food processor along with a sprinkling of salt and pepper and purée until finely chopped. Season with more salt, pepper, and lemon juice to taste.

PAIRINGS: Try this purée with sautéed halibut (page 42) or with a grilled steak (page 75).

SHELF LIFE: Up to four days in the refrigerator.

Green Olive Tapenade

Tapenade is a versatile olive paste: spread it on a sandwich, toss it with sautéed vegetables, or spoon it over fish. Because green olives are milder than black, I like filling this paste out with toasted almonds and fresh parsley.

YIELD: ¾ CUP, 6 SERVINGS
PREP TIME: 8 minutes
COOK TIME: 4 minutes (for the almonds)

¾ cup pitted green olives (like picholine)
¼ cup toasted slivered almonds
2 anchovy filets, drained well and coarsely chopped (optional)
2 tablespoons chopped fresh parsley
1 tablespoon lemon juice
¼ cup olive oil
About ¼ teaspoon kosher salt
About ¼ teaspoon freshly ground black pepper

Set the olives, almonds, anchovies (if using), parsley, and lemon juice in a mini-chop or food processor and pulse to chop. While the motor is running, drizzle in the olive oil and then 2 or 3 tablespoons water to loosen the mixture to a smooth, but not loose, paste. Season with a sprinkling of salt and pepper to taste.

PAIRINGS: Toss this paste with sautéed cauliflower (page 52) and sprinkle with toasted panko bread crumbs. Or spoon over sautéed cod (page 44) and serve with steamed artichokes and a crusty baguette.

SHELF LIFE: Up to five days in the refrigerator.

Black Olive and Mint Tapenade

I like pairing fresh mint with anchovies. It freshens up the fish's slight funkiness, making this mixture bright and balanced.

YIELD: 1 CUP, 8 SERVINGS
PREP TIME: 8 minutes
COOK TIME: N/A

1 cup pitted black olives (like Kalamata or gaeta)
2 anchovy filets, drained well and coarsely chopped (optional)
1 tablespoon chopped nonpareil capers
1 tablespoon freshly squeezed lemon juice
1 teaspoon chopped fresh thyme
3 tablespoons olive oil
About ¼ teaspoon freshly ground black pepper

Set the olives, anchovies (if using), capers, lemon juice, and thyme in a mini-chop or food processor and purée. While the motor is running, drizzle in the olive oil and then 2 or 3 tablespoons water to loosen to a smooth, but not loose, paste. Sprinkle with pepper to taste.

PAIRINGS: Spoon this purée over sautéed tuna (page 42) and serve with boiled new potatoes and sautéed green beans (page 50) for a deconstructed Niçoise salad.

SHELF LIFE: Up to five days in the refrigerator.

Spicy Chipotle and Sun-Dried Tomato Paste

This is one of a couple of recipes in which I pair chipotle peppers and sun-dried tomatoes (see Chipotle and Cilantro Cream on page 108 and Chipotle-Balsamic Vinaigrette on page 184). The two simply work together—the concentrated sweetness of the tomatoes complements the smoky spice of the peppers, making this the perfect D.D.H.S. (designated dinner hot sauce).

YIELD: ¾ CUP, 6 TO 8 SERVINGS
PREP TIME: 8 minutes
COOK TIME: N/A

1 cup lightly packed chopped fresh cilantro (from about 1 bunch)
6 oil-packed sun-dried tomatoes, coarsely chopped (about ¼ cup)
1 canned chipotle chile, chopped plus 1 tablespoon adobo sauce
2 tablespoons olive oil
2 teaspoons cider vinegar
1 teaspoon light brown sugar
1 small garlic clove, minced and mashed to a paste using the side of a chef's knife, about ½ teaspoon (see page 153)
½ teaspoon ground cumin
About ¼ teaspoon kosher salt
About ¼ teaspoon freshly ground black pepper

Set all of the ingredients in a food processor along with a light sprinkling of salt and pepper and purée until finely chopped and smooth. Season with more salt and pepper to taste.

PAIRINGS: This paste was made for pork, either as a top crust for broiled chops (page 64) or smeared over grilled tenderloin (page 75). Serve with grilled corn on the cob (page 82) and steamed long-grain rice.

SHELF LIFE: Up to five days in the refrigerator.

Spicy Chinese Black Bean Paste

I very well could have included this sauce in the stir-fry section (it's like a fresher version of the jarred stuff), but I like to pair it more with grilled or broiled fare as an intense Asian dipping sauce.

YIELD: ½ CUP, 4 SERVINGS
PREP TIME: 7 minutes
COOK TIME: 2 minutes

2 tablespoons canola oil
2 medium garlic cloves, chopped (about 1½ teaspoons)
2 tablespoons coarsely chopped ginger
2 tablespoons fermented black beans, coarsely chopped
½ teaspoon crushed red pepper flakes
2 tablespoons soy sauce
1 tablespoon balsamic vinegar (or Chinese black vinegar if you have)
2 teaspoons toasted sesame oil
2 teaspoons granulated sugar

Set the canola oil, garlic, ginger, black beans, and red pepper flakes in a medium skillet over medium heat and cook, stirring, until they sizzle steadily and the garlic just starts to brown lightly at the edges, about 2 minutes. Remove from the heat and let cool for a minute or two. Transfer to the blender along with the remaining ingredients and purée until smooth.

PAIRINGS: The flavors in this sauce bridge the essence of stir-frying with grilled fare. Serve alongside grilled chicken breasts (page 71) or grilled flank steak (page 75) with grilled asparagus (page 80) and steamed jasmine rice, or toss with stir-fried beef (page 60) and snap peas.

SHELF LIFE: Up to one week in the refrigerator.

Fiery Chinese Peanut and Ginger Sauce

For me, it's essential that a peanut sauce have big flavors to give it complexity. Here, ginger, Thai chiles, and scallions do the job; seed the chiles if you want this sauce to be simply smoldering.

YIELD: 1¼ CUPS, 6 SERVINGS
PREP TIME: 8 minutes
COOK TIME: N/A

½ cup peanut butter (either smooth or chunky is fine)
2 Thai chiles or 1 jalapeño, stemmed and coarsely chopped (about 3 tablespoons)
2 tablespoons chopped fresh ginger
2 tablespoons soy sauce
1 tablespoon rice vinegar
1 teaspoon Thai chile paste (like Sriracha)
¼ cup peanut or canola oil
2 scallions (both white and green parts), trimmed and thinly sliced (about ¼ cup)
2 tablespoons chopped fresh cilantro (optional)

In a food processor, purée the peanut butter with the chiles, ginger, soy sauce, rice vinegar, and chile paste. While still puréeing, drizzle in the oil so the mixture becomes smooth and uniform. Drizzle in 2 or 3 tablespoons of water to loosen the texture if you like. Stir in the scallions and cilantro, if using, and add more vinegar to taste.

PAIRINGS: Serve this sauce for dipping with grilled chicken (page 71) or beef (page 75) satays. Or toss with stir-fried vegetables (page 50) and fresh Chinese egg noodles.

SHELF LIFE: Up to one week in the refrigerator.

Toasted Chermoula Sauce

This traditional North African herb and spice purée may sound so exotic you'll need a passport just to prepare it, but it's rather easy and tasty and goes well with grilled steaks or fish.

YIELD: 1 CUP, 6 TO 8 SERVINGS
PREP TIME: 8 minutes
COOK TIME: 2 minutes

¼ cup olive oil
2 large cloves garlic, chopped (about 2 teaspoons)
1 teaspoon ground cumin
½ teaspoon ground coriander
½ teaspoon pimentón de la Vera
½ cup lightly packed fresh parsley leaves
½ cup lightly packed fresh cilantro leaves
2 tablespoons freshly squeezed lemon juice plus 1 teaspoon freshly grated zest
About ¾ teaspoon kosher salt
About ½ teaspoon freshly ground black pepper

Heat the oil with the garlic in a small saucepan over medium heat until the garlic starts to sizzle steadily and become fragrant, about 2 minutes. Add the spices, remove from the heat, and let cool for a couple of minutes.

Set the herbs in a blender and top with the oil mixture. Blend to purée and while the motor is still running, add the lemon juice, lemon zest, and up to ¼ cup water (1 tablespoon at a time) so the mixture becomes smooth. Season generously with salt and pepper to taste.

PAIRINGS: Toss with grilled shrimp (page 78) and serve with Buttery Herbed Couscous (page 237). Or drizzle over a mild vegetable like sautéed cauliflower (page 52).

SHELF LIFE: Up to four days in the refrigerator.

Warm Green Chile and Cheddar Purée

This sauce is the kind of mildly spicy comfort food I like to turn to when it's cold or rainy or both.

YIELD: 1½ CUPS, 6 SERVINGS
PREP TIME: 8 minutes
COOK TIME: 6 minutes

1 jalapeño, cored and coarsely chopped (about 2 tablespoons)
2 cloves garlic, finely chopped (about 1½ teaspoons)
2 tablespoons olive oil
1 teaspoon ground cumin
About ½ teaspoon kosher salt
About ½ teaspoon freshly ground black pepper
1 (7-ounce) can chopped green chiles, drained
½ cup low-sodium chicken broth
2 tablespoons heavy cream
1 cup grated sharp cheddar cheese (about 4 ounces)
1 tablespoon freshly squeezed lime juice

Cook the jalapeño and garlic with the oil in a large sauté pan over medium-high heat, stirring occasionally, until the garlic starts to turn a light golden color, about 2½ minutes. Add the cumin and a sprinkling of salt and pepper and cook, stirring, for 20 seconds so the spice becomes fragrant. Add the chiles, chicken broth, and cream and bring to a boil. Stir in the cheddar and lime juice and remove from the heat. Transfer to a blender or food processor and purée. Season with more lime juice, salt, and pepper to taste.

OPTIONS: Substitute a couple of roasted Anaheim, poblano, or Hatch chiles for the canned. Core, seed, and skin the peppers before puréeing.

PAIRINGS: Spoon this sauce in the center of dinner plates and top with sliced grilled chicken thighs (page 71) or grilled skirt steak (page 75). Serve with Spanish Yellow Rice (page 234) and warm pinto beans.

SHELF LIFE: Up to three days in the refrigerator; reheat over low heat on the stove top.

Fresh Tomato and Chive Coulis

Coulis may sound fancy and French but it's just a thick fruit or vegetable purée. Here, tomatoes are the star. I like to leave them raw and the sauce relatively simple so their flavor shines through.

YIELD: 1 CUP, ABOUT 4 SERVINGS
PREP TIME: 8 minutes
COOK TIME: N/A

1 pound ripe plum tomatoes (about 5), cored and cut in ½-inch dice (about 2 cups)
1 teaspoon balsamic vinegar
About 1 teaspoon kosher salt
About ½ teaspoon freshly ground black pepper
3 tablespoons extra-virgin olive oil
¼ cup thinly sliced fresh chives

Purée the tomatoes in a blender with the vinegar and a generous sprinkling of salt and pepper. While still puréeing, drizzle in the olive oil. Strain through a fine mesh sieve and then stir in the chives and season with salt and pepper to taste.

PAIRINGS: This light tomato mixture is somewhere between a broth and a sauce in texture—spoon it into a shallow bowl and top with grilled shrimp (page 78) or sautéed scallops (page 46) along with Herbed Goat Cheese Polenta (page 237).

SHELF LIFE: Up to two days in the refrigerator.

Roasted Red Pepper and Cucumber Purée

This pretty Mediterranean sauce is kind of like a gazpacho without the tomatoes, light and perfect for summery, outdoor eating.

YIELD: 1 CUP, ABOUT 4 SERVINGS
PREP TIME: 7 minutes
COOK TIME: N/A

1 large jarred roasted red pepper, drained and
    coarsely chopped (about ½ cup)
½ cup diced English cucumber (about ⅓ cucumber)
1 slice sandwich white bread, torn into pieces
2 tablespoons sherry vinegar
1 medium garlic clove, chopped (about ¾ teaspoon)
¼ teaspoon ground cumin
About ¾ teaspoon kosher salt
About ½ teaspoon freshly ground black pepper
¼ cup olive oil
2 tablespoons chopped fresh parsley

In a food processor, purée the red pepper, cucumber, bread, vinegar, garlic, cumin, and a generous sprinkling of salt and pepper. While puréeing, drizzle in the oil so the mixture becomes smooth and uniform. Drizzle in 1 or 2 tablespoons of water to loosen if you like. Stir in the parsley and season with more salt, pepper, and vinegar to taste.

PAIRINGS: This light sauce goes nicely with fish and seafood. Serve with grilled tuna steaks (page 78) or sautéed cod (page 44) along with a green salad and a loaf of olive bread.

SHELF LIFE: Up to three days in the refrigerator.

TIP: Bread in sauces: Stale bread has always been a staple of peasant cuisines. Historically, it was one of those foodstuffs always in abundance, no matter one's social status. Here the bread (which doesn't need to be stale) helps thicken the sauce, acting like a lighter, cheaper alternative to heavy cream.

Piquillo Pepper Romesco Sauce

I always wonder who the first one was—in this case, the first Catalonian from Northwest Spain—to pair strange ingredients like roasted red peppers and almonds together. Whoever that curious fellow was, I'm glad he did. Romesco is intense and tangy and the perfect complement to grilled or sautéed fish.

YIELD: 1 CUP, ABOUT 4 SERVINGS
PREP TIME: 7 minutes
COOK TIME: N/A

3 jarred piquillo peppers or 1 large roasted red pepper, drained and coarsely chopped (about ½ cup)
¼ cup blanched almonds
1 slice sandwich bread, torn into pieces
2 tablespoons red wine vinegar
1 teaspoon chopped fresh thyme
1 large garlic clove, chopped (about 1 teaspoon)
⅛ to ¼ teaspoon crushed red pepper flakes
About ¾ teaspoon kosher salt
About ½ teaspoon freshly ground black pepper
¼ cup olive oil

In a food processor, purée the peppers, almonds, bread, vinegar, thyme, garlic, pepper flakes, and a generous sprinkling of salt and pepper. While puréeing, drizzle in the oil so the mixture becomes smooth and uniform. Drizzle in 2 or 3 tablespoons water to loosen the mixture if you like.

PAIRINGS: Spoon over grilled shrimp (page 78) or swordfish (page 78), and pair with Traditional Rice Pilaf (page 234) and grilled eggplant (page 80).

SHELF LIFE: Up to three days in the refrigerator.

RELISHES, SALADS, CHUTNEYS, AND QUICK PICKLES

The sauces in this section have a fruit or vegetable base that's perked up with something acidic (like vinegar or citrus) as well as herbs and spices. Relishes and chutneys sound exotic, but they can be made with ingredients you can find at your local market. Both are chopped vegetable or fruit mixtures. Relishes tend to have some level of sweetness to go with the acidity while chutneys veer in a spiced, Eastern direction.

By "salads," we're not talking Caesar, nor will the pickles be big honkin' dills. Rather, these mixtures fit my one-bite sauce definition (page 9) in that they are small, chopped bits that are meant to be eaten bite for bite with whatever you've seared; kind of like a vegetal vinaigrette. Only here the ratio is inversed with the vegetables and aromatics (like onions, garlic, shallots, ginger, etc.) starring in the lead role and the oil and vinegar playing supporting, albeit still assertive, parts.

RELISHES, SALADS, CHUTNEYS, AND QUICK PICKLES METHOD

Toss finely diced or thinly sliced vegetables or fruit with acidic dressings, spices, and herbs and serve as a crunchy, tangy counterpoint to grilled or broiled ingredients.

Jimmy's Mom's Greek Cherry Tomato and Cucumber Salad

As a teenager, I waited tables at the No Name restaurant on Boston's Fish Pier. The restaurant was owned by Nick Contos, a brilliant man who bused tables to get through Harvard Business School. Pretty much all of the waitstaff was native Greek and lunch was whatever fish was freshest and some sort of salad. Young Jimmy, one of Nick's extended cousins, used to bring in this salad from his mom. One day, I asked Jimmy how she made it. "Do you like it?" he asked, staring at me through his thick glasses. I nodded. "So what's the difference?" he asked dismissively. I think I've accurately re-created the original, going a little heavier on the oil and vinegar to make this sort of a chunky vinaigrette.

YIELD: ABOUT 2 CUPS, 4 TO 6 SERVINGS
PREP TIME: 12 minutes
COOK TIME: N/A

1 cup ripe cherry or grape tomatoes, halved or quartered if large
1 cup diced English seedless cucumber (about ½)
4 scallions (both white and green parts), trimmed and thinly sliced (about ½ cup)
About ¾ teaspoon kosher salt
About ½ teaspoon freshly ground black pepper
6 tablespoons olive oil
2 tablespoons red wine vinegar
1 tablespoon chopped fresh oregano or ½ teaspoon dried oregano

In a medium bowl, toss the tomatoes, cucumber, and scallions with a generous sprinkling of salt and pepper and let sit for a couple of minutes. Then toss with the oil, vinegar, and oregano and season with salt and pepper to taste.

PAIRINGS: Do as we did at the No Name and spoon this chunky sauce over grilled halibut (page 78) or broiled cod (page 66). Serve with grilled corn (page 82) or Roasted Yukon Wedges with Bacon and Thyme (page 236)

SHELF LIFE: Up to three days in the refrigerator, though best served fresh.

Chopped Cucumber, Scallion, and Hoisin Sauce

I love the interplay between these three main ingredients. For me it's vaguely reminiscent of Peking duck, without the need to call a restaurant 24 hours ahead to order it.

YIELD: 1 ¼ CUPS, ABOUT 4 SERVINGS
PREP TIME: 6 minutes
COOK TIME: N/A

⅓ English cucumber, cut in ½-inch dice (about 1 cup)
2 scallions (both white and green parts), trimmed and thinly sliced (about ¼ cup)
About ½ teaspoon kosher salt
2 tablespoons hoisin sauce
1 tablespoon rice vinegar
1 teaspoon toasted sesame oil
1 teaspoon soy sauce
1 teaspoon toasted sesame seeds
½ teaspoon Thai chile paste

In a medium bowl, toss the cucumber and scallions with a generous sprinkling of salt. Let sit for a couple of minutes so that the cucumber starts to soften. Add the remaining ingredients and toss well.

PAIRINGS: Create a home-style take on Peking duck, only with chicken. Grill or broil boneless skinless chicken thighs (pages 71 or 63), brush with the Chinese BBQ Sauce (page 94), and then thinly slice and wrap in flour tortillas with this sauce.

SHELF LIFE: Up to three days in the refrigerator.

Herb-Marinated Chopped Summer Tomatoes

I always marvel at the transformation that a ripe summer tomato undergoes when it's paired with savory ingredients. Here, fresh herbs, sliced garlic, and a generous sprinkling of sea salt, shape into an intensely flavored sauce. I only use a light drizzle of balsamic so it offers a hint of sweetness without overpowering of the tomatoes.

YIELD: 2 CUPS, 4 TO 6 SERVINGS
PREP TIME: 8 minutes
COOK TIME: N/A

2 ripe tomatoes (about 1¼ pounds), cored and cut in ¾-inch dice (about 2 cups)
2 cloves garlic, smashed
2 teaspoons chopped fresh thyme or 1 teaspoon chopped fresh rosemary
2 teaspoons balsamic vinegar
About 1¼ teaspoons sea salt or kosher salt
About ½ teaspoon freshly ground black pepper
6 tablespoons olive oil

In a medium bowl, toss the tomatoes with the garlic, thyme, vinegar, and a generous sprinkling of salt and pepper. Let sit for a couple of minutes, tossing occasionally, and then toss with the oil. Mix before serving to emulsify the oil with the tomato juices and sprinkle lightly with salt.

PAIRINGS: Spoon this chunky sauce over grilled chicken breasts (page 71) or steaks (page 75). Thinly slice the meat and set atop Buttery Herbed Couscous (page 237).

SHELF LIFE: Up to three days in the refrigerator, though best served fresh.

TIP: Double salt: I like to season these tomatoes twice. The first seasons and "marinates" the tomatoes while the second offers a little texture (use coarse sea salt if you can for this) and punch.

Pickled Red Onions

I've become consumed with pickling over the last couple of summers, and these tart strips have become a mainstay in my fridge. They keep for a while (at least a week) and go great with beef and chicken. Heat the red wine vinegar before adding the onions both to incorporate the salt and sugar and to wilt the onions.

YIELD: 1½ CUPS, ABOUT 10 SERVINGS
PREP TIME: 6 minutes
COOK TIME: 4 minutes

½ cup red wine vinegar
3 tablespoons granulated sugar
3 bay leaves, broken into pieces
2 teaspoons kosher salt
2 medium red onions (about ¾ pound), thinly sliced (about 2½ cups)

In a medium saucepan bring the vinegar, ¼ cup water, sugar, bay leaves, and salt to a simmer, stirring occasionally. Add the onion, remove from the heat and let cool for a couple of minutes before serving or cool to room temperature before storing in the refrigerator.

PAIRINGS: For an excellent burger, top a grilled chuck patty (page 76) with a good aged provolone or cheddar, these red onions, and baby arugula. Serve on a sourdough roll with the Smashed Garlic and Rosemary Chimichurri (page 164) for dipping.

SHELF LIFE: At least one week in the refrigerator; their flavor only improves after a couple of days.

TIP: Bay leaves: Though the bay leaves don't impart much flavor during the initial simmer, they continue to marinate the onions as they sit. You can omit them if you're making the onions strictly for eating right now.

Quick Dill Cucumber Chips

Any cucumber will work for these slices though I recommend pickling cukes which have a firm texture and relatively small seed core. You can cut the cucumbers into spears, though I like how rounds go with burgers and sandwiches.

YIELD: 1½ CUPS, ABOUT 6 SERVINGS
PREP TIME: 8 minutes
COOK TIME: N/A

1 pound cucumber (3 large pickling cucumbers or 1 English seedless), cut into thin disks (about 2¼ cups)
About 1¼ teaspoons kosher salt
About ¾ teaspoon freshly ground black pepper
2 tablespoons white wine vinegar
1 tablespoon chopped fresh baby dill
1 garlic clove, smashed

Set the cucumbers in a large bowl and toss with a generous sprinkling of salt and pepper and let sit for a couple of minutes. Toss with the remaining ingredients and let sit for a couple of more minutes before serving or refrigerating.

PAIRINGS: My favorite burger is one of the simplest: these pickle chips, a medium rare burger (page 76), and a thick slice of Vermont sharp cheddar. At our b.good stores, this is the Monty and, despite its simplicity, it sells like crazy. I also like pairing these cucumber slices with sautéed salmon (page 42); drizzle any of the pickling juice over the filets for a cooked twist on gravlax.

SHELF LIFE: At least five days in the refrigerator; discard the garlic after the first day.

Ginger-Cranberry Relish

This is one of the sauces that will take you past the fifteen-minute window if you let it properly cool. Serve it warm if you're on the go, or go with canned cranberries and just toss them with the apple, orange, and ginger if you're hell-bent on a shortcut. It is a large portion, but you might as well use up the whole bag of cranberries.

YIELD: 3 CUPS, 12 SERVINGS
PREP TIME: 6 minutes
COOK TIME: 8 minutes

3 cups fresh or frozen cranberries (about 12 ounces)
1½ cups granulated sugar
½ cup ¼-inch dice Granny Smith apple (about ½ apple)
1 navel orange, zested (about 2 teaspoons) and juiced (about ½ cup)
1 tablespoon freshly grated ginger
About ¼ teaspoon kosher salt

Set all the ingredients in a medium saucepan over medium-high heat and cook, stirring every minute or so, until the cranberries just start to pop, about 8 minutes. Remove from the heat and let cool to room temperature before serving or refrigerating.

PAIRINGS: Spoon over sautéed pork chops (page 38) or turkey cutlets (page 36) and serve with sautéed Brussels sprouts (page 52) and Wild Rice with Dried Cherries and Toasted Walnuts (page 236) for an impromptu holiday meal.

SHELF LIFE: Up to two weeks in the refrigerator.

Fennel and Red Onion Relish

This colorful fennel and red onion sauce may be quite different from a dill pickle relish, but it does have the prerequisite tang, and its sweet/crunchy balance makes it a perfect pairing for fish or meat.

YIELD: 1¼ CUPS, ENOUGH 4 TO 6 SERVINGS
PREP TIME: 8 minutes
COOK TIME: N/A

1 fennel bulb (about ½ pound), trimmed, quartered, cored, and cut in ¼-inch dice (about 1 cup)
¼ cup finely diced red onion (about ½ small onion)
About ¾ teaspoon kosher salt
About ½ teaspoon freshly ground black pepper
2 tablespoons extra-virgin olive oil
1 tablespoon red wine vinegar
1 tablespoon nonpareil capers, drained and chopped
1 tablespoon chopped fresh tarragon

Set the fennel and red onion in a medium bowl, toss with a generous sprinkling of salt and pepper, and let sit for a couple of minutes to soften. Toss with the oil, vinegar, capers, and tarragon and taste for salt and pepper before serving.

PAIRINGS: This full-flavored relish goes nicely with broiled lamb chops (page 64) or a grilled flank steak (page 75). Serve with Bulgur with Cherry Tomatoes, Mint, and Mozzarella (page 236).

SHELF LIFE: Up to three days in the refrigerator.

Grilled Sweet Corn and Pepper Relish

Grill the corn and pepper in this relish just long enough to pick up a little color and flavor, but not so much that they cook through. The acidity of the relish should match the natural sweetness of the vegetables.

YIELD: 1½ CUPS, 4 TO 6 SERVINGS
PREP TIME: 9 minutes
COOK TIME: 6 minutes

2 ears corn, husked
1 red bell pepper, cored, and quartered
3 tablespoons olive oil
About ¾ teaspoon kosher salt
About ½ teaspoon freshly ground black pepper
½ small red onion, finely diced (about ¼ cup)
2 tablespoons red wine vinegar
1 tablespoon chopped fresh dill
1 teaspoon granulated sugar

Light a gas grill to high or prepare a medium-hot charcoal fire. Set the corn and pepper on a rimmed baking sheet and toss with 1 tablespoon of the oil and a generous sprinkling of salt and pepper. Grill the corn and pepper, flipping after a couple of minutes, so they get nice grill marks and the peppers just start to soften, about 5 minutes.

Let cool for a couple of minutes, then coarsely chop the peppers, remove the kernels from the cob, and toss both in a medium bowl with the onion, vinegar, dill, sugar, and the remaining 2 tablespoons oil. Season with salt and pepper to taste.

PAIRINGS: Set this summery sauce atop a grilled steak (page 75) or grilled swordfish (page 78). Serve with Warm Farro Salad with Orange and Asparagus (page 236).

SHELF LIFE: Up to three days in the refrigerator.

Roasted Red Pepper and Cornichon Relish

Two pantry foodstuffs—roasted red peppers and cornichons, or tiny, pickled gherkins—power this simple but dressy relish.

YIELD: 1 CUP, 4 SERVINGS
PREP TIME: 8 minutes
COOK TIME: N/A

2 tablespoons olive oil
1 tablespoons white wine vinegar
1 teaspoon chopped fresh thyme
½ teaspoon granulated sugar
1 small garlic clove, minced and mashed to a paste using the side of a chef's knife, about ½ teaspoon (see page 153)
About ¼ teaspoon kosher salt
About ½ teaspoon freshly ground black pepper
1 large roasted red pepper, cut in ¼-inch dice (about ½ cup)
½ cup chopped dill cornichons (about 5)

In a small bowl, whisk together the oil, vinegar, thyme, sugar, garlic, and a sprinkling of salt and black pepper. Set the remaining ingredients in a medium bowl, toss with this oil mixture, and season with more salt and pepper to taste.

PAIRINGS: The sweet and sour tang of this relish is a good fit with a full-flavored fish like grilled salmon (page 78) or sautéed swordfish (page 78). Serve with Quinoa with Fennel and Feta (page 236).

SHELF LIFE: Up to three days in the refrigerator.

Mango and Grilled Pepper Chutney

Kind of like with a tomato, it's important to season the mangoes in this sauce generously so they have a sharp, savory edge. Cumin and curry do the spicing while a mix of peppers and chiles adds heat.

YIELD: 1½ CUPS, 6 SERVINGS
PREP TIME: 10 minutes
COOK TIME: 6 minutes

1 red bell pepper, cored and cut in 4 pieces
1 Anaheim or poblano pepper, cored and cut in 4 pieces
1 tablespoon olive oil
1 teaspoon curry powder
1 teaspoon ground cumin
About ¾ teaspoon kosher salt
About ½ teaspoon freshly ground black pepper
2 medium-ripe mangoes (about 1 pound), cut in ½-inch dice (1½ cups)
2 tablespoons chopped fresh cilantro
1 tablespoon minced fresh ginger
1 tablespoon freshly squeezed lime juice

Prepare a medium-hot fire on a gas or charcoal grill. Toss the red pepper and Anaheim pepper with the oil, curry powder, cumin, and half of the salt and black pepper. Set the peppers on the grill and cook, flipping every couple of minutes, until they brown and start to become tender, 5 to 6 minutes. Transfer to a cutting board to cool.

Coarsely chop the peppers and set in a medium bowl along with the mango, cilantro, ginger, and lime juice. Season with the remaining salt and pepper and more lime juice to taste.

PAIRINGS: Direct this sauce toward light and delicate seared ingredients like grilled shrimp (page 78) or sautéed scallops (page 46). Serve with Spanish Yellow Rice (page 234).

SHELF LIFE: Up to two days in the refrigerator.

Spicy Indian Tomato-Onion Chutney

This staple Indian condiment is one of my favorites. Mustard seeds offer the aromatic spice while jalapeños and a spoonful of chile paste bring the heat.

YIELD: 1½ CUPS, ABOUT 8 SERVINGS
PREP TIME: 8 minutes
COOK TIME: 7 minutes

2 tablespoons canola or peanut oil
1 teaspoon mustard seeds
1 medium Spanish onion, cut in ¼-inch dice (about 1¼ cups)
1 jalapeño, chopped (remove the seeds if you don't want the chutney too spicy) (about 3 tablespoons)
About 1 teaspoon kosher salt
½ teaspoon freshly ground black pepper
¼ teaspoon curry powder
⅛ to ¼ teaspoon saffron threads
¾ cup canned diced tomatoes, drained and puréed
1 to 2 teaspoons Thai chile paste

Heat the oil and mustard seeds in a large skillet over medium-high heat until the seeds start to sizzle and pop, about 1½ minutes. Add the onion and jalapeño, sprinkle generously with salt and pepper, and cook, stirring, until the onion softens and starts to turn light brown, about 3 minutes.

Stir in the curry powder and saffron and cook, moving around the pan, for 30 seconds so the spices become fragrant. Add the puréed tomato and simmer for a couple of minutes, stirring, so the onions soften a bit and the flavors of the spices become integrated. Let cool to room temperature, season with salt and pepper to taste, and serve.

PAIRINGS: I love this sauce with grilled chicken thighs (page 71) or broiled lamb chops (page 64). If you have the time, soak either in the Tandoori Yogurt Marinade (page 17) or simply sprinkle with a light dusting of curry powder and cayenne before searing. Serve with steamed basmati rice.

SHELF LIFE: Up to five days in the refrigerator.

Indian Mint and Cilantro Chutney

Along with Spicy Indian Tomato-Onion Chutney (page 223) and Tamarind Sauce (on right), this sauce forms the holy trinity of condiments that are often set on the table at Indian-American restaurants. Though this sauce plays a cooling foil to spiced tandoori meats and fish, it's not all soothing; chiles, ginger, and garlic give it a little punch.

YIELD: 1 CUP, 8 SERVINGS
PREP TIME: 10 minutes
COOK TIME: N/A

½ cup chopped fresh mint
½ cup chopped fresh cilantro
½ cup yogurt (preferably a full-fat Greek yogurt)
1 Thai chile or 1 jalapeño, stemmed and chopped
2 tablespoons chopped fresh ginger (from a 1-inch knob)
1 garlic clove, chopped (about ¾ teaspoon)
1 tablespoon freshly squeezed lime juice
About ½ teaspoon kosher salt
About ½ teaspoon freshly ground black pepper

Set all the ingredients with a generous sprinkling of salt and pepper in a food processor and purée until uniform. Season with more salt, pepper, and lime juice to taste.

PAIRINGS: Serve for dipping with spiced grilled chicken skewers (page 71) or sautéed lamb chops (page 38), basmati rice, and sautéed cauliflower (page 52).

SHELF LIFE: Up to two days in the refrigerator.

Tamarind Sauce

Though it's not chunky, this traditional Indian sauce has the prerequisite spice and sweet and sour tang that marks all good chutneys. Its base is made with tamarind available at your local Asian grocer.

YIELD: 1 CUP, 8 SERVINGS
PREP TIME: 5 minutes
COOK TIME: N/A

1 tablespoon tamarind (from a pliable block)
½ teaspoon fennel seeds
2 tablespoons canola oil
½ cup finely diced yellow onion (1 small)
2 tablespoons minced fresh ginger
1 tablespoon light brown sugar
2 teaspoons ground cumin
1 teaspoon garam masala
¼ teaspoon cayenne
About ½ teaspoon kosher salt
About ½ teaspoon freshly ground black pepper
1 tablespoon tamarind paste

In a medium bowl, mash the tamarind with ½ cup boiling water until softened. Strain through a fine mesh sieve and discard the solids. Heat the fennel seeds with the oil in a sauté pan over medium high heat until they start to sizzle, about 1½ minutes. Add the onion and ginger and cook, stirring, until the onion starts to soften and become translucent, about 4 minutes. Stir in the sugar, spices, and a sprinkling of salt and pepper and cook for 1 minute, stirring, so the spices become fragrant.

Stir in the tamarind liquid and bring to a simmer. Cook, stirring, until the onions become tender, about 4 minutes. Purée using an immersion blender, then season with salt and pepper to taste.

PAIRINGS: Serve with grilled shrimp (page 78) or drizzle over broiled lamb chops (page 64). Serve with Curried Basmati Rice with Currants and Almonds (page 234).

SHELF LIFE: Up to five days.

Apricot and Toasted Pistachio Chutney

No doubt this sauce is probably out of your comfort zone, but its flavors are familiar, making it just exotic enough to please, but not overwhelm on a weeknight.

YIELD: 1½ CUPS, ABOUT 6 SERVINGS
PREP TIME: 8 minutes
COOK TIME: 6 minutes

2 tablespoons olive oil
1 small yellow onion, finely diced (about ½ cup)
About ½ teaspoon kosher salt
About ½ teaspoon freshly ground black pepper
1 teaspoon ground cumin
¼ teaspoon pimentón de la Vera or chipotle powder
10 dried apricots, coarsely chopped (about ½ cup)
¼ cup freshly squeezed orange juice
¼ cup chopped toasted pistachios
2 tablespoons chopped fresh cilantro
1 tablespoon honey

Heat the oil in a large skillet over medium-high heat until shimmering hot, about 1½ minutes. Add the onion, sprinkle with salt and pepper, and cook, stirring, until the onion softens and starts to turn light brown, about 3 minutes. Stir in the spices and cook for 30 seconds, stirring, so they become fragrant. Stir in the remaining ingredients and remove from the heat.

PAIRINGS: Spoon over a grilled steak (page 75) or broiled chicken thighs coated with the Moroccan Spice Crust (page 14). Serve with Spiced Grilled Vegetable Couscous (page 237).

SHELF LIFE: Up to four days in the refrigerator; it improves after a day or two as the dried fruit soaks up the surrounding flavors.

SEARED VEGETABLES

These toppings occupy a funny place between "sear" and "sauce." Many of the techniques for searing the vegetables are covered in chapter 2. But they become "sauces" by adding intense flavorings, which make them perfect accompaniments for seared meat, chicken, or fish. If you have any doubt as to their sauciness or their adherence to the One-Bite Principle (page 9), try the Grill-Marinated Peppers and Capers (page 230) with grilled halibut (page 78) or the Chinese Seared Jalapeños and Scallions (page 228) with broiled shrimp. You'll buy in.

BASIC SEARED VEGETABLES METHOD

Brown vegetables in a hot skillet, on the grill, or under the broiler, then toss with bright flavors (like fresh herbs or vinegar) as well as something rich like butter or cream.

Browned Sherry Onions

So as not to upset the culinary police, I've called these onions "browned" and not "caramelized." True caramelized onions, like a caramel itself, must be slowly guided to that delicate browned stage, so they perilously teeter on the brink of burning without quite crossing over. That process can take up to forty-five minutes; I like to speed things along by cooking over relatively high heat and stirring often to avoid burning.

YIELD: ABOUT 1 CUP, 4 TO 6 SERVINGS
PREP TIME: 4 minutes
COOK TIME: 12 minutes

2 tablespoons olive oil
1 large Spanish onion (about 1 pound), thinly sliced (about 2½ cups)
About 1 teaspoon kosher salt
⅓ cup dry sherry
1 teaspoon chopped fresh thyme (optional)

Heat the oil in a large skillet over medium-high heat until shimmering hot, about 1½ minutes. Add the onion, sprinkle generously with salt, and cook, stirring often to avoid burning, until the onions wilt uniformly and color in places, about 4 minutes.

Add the sherry and thyme, if using, and cook, stirring, until the sherry almost completely reduces, about 2 minutes. Reduce the heat to medium and continue to cook, stirring, until the onions color a light brown and become tender, about 5 minutes; add a couple of tablespoons of water if the onions start to brown or stick.

PAIRINGS: Pair with sautéed steaks (page 64), or stuff in chicken breasts along with some Parmigiano and sun-dried tomatoes and broil (page 33). Serve either with roasted potatoes and sautéed spinach (page 53).

SHELF LIFE: Up to one week in the refrigerator.

Pernod-Infused Caramelized Fennel Wedges

Pernod is an anise-flavored green liquor. Here it harmonizes with the front-man fennel. I like to use an ample amount of butter both so the fennel properly browns and so the extra fat mellows the flavor of the Pernod.

YIELD: 1 CUP, 4 TO 6 SERVINGS
PREP TIME: 4 minutes
COOK TIME: 12 minutes

3 tablespoons unsalted butter
1 medium bulb fennel (about ¾ pound), trimmed, quartered, cored, and cut in thin wedges
About ¾ teaspoon kosher salt
About ½ teaspoon freshly ground black pepper
⅓ cup Pernod
1 teaspoon chopped fresh thyme (optional)
¼ cup low-salt chicken broth or water

Melt the butter in a large skillet over medium-high heat. Add the fennel, sprinkle generously with salt and pepper, and cook, flipping after a couple of minutes, until the fennel browns lightly and starts to soften, about 4 minutes.

Add the Pernod and thyme, if using, and cook, stirring, until the Pernod almost completely reduces, about 2 minutes. Add the chicken broth or water and cook, stirring occasionally, until it almost completely reduces and the fennel softens, about 4 minutes.

OPTIONS: Add a third layer of anise flavor to this dish with a tablespoon of chopped fresh tarragon. Or toss with some shaved Parmigiano.

PAIRINGS: Fennel and beef are a good match. Spoon these flavored wedges over a hearty cut like a broiled top sirloin (page 64). Or toss with broiled shrimp skewers (page 66). Serve either with Parmesan and Sun-Dried Tomato Polenta (page 237).

SHELF LIFE: Up to three days in the refrigerator

Sautéed Red Wine Shallots

Smaller and quicker cooking than onions, these shallot rings race to an even, browned doneness in short order. They are more apt to burn, though, so take care to stir often.

YIELD: ½ CUP, 6 SERVINGS
PREP TIME: 4 minutes
COOK TIME: 11 minutes

2 tablespoons olive oil
3 large shallots (about 6 ounces), thinly sliced (about
    1¼ cups)
About ½ teaspoon kosher salt
¼ cup dry red wine
1 teaspoon chopped fresh thyme (optional)
½ teaspoon granulated sugar

Heat the oil in a large skillet over medium-high heat until shimmering hot, about 1½ minutes. Add the shallots, sprinkle generously with salt, and cook, stirring often to avoid burning, until they wilt and start to soften, about 3 minutes.

Add the red wine, thyme, and sugar, if using, and cook, stirring, until the wine almost completely reduces, about 2 minutes. Reduce the heat to medium and continue cooking and stirring until the shallots soften completely, about 4 minutes; add a splash of water if the shallots start to stick or burn.

PAIRINGS: The red wine and shallots pair perfectly with beef. Go with a sautéed dressy cut like filet mignon or strip steak (page 38) and serve with Rosemary-Parmesan Mashed Yukon Potatoes (page 235) and sautéed broccolini (page 50).

SHELF LIFE: Up to one week in the refrigerator.

Truffled Wild Mushrooms

This recipe can include any mix of wild mushrooms that you can find or afford. Sauté the mushrooms in a very hot pan without touching for a minute or two so they caramelize and then stir until soft and tender.

YIELD: 1¼ CUPS, 6 SERVINGS
PREP TIME: 7 minutes
COOK TIME: 6 minutes

3 tablespoons unsalted butter
2 cloves garlic, halved
8 ounces wild mushrooms (like shiitakes, oyster,
    chanterelles, morels, maitake), stemmed and thinly sliced
About ¾ teaspoon kosher salt
1 teaspoon chopped fresh thyme
1 teaspoon sherry vinegar
Light drizzle white truffle oil (about ½ teaspoon)

Melt 2 tablespoons of the butter with the garlic in a large skillet over medium-high heat until the butter's foam cooks off and the garlic starts to sizzle steadily and becomes fragrant, about 1½ minutes. Discard the garlic cloves and add the mushrooms. Cook, without touching, until they start to brown (you can peek underneath), about 2 minutes.

Sprinkle generously with salt, add the thyme, and then cook, stirring, until the mushrooms soften completely and brown more uniformly, 1 to 2 more minutes. Toss with the remaining 1 tablespoon butter, the sherry vinegar, and truffle oil, and season with salt to taste.

OPTIONS: Though truffle oil is increasingly available in supermarkets, white truffle butter can be harder to find, but it's worth it. Fold in 1 to 2 tablespoons at the end of cooking in place of the truffle oil and the last pat of butter.

PAIRINGS: These mushrooms go nicely with sautéed chicken or veal cutlets (page 36). Serve with sautéed spinach (page 53) and Buttered Egg Noodles with Chives (page 233).

SHELF LIFE: Up to three days in the refrigerator, though these are best right out of the pan.

TIP: Go light on the truffle oil; a drizzle bolsters the mushrooms, a splash will make them taste like burnt plastic.

Sautéed Vinegar Peppers

This Italian-American preparation is a perfect example of how seared vegetables can become a sauce. The vinegar combines with the peppers to create intense sweet and sour strips, which give pork chops or steak a tangy boost.

YIELD: 1¼ CUPS, 4 TO 6 SERVINGS
PREP TIME: 4 minutes
COOK TIME: 9 minutes

3 tablespoons olive oil
2 red bell peppers (or orange or yellow peppers), cored and cut in ½-inch strips (about 2 cups)
About ¾ teaspoon kosher salt
About ½ teaspoon freshly ground black pepper
1 large garlic clove, chopped (about 1 teaspoon)
3 tablespoons red wine vinegar
1 teaspoon granulated sugar
1 tablespoon fresh oregano

Heat the oil in a large skillet over medium-high heat until shimmering hot, about 1½ minutes. Add the peppers, sprinkle with salt and pepper, and cook, stirring occasionally, until the peppers brown in places and start to soften, 3 to 4 minutes. Add the garlic and cook, tossing, until it becomes fragrant and starts to turn light brown at its edges, about 1 minute.

In a small bowl, mix ¼ cup water with the vinegar and sugar and add to the peppers. Cook, stirring occasionally, until the liquid almost completely cooks off and the peppers soften, about 2 minutes. Stir in the oregano and season with more salt and pepper to taste.

PAIRINGS: The traditional pairing for these peppers is sautéed pork chops (page 38). Nestle the chops into the pan with the peppers so they soak up all of the flavors and then serve with sautéed greens and Herbed Goat Cheese Polenta (page 237).

SHELF LIFE: Up to three days in the refrigerator; they're fine served at room temperature.

Chinese Seared Jalapeños and Scallions

One of my favorite Chinese restaurant preparations is "salt and pepper" shimp or pork or anything for that matter. The main ingredient is generally fried and then tossed with a mix of jalapeños and scallions so the fried coating picks up their flavors. This sauce applies that concept to seared food.

YIELD: ¾ CUP, 4 TO 6 SERVINGS
PREP TIME: 5 minutes
COOK TIME: 6 minutes

2 tablespoons canola or peanut oil
3 jalapeños, stemmed and sliced into thin rings
4 scallions (both white and green parts), trimmed and thinly sliced
About ¾ teaspoon kosher salt
About ¾ teaspoon freshly ground black pepper
Pinch 5-spice powder (optional)
2 teaspoons soy sauce
1 teaspoon toasted sesame oil
1 teaspoon white vinegar

Heat the oil in a large skillet over medium-high heat until it's shimmering hot, about 1½ minutes. Add the jalapeños and scallions, sprinkle generously with salt and pepper, and cook, stirring occasionally, until the vegetables brown in places and start to soften, about 2 to 3 minutes. Sprinkle with the 5-spice powder, if using, and cook, tossing, for 20 seconds. Remove from the heat and toss with the soy sauce, sesame oil, and vinegar.

PAIRINGS: Nap this spicy mixture over steaks or chops, or toss with broiled shrimp (page 78). Serve with stir-fried baby bok choy (page 50) and steamed rice.

SHELF LIFE: Up to three days in the refrigerator.

Grilled Vinegar-Soaked Jalapeños

Grill these jalapeños long enough so they pick up some smokiness and start to become tender, but not so long that they shrivel or char (which chiles are apt to do if left on the grill too long).

YIELD: 1 CUP, 6 SERVINGS
PREP TIME: 3 minutes
COOK TIME: 5 minutes

3 jalapeños, stemmed
4 tablespoons olive oil
About ½ teaspoon kosher salt
About ½ teaspoon freshly ground black pepper
3 tablespoons red wine vinegar
1 tablespoon chopped fresh oregano

Light the gas grill to medium-high or prepare a medium charcoal fire. Toss the whole jalapeños with 1 tablespoon of the oil and a sprinkling of salt and pepper.

Grill the jalapeños, flipping every minute or so, until they have good grill marks and just start to soften (you don't want them to shrivel or char), 3 to 5 minutes. Transfer to a large cutting board and let cool for a minute or two, then thinly slice and toss with the remaining 3 tablespoons oil, the vinegar, and oregano. Stir well just before serving.

PAIRINGS: Spoon these jalapeños into a fajita or taco with sautéed beef (page 38), chicken (page 31), or vegetables (page 50) and let their heat get folded into the whole of the dish. Or sprinkle them on grilled or broiled fare and eat them one at a time with bitefuls of meat or fish.

SHELF LIFE: Up to one week in the refrigerator.

Grilled Balsamic Onions

I prefer red onions for grilling—they tend to burn less and have a measured sweetness. Use slightly lower heat if grilling a yellow onion.

YIELD: 1 CUP, 4 SERVINGS
PREP TIME: 4 minutes
COOK TIME: 8 minutes

1 large (or 2 small) red onion, peeled and cut in disks between ½- and ¼-inch thick
2 tablespoons olive oil
About ¾ teaspoon kosher salt
About ½ teaspoon freshly ground black pepper
2 tablespoons balsamic vinegar
1 teaspoon chopped fresh thyme

Light the gas grill to medium-high or prepare a medium charcoal fire. Sprinkle the onion with 1 tablespoon of the oil and a generous sprinkling of salt and pepper. Grill the onion disks until they have good grill marks, 3 to 4 minutes. Flip and cook until the other sides brown and start to soften (you don't want them to shrivel or char), 3 to 4 more minutes. Transfer to a large shallow bowl, toss with the vinegar and thyme and the remaining oil, and cover tightly with plastic wrap. Let sit for 5 minutes before serving.

PAIRINGS: These grilled onions go with most anything, but best with beef. The balsamic gives the onions a refined edge to match a good grilled steak (page 75), but they're also assertive enough to star on a grilled burger (page 76).

SHELF LIFE: Up to one week in the refrigerator.

TIP: Thread the onions onto metal or wooden skewers, if you like, to prevent them from breaking apart.

Grill-Marinated Peppers with Capers

Use a couple of different colors of peppers here if you have them. After grilling, cover the peppers with plastic wrap for a couple of minutes to steam off their skins and soften their fleshy texture.

YIELD: 1 CUP, 6 SERVINGS
PREP TIME: 2 minutes
COOK TIME: 8 minutes

2 red bell peppers, quartered and cored
4 tablespoons olive oil
About ¾ teaspoon kosher salt
About ½ teaspoon freshly ground black pepper
1 tablespoon sherry vinegar or red wine vinegar
2 tablespoons nonpareil capers, drained well
1 tablespoon chopped fresh parsley

Light the gas grill to medium-high or prepare a medium charcoal fire. Toss the peppers with 1 tablespoon oil and a generous sprinkling of salt and pepper. Grill the peppers, flipping every couple of minutes, until they have good grill marks and are just starting to soften, about 5 to 8 minutes.

Transfer to a large shallow bowl and cover with plastic wrap. Let sit for a couple of minutes, then uncover and scrape off any loose skins. Lay the peppers on a large plate and sprinkle with the vinegar, the remaining 3 tablespoons of oil, the capers, and parsley.

PAIRINGS: I like making these peppers the base for grilled swordfish or tuna (page 78) or for broiled cod (page 66). Set some thinly sliced roasted potatoes on the plate, top with the fish, and finish with the peppers.

SHELF LIFE: Up to one week in the refrigerator.

Grilled Herb-Crusted Plum Tomatoes

Plum (or Roma) tomatoes are sturdier and less watery than round tomatoes so they hold up better on the grill.

YIELD: 2 CUPS, 6 SERVINGS
PREP TIME: 2 minutes
COOK TIME: 8 minutes

1½ pounds ripe plum tomatoes (about 6), cored and halved
3 tablespoons olive oil
2 teaspoons chopped fresh thyme
1 medium garlic clove, chopped (about ¾ teaspoon)
About 1¼ teaspoons kosher salt
About ½ teaspoon freshly ground black pepper
2 teaspoons red wine vinegar
2 tablespoons chopped fresh parsley

Light the gas grill to medium-high or prepare a medium charcoal fire. Toss the tomato with half of the oil, thyme, the garlic, and a generous sprinkling of salt and pepper. Let marinate for up to ½ hour if you have the time.

Grill the tomatoes, cut side down, until they start to get good grill marks, 2 to 3 minutes. Flip the tomatoes and cook until the other sides have good grill marks, too, and start to soften, about 3 more minutes. Transfer to a large plate, drizzle with the remaining oil and vinegar, sprinkle with the parsley and serve.

PAIRINGS: Pair these tomatoes with a grilled steak (page 75); top with fresh mozzarella, chopped fresh basil, and a drizzle of good olive oil, and serve with a fresh baguette.

SHELF LIFE: Up to three days in the refrigerator.

Blistered Cherry Tomatoes with Fresh Herbs

I like broiling cherry or grape tomatoes just until they're about to pop, and then serving them as is or mashing them into a chunky sauce with the tines of a fork.

YIELD: 1½ CUPS, 4 SERVINGS
PREP TIME: 3 minutes
COOK TIME: 7 minutes

1 pint cherry or grape tomatoes, stemmed
2 tablespoons olive oil
1 teaspoon chopped fresh thyme or rosemary or 1 tablespoon chopped fresh oregano
About 1 teaspoon kosher salt
About ½ teaspoon freshly ground black pepper
1 teaspoon balsamic vinegar

Heat the broiler to high and position an oven rack about 6 inches away from the element. In a small roasting pan or baking dish, toss the tomatoes with half of the oil, the herbs, and a generous sprinkling of salt and pepper.

Broil the tomatoes until they start to brown and blister, about 3 minutes. Give the pan a shake so the tomatoes flip and then continue to broil until they brown and blister more uniformly, 1 to 2 more minutes. Remove from the oven, toss with the balsamic vinegar and the remaining oil, and serve.

PAIRINGS: Spoon the warmed tomatoes over (page 66). Or toss with broiled shrimp (page 66), asparagus (page 65), and orzo.

SHELF LIFE: N/A; these tomatoes lose their freshness and texture upon refrigerating.

TIP: Season the outsides of the tomatoes generously so they have a charred, savory crust.

TIP: Bread Crumbs, a Southern Italian "Sauce"
In the south of Italy, where it's hot and dry and where there's little dairy, bread crumbs are sprinkled on pastas and meats as a finishing touch in much the same way Italians in the fertile North use Parmigiano. Economics were also a factor in the evolution of bread crumbs in southern Italian cooking—stale bread was a lot easier to come by than expensive, aged cheese. As with most staples of peasant cuisine, crisped crumbs are a smart technique that still has merit. Bolster them with some chopped fresh herbs (like thyme or rosemary), aromatics (like chopped garlic or lemon zest), some shredded aged cheese and sprinkle on seared foods to add texture and intense flavor.

CHAPTER: 5

SERVE WITH STARCHY SIDES

BASIC MASTER RECIPES (AND A HANDFUL OF VARIATIONS) FOR SIMPLE THINGS TO SERVE WITH SEAR-AND-SAUCE MAIN COURSES; ALL ARE ACCOMPANIMENTS THAT CAN BE QUICKLY STIRRED, SAUTÉED, CHOPPED, OR MASHED TOGETHER.

ALL SIDES YIELD FOUR GENEROUS SERVINGS.

PASTA

Infused Pastas (Boil and Toss)

Cook ¾ *pound pasta* in a generous amount of well-salted water (a couple tablespoons of salt for 4 quarts water), stirring occasionally, until tender (follow the package instructions for times, though taste early and often for doneness), and then toss with the different flavorings.

Buttered Egg Noodles with Chives: Toss the *noodles* just after straining with *2 to 3 tablespoons unsalted butter* (cut into smaller pats), *3 tablespoons thinly sliced fresh chives*, and plenty of *salt* and *pepper* to taste; add a couple tablespoons of the pasta cooking water to loosen the mixture if you like.

Spaghetti with Pecorino and Black Pepper: Toss the *noodles* just after straining with *2 tablespoons unsalted butter* (cut into smaller pats), *1 cup freshly grated Pecorino Romano*, and *1¼ teaspoons coarsely cracked black pepper*. Season with more pepper and *salt* to taste; add a couple tablespoons of the pasta cooking water to loosen the mixture if you like.

Penne with Broccoli and Sun-Dried Tomatoes: Add *3 cups broccoli florets* to the boiling water with the *pasta* for the final minute or two of cooking—you just want to soften its crunch—then drain well and toss with *2 tablespoons olive oil*, *2 thinly sliced scallions*, *4 oil-packed sun-dried tomatoes* (thinly sliced), *4 ounces crumbled feta* (about 1 cup), and *salt* and *pepper* to taste.

Elbows with Peas and Farmers' Cheese: Toss the *pasta* immediately after straining with *8 ounces farmers' cheese* (sub in ricotta or crumbled feta if you like), *1 cup thawed frozen peas*, *1 teaspoon freshly grated lemon zest*, and *salt* and *pepper* to taste. Drizzle with *olive oil* before serving.

Cold Peanut Noodles with Mint and Thai Chiles: While the *spaghetti* or *linguine* cooks, purée *¼ cup peanut butter*, *2 tablespoons canola oil*, *1 tablespoon soy sauce*, *1 tablespoon rice vinegar*, *1 tablespoon minced ginger*, and *1 chopped Thai chile* in a blender with enough water to thin the mixture, 2 or 3 tablespoons. Drain the pasta under cool, running water to room temperature, then toss with the peanut mixture and *2 tablespoons chopped fresh mint*.

Stir-Sautéed Pastas

While the *pasta* is cooking (see at left for cooking instructions), sauté vegetables, aromatics, and pantry ingredients. Add the pasta and toss over high heat for 1 to 2 minutes so it picks up the flavorings.

Orzo with Wild Mushrooms and Baby Spinach: Heat *3 tablespoons olive oil* with *2 smashed garlic cloves* in a large skillet over medium-high heat until the garlic starts to sizzle steadily, about 1½ minutes. Add *3½ ounces thinly sliced oyster mushrooms*, sprinkle with *½ teaspoon salt*, and cook, stirring, until browned and tender. Add *6 ounces baby spinach* and cook, tossing, until just wilted, 1 to 2 minutes. Add the cooked pasta and cook, tossing, for a minute or two. Season with *salt* and *pepper* to taste and discard the garlic.

Spaghetti with Garlic, Oil, and Hot Pepper Flakes: Heat *4 tablespoons olive oil* with *2 cloves chopped garlic* in a large skillet over medium heat until the garlic colors a light, golden brown and becomes very aromatic, about 2½ minutes. Add *½ teaspoon crushed red pepper flakes* and cook, stirring, for 15 seconds. Add the *spaghetti* and cook, tossing, for 1 minute so it picks up the different flavors. Stir in *1 tablespoon chopped fresh parsley* and season with salt to taste.

Chinese Egg Noodles with Scallions and Shiitakes: Heat *2 tablespoons canola oil* in a large nonstick skillet over medium-high heat until shimmering hot, about 1 minute. Add *3½ ounces thinly sliced shiitake mushrooms* and *4 thinly sliced scallions* and sprinkle with *½ teaspoon salt*. Cook, stirring, until the mushrooms soften and brown in places, about 3 minutes. Add cooked *fresh egg noodles* and stir-fry until the noodles heat through, about 2 minutes. Toss with *1 tablespoon soy sauce*, *2 teaspoons sesame oil*, *1 teaspoon rice vinegar*, and a *sprinkling of toasted sesame seeds*.

Curried Rice Noodles: Soak *6 ounces rice noodles* in 1 quart boiling water until soft and pliable, about 5 minutes. Drain under cold running water. Heat *2 tablespoons canola oil* in a large nonstick skillet over medium-high heat until shimmering hot, about 1 minute. Add *1 yellow onion* (thinly sliced) and *1 cup julienned carrot*, sprinkle with *½ teaspoon salt*, and cook, stirring, until softened and lightly browned, about 3 minutes. Add *2 teaspoons curry powder* and cook, stirring, for 15 seconds. Add the noodles and cook, tossing, until browned in places and heated through; add stir-fried egg, ham, or shrimp if you like.

Spanish Fideos with Garbanzos: Heat *1 minced garlic clove* with *3 tablespoons olive oil* in a large skillet over medium-high heat until the garlic starts to sizzle steadily and become fragrant. Add *1 teaspoon ground cumin* and *¼ teaspoon pimentón de la Vera* and cook, stirring, for 15 seconds. Add *1 cup canned diced tomato* and *1 cup canned garbanzos* (rinsed and drained), sprinkle with *¾ teaspoon salt*, and cook stirring until the mixture heats through and the spices are evenly incorporated. Add 10 ounces cooked *fideo noodles* (thin egg noodle sticks or angel hair pasta) and cook, tossing, for a couple of minutes so they absorb the surrounding flavors.

Israeli Couscous with Lemon Cream and Fresh Oregano: Sauté *1 large finely diced shallot* with *2 tablespoons unsalted butter* and *½ teaspoon salt*, in a medium saucepan over medium-high heat, stirring, until it becomes tender and translucent, about 3 minutes. Add *⅓ cup heavy cream* and bring to a boil. Stir in *⅓ cup Parmigiano*, *2 tablespoons chopped fresh oregano*, the *zest of 1 lemon*, and *salt* and *pepper*, about ¾ teaspoon each. Add 10 ounces of cooked *Israeli couscous* (or fregola) and cook, stirring, for a minute or two so it absorbs the sauce; add a splash of pasta water if it becomes too dry.

Rice Pilaf

Heat *2 to 3 cups chicken broth* in the microwave. Meanwhile, cook chopped *onion, garlic, ginger,* or *shallots* with *2 to 3 tablespoons oil (or butter)* in a large saucepan. Add the *rice* and cook, stirring, for 1 minute so the oil coats it. Add the broth and cook, stirring occasionally, until the rice absorbs most of the liquid. Cover, reduce the heat to low, and cook without touching for 20 minutes so the grains become tender. Fluff with a fork and serve.

Traditional Rice Pilaf: Heat *3 cups chicken broth*. Meanwhile, cook *1 yellow onion* (cut in ¼-inch dice) with *3 tablespoons olive oil* and *½ teaspoon salt* in a large saucepan over medium-high heat until the onion softens and becomes translucent, about 4 minutes. Add *1¼ cups long-grain rice* and *¼ cup orzo* and cook, stirring, for 1 minute. Add the broth and cook following the directions above.

Curried Basmati Rice with Currants and Almonds: Heat *1¾ cups chicken broth* and *½ cup coconut milk*. Meanwhile, cook *1 finely diced shallot* with *3 tablespoons unsalted butter* and *½ teaspoon salt* in a large saucepan over medium-high heat until the shallot softens and becomes translucent, about 2 minutes. Stir in *1 teaspoon curry powder* and *1 teaspoon ground cumin*. Add *1½ cups basmati rice* and *¼ cup currants* and cook, stirring, for 1 minute. Add the coconut broth and cook following the directions above. Sprinkle with *½ cup toasted sliced almonds* and serve.

Spanish Yellow Rice: Heat *3 cups chicken broth*. Meanwhile, cook *1 yellow onion* (cut in ¼-inch dice) and *1 garlic clove* (minced) with *2 tablespoons olive oil* and *½ teaspoon salt* in a large saucepan over medium-high heat until the onion softens and becomes translucent, about 4 minutes. Add *½ teaspoon cumin, ¼ teaspoon pimentón de la Vera,* and *¼ teaspoon saffron threads* and cook, stirring, for 15 seconds. Add *1½ cups long-grain rice* and cook, stirring, for 1 minute. Add the *broth* and cook following the directions above.

Dirty Rice: Heat *3 cups chicken broth*. Meanwhile, cook *1 yellow onion, 1 carrot, ½ green bell pepper*, and *1 stalk celery* (all cut in ¼-inch dice) with *2 tablespoons olive oil* and *¾ teaspoon salt in* in a large saucepan over medium-high heat until the onion softens and becomes translucent, about 4 minutes. Add *1 ½ cups long-grain rice* and *1 tablespoon tomato paste* and cook, stirring, for 1 minute. Add the *broth* and *2 bay leaves* and cook following the directions above.

POTATOES

There really isn't much to making a baked potato, so I'll leave you on your own for that. And fried potatoes (or French fries) are both labor-intensive and somewhat complicated to cook so I also stay away from those in this book. What's left are basic potato methods, relatively quick, full of flavor, and easy to pair with different seared main courses.

Mashed Potatoes

Peel *2 pounds potatoes*, cut in ½-inch pieces, set in a large saucepan, and cover with water or milk by a couple of inches. Stir in a generous sprinkling of *salt*, about 1 teaspoon, and bring to a boil. Reduce to a simmer, cover, and cook, until the potatoes are completely tender, about 10 minutes. Drain well and mash with *unsalted butter*. Season with *salt* and *pepper* to taste.

Garlicky Smashed Red Potatoes: Quarter small *red creamer potatoes* (leave the skins on), boil following the directions above with *2 smashed garlic cloves*, and cook until the potatoes are completely tender. Drain well and mash with *4 tablespoons unsalted butter* and *¼ cup thinly sliced fresh chives*.

Rosemary-Parmesan Mashed Yukon Potatoes: Boil peeled *Yukon Gold potatoes* and *2 smashed garlic cloves* following the directions above. Drain, return the potatoes to the saucepan, and mash with *4 tablespoons*

unsalted butter, ¾ cup freshly grated Parmigiano, 1 ½ teaspoons chopped fresh rosemary, and a generous sprinkling of *black pepper*, about ¾ teaspoon.

Pesto Mashed Potatoes: Boil peeled *russet potatoes* and *2 smashed garlic cloves* following the directions on left. Drain, return the potatoes to the saucepan, and mash with *½ cup basil pesto* (page 210).

Horseradish Mashed Potatoes: Boil peeled *russet potatoes* and *2 smashed garlic cloves* following the directions on left. Drain, return the potatoes to the saucepan, and mash with *⅓ cup heavy cream, 1 tablespoon prepared horseradish*, and a generous sprinkling of *black pepper*, about ¾ teaspoon.

Roasted Potatoes

Heat the oven to 450°F. Cut *2 pounds of potatoes* into ½-inch to 1-inch pieces or wedges (for small creamer or fingerling potatoes, leave them whole or halve them). Toss with a *couple tablespoons of olive oil*, some *smashed garlic cloves* or *wedges of shallots*, *chopped fresh herbs* or *spices*, and a generous sprinkling of *salt* and *pepper*, about 1 teaspoon and ½ teaspoon respectively. Transfer to a large rimmed baking sheet lined with foil or parchment paper and roast, tossing every 10 minutes or so, until the potatoes are browned and tender, 25 to 30 minutes.

Roasted Rosemary Fingerling Potatoes: Toss *2 pounds fingerling potatoes* (halved or quartered) with *2 tablespoons olive oil, 3 smashed cloves garlic, 2 teaspoons chopped fresh rosemary, 1 teaspoon salt*, and *½ teaspoon pepper*. Roast following the directions above.

Spiced Oven Hash Browns: In a small bowl, mix *1 teaspoon salt, 1 teaspoon Hungarian* paprika, *½ teaspoon each black pepper, granulated sugar*, and *garlic powder*, and *¼ teaspoon pimentón de la Vera*. In a large bowl, toss this spice mixture with *2 pounds russet potatoes* (½-inch dice) and *3 tablespoons olive oil*. Roast following the directions above.

Roasted Yukon Wedges with Bacon and Thyme: Slice *2 pounds Yukon Gold potatoes* into ¾-inch wedges lengthwise and toss with *1 tablespoon olive oil, 2 slices thick bacon* (cut in ½-inch pieces), *2 shallots* (cut in ¼-inch wedges), *2 teaspoons chopped fresh thyme, ¾ teaspoon salt,* and *½ teaspoon pepper.* Roast following the directions on page 235.

Roasted Red Potatoes with Artichokes and Black Olives: Halve *2 pounds red creamer potatoes* and toss with *2 tablespoons olive oil, 1½ teaspoons chopped fresh rosemary, ¾ teaspoon salt,* and *½ teaspoon pepper.* Roast following the directions on page 235 and then toss with *1 cup thinly sliced canned artichoke hearts, ½ cup pitted Kalamata olives, 1 tablespoon fresh lemon juice, 1 additional tablespoon olive oil,* and *1 tablespoon chopped fresh oregano.*

GRAINS

We all should eat more grains. The easiest way to prepare them is tossed in warm or room-temperature salads with vegetables, cheeses, and fresh herbs. The following sides all adhere to this simple formula.

Steam or boil the grains until tender. While they're still warm, toss with sliced vegetables, cheese, and fresh herbs and serve warm or at room temperature.

Bulgur with Cherry Tomatoes, Mint, and Mozzarella: *Bring 1½ cups water* and *2 tablespoons olive oil* to a boil in a medium saucepan. Stir in *¾ teaspoon salt* and *1½ cups bulgur,* cover, and remove from the heat. Let sit for 10 minutes so the bulgur absorbs all of the water and then transfer to a large bowl and toss with *1 cup halved cherry tomatoes, ¾ cup fresh mozzarella* (½-inch pieces), *2 scallions thinly sliced, 2 tablespoons chopped fresh mint,* and a *squirt of fresh lemon juice.* Season with more salt to taste.

Quinoa with Fennel, Roasted Red Pepper, and Feta: Bring *1½ cups water* and *1 tablespoon olive oil* to a boil in a medium saucepan. Stir in *¾ teaspoon salt,* and *1½ cups quinoa,* cover and remove from the heat. Let sit for 5 minutes so the quinoa absorbs all of the water and then transfer to a large bowl and toss with *1 cup ¼-inch diced fennel, ¾ cup crumbled feta, 2 sun-dried tomatoes* (chopped), *1 tablespoon chopped fresh dill,* and *2 teaspoons freshly squeezed lemon juice.* Season with more salt and lemon juice to taste.

Warm Farro Salad with Orange and Asparagus: Bring 2 quarts well salted water to a boil. Reduce to a steady simmer, add *1½ cups farro,* and cook, stirring occasionally, until it becomes tender, about 20 minutes. Drain well and then toss with *2 cups blanched asparagus* (cut in 1-inch pieces), *1 navel orange* (peeled and diced), *½ cup grated Parmigiano, 3 tablespoons olive oil,* and *1 tablespoon chopped fresh tarragon.*

Wild Rice with Dried Cherries and Toasted Walnuts: Bring 2 quarts well salted water to a boil in a medium saucepan. Add *1 cup wild rice* and cook at a gentle simmer until the grains just start to open up and the rice becomes tender, about 45 minutes. Drain well. Meanwhile, sauté *1 finely diced yellow onion* and *1 finely diced carrot* with *2 tablespoons unsalted butter* in a large skillet over medium heat until tender, about 6 minutes. Add the wild rice and toss with *⅓ cup dried cherries, ⅓ cup chopped toasted walnuts,* and *2 tablespoons chopped fresh parsley.*

Couscous

In a medium saucepan, sauté aromatics and spices if using,, then add *1 cup chicken broth* (or *1 cup water and ½ teaspoon salt*), and bring to a boil. Stir in *1 cup couscous*, cover, and remove from the heat. Let sit for 5 minutes so that the couscous absorbs the water, then stir in any other flavorings, fluff with a fork, and serve.

Buttery Herbed Couscous: Cook the couscous following the directions above, then stir in *2 tablespoons unsalted butter, 2 tablespoons chopped fresh parsley,* and *1 teaspoon chopped fresh thyme* or *rosemary.*

Couscous with Cinnamon and Oranges: Set *2 tablespoons olive oil* and *1 yellow onion* (finely diced) in a medium saucepan over medium-high heat, sprinkle with *½ teaspoon salt,* and cook, stirring, until the onion softens and browns in places, about 4 minutes. Sprinkle with *½ teaspoon ground cumin* and *¼ teaspoon cinnamon* and cook, stirring, for 15 seconds. Add the *broth* or the water and *salt,* bring to a boil, stir in the *couscous,* and cook following the directions above. Stir *1 navel orange* (peeled and cut in ½-inch pieces) and *3 tablespoons chopped fresh cilantro* into the cooked couscous.

Spiced Grilled Vegetable Couscous: Grill *1 medium zucchini, 1 red bell pepper,* and *1 medium red onion* (follow the techniques on pages 80 and 82). Coarsely chop, add to the boiling *broth* or the water and salt along with the *couscous, 1 tablespoon olive oil, ½ teaspoon chile powder,* and a *large pinch cinnamon.* After cooking, stir in a *couple squirts fresh lime juice.*

Couscous with Zucchini, Sun-Dried Tomatoes, and Black Olives: Sauté or grill *1 medium zucchini* (following the techniques on page 50 or 80). Cut in ½-inch dice and then add to the boiling *broth* or water at the same time as the *couscous.* Cook following the directions above. Then stir in *¼ cup pitted Kalamata olives, 2 sun-dried tomatoes* (chopped), *1 tablespoon olive oil, 1 tablespoon chopped fresh basil,* and a *squeeze fresh lemon juice.*

Polenta

I love the rich, hearty texture of coarse polenta, but it can take up to 45 minutes to cook. I suggest going with the quick-cooking stuff for these recipes. It only takes about 5 minutes and vibes with the convenience of our approach. You can make the recipe for grits (see below) with either polenta or grits (which are just ground hominy).

Bring *1¼ cups chicken broth* (or *1¼ cups water and ¾ teaspoon salt*) to a boil in a medium saucepan. Whisk in *1¼ cups polenta,* reduce the heat to low and cook, stirring, until the polenta absorbs all of the water and acquires a smooth, thick texture, about 5 minutes.

Herbed Goat Cheese Polenta: Stir into the cooked *polenta 4 ounces crumbled goat cheese, 2 teaspoons chopped fresh rosemary,* and *½ teaspoon black pepper.* Season with more *salt* and *pepper* to taste.

Roasted Red Pepper and Thyme Polenta: Add *1 roasted red pepper* (coarsely chopped), *⅓ cup heavy cream,* and *2 teaspoons chopped fresh thyme* to a blender and purée until smooth. Stir into the cooked *polenta* and cook, stirring, until heated through. Season with *salt* and *pepper* to taste.

Parmesan and Sun-Dried Tomato Polenta: Stir into the cooked *polenta ¾ cup Parmigiano, 3 sun-dried tomatoes* (finely chopped), *2 tablespoons unsalted butter, 1 teaspoon chopped fresh thyme,* and *salt* and *pepper* to taste.

Cheddar Cheese Grits: Stir into the cooked *grits* or *polenta 1¼ cups grated sharp cheddar cheese, 2 tablespoons unsalted butter, 1 tablespoon chopped fresh parsley, ½ teaspoon pepper,* and *¼ teaspoon Tabasco.* Season with *salt* and *pepper* to taste.